Access EAP

FRAMEWORKS

Course Book

Sue Argent
Olwyn Alexander

Garnet EDUCATION

Published by
Garnet Publishing Ltd.
8 Southern Court
South Street
Reading RG1 4QS, UK

www.garneteducation.com

First published 2013.

ISBN: 978 1 85964 558 1

British Cataloguing-in-Publication Data
A catalogue record for this book is available from the
British Library.

Production

Project manager:	Sophia Hopton
Editorial team:	Sophia Hopton, Kate Kemp, Karen Kinnair-Pugh
Design and layout:	Madeleine Lane, Ian Lansley, Mike Hinks
Photography:	iStock, Shutterstock
Audio:	Recorded at Silver Street Studios, Reading, UK

Every effort has been made to trace copyright holders
and we apologize in advance for any unintentional
omission. We will be happy to insert the appropriate
acknowledgements in any subsequent editions.

Printed and bound in Lebanon by International Press:
interpress@int-press.com

Author acknowledgement

We would like to thank all those who gave us feedback
on early drafts of this book, including the readers and
editors at Garnet Education and our colleagues, Kester
Newill and June Nimmo, who piloted the draft material
with their students and provided tremendously helpful
comments. We are particularly grateful to Mike Wallace
and Alison Wray for their clear analysis of critical reading
and to George Woolard for his invaluable suggestions on
spoken communication.

Thanks are also due to the following for their subject-
specific expertise and advice: Dr Alan Marshall on
mathematical modelling; Dr George Argent on tropical
rainforest; Jennifer Argent and Paul Howden-Leach on
Environmental Science; Iain Argent on Computer Science.
To all the academic writers, whether experts or students,
who allowed us to use their texts we owe a great debt of
gratitude.

Finally, many thanks to teaching colleagues who discussed
with us the scholarship of teaching and learning at
university and gave us permission to present them in the
pages of this book as staff at Gateway University.
Any errors in the book are our fault and result from not
asking these people the right questions.

Contents

	Unit themes	Functions	Texts	Academic language
1	**Starting points** **Section 1** New places and new faces **Section 2** Making contact and first impressions **Section 3** Nouns and noun phrases **Section 4** Academic writing **Section 5** An introductory lecture	• introduction to functions • stating purpose and method • defining and classifying	**Reading:** university websites; student e-mails; a student assignment; textbook contents **Listening:** conversations; an ecology lecture	• purpose statements • prepositional phrases • types of nouns • noun phrases • academic style • positive and negative words for viewpoint
2	**Looking backwards and forwards** **Section 1** Reviewing **Section 2** Coaching **Section 3** Reporting **Section 4** Reporting ideas from sources **Section 5** Writing clearly and logically	• reviewing • reporting • evaluating	**Reading:** report writing guidelines; a research report **Listening:** tutorial discussions	• two-part questions • reporting tenses • reporting verbs
3	**Key concepts and tools** **Section 1** The concept of autonomy **Section 2** Tools for researching vocabulary **Section 3** Key concepts and tools **Section 4** From metaphors to models **Section 5** Concepts and tools that cross disciplines	• defining • explaining	**Reading:** dictionary entries; concordance lines; textbooks; lecture handouts **Listening:** instructions for using concordancers; a lecture on mathematical models	• types of definition and purposes • structure of definitions: *an X is a Y that …; an X is a Y for verb + ing / to + verb* • synonyms and acronyms
4	**Resources for research** **Section 1** Exploring the concept of research **Section 2** Tools for searching online **Section 3** Reviewing the language of comparison and contrast **Section 4** Surveying sources **Section 5** Using abstracts to select and compare sources	• comparing • contrasting • evaluating	**Reading:** a list of references; a set of abstracts **Listening:** a seminar introducing research; a talk on searching online databases	• metaphors for research • noun phrases in titles • grammar patterns for comparison and contrast
5	**Speaking for yourself** **Section 1** Learning from experience **Section 2** Setting the right tone for enthusiasm and agreement **Section 3** Telling problem stories **Section 4** Setting the right tone for listing and new information **Section 5** Setting the right tone for familiar and contrasting information	• classifying • explaining problems and solutions • making recommendations	**Reading:** case studies of problems; job interview guidelines **Listening:** a discussion about working overseas	• positive and negative words for problems and solutions: *too, not enough* • modals in the past • word and sentence stress • key intonation patterns • emphasizers and emphatic *do*
6	**Cultures and systems** **Section 1** Crossing cultures **Section 2** Negotiating the system: brick walls and gatekeepers **Section 3** Setting the right tone for negotiating the system **Section 4** Presenting a case for change: Part 1 **Section 5** Presenting a case for change: Part 2	• explaining causes and effects • explaining problems and evaluating solutions • negotiating	**Reading:** a textbook; Internet sources; a lecturer's webpage and e-mail; case studies **Listening:** staff–student negotiations; a committee meeting	• metaphors for cross-cultural communication • comparatives • positive and negative words for evaluating sources • *too* + adjective • strategic language for diplomacy, assertiveness • sentence stress
7	**Academic integrity** **Section 1** Understanding ethical thinking **Section 2** A lecture on ethics **Section 3** What is scholarship? **Section 4** An academic misconduct hearing **Section 5** Discussing ethical case studies	• making ethical decisions • expressing probability • describing procedures	**Reading:** a lecture handout; a 'cheat' website; a student code of conduct; a Turnitin® report; ethical case studies **Listening:** a lecture on ethics; an academic misconduct hearing	• *If* clause + result clause + tense choice • *The more … the more …* • tenses to show viewpoint
8	**Critical reading and academic argument** **Section 1** A point of view **Section 2** Reasonable scepticism: how to be a critical reader **Section 3** Writer's voice: reasonable persuasion **Section 4** Arguing from sources: assignments **Section 5** Arguing from data	• arguing • persuading • evaluating arguments	**Reading:** a textbook; Internet sources; published data; student writing **Listening:** an argument about data	• strengthening: *clearly, obviously* • hedging: *some, possibly, may* • distancing: *a widespread view* • evaluating: *primitive, failed* • emphasizers and highlighters: *only, over, particularly* • numerical comparison: *four times*
9	**Evidence from research** **Section 1** Communicating research transparently: where is the evidence? **Section 2** Research across the disciplines: what counts as evidence? **Section 3** Evaluating research: how good is the evidence? **Section 4** The role of the literature review: linking theory to research design **Section 5** Critical reading of a research paper	• linking evidence to claims • evaluating evidence and the methods that produced it • communicating research	**Reading:** newspaper articles; research papers; student projects **Listening:** a lecture on research approaches; a focus group discussion	• research terms: *cohort, control, conditions, variables* • informal register for research quality: *reliable, robust, significant, elegant* • reporting claims: *as predicted, it is well known*
10	**Entering university** **Section 1** Assessing readiness for university study **Section 2** Teamwork in group projects **Section 3** Reflection for assessment	• arguing and persuading • evaluating • comparing • solving problems	**Reading:** extracts from CEFR; table comparing SELTs; FAQs from test website; SELT and subject exam questions; group project briefs; a student peer review and self-reflection	• exam questions and instructions • describing team roles and team skills: *delegate, adaptive, facilitator* • self-reflection: *perceptions, complemented, insights*

ACCESS EAP: Frameworks • Book map

Writing and speaking	Academic competence	Thinking critically
Writing: e-mails; an exam answer; redrafting in academic style **Speaking:** word stress	• explore expectations of students and universities • develop awareness of writer's purpose and intended reader • prepare for a lecture • listen and make notes effectively	• interpret a general statement by selecting specific examples • evaluate e-mails and other texts – guess, speculate and justify answers
Writing: a tutorial record form; an e-mail to a lecturer; reporting ideas from sources **Speaking:** advice about study	• set, implement and review goals • record key information • use general to specific and familiar to new principles to structure texts • understand moves in texts	• evaluate performance • set SMART objectives • compare report formats and purposes • understand a writer's viewpoint
Writing: definitions and explanations; summaries from a textbook and a lecture; a definition of a concept in your field **Speaking:** short presentations of concepts	• understand autonomy • identify moves in an explanation • check vocabulary using a concordance tool • practise strategies to find information in a book • tolerate uncertainty about difficult concepts in a lecture	• distinguish definitions from descriptions • infer implicit definitions • identify writer's purpose in defining • evaluate your own learning approach • relate general concepts to your own examples
Writing: answers to FAQs; an e-mail; a comparison of online search tools; a summary from notes **Speaking:** an oral summary	• understand the purpose of library research use keyword searching • compare familiar with new concepts • categorize sources • use abstracts to preview articles	• identify types of research • explore the limits of a metaphor • evaluate online search tools • identify general and specific research titles • identify the purpose of abstracts • link concepts to your own experience
Writing: guidelines for working overseas **Speaking:** problem narratives; responding effectively in discussions; contrasting, listing and giving examples orally; suggesting alternative solutions; advice on working in your country, a presentation	• analyze problems and solutions • acknowledge and respond to the ideas of others • identify learning outcomes • research and plan for a written assignment	• infer the impact of experiences • evaluate solutions • infer the causes of problems • apply job interview criteria
Writing: e-mails; a personal statement for a funding proposal; an article for a student newsletter; meeting minutes; a report **Speaking:** negotiation role plays, a meeting	• take a stance and negotiate • follow the writing process • understand roles and responsibilities within the university system • follow conventions for meetings	• evaluate sources for specific purposes • analyze problems and solutions • compare negotiating conventions across cultures • evaluate negotiations and contributions to a meeting
Writing: advice on cultural differences; an e-mail about cheating; a formal letter; a case study report **Speaking:** discuss cultural differences; advise a student on plagiarism; a case study presentation	• reflect on hypothetical situations • choose levels of probability and certainty • plan and adapt listening and note-taking strategies • summarize accurately • show viewpoint • use and reference ideas from a source	• relate ethical options and choices to your own experience • infer lecturer's purpose • evaluate a 'cheat' website • find evidence for answers • ask sceptical questions
Writing: to what extent arguments; interpretive summaries; a persuasive report of research data; a defended stance; a critical evaluation of a key concept **Speaking:** discussion of viewpoints – brainstorming for definitions	• take a nuanced stance and defend it • read sources and data critically • understand assignment titles • write from sources and data with an academic voice	• infer viewpoints from context • suggest improvements • anticipate problems • identify data to answer a question • interpret research data
Writing: diagrammatic notes from a lecture; a summary of two research papers **Speaking:** discussions: claims and research evidence; research types and quality; experience of being an international student	• understand and compare research designs • classify types of research • record points in a lecture and discussion • formulate research questions	• assess research evidence • identify stance in a paper or lecture • evaluate the quality of methods and results • identify limitations in research • draw independent conclusions from research data
Writing: advice about working in teams; a reflective log **Speaking:** negotiation in teamwork; reflective discussion	• recognize university-level competence and assess current ability • analyze exam questions • analyze project briefs • undertake autonomous, self-directed learning • assess process, peers and self	• evaluate type of evidence • recognize limitations of SELTs • identify assessment criteria • assess student project reports

Introduction
What is different about this book?

It's about university

Access EAP: Frameworks is based on real university life and prepares you for many of the tasks and situations that you will face in your studies. Each unit has an **academic theme** and takes you through conversations and discussions, seminars and lectures, reading texts and assignments that relate to the theme, helping you to make choices about how to study.

Access EAP: Frameworks follows on from the lower-level book *Access EAP: Foundations*. However, it is not necessary to have studied *Access EAP: Foundations* first – the short preface will help you to familiarize yourself with the students in the book and their areas of study.

The themes

Each theme explores an aspect of what lecturers will expect you to do at university. You will develop the language and skills you need to meet these expectations; for example, explaining concepts and using data to support arguments, as well as writing assignments and e-mails and negotiating with staff. Each theme determines the content of the unit and the choice of **authentic academic reading and listening texts**, which help you practise study strategies and develop vocabulary and grammar patterns that you can use in your academic studies. Look at the Book map on pages 4–5 to see how it works.

The units

Access EAP: Frameworks has ten units, each divided into five sections, apart from the final unit which has three. The first section introduces the theme, for example, reports, key tools and concepts, and research. The listening, reading, speaking and writing tasks are linked together around each theme, just as they are at university. There are regular tasks in each section to develop your ability to think critically and to study effectively.

We recognize that you need to develop your writing specifically for your target subject, yet you may share a class with EAP students intending to study in a wide range of disciplines. An important part of each section is the **Self study** task which directs you to investigate how the vocabulary, grammar and skills introduced in the section are applied in your particular subject area.

To help you to build your academic vocabulary, there are lists of **key academic words and phrases** beside the texts in which they appear. You will learn the important **grammar patterns** that are needed for understanding and producing a range of academic texts. This means that you will focus on nouns and noun phrases rather than verbs. You will also learn that academic texts develop from general to specific ideas, and from what is familiar to what is new. These aspects of academic grammar are essential for understanding **academic style**.

Progress

Access EAP: Frameworks is designed to help you to make progress and achieve a high level of academic performance by providing you with **frameworks of language** and **study skills** through which you can build your own experience and learning. These frameworks may be checklists and procedures to follow, or language patterns and structures to use. You will revisit the same key concepts and key language within increasingly more difficult texts and tasks, helping you to remember them as you work through the book.

Access EAP: Frameworks consists of:

- a students' **Course Book**, including audio transcripts
- a **Teacher's Book**, which provides detailed guidance on each section, answers to tasks and additional photocopiable resources
- an **audio DVD** with lectures, conversations, discussions and seminar excerpts

Preface

Gateway University students

Maysoun, Chen, Guy and Xiaohua are all studying at Gateway University in Summerford, in the UK, where there is a large population of international students studying both on campus and by open learning[1]. They appeared in *Access EAP: Foundations* and have successfully completed Semester 1; *Access EAP: Frameworks* follows their progress through Semester 2, examining the tasks they do and the choices they make. Their experiences illustrate clearly and in personal detail the sometimes problematic situations you are likely to encounter at university, and demonstrate ways that you can meet these challenges.

Maysoun

Maysoun is the oldest of the students in this book and is a postgraduate. She met Chen when they were both studying on the university's pre-sessional course. They studied English for Academic Purposes (EAP) for eight weeks in order to prepare for their university studies. She lives off campus and is married with a small child, a little boy who attends a local primary school. Her husband is studying for a PhD in Education and she is studying for a Master's degree in Environmental Science. Her first degree, which she gained in her home country, Syria, was in Geography. Her main concern is that she has not studied biology before and so she has to learn a lot about this subject in a short space of time. She has also experienced some new ways of learning – for example, in the first semester she had her first laboratory practical classes and she had to go on a residential field trip.

Chen

Chen is from China and is in his first year of a BSc in Computer Science. In the first semester, he lived on campus in the room next to Guy and they became friends. Chen helps Guy with any computer problems. They are also language partners, so Guy helps Chen with his English and Chen is helping Guy to learn Chinese. Chen expected that he wouldn't have to write or speak much English on his course, but he soon found that he was wrong. For one of his essays, he considered using ideas from another student's essay by just changing the words, but Maysoun convinced him that this is unacceptable at university. He hates speaking in class, but when he had to give a presentation, Maysoun and Guy helped him. He also joined the International Student Committee, and that gave him a little more confidence in speaking English. He met his girlfriend, Xiaohua, when he went to talk to a new group of international students at the university.

Guy

Guy is from Wales in the UK and he is in his second year of a degree in International Business. He has to study a language module as part of his degree and has chosen Chinese. His first year at the university was not very successful. He avoided the library because he was not really sure how to use the resources there, instead relying heavily on the Internet to find information for his assignments. He missed assignment deadlines and even failed some of his exams; however, he took them again during the holidays and managed to pass them. During the next semester, he struggled to understand how to write good academic texts and so he got some help from a tutor in the Writing Centre. She showed him the correct way to use ideas from the library sources he found and how to reference them. He started to enjoy his studies when he became interested in ethical trading and found some good journal references.

Xiaohua

Xiaohua is the youngest of the group. She wants to study Computer Science next year and so she is studying on the one-year Foundation programme. Because she arrived late, she missed some important work and it was very difficult for her to understand what was expected of her writing. Chen helped her to understand the difference between the essays she used to write for her high school English class and the academic assignments that are required at university.

Key words & phrases

- a population
- international
- on campus
- by open learning
- problematic
- meet challenges
- off campus
- main concern
- practical classes
- a residential field trip
- unacceptable
- a module
- relied heavily
- managed to
- to reference
- ethical trading
- journal references
- academic assignments

[1] Many universities offer whole or part of degree studies in a student's own country. This is called 'open' or 'distance' learning.

Unit 1

Starting points

Section 1 New places and new faces

What the university expects:

• a global and ethical understanding – identify your global responsibilities

Contexts:

• studying and working in international contexts

Aims:

• to explore the expectations of universities and of international students
• to consider the purposes and readers of texts
• to use purpose statements and prepositional phrases

Welcome!

Gateway University attracts staff and students from all around the world and we are proud of our international reputation. The university is dedicated to helping all our students to become successful future professionals by developing their graduate attributes. Graduate attributes are key academic abilities, personal qualities and transferable skills that transcend the specific knowledge and skills of your subject discipline. One of these is awareness of your global responsibilities.

Studying at university is an opportunity to become a member of a global academic community, with shared goals, shared understanding and a shared language: English. You will meet many different people from different backgrounds and different countries. It's an exciting time; it's also a time when you have to be prepared to leave your comfort zone. Life will be very different from what you are used to and you will face many challenges. However, there are steps that you can take to prepare yourself before you arrive.

GATEWAY UNIVERSITY

Key words & phrases

reputation
is dedicated to
professionals
graduate attributes
transcend
an opportunity to
a global community
goals
be prepared to
comfort zone
face challenges
take steps

Task 1 Reading and thinking critically

1.1 Who are the intended readers of this *Welcome!* statement and what is the university's purpose in putting it on its website?

1.2 Think of specific examples to illustrate these ideas from the website extract:

   a global communities and global academic communities

   b leaving your comfort zone

1.3 What might be the challenges for you personally and what steps can you take to prepare yourself? Write down your ideas.

Chen and Guy became friends in the first semester. They are planning to move off campus to cheaper accommodation in a flat[1] in the city centre. They are looking for two flatmates, so they write an advertisement to put on the Student Union noticeboard.

Two students needed to share a comfortable flat in the centre of Summerford

Close to shops – overlooking Victoria Park – 5 mins from station

Reasonable rent and shared bills

Contact: Chen z.q.chen@gwu.ac.uk or Guy 0779 602 138

Task 2 Preparing to listen

Discuss in small groups whether you would prefer to live on campus in a hall of residence, or off campus in a flat. Why?

Task 3 Listening for specific information

Three students apply. Guy and Chen meet in the campus coffee shop to discuss progress in their search for flatmates.

3.1 ⊚T01 **Listen to their discussion and make notes about the three applicants.**

Matt

Khalid

Dimitri

3.2 Complete these sentences:
 a Khalid wants to leave his present accommodation to _____.
 b Matt wants to leave his present accommodation to _____.
 c Dimitri wants to leave his present accommodation to _____.
 d Chen wants to share the flat to _____.
 e Guy and Chen decide to ask the three students some questions so that _____.

3.3 Work in pairs to listen again and/or read the transcript on page 286 to check your answers.

[1] *apartment* in US English

Task 4 Investigating grammar patterns

4.1 Find the purpose statements in the transcript on page 286 that use the patterns in the table below, and add an example of each.

pattern	example from the transcript
to + verb	
so that + sentence	

4.2 Prepositional phrases (preposition + noun) can be used for different functions. Find another example of each in the transcript and add it to the table below.

purpose	pattern	examples from the transcript
to show location (place)	*from, in, at, on, to, around* + noun	*from Libya,*
to show duration (how long)	*for, until* + noun	*for one semester,*
to show method (how)	*by* + noun	*by e-mail,*

4.3 Write sentences about your classmates using these patterns.

Task 5 Thinking critically about international study

Make links between the statement on the Gateway University website and the students' conversation by answering these questions.

5.1 In what respects are these students becoming members of a global community, with shared goals, shared understanding and a shared language?

5.2 To what extent are their backgrounds and countries different?

5.3 From the conversation in Task 3, find an example of any student who is prepared to leave his or her comfort zone and justify (give reasons for) your choice to another student.

Task 6 Reading quickly for style and layout

Quickly read the two e-mails that were sent to Chen.

6.1 Which is more formal in style? What impression does this give?

6.2 What is the main difference between the two e-mails in terms of layout?

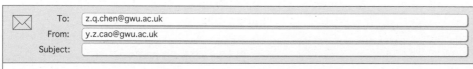

To:	z.q.chen@gwu.ac.uk
From:	y.z.cao@gwu.ac.uk
Subject:	

Hi Chen,

I'm Cao Yong Qiang but everyone calls me Matt. I think U must be Chinese like me. Anyway I write now in English but sorry my English is not good. How come I don't see you last semester? Maybe in different dormitory. I'm a boy from Wenzhou of Zhejiang Province, I'm 20 and I study BSc Building and Estate Management in first year. My parents have import–export business but not very big and they support me in my studies here, money, advice, everything. Last semester was my first time to study in UK and I wanted to study very hard. But the money to stay on campus was a big shock, so now I decide to spend less for accommodation and maybe find a part time job in city centre. I saw Ur ad on Student Union noticeboard. What can I tell U about myself? I am quiet and hard working. I don't smoke. I can cook and clean and be a good flatmate if you give me a chance. I hope I can join your flat. You can phone my cell phone on 0781 042 942.

Bye bye

Key words & phrases

an import–export business

a shock

To:	z.q.chen@gwu.ac.uk
From:	dimitri_andreou7@hotmail.com
Subject:	Flat vacancy

Dear Mr Chen,

I am writing to express my interest in renting a room in your flat, as recently advertised on the Student Union noticeboard.

I am a mature student from Athens in the final year of a BA in Business Studies (Accounting). I successfully completed the first two years as an external student of Gateway University, but this part of my studies took me five years because I was working full time. Last semester I lived with my uncle's family but the accommodation was very crowded and I had insufficient space for my books, computer, etc. This semester I am looking for my own study bedroom so that I can complete my degree quickly and successfully.

I am a quiet, hard-working family man. I enjoy cooking and am good at DIY. I can provide financial and character references. I hope that you will consider my application carefully. You can contact me on my mobile phone on 0779 882 071 or by e-mail.

Yours faithfully,

Dimitri Andreou

Task 7 Reading and note-making

Read the e-mails from Matt and Dimitri, and the section of the transcript relating to Khalid on page 286. Make notes comparing and contrasting these students in terms of their suitability as flatmates for Chen and Guy.

Task 8 Writing an e-mail

Use your notes to write an e-mail to Chen to compare the three applicants, Khalid, Matt and Dimitri. Suggest which two are the most suitable to be Chen and Guy's flatmates and why. Think about what style of e-mail is most appropriate for you to use. Write about 150 words.

Discussion

- Which of the students in this section do you most closely resemble? Reread the *Welcome!* statement at the beginning of this section. What will be exciting and what will be difficult for you when you go to university? In what ways do you think you will have to leave your comfort zone?
- Read the seven Gateway University graduate attributes at the top of page 12 and discuss what they mean at university and at work. For each one, think of ways that you could develop your own abilities, qualities and skills. Do any of them surprise you?

Graduate Attributes

In addition to academic excellence, Gateway University offers students the opportunity to develop seven key graduate attributes that will ensure our graduates are able to perform to the highest possible professional standards in their future careers.

1 Critical reflection
2 Awareness of how knowledge is advanced
3 A spirit of enquiry
4 A global and ethical understanding

5 Effective communication
6 Autonomy
7 Team-working

GATEWAY UNIVERSITY

Self study

Find a university website in English. Read the introduction or welcome page for new or prospective students. Find examples of purpose statements and prepositional phrases to show other students. Write an e-mail to Chen about renting one of the rooms in his flat. Look at the card on the noticeboard and think about what other information you need.

Section 2 Making contact and first impressions

What the university expects:

• effective communication – interact with a wide range of audiences

Contexts:

• communicating with university staff and professional colleagues

Aims:

• to understand names and e-mail writing conventions at university
• to evaluate some student e-mails
• to write formal e-mails

The impression that students make through their written communications, such as e-mails, is vitally important. Computer technology makes this process quicker and easier than traditional letter writing, but even for electronic communication there are some important conventions (rules) that are designed to help the reader and which everyone needs to follow. Instead of moving in with Chen and Guy, Matt decides to share a flat in town with some Chinese friends. He meets Chen to explain this, but also to ask for some advice. Matt's exam results at the end of the first semester were not good. His tutor told him that he needed to improve his writing and should get some help from the writing support teacher, Mrs Jenifer Spencer. He writes an e-mail to her, but before sending it, he asks Chen to check it for mistakes.

Task 1 Reading critically

1.1   Evaluate Matt's e-mail on page 13. Is the style formal or informal?

1.2   What impression does he give? Is this a problem? If so, why?

To:	j.a.spencer@gwu.ac.uk
From:	y.z.cao@gwu.ac.uk
Subject:	

Hi Jenifer,

I hope U R well. I am very sorry to disturb U but my tutor says U are good teacher and help students alot ☺. I am sure this is very true, because everyone here at Gateway University is very kind. I have too many problems with my writing so that my exam grade was BAD and I want U to help me every Wed afternoon. I want my writing to be prove too much. Can U do this? I hope so. And should I send U some of my bad writing for U 2 see how HORRIBLE ☹? I can send you all my essays if U say me. I will work very hard.

Bye Bye from Yong Qiang (Matt).

Task 2 Reading quickly for content overview

Jenifer Spencer was annoyed by some of the e-mails that students sent because they sounded very impolite; for example, they would begin *Hi Jenny*[2] and end *Bye for now*. They did not understand the effect that their e-mails had on the reader. She realized that this would be a disadvantage for them when they applied for a job, so she wrote a set of guidance notes for the university website. Chen shows Matt these guidance notes.

Read the guidance notes quickly. What types of information are given?
Choose three from the box.

> instructions   references   reasons   examples   hyperlinks to other websites

E-mail Guidance Notes

GATEWAY UNIVERSITY

Before coming to university, all students are familiar with e-mails and have probably sent thousands to their friends. E-mail is also the most frequent way of communicating professionally, i.e., in fields such as industry, government and the academic world. However, a professional e-mail has to be written with much more care than an e-mail to a friend and looks very different. At university, you will have to write professional e-mails to the staff, e.g., professors, lecturers and secretaries, and to other students and outside organizations. What you write will depend on your purpose and your reader. You should always think about your reader because they will evaluate you on the basis of how you write.

There are conventions to help you to make your e-mail communication more effective and to give a good impression. Here are some key points to remember, together with the reasons for them.

1 Write something in the subject field at the top of the e-mail page to give the reader some idea of what the e-mail is about, especially when it appears in the list in the Inbox. If you don't write anything, the reader has to pre-read the e-mail to find out its content, which wastes time.

2 E-mail messages should be short and simple, with short, simple sentences. Reading a computer screen is much more difficult and tiring for the eyes than reading a sheet of printed paper, and you want your reader to understand your message without getting tired and bored. Written communication in English, even for formal letters, is simple and direct and gets to the point quickly in a way that might seem very impolite in many languages and cultures.

3 Be formal, but friendly. You should not use the kind of abbreviations used in mobile phone text messages, e.g., *CU* for *I will see you*. Some readers may not understand these and they make your text look childish and unprofessional.

4 Use capitals and lower-case letters correctly. If you want to emphasize, you can use bold, italics or underline. The use of capitals for emphasis looks like SHOUTING. On the other hand, forgetting to use capitals in the right places looks lazy.

5 Because it is difficult to read on a computer screen, it is important to write short paragraphs with blank lines between them. Make one point in each paragraph. Use paragraphs, numbers and bullet points to help organize your message clearly for your reader.

Key words & phrases

familiar with
fields
outside organizations
evaluate
on the basis of
conventions
give a good impression
the subject field
the Inbox
to pre-read
wastes time
formal
direct
gets to the point
impolite
abbreviations
childish
unprofessional
capitals
lower case
to emphasize
bold
underline
a computer screen
blank lines
bullet points

---

[2] 'Jenifer' is her first name and she does not like it to be shortened.

Task 3 Reading carefully for reasons

3.1 Read the first paragraph of the e-mail guidance notes carefully and find the sentence that summarizes the main idea of all these notes.

3.2 Read the guidance notes again and give a reason, in your own words, for each of the notes.

    a Give the subject so that _____.

    b Keep it short so that _____.

    c Use formal English so that _____.

    d Use capitals correctly so that _____.

    e Use short, clear paragraphs and bullet points so that _____.

Task 4 Thinking critically about e-mails

4.1 Which guidance notes could Matt use to improve the draft e-mail that he shows to Chen?

4.2 Look again at the e-mails from Matt and Dimitri about the flat in Section 1. What impressions do they give? Use the guidance notes to suggest improvements.

4.3 Think of another guidance note of your own to add to the lecturer's list and give a reason.

Discussion

The guidance notes suggest that e-mail conventions might be different in other languages. Is what they say relevant for your language? How could this affect your e-mails to staff at university in the UK?

Task 5 Investigating evaluative language: positive and negative words

In the guidance notes, positive words (e.g., *effective*) and negative words (e.g., *lazy*) are used to show the impression that you might give a reader from your e-mails.

Sort these words from the guidance notes into a positive group and a negative group.

> effective   waste   short   simple   difficult   tiring   bored   direct
> impolite   friendly   childish   unprofessional   lazy   clearly

It is important for students to make a good impression on members of staff and this means learning the correct way to address them. Chen and Matt find the staff list for Matt's department on the university website.

Task 6 Understanding names at university

Read the table on page 15 showing the staff of the School of the Built Environment. How are the names arranged?

a in order of importance, from Head of Department down

b in order of academic qualifications, from Professor down

c in alphabetical order of family names (except the Head of Department is first)

d in alphabetical order of first names (except the Head of Department is first)

Staff	Position
Prof Robert Morris	Head of Department
Dr Carlos Gonzales Munoz	Senior Lecturer
Dr Thomas Graham	Lecturer
Dr Yasmin Hakim	Lecturer
Prof Hu Ke Li	Visiting Professor
Dr Anna Lewis	Course Administrator
Dr Nicholas Robertson	Lecturer
Mr Alistair Stewart	Course Assistant
Dr Liz Walters	Lecturer

Task 7 Thinking critically about teaching staff

Answer these questions and justify your answers.

7.1 Why do you think the staff chose this way to order the information?

7.2 What does the word *position* mean?

7.3 What do you think a *visiting professor* is?

7.4 Which members of staff mainly teach students and which are mainly concerned with administration work?

Task 8 Writing

8.1 Begin an e-mail message to each member of staff in the table in Task 6. For example, 'Dear Professor Morris'.

8.2 How would you end each message?

Study smart: making a positive impression
Busy lecturers can get a very negative impression of a student if the first contact they receive is a badly constructed e-mail. Always think about your purpose and your intended readers when you write. Consider what impression you want to give.

Task 9 Writing

Write an improved draft of Matt's e-mail to Jenifer Spencer about help with his writing. Compare with another student.

Self study

Write an e-mail to one of the School of the Built Environment staff about one of the following:

* to arrange a meeting to discuss feedback on a draft assignment
* to ask if you can visit the university department and sit in on a lecture or seminar
* to explain why you missed a lecture or class
* to offer help with a visit to your university department from a local school
* to ask for a timetable for the second semester

Section 3 Nouns and noun phrases

What the university expects:
• effective communication – present complex ideas

Contexts:
• written communication for study and work

Aims:
• to understand the importance of noun phrases
• to recognize noun phrases in texts
• to explore the grammar and meaning of noun phrases

Task 1 Reviewing learning

1.1   Write down the ten most useful words and phrases that you have learnt in Sections 1 and 2.

1.2   Compare with two other students.

1.3   Combine your lists and label the verbs, nouns and adjectives. Which group – verbs, nouns or adjectives – is the largest? Why?

Task 2 Investigating grammar patterns: word families

2.1   Find the verbs, nouns and adjectives in this extract from the *Welcome!* statement in Section 1.

> Studying at university is an opportunity to become a member of a global community, with shared goals, shared understanding and a shared language: English. You will meet many different people from different backgrounds and different countries.

2.2   Complete the word families in the table. Use a dictionary if you need to.

nouns	verbs	adjectives*
studying		
		global
		shared
understanding		
	meet	
		different

*many past participles can be used as adjectives

2.3   Use words from the table to complete the following text.

There is an important _____ between the UK universities of 30 years ago and those of today. One significant effect of _____ is the large number of international students that now _____ on courses here. _____ people from all over the world and _____ our ideas are important ways to _____ how others think and behave.

2.4   As well as *studying*, what other nouns come from the verb *study*?

Task 3 Investigating grammar patterns: types of noun

3.1 Five nouns for *study* are shown in the first row of the word family table below. Use them to complete the following text.

Chen is a _____ at Gateway University. He shares a flat and his bedroom is also his _____. He enjoys _____ programming, but he also has a compulsory module called Management _____, which he doesn't like. Chen is good at managing his time and organizes one hour every evening for language _____.

verb	person noun	thing noun	doing noun	instance noun	idea noun
'study	a 'student	a 'study	'studying	a 'study / 'studies	'study
apply	an applicant		applying	an application	application
con'sider					
		a 'globe			
				an 'extract	
'advertise					
				an organi'zation	
	ad'ministrator				

3.2 Dimitri wrote in his e-mail about the flat: *I hope that you will consider my application carefully.* The noun *application* is one of four nouns for the verb *apply* shown in the second row of the table.

Add a stress mark where appropriate to show how each word in the row is stressed.

3.3 Complete the word families for the other words in the table in the same way. Note that not all families have a complete set of five nouns. Check that you can find this information in a good English–English dictionary.

Task 4 Understanding types of noun

There are five types of nouns in the table. They are used to name different things. Complete the following descriptions.

a A(n) _____ noun names the general idea shared by the verb and the nouns in the family.

b A(n) _____ noun names the person or group of people that carry out the verb.

c A(n) _____ noun names the activity carried out.

d A(n) _____ noun names something physical, i.e., that can be seen or touched.

e A(n) _____ noun names something specific that happens or exists.

One word family can contain all these different kinds of nouns. However, we have to see a noun in context to see what type it is. For many nouns, the same form can be several different noun types, for example, *study*.

Investigating grammar patterns: countable and uncountable nouns

type of noun	pattern	examples
person noun	countable	*She is an administrator.* *There are three applicants.*
thing noun	mainly countable[3]	*The Earth is a globe.* *His study is also his bedroom.*
instance noun	countable	*Applications can be e-mailed.* *Corrupt administrations can't fight poverty.*
doing noun	uncountable	*TV advertising is effective, but costly.*
idea noun	uncountable	*The administration of most exams is tightly controlled.*

- Countable nouns can be plural and can take the indefinite article *a* or *an*:
 an administrator, administrators, an administration; a globe, globes; an application, applications.

- Uncountable nouns do not have plural forms and do not take the indefinite article (*a* or *an*):
 advertising, administration, globalization. This form tends to be used for general reference.

- Both countable and uncountable nouns can take the definite article *the* when the noun has unique reference (e.g., *the Earth*) or is already familiar to the reader or listener from the context:

	context	familiar noun
countable	*Two students needed to share a **comfortable flat** in the centre of Summerford.*	*Let's interview them this evening and take them around **the flat**.*
uncountable (idea noun)	*Last semester I lived with my uncle's family …*	*… but **the accommodation** was very crowded.*

- The definite article *the* is also used with a countable or uncountable noun when its exact reference is specified by a following prepositional phrase or relative clause:
 *Here are some key points to remember, together with **the reasons** for them.*
 *Thank you for **the feedback** you sent.*

Task 5 Practising grammar patterns: countable and uncountable nouns

5.1 **Complete these sentences using an instance noun and an idea noun of the word given.**

a *application*
An important use of computer modelling is in its _____ to climate research.
Computer _____ can help researchers to use statistics to process their data.

b *communication*
Conflict in teams can result from breakdowns in _____.
It is important for managers not to send private _____, such as a dismissal notice, by e-mail.

c *evaluation*
Management teams can improve their effectiveness by regular review and _____.
Detailed _____ of the model were carried out before publication.

d *argument*
EAP students have to learn the organization and language of _____.
In a seminar, _____ can occur, but not frequently.

5.2 **Check that you can find this information in a good English–English dictionary.**

---

[3] Some nouns in this group are uncountable, e.g., *rice, water, air, money, software, traffic, accommodation.* However, note that there is a plural noun, *monies*, which means 'amounts of money'.

Task 6 Practising grammar patterns: common errors

There are some nouns which do not have a countable form, but students often mistakenly make them plural: *researches, accommodations, informations, attentions*

With some of these nouns, instead of making them plural, you can make a plural, countable noun phrase; others stay singular and uncountable.

Complete these sentences using the noun in brackets. Use a dictionary if you need to.

a They carried out three major _____. (*research*)

b Khalid, Matt and Dimitri needed to find _____. (*accommodation*)

c There are several important _____ that you have left out of your report. (*information*)

d Once they had discovered that the computer programme was not working properly, they focused their _____ on debugging. (*attention*)

Task 7 Investigating academic nouns

Noun formation in academic English

In academic English, nouns are extremely important. They are often derived (formed) from verbs and from adjectives. This table shows the most frequent endings for these derived nouns in academic English, together with some examples derived from verbs and adjectives in Sections 1 and 2[4].

ending	examples
~tion	*abbreviation, accommodation, communication, convention, duration, evaluation, location*
~ity	*clarity, familiarity, formality, priority, probability, simplicity, suitability*
~er	*computer, lecturer, reader, writer*
~ness	*childishness, effectiveness, friendliness, laziness, politeness*
~ment	*advertisement, government, management, statement*

7.1 Which endings show that the noun is formed from a verb and which from an adjective?

7.2 The two most frequent academic noun endings, *~tion* and *~ity*, are always stressed in the same place in the words. Write the stress mark in the examples in these rows in the table and practise saying them.

Investigating grammar patterns: noun phrases

A noun phrase is a word or group of words that names or labels a person, action, thing or idea; in other words, that behaves like a noun[5]. It can be the subject of a verb and it always contains at least one noun, the main or head noun. Identifying the noun phrases and what they are doing in a text helps you to read more effectively.

---

[4] Table based on Biber et al. (1999). *Longman grammar of spoken and written English*. Harlow: Pearson, pp318–325. **Note:** *~ism* is not included here.
[5] Pronouns can stand in for noun phrases in the same way that they stand in for nouns.

Task 8 Understanding noun phrases

In this extract from Dimitri's e-mail, the noun phrases are underlined.

> <u>Last semester</u> I lived with <u>my uncle's family</u> but <u>my accommodation</u> was very crowded and I had <u>insufficient space for my books, computer, etc</u>. <u>This semester</u> I am looking for <u>my own study bedroom</u> so that I can complete <u>my degree</u> quickly and successfully.

8.1 **a** Which two noun phrases label times and which two label places?

    b Which noun phrase labels people, which labels a problem and which labels a qualification?

8.2 Highlight the main or head noun in each noun phrase. The first one has been done for you.

Here is one of the guidance notes from the website you studied in Section 2.

> 2 E-mail <mark>messages</mark> should be short and simple, with short, simple sentences. Reading a computer screen is much more difficult and tiring for the eyes than reading a sheet of printed paper and you want your reader to understand your message without getting tired and bored. Written communication in English, even for formal letters, is simple and direct and gets to the point quickly in a way that might seem very impolite in many languages and cultures.

8.3 Underline the noun phrases and highlight the head nouns. The first one has been done for you.

8.4 Find three noun phrases that name actions. These have doing nouns as the head nouns.

Investigating grammar patterns: the components of noun phrases

The components which can be in a noun phrase are:

determiner + adjective + noun + (*of*) + noun + prepositional phrase + relative clause

All these components are optional in a noun phrase, but there must be a head noun. There can be more than one relative clause or prepositional phrase, and they can be in either order. The longer the noun phrase is, the more specific the label is, and the easier it is for the reader to identify what you are talking about. Academic texts use long noun phrases to label ideas very precisely.

Task 9 Analyzing noun phrase components

This table shows how noun phrases are constructed.

Find an example from the guidance note in Task 8.2 for each pattern and add it to the table. Highlight the head noun. The first one has been done for you.

noun phrase pattern	example
1. determiner + noun	*the eyes*
2. adjective(s) + noun	
3. noun + noun	
4. doing noun + adjective(s)	
5. doing noun + noun + noun	
6. adjective + noun + prepositional phrase	
7. doing noun + determiner + noun + *of* + adjective + noun	
8. determiner + noun + relative clause	

Task 10 The noun phrase game

Work in groups. Write down a noun and then add components to make longer and longer noun phrases. Try to make the longest noun phrase in the class.

Task 11 Constructing noun phrases

Reconstruct the jumbled noun phrases highlighted in the following sentences. They are all from texts you have read.

a university at Studying is an opportunity …

b I am from a student mature Athens.

c The of for use emphasis capitals looks like shouting.

d … become member community. a a of global

e They are planning to move to city flat centre. accommodation cheaper in a in the

f You should not use mobile messages. text phone used the abbreviations kind of in

g There is campus. studying students on a population large international of

h You will meet different many different different and from countries. people backgrounds

Self study

Find a textbook in your subject area and identify ten useful academic noun phrases. Share them with other students at your next class. You could make some jumbled noun phrases for them to reconstruct.

Section 4 Academic writing

At university, lecturers expect students to read academic sources in order to understand key concepts in their discipline. Students then have to use what they have learnt to write their assignments. The writing style expected at university can be very different from the kinds of texts that are studied in general English courses in high school.

Task 1 Reading quickly to identify text type and topic

Chen is interested in Khalid's field, robotics, and he has been reading a newspaper article about the study of robotics at Gateway University. Khalid has also given him one of his own robotics assignments to read.

Read Texts A and B quickly.

1.1   Look at the title and the layout of each. Which text is part of the newspaper article and which is part of Khalid's assignment? How do you know?

1.2   Do they contain similar information or very different information?

Text A

What is a robot?

You probably know about fictional robots from films like *2001: A Space Odyssey, I, Robot* and *Enthiran: The Robot*, but the truth about robots is stranger and much more interesting than the fiction. We use these machines that think for all kinds of tasks in every environment you can imagine, from operating theatres to outer space.

You might not recognize a robot at first meeting as they do not always look like humans. Robot engineers have produced a wide range of designs for how they are driven and how they move, with some that resemble insects and walk on legs, others that are small submarines for under water and even airplanes that fly. However, all robots have something in common – they need humans to program them, and that's why so many computer science graduates work in the field of robotics, according to Prof John Dunbar of Gateway University.

Scientists use robots with sophisticated computer programs for research under water and out in space. They are particularly useful where conditions are too dangerous or too difficult for humans, for example, checking pipelines on the ocean floor or finding casualties in burning buildings. Workers in the chemical and nuclear industries use robots to pick up dangerous materials, such as explosives and radioactive items, which humans could not even get close to. Space scientists can send robots on a one-way ticket to the Moon or to Mars to send home images of the alien planet surface and skies. Robots can even collect dust and carry out sophisticated experiments, sending back valuable data to scientists on Earth. According to Prof Dunbar, robot engineers need all their expertise to find designs and materials to meet the challenges of these environments.

Key words & phrases

fictional
truth is stranger than fiction
environment
operating theatres
outer space
a wide range of
designs
resemble
submarines
have … in common
to program
in the field of
according to
sophisticated
casualties
a one-way ticket
images
alien planet
dust
expertise

Text B

Issues in robot design
1 Introduction

1.1 A definition – Robotics has been defined as, 'the science which studies the intelligent connection between perception and action'[1]. A robot is thus a machine that can interact intelligently with its environment in order to perform physical tasks autonomously, under the control of a programmed computer.

1.2 Robot classification – Robots can be classified according to various criteria of design, function or domain. Design features include the range of possible movements in space, the drive technology, the type of movement in the working environment and the motion characteristics[2]. Alternatively, function can be the basis of robot categories. A major distinction is often made between robots that simply manipulate objects and those that use sensors to gather information. A third possibility is to classify robots in terms of their domain of operation, i.e., surface, underwater, aerial or microgravity (space) environments. Robots are often used in the field to perform tasks that are too hazardous for humans. For example, in the underwater domain they can perform inspection and maintenance on dams, offshore oil installations and pipelines. Surface robots can also be used to minimize risk to humans in the manipulation of toxic materials such as nuclear fuel rods or very corrosive acids, and in search and rescue operations following an earthquake, for instance[3]. These environments can be a severe test of materials and design.

[1] Siciliano, B., & Khatib, O. (Eds.). (2008). *Springer Handbook of Robotics*. Berlin: Springer (pp. 2–3).
[2] *ibid.* (pp. 9–15)
[3] Tsai, W. M. (2009). *Robotics for hostile environments*. London: Roadhouse.

Key words & phrases
issues
perception
to perform tasks
autonomously
under the control of
classification
according to
criteria
function
domain
type
categories
a distinction is made
sensors
domain of operation
aerial
microgravity
in the field
inspection
maintenance
offshore oil installations
minimize risk
manipulation
toxic materials
corrosive
operations
a severe test
hostile environments

Task 2 Reading critically for audience and purpose

Who are the intended readers of the two texts and what are the writers' purposes? Complete the table.

	Text A	Text B
intended readers		
writers' purposes		

Task 3 Reading critically for style and organization

How is the style and organization of the two texts influenced by the writer's purpose and intended readers? Work with another student to make a comparison table to show the differences in the way the texts are written. Use these features to help you:
a layout
b starting point of the texts
c style of presentation of information
d organization of information
e language

Task 4 Identifying topic differences

4.1 Work in small groups. Find and underline the main verbs in the sentences in each text.

4.2 Find and highlight the noun phrase at the starting point of each sentence. The noun phrase is the subject and it shows the theme, i.e., what the sentence is about. What aspects of the topic of robots are covered in each text?

Task 5 Investigating language patterns: language for analyzing a concept

In Text B, Khalid analyzes the concept of a robot in two clearly identified steps: first, he gives a definition of robots, then he classifies them, i.e., he explains different types of robots with examples.

5.1 In Text B, find and underline key language for defining and classifying.

5.2 Add the key language to the table according to the purpose.

purpose	key language
1. to introduce a definition of robots	
2. to introduce types of robots	
3. to explain the reasons for the types of robots	
4. to contrast types	
5. to give examples	
6. to use another word for 'types'	

Task 6 Thinking critically

Here is Matt's introduction to an assignment. The introduction is not satisfactory for a number of reasons.

Work in pairs to identify any features that are not academic.

Key words & phrases

component
relates to
construction
concrete
layer
cavity
insulating

Assignment:

Choose a component of a building and explain how the design relates to the function.

Have you ever thought about walls? I mean the walls that surround you in the classroom where you are now sitting. Everyone wants to feel safe, private, warm and comfortable and for these things we need walls. We want to be sure that the roof won't fall on us, that we have our own quiet space within a large building like a school and that we keep the weather out. Construction engineers know what type of wall to build for all our needs, whether they use brick, concrete, wood or steel. They use single walls, made of one layer of material, for dividing the school into rooms. When they know that the wall has to support a roof, or has to keep out noise, construction engineers use double walls. Where we need outside walls to keep us from the weather, they build cavity walls and fill the space between the layers with an insulating material that keeps us warm.

Task 7 Understanding key features of notes

Chen wrote some notes from Khalid's text on robots to make sure he could understand the range of their applications.

In what ways are his notes different from Khalid's text?

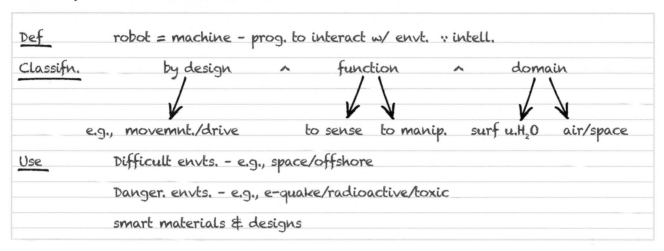

| Def | robot = machine – prog. to interact w/ envt. ∴ intell. |

Classifn.   by design   ᴧ   function   ᴧ   domain

e.g., movemnt./drive   to sense to manip.   surf u.H_2O air/space

Use   Difficult envts. – e.g., space/offshore

Danger. envts. – e.g., e-quake/radioactive/toxic

smart materials & designs

Task 8 Writing: redrafting in an academic style

Make notes on Matt's introduction and redraft it so that it is a more academic text. Use the language you identified in Khalid's text to define and classify walls. Review your draft with another student.

Self study

Write a short academic text to explain to a classmate something that you are interested in. For example, explain a sport such as football or basketball, an activity using a computer, a fashion style or a traditional festival. Write 150–200 words.

Section 5 An introductory lecture

What the university expects:
• awareness of how knowledge is advanced and communicated

Contexts:
• preparing for lectures and seminars

Aims:
• to understand how university students prepare to listen to a lecture
• to listen to a lecture and make notes for a purpose
• to use an understanding of functions to support listening

Reading and lectures are two of the main methods by which university students learn. In order to remember what they are learning and to use the ideas in their assignments, students need to make notes.

Discussion

Why do you make notes while reading? How do you make notes? How are notes different from text? How are notes made while reading different from notes made while listening?

Study smart: a checklist for making notes

• Have a purpose.
• Select information for this purpose. Do not make notes on everything.
• Use an appropriate note format to organize the information according to its function or purpose – a list, a table (to compare and contrast), a tree diagram (to classify), a flow diagram (for causes and effects or processes), etc. Use clear headings.
• Do not write in sentences. Use symbols or abbreviations. You can personalize these when the notes are for you only to read (spelling and grammar are not important).

Task 1 Listening for information

Maysoun is a postgraduate Environmental Studies student. She is helping to organize a public lecture by a famous visiting professor on the environmental significance of tropical rainforests. She wants as many people to attend as possible so she makes an announcement at the end of the International Students' Association meeting. You think your friend might be interested in this lecture because he is going to research rainforest products and the fair-trade movement.

1.1   ⊚T02 and T03 **Listen to Maysoun's announcement and make notes on what to tell your friend.**

1.2   **Maysoun misses out some important information. What is it and how can your friend find it?**

Task 2 Listening for practice/ear training

⊚ T03 **Listen again carefully to Maysoun's last two sentences and try to write down exactly what she says. Listen as often as necessary.**

Discussion
- Why is it more difficult to make notes when you are listening to a lecture than when you are reading something?
- How can you prepare to listen to a lecture?

Task 3 Reading carefully for relevant content

Maysoun wants to prepare by finding information on what exactly is meant by *tropical rainforests*, and where they are located. She takes a book out of the library to make some notes.

3.1 Read the contents page of Maysoun's book. Which chapters have the information she needs to answer the following questions: *What exactly is meant by tropical rainforests? Where are they located?*

3.2 Which sections of the book will help her to find:

a the meanings of any technical words she doesn't know?

b where the author got his information from?

Key words & phrases
tropical
rainforest
climate
geological
distribution
structure
nutrients
interaction
diversity
modelling
sustainability
references
glossary
index
ecosystem

CONTENTS

Richmore, P. T. (2009). *Tropical Rainforests: An Introduction to a Vital Ecosystem.* Summerford: Gateway University Press.

Task 4 Understanding chapter titles

4.1 Khalid organized the information in his robots text using functions such as defining and classifying. He used key language to express these functions: *has been defined as*; *can be classified according to*. Richmore also uses functions in some of the chapters of his book to organize information about tropical rainforests.

Write the chapter titles in the appropriate place in the table and underline the key language that shows the function. The first one has been done for you.

function	examples
1. comparing and contrasting	*Chapter 8 Measuring <u>diversity</u>*
2. defining and classifying	
3. describing spatial location	
4. describing change and development	
5. describing causes and effects	
6. describing problems and solutions	

4.2 Find and highlight the head nouns in the book and chapter titles.

Discussion

Before the lecture, discuss the lecture handout and try to predict what the lecturer will say.

Lecture handout:

1. **A visit to the tropical rainforest**

   Outline
   - Definition
     - Locations
     - Types
   - Structure
   - Animal and plant adaptations
   - Threats

2.

   Notes:

3.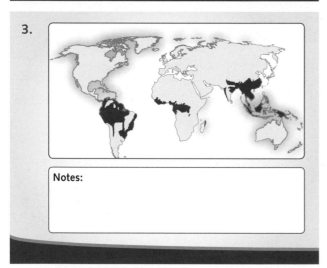

   Notes:

4.

   Notes:

5.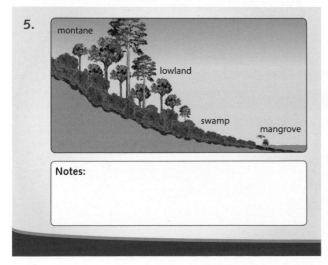

   Notes:

6.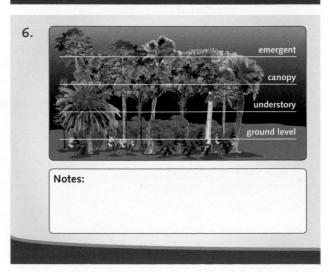

   Notes:

Task 5 Using functions to support listening

Following Maysoun's introduction, Professor Mogea begins his lecture with an outline of the key functions that he will use to organize his lecture.

T04 Listen to the outline of the lecture carefully. Write phrases that he uses to show the functions in the table. The first one has been done for you.

function	examples
1. comparing and contrasting	*a very different place; the richest biodiversity of any system on Earth*
2. defining	
3. classifying	
4. describing spatial location	
5. describing change and development	
6. describing causes and effects	
7. describing problems and solutions	

Task 6 Listening and note-making: shared listening

6.1 **T05 Listen to the rest of the lecture. Work in groups of four to make notes on the lecture handout. You will each focus on a different part of the lecture.**

Student A: What is a tropical rainforest?

Student B: Where is it found and why is it found there?

Student C: What are some of the different types of rainforest?

Student D: What is the structure of the rainforest?

6.2 **Rewrite your notes together to combine all the information into one set of notes.**

Discussion

Is shared listening a useful strategy? Is recognizing functions helpful to understand the lecture?

Self study

Using only your notes, write a short exam answer in 50–100 of your own words to each of the following questions:

* What exactly is meant by 'tropical rainforest'?
* What are the reasons for the geographical locations of tropical rainforest?
* Describe the structure of a typical tropical rainforest.

Unit 2

Looking backwards and forwards

Section 1 Reviewing

> **What the university expects:**
> • autonomy – assess yourself rigorously and conscientiously
>
> **Contexts:**
> • interviews or appraisals for study and work
>
> **Aims:**
> • to understand how to plan, implement and evaluate good study strategies
> • to understand the main points in a tutorial meeting
> • to use language for planning, implementing and evaluating

At university, undergraduate students are assigned an academic tutor whose role is to have an overview of a student's academic performance and provide guidance throughout their degree. They can also help students to deal with study or personal problems. Students meet their academic tutors regularly to review their progress. Reviewing involves reporting and also evaluating actions. Guy's academic tutor is Dr Malik, who is also a lecturer on his International Marketing course. They meet to review Guy's recent exam results.

> **Study smart:** the PIE cycle
>
> The PIE cycle can be used to review study performance and strategies.
> **Planning:** objectives are specified, together with the actions needed to achieve them.
> **Implementation:** the action plans are implemented and the results of this implementation are recorded.
> **Evaluation:** the plans are evaluated by comparing the results with the original objectives. This analysis leads to the specification of a new set of objectives and action plans.

Task 1 Thinking critically about PIE

1.1 **At which point in the PIE cycle do you think Guy and Dr Malik will start their discussion? Give reasons for your answer.**

1.2 How will Guy know if his study strategies were successful in Semester 1?

Task 2 Listening for the main ideas

🎧T06 Listen to Guy discussing his studies with Dr Malik.

2.1 **Were his study strategies more successful in Semester 1 than in his first year? How do you know?**

2.2 **What did he do to improve the way he studied? Make a list. How does he feel now?**

Task 3 Listening and recording

3.1 At the end of the tutorial, Dr Malik asks Guy to check the record he has made of their meeting.

🔊**T06 Listen to the conversation again, using the transcript on page 288 if you want to, and complete the form. Add specific actions for Guy's objectives in Semester 1. Record the results of Guy's actions and his evaluation. Were his evaluations positive?**

3.2 In his discussion with Dr Malik, Guy mentions some of the new actions he will take in Semester 2.

For each of the objectives for Semester 2 listed in the meeting record, record what action Guy plans to take.

RECORD OF MEETING

GATEWAY UNIVERSITY

Student　　　Guy Edwards

Course　　　International Business　　Year of study 1 ❨2❩ 3 – 4

Date of meeting　21st January

Study objectives and actions for Semester 1

To study smarter　　　　Action: _____

To organize time better　Action: make specific times to prepare for seminars

To use the library more　Action: _____

Results

1 _____

2 _____

3 _____

4 Achieved A grades in an essay and exam _____

Evaluation *positive/negative* + comments

1 _____

2 _____

3 _____

4 felt more motivated and has a better attitude because he knows which topics interest him

Study objectives and actions for Semester 2

To organize time for study　Action _____

To find quiet study time　　Action _____

To focus on practical aspects　Action _____

A copy of this record should be forwarded to the administrative officer responsible for student records.

Study smart: SMART objectives

SMART objectives are Specific, Measurable, Achievable, Realistic, Time-bound. Students sometimes say *I will do my best* or *I want to get a good degree*. These are very general aims and are hard to evaluate. Specifying study objectives as SMART objectives helps to make them easier to evaluate.

Discuss with other students: to what extent do you think Guy specified SMART objectives?

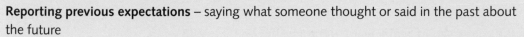

Investigating grammar patterns for PIE

Dr Malik and Guy used these patterns to plan, implement and evaluate Guy's study strategies:

Reporting previous expectations – saying what someone thought or said in the past about the future

| *thought* + clause (future in the past) | *I thought it would just be a repeat of things I learnt at school …* |
| *said* + clause (future in the past) | *You said you would try to organize your time better and study smarter this year.* |

Planning – stating intentions

| *going to* + verb | *So I'm going to … make another study plan for this semester.* |
| *will* + verb | *… I'll [probably] go to the library [whenever I need quiet study time].* |

Implementation – reporting actions

| verb (past simple) | *I put specific times in the plan [to read and prepare for the seminars] …* |
| | *I went … to a lecture … given by one of the librarians [about how to use the library].* |

Evaluation – reporting the effects of actions

verb (present simple) + purpose verb (past simple) + reason	*… I understand how hard I have to work to get the grades I want.*
	… that really motivated me because the ideas weren't only from books …
	I was pretty surprised because I didn't see myself as an A-grade student.

Task 4 Practising grammar patterns for PIE

4.1 **Think about your own experience of studying academic English. Use each of the grammar patterns in the PIE cycle to write statements about your expectations, plans and actions, and your evaluation of these.**

4.2 **Write some SMART objectives and actions for your learning goals in the next semester.**

Self study

Find the website of a university where you would like to study and look for a degree that interests you. Write down the titles of some modules or courses listed for this degree. Try to decide why you find these modules interesting. Bring the titles to class to compare with other students.

Section 2 Coaching

What the university expects:
- autonomy – set goals and direct your own learning

Contexts:
- interviews or appraisals for study and work

Aims:
- to understand how coaching can be used to improve performance
- to use comparisons for thinking critically
- to use language for reporting and asking two-part questions

Academic tutors conduct their sessions with students in a variety of ways. Chen has a meeting with his tutor, Dr Michaelson, who is a lecturer in computer science, but also a keen football supporter. His approach is similar to the way football coaches prepare their teams for important matches. He uses a performance coaching technique called GROW.

Task 1 Thinking critically about coaching

1.1   How does a coach encourage the members of his team to improve their game and give their best performance? How do you think Dr Michaelson will use these ideas in his tutorial with Chen?

1.2   What words do you think the letters stand for in the acronym GROW?

Task 2 Listening for the main ideas

🎧T07 Listen to the conversation between Chen and Dr Michaelson.

2.1   What problem or weakness does Chen identify that he would like to improve?

2.2   How does Dr Michaelson try to build Chen's confidence to make these improvements?

Task 3 Thinking critically by comparing

3.1   Dr Michaelson guides Chen to compare himself with a Greek student in his seminar class and with football players in a team.

   What is his purpose in making these comparisons?

3.2   In their discussion, do Chen and Dr Michaelson mainly look back or look forward? How is this similar or different to Guy's tutorial with Dr Malik in Section 1?

3.3   Who seems to be more in control of the direction taken in each tutoring session – the lecturer or the student? Which type of tutoring session would you prefer?

Task 4 Listening and analyzing

4.1   🎧T07 Listen to the conversation again, using the transcript on page 290 if you need to. Dr Michaelson uses a performance coaching technique called GROW. Complete the questions below to show what the letters in this acronym stand for.

G   What _____ does the performer want to achieve?

R   What is the current situation or current _____?

O   What _____ for change are available to the performer?

W   What _____ the performer do to achieve the goals?

4.2   During their conversation, Dr Michaelson reports Chen's ideas back to him and then asks a question.

Why does he use this two-part structure?

4.3   **Find places in the transcript where Dr Michaelson reports what Chen says. Highlight Chen's actual words. How does Dr Michaelson change Chen's words in his report?**

Investigating grammar patterns for reporting

Reports can be *direct* – the exact words that were said – or *indirect* – a summary of the ideas in the words of the reporter. Reports come first in two-part questions to link what a speaker has said to a question which takes him or her in a new direction.

Reporting words directly

think/say + exact words in inverted commas '...'	*I think, 'I know that! I could say that!'*

Summarizing and reporting words indirectly

think + *that* + report clause (present simple)	*OK, so you think that you need to check the grammar of your answer ...*
say + report clause (present simple)	*... but you say it's easy for you.*

noun phrases: ~*ing* + adjective
               ~*ing* + prepositional
               ~*ing* + object
	being silent
	 speaking in class
	 making grammar mistakes

general noun	*... your goal [is to feel confident contributing in seminars] ...*

Asking two-part questions

Report (question) + checking question	*Are you happy with ... being silent in class? Is that OK for you?*
Report (clause) + checking question	*OK, so you say that you want to speak ... but you don't speak because you don't feel confident ... Is that right?*
Question + *when* + report (subordinate clause)	*What happens now when you know the answer and you want to say something?*
If + report (subordinate clause) + question	*So if it's OK for the Greek student to make mistakes and to give the wrong answer, is it OK for you to do that, too?*
Report (noun phrase) + question	*Good, but the football players who miss the goal or lose the ball ... what do they do about that?*

Task 5 Practising grammar patterns for reporting

Work in pairs to make a list of things you find difficult about studying or about academic English. Exchange your list with another pair of students. Read their list and together with your partner think of some suggestions that might help them to overcome the difficulties. Offer your suggestions to the other pair of students using two-part questions, e.g., *You say that you find it difficult to study on your own. Could you try studying in a group with other students?*

Task 6 Keeping a record

Write the e-mail which Chen sends to Dr Michaelson. Use the GROW framework to structure the e-mail.

Self study

The PIE cycle, SMART objectives and the GROW technique are management tools. They are given these labels so that they can be easily recognized and referred to by people who use them. They become part of the jargon of the discipline. Do you know any acronyms for tools or techniques in your field? Find an example to bring to class. Be prepared to explain the meaning of the acronym and how the tool or technique is used.

Section 3 Reporting

What the university expects:
- effective communication – present complex ideas in response to the needs of a wide range of audiences

Contexts:
- written reports for study and work

Aims:
- to use guidelines to compare the structure of reports in different fields
- to identify sections and their purposes in a published research report
- to understand how to keep a record of sources you read

Written reports are a common type of document which students have to read and use as sources in their assignments. Khalid, who studies robotics, and Guy, who studies international business, each have a report to write for one of their modules. They have found some guidelines on their department websites about how to write reports.

Discussion

What is the purpose of a report? Who is it written for? Do you think the reports that Khalid and Guy have to read and write will be similar or different? Discuss with other students what sections each report will contain. Do you know the names for any of these sections?

Study smart: the purpose of reports

Written reports are important documents which look back to record activities carried out; for example, an experiment, a site visit, a new software design or the analysis of a problem. A reader has to understand what was done in order to look forward to future research or to act on recommendations. The report communicates the results of the activity clearly for the intended audience because it uses a standard structure. It usually begins by introducing the topic and the aims, then describes the methods used to produce the results, the design, or the analysis, and ends with a discussion of the results, conclusions or recommendations. The specific detail of the structure varies depending on the purpose of the report and its context, e.g., a professional report at work is different from a laboratory report at university.

The report mediates the interaction between the real academic or professional worlds in which people carry out research and analyze problems, and the virtual, textual world in which they communicate their results. The list of report sections in Task 1 illustrates this interaction with a general-to-specific introduction, and a specific-to-general discussion, which looks back and forward to the real academic or professional worlds.

Key words & phrases

written reports
record
an experiment
a site visit
a software design
to act on
recommendations
the intended audience
varies
depending on
context
professional
mediates
illustrates

Task 1 Reading to understand the structure of reports

1.1 The names for each section in a basic report are:

- Introduction
- Aims
- Methods
- Results
- Discussion
- Conclusion

Read both sets of guidelines below and opposite, and decide in which section you would place each of the elements listed under *Report structure*.

1.2 Did you have difficulty deciding where to place some of the elements listed?

Department of Computer Science

Guidelines for writing laboratory reports

Introduction

There are two principal kinds of laboratory report. In the first kind, the scientist or engineer reports experiments to test a particular theory. For example, the theory of gravity can be tested by measuring the velocities and accelerations of falling objects and comparing these results with the formulae that describe gravitational motion. In the other kind of report, the scientist or engineer designs some software or hardware to perform a particular task, e.g., a digital filter to filter out noise from an audio signal. In that case, the report presents the theoretical approach to filter design in general and then explains how a particular filter design was implemented. It then compares the results before and after filtering, with the performance predicted by the theory.

GATEWAY UNIVERSITY

Key words & phrases

guidelines
laboratory report
to test a theory
theory of gravity
velocities
accelerations
formulae
gravitational motion
to design
a digital filter
an audio signal
the theoretical approach to
to filter out noise
filter design

The report must critically evaluate any limitations in measurement or design so that the reader knows to what extent the results are reliable, i.e., if the experiment or design was repeated, the results would be the same. The writer also has to discuss the implications of the results, i.e., what was achieved, how this contributed to understanding the problem and what further work would be necessary.

Report structure

Typically, a well-structured report will include some or all of the following elements:

1 Title page
2 Abstract
3 Introduction
4 Aims and objectives
5 Explanation of theory or development of design
6 Procedures followed to test the theory or to evaluate the design
7 Presentation of results in comparison with the theory or design
8 Conclusions and further work
9 References
10 Appendices (e.g., code listings)

All reports should be typed using word-processing software. All diagrams should be drawn neatly with an appropriate design package and the axes of graphs should be labelled with both variables and units. Where possible, use graphs rather than tables. Write as briefly as possible in plain, precise English.

School of Management

Guidelines for writing business reports

Introduction

GATEWAY UNIVERSITY

A business report records the analysis of a business problem and recommended solutions. The analysis is intended to establish and interpret the facts which relate to the problem and to persuade a reader, e.g., a manager, to accept and implement the recommendations.

The analysis is often supported by references to previous research and to theoretical models of the way organizations operate. The report links this theory to practice within a business context in order to justify the recommendations. A business report is successful if it can be read and understood quickly and easily by its intended reader, who will accept the facts, findings and conclusions it contains and decide to take the recommended actions. Busy managers do not have time or may not need to read a whole report, so they read the executive summary which provides an overview of the key information. It outlines as briefly as possible the topic and the problem, the scope of the investigation, methods of analysis and important findings, issues raised, conclusions and recommendations. It is designed to be read and understood without reference to the main report.

Report structure

Typically, a well-structured business report will include some or all of the following elements:

1 Title page
2 Executive summary
3 Contents
4 Introduction
5 Terms of reference
6 Review of previous research or explanation of models relevant to the problem
7 Analysis of the problem to establish the facts
8 Discussion of the analysis in comparison with the research or models
9 Conclusions and recommendations
10 References
11 Appendices (e.g., complete data sets)

The report should follow a format that is acceptable to the intended audience. This is often specified in detail for company reports which usually have a house style. The language should be neutral and objective with no unnecessary repetition.

Task 2 Reading carefully to understand the purpose of each section

2.1   The table below contains purposes for different sections of a report.

Choose the set of guidelines which is closest to your field and reread them carefully. Complete the table for your set of guidelines.

2.2   **Compare your answers with a student who read different guidelines. Are any of your answers different? Try to explain the difference.**

purpose of a section	laboratory report	business report
1. to identify the report and author		
2. to give a brief overview of the study	abstract	
3. to describe the background of the study		
4. to briefly state the purpose		
5. to explain how the study fits with previous work		
6. to present theories or models to evaluate results		
7. to describe the methods	procedures followed	
8. to present the findings		
9. to compare results / analysis with theory		comparison with models
10. to summarize what was achieved / suggest action		

Task 3 Thinking critically about report structure and style

3.1   **Why are there differences in structure between the different types of reports?**

3.2   Often in professional reports, complete sections, e.g., methods, can be cut and pasted from other similar reports.

Is this acceptable practice at university? Why/Why not?

3.3   **Decide which sections of a report look back and which sections look forward. Think about the relationships between sections and the grammar patterns you expect to find in each section. Explain to another student the reasons for your answers.**

3.4   **What should students do to make sure that they write reports using the correct format and style?**

Task 4 Identifying sections and purposes in a published research report

Khalid intends to write his report on the design of safety systems in cars; specifically, Advanced Driver Assistance Systems (ADASs), which are designed to help people to drive safely in busy traffic. He needs to read other reports on this topic and use them as sources in his assignment. He has found a research report which compares attitudes to driving and to ADASs in China and in Sweden.

4.1   On page 39 are seven extracts (a–g) from the report.

For each extract, identify the section of the report it comes from. Look back to Tasks 2 and 3 to help you remember the names of the sections and their purpose.

4.2   **Put the extracts in the order you would expect to find them in the report.**

a Section: _____

Sixty participants (56 male, 4 female) in Beijing were asked to complete questionnaires. The questionnaire was based on the Manchester Driver Behaviour Questionnaire (developed by Reason, Manstead, Stradling, Baxter, & Campbell, 1990) which contained questions about traffic problems.

b Section: _____

Active safety systems, also known as Advanced Driver Assistance Systems (ADASs), are a type of independent electronic system designed to help drivers move safely through busy traffic. Their overall aim is to reduce traffic accidents and to make the driving experience easier and more efficient. Recently, there has been an increasing amount of research on the technical aspects of ADAS development, with many of these publications coming from China (Gong et al., 2008; Zhao et al., 2008; Wu et al., 2008).

c Section: _____

The traffic problems identified in China indicate strong cultural factors regarding patterns of thought and patterns of behaviour. The participants found that problems with drivers using the hard shoulder (emergency lane), illegal overtaking and speeding were the main factors likely to cause accidents. These results agree with results showing that unsafe behaviour is a contributing factor in more than 90% of accidents worldwide (Rumar, 1985).

d Section: _____

There are very few studies that have investigated what kind of ADAS is needed for drivers to cope with the traffic problems in China. The purpose of this study is to identify the most common traffic problems Chinese drivers face, and to ask their opinions about the introduction of ADASs into their cars.

e Section: _____

There were nine traffic problems that most participants considered serious. These problems are presented in Table 1.

f Section: _____

Advanced Driver Assistance Systems are intended to reduce traffic accidents and fatalities. The design of these systems is usually based on research on driving in Western countries. However, with the increase in car ownership in countries such as China, there is a need to investigate how these systems should be designed for developing markets. This study aimed to discover the most common traffic problems facing Chinese drivers, how those problems differ from those in a country with a more developed driving culture (Sweden), and what consequences these differences will have for the design of Advanced Driver Assistance Systems. Results show that, even though Swedish and Chinese traffic rules and regulations are similar, driver behaviour is very different. The observed differences suggest that Advanced Driver Assistance Systems designed for roads in Sweden may not necessarily be suitable in other markets.

g Section: _____

Chinese roads are often dangerous, with high numbers of fatalities. Drivers have to share the road with many vulnerable users, such as pedestrians and cyclists (Huang, Zhang, Roetting, & Melton, 2006; Lindgren et al., 2007). Road signs tend to be poorly designed or even missing at road construction areas (Lindgren, Chen, Jordan, & Ljungstrand, n.d.). In addition, driver behaviour is considered a major safety problem. Huang et al. (2006) found that Chinese drivers are more aggressive than drivers in the USA, because the Chinese tend to drive more forcefully and disobey traffic rules.

Source: Lindgren, A., Chen, F., Jordan, P. W., & Zhang, H. (2008). Requirements for the design of Advanced Driver Assistance Systems: The differences between Swedish and Chinese drivers. _International Journal of Design_, 2(2), 41–54.

Key words & phrases
participants
to complete questionnaires
contained
electronic system
to move through traffic
the driving experience
the technical aspects
publications
cultural factors
patterns of thought
hard shoulder
emergency lane
illegal overtaking
speeding
likely to cause
accidents
a contributing factor
worldwide
to cope with
to face problems
the introduction of … into …
considered
serious
fatalities
car ownership
to investigate
developing markets
to discover
driving culture
consequences
show that
even though
driver behaviour
the observed differences
suggest that
necessarily
vulnerable users
pedestrians
cyclists
tend to be
poorly designed
road construction areas
in addition
a major problem
aggressive
forcefully

Task 5 Thinking critically about reading a published research report

5.1 Below is a list of purposes that Khalid might have for reading this report.

For each purpose, how would Khalid read the report? For example, would he read slowly or quickly, and which sections would he read:

a to see if the topic is related to his research?

b to find other research reports on ADASs?

c to see if the results agree with his results?

d to decide if he will use the same research method?

e to see if the conclusions could help him make decisions about the design of a new ADAS?

5.2 **What information should Khalid record from this report if he wants to use it later in his own report?**

5.3 **Would Khalid copy phrases and sentences from the report or write in his own words? Why?**

Study smart: keeping a record of your reading

It is important for you to keep a record of what you read so you can easily find and use the information later in an essay or report or in an exam. You can record the following information:

- bibliographic reference – so you can find the text to read again or reference it in your report
- key words – to help you identify quickly what the text was about
- a short summary – so you can remember the key points you thought were important
- a comment – so you can remember your thoughts when you first read the text

---

Task 6 Keeping a record of your reading

Below is part of Khalid's record for the ADAS report he found.

Read the extracts from Task 4 again and complete the record below by adding a summary of the key points Khalid might want to remember. In deciding what he would record, think carefully about what Khalid knows already, e.g., the definition of ADASs, and what is new for him. Compare with other students.

Reference Lindgren, A., Chen, F., Jordan, P. W., + Zhang, H. (2008). Requirements for the design of Advanced Driver Assistance Systems: The differences between Swedish and Chinese drivers. International Journal of Design, 2(2), 41–54.

Key words ADAS, cross-cultural differences, driver assistance, driver behaviour, traffic safety

Summary

Comment Contexts: Sweden + China (= Libya??) similar driving culture + problems (check accident rate in Libya)
Method (questionnaire) not useful for my report
Results: factors likely causing accidents + driver attitudes – relevant for determining design and type of ADASs

Section 4 Reporting ideas from sources

What the university expects:
• awareness of how knowledge is advanced and communicated

Contexts:
• written reports for study and work

Aims:
• to understand why writers need to report ideas from sources
• to understand how writers manage their own and others' voices in their reports
• to use language for reporting the ideas of other writers

Discussion

The guidelines for writing reports specify that writers have
to review previous research or explain models, theories or
developments in design which are relevant to the problem.
Why do they have to do this? What is the purpose of this review? Where is it
usually found?

Task 1 Preparing to read critically

1.1 The following extract from the report by Lindgren et al. (2008) provides
the rationale for the research (the reasons why it is worth doing) and the
purpose of the study.

**Read the extract and discuss with a partner what information you need the
writers to provide in the introduction of the report to help you to understand
the context for this research, e.g., a definition of ADAS.**

There are very few studies that have investigated what kind of ADAS is
needed for drivers to cope with the traffic problems in China. The purpose
of this study is to identify the most common traffic problems Chinese
drivers face, and to ask their opinions about the introduction of ADASs into
their cars.

1.2 In what order do you expect to read the information you need?

Task 2 Reading to check your expectations

Read the introduction to the research report quickly to find out if your needs and expectations were met.

Introduction

In recent years, safety has become an increasingly important concern for the automotive industry and manufacturers have been putting effort into *active* safety. Active safety systems, also known as Advanced Driver Assistance Systems (ADASs), are a type of independent electronic system designed to help drivers move safely through busy traffic. Their overall aim is to reduce traffic accidents and to make the driving experience safer and more efficient. However, the design and development of these systems has concentrated on the needs of motorists in Western markets. A question remains as to whether the systems currently available can offer similar benefits to drivers in other parts of the world.

As Shneiderman and Plaisant (2005) point out, good design begins with an understanding of the intended user's attitudes and needs. When designing products for global use, it is important to understand how needs differ around the world. This may be particularly relevant for the design of ADASs since not only the rules of the road, but also social environments, norms and driver behaviour may vary significantly from country to country and could have a notable influence on the attitudes and behaviours of drivers (Zeidel, 1992). Consequently, as Lindgren et al., (2008) note, an ADAS that is of great value to drivers in one country might be of less value to those in another.

Today, automotive manufacturers design different products for different markets. For example, manufacturers such as Toyota have different in-car control and display designs depending on whether the vehicle is intended for the Asian, American or European market. Nevertheless, the design of ADASs for particular markets still seems to be in the early stages (Krum, Faenger, Lathrop, Sison, & Lien, 2008). Since the West is the dominant market, the design is generally based on perceptions of the needs of drivers in Western countries. Although there has been an increasing amount of research on the technical aspects of ADAS development coming from China (Gong et al., 2008; Zhao et al., 2008; Wu et al., 2008), there is still a lack of research about the attitude of Chinese drivers to ADASs in their cars.

The Chinese automotive industry is booming and the Chinese government is beginning to introduce intelligent systems into the transport network to prepare for new generations of vehicles to come (Zhang et al., 2005). In just over 20 years, the production of passenger cars in China has increased from 220,000 to 2.34 million units

Key words & phrases

an important concern
automotive industry
to put effort into
active safety
to point out
the intended user
attitudes
for global use
particularly relevant
not only … but also
the rules of the road
social environments
norms
vary significantly
have an influence on
consequently
of value to
in-car control
seems to be
in the early stages
since
dominant market
perceptions
although
a lack of research
is booming
intelligent systems
the transport network
new generations
to come

(China Statistical Yearbook, 2004). At the same time, the Chinese driver population has changed from a majority of professional drivers, such as taxi drivers, to more than half private drivers. This rapid increase in the number of novice drivers is becoming a major challenge to traffic safety, with traffic fatalities increasing (Zhang, Huang, Roetting, Wang, & Wei, 2006) and almost 110,000 people being killed every year (China Road Traffic Accident Statistics, 2003). With China's rapid economic development, it is expected that this problem will increase. It has been projected that the number of vehicles per capita will increase faster than the fatalities per vehicle will decrease (Zhang et al., 2006), which forecasts a worrying future.

There are other reasons why Chinese roads are often dangerous, with high numbers of fatalities. Drivers have to share the road with many vulnerable users, such as pedestrians and cyclists (Huang, Zhang, Roetting, & Melton, 2006; Lindgren et al., 2007). Road signs tend to be poorly designed or even missing at road construction areas (Lindgren, Chen, Jordan, & Ljungstrand, n.d.). In addition, driver behaviour is considered a major safety problem. Huang et al. (2006) found that Chinese drivers are more aggressive than drivers in the USA, because the Chinese tend to drive more forcefully and disobey traffic rules. A study by Xie and Parker (2002) showed that these aggressive violations significantly contributed to traffic accidents in China. Moreover, they speculated that this deliberate behaviour may be a result of culturally specific norms, such as a sense of social hierarchies or challenging legitimate authority. In further emphasizing the role culture plays, Lee (2006) criticizes past research done solely on driver behaviour as it focused only on individual differences of drivers as contributors to traffic dangers. He claims that the extreme difference in the rate of fatalities between countries suggests that culture has an important influence on driving behaviour, as well as playing a critical role in general driving safety.

Source: Lindgren, A., Chen, F., Jordan, P. W., & Zhang, H. (2008). Requirements for the design of Advanced Driver Assistance Systems: The differences between Swedish and Chinese drivers. *International Journal of Design*, 2(2), 41–54.

Key words & phrases
professional drivers
taxi drivers
private drivers
novice drivers
is becoming
a challenge
rapid economic development
it is expected
it has been projected
vehicles per capita
forecasts
a worrying future
violations
speculated that
deliberate behaviour
culturally specific norms
social hierarchies
challenging legitimate authority
in further emphasizing
to play a role
criticizes
individual differences
contributors
claims that
critical

Task 3 Understanding points in the writers' research story

The list of statements below constitutes a paraphrase of the main points in the writers' research story.

Read the introduction again carefully and number each point in the list below to show its order in the review.

____ **a** Most ADASs are developed for drivers in Western countries.

____ **b** Chinese roads are dangerous because many different types of road users share the road.

____ **c** Chinese drivers tend to be aggressive and do not always follow rules.

____ **d** Car manufacturers design some of their products for different markets, but not ADASs currently.

____ **e** Cultural attitudes influence driving behaviour and driving safety.

____ **f** Car manufacturers have been improving the safety of cars with active safety systems.

____ **g** The number of cars on the road is increasing rapidly in China.

____ **h** Most users are no longer experienced drivers, which has resulted in a sharp rise in the number of fatal accidents.

____ **i** The design of products for global use must consider different needs in different countries.

____ **j** A lot of research is being done in China on the technical aspects of ADASs, but not on driver attitudes.

____ **k** The purpose of Advanced Driver Assistance Systems is to make cars safer to drive on busy roads.

____ **l** Aggressive behaviour by Chinese drivers can lead to accidents.

In their introduction, writers first present ideas which the research community accepts as common knowledge as a background for their research. They then review research published by other writers (the literature) in order to provide a foundation for their own research and persuade readers that their study will contribute to knowledge in their field. This published research supports and strengthens the new claims. Quoting or paraphrasing ideas from other writers gives them a *voice* in the review. Although it is essential to include these other voices, dominant writers make sure their own voice stands out clearly so that they stay in control of their review. Their own voice is heard through the series of points they make in their literature review, in order to tell their research story. They control other voices by limiting the amount of space they give to them in the review and by imposing their own viewpoint on the findings and conclusions they report.

Task 4 Investigating grammar patterns for organizing the review

This review has a general-to-specific organization. The writers chose to present ideas as accepted facts, as trends and developments, or as the outcome of specific studies which are still under discussion by the research community. Examples from the review are shown in the table below.

4.1 **Read the review again and try to find more examples of these patterns to add to the table.**

4.2 **Underline the verbs and say what form they have, e.g., present perfect, as has been done in the examples given.**

purpose	example	verb form
to present accepted ideas and facts	… *good design <u>begins</u> with an understanding of the intended user's attitudes and needs.*	present simple
to summarize trends and developments in the research area	*In recent years, safety <u>has become</u> an increasingly important concern for the automotive industry … However, the design and development of these systems <u>has concentrated</u> on the needs of motorists in Western markets.*	present perfect
to present ideas from one study	*A study by Xie and Parker (2002) <u>showed</u> that these aggressive violations significantly contributed to traffic accidents in China.*	past simple

Study smart: giving space to other voices in a review

Writers can choose whether to let other voices into their review *directly*, by reporting their actual words, or *indirectly* by paraphrasing their ideas. These voices can be allowed to speak for themselves as actors in the reporting sentence, using *integral citation*, or simply referred to in brackets following the reported idea, using *non-integral citation*. Integral citation focuses on the source, giving more space and hence relevance to the ideas. It tends to be used to report findings and claims that are more central to the research story. Non-integral citation focuses on the ideas. It tends to be used to present background ideas and facts, which are accepted in the field, e.g., by showing that multiple sources all support a particular idea.

integral citation	examples
focus on the source using a reporting structure: *X found that* + report [clause]	*Huang et al. (2006) found that Chinese drivers are more aggressive than drivers in the USA …*
As X point out + report [clause]*	*As Shneiderman and Plaisant (2005) point out, good design begins with an understanding of the intended user's attitudes and needs.*
non-integral citation	
focus on the ideas and put the source in brackets at the end of the sentence.	*Nevertheless, the design of ADASs for particular markets still seems to be in the early stages (Krum, Faenger, Lathrop, Sison, & Lien, 2008).*

* Could also be paraphrased *According to X* + report [clause]: *According to Schneiderman and Plaisant (2005), good design begins with an understanding of the intended user's attitudes and needs.*

Task 5 Understanding how the writers support their points

5.1 The writers support the points in their review by referring to sources.

Which points from the list in Task 3 are supported by each of the sources in the table below? Write the letter of the point next to the reference in the table. Some points may have more than one reference to support them. Sources 10 and 12 (shown with a ✓) support minor points which were not included in the list in Task 3.

5.2 The writers support the points in their review using both integral and non-integral citation.

Identify the type of citation used for each source.

sources	support points	integral citation	non-integral citation
1. Shneiderman and Plaisant, 2005	i		
2. Zeidel, 1992			
3. Lindgren et al., 2007			
4. Krum, Faenger, Lathrop, Sison, and Lien, 2008			
5. Gong et al., 2008; Zhao et al., 2008; Wu et al., 2008			
6. Zhang et al., 2005			
7. China Statistical Yearbook, 2004			
8. Zhang, Huang, Roetting, Wang, and Wei, 2006			
9. China Road Traffic Accident Statistics, 2003			
10. Zhang et al., 2006	✓		
11. Huang, Zhang, Roetting, and Melton, 2006; Lindgren et al., 2007			
12. Lindgren, Chen, Jordan, & Ljungstrand, n.d.	✓		
13. Huang et al., 2006			
14. Xie and Parker, 2002			
15. Lee, 2006			

Task 6 Thinking critically about referencing sources

6.1 Integral citation tends to be used to report findings and claims, while non-integral citation tends to be used to present background ideas and facts.

Which sources in the table do not follow this pattern?

6.2 Which points in the writers' review are not supported by sources? Why did the writers decide not to support these points?

Task 7 Choosing a reporting verb to show stance

Writers can impose their own viewpoint on the findings and conclusions they report through their choice of reporting verbs. These verbs enable writers to show different levels of agreement with the source.

7.1 **Find and highlight the reporting verbs used by the writers of the report you read in Task 2.**

7.2 There are more than 400 reporting verbs, but the 21 most common are listed in the box below.

Sort them into two lists: verbs which report research activity, e.g., _analyze_, or verbs which report thinking and writing activity, e.g., _argue_.

analyze	argue	criticize	claim	demonstrate	describe	develop
discuss	examine	explain	find	identify	indicate	note
observe	propose	point out	report	show	study	suggest

7.3 **Within each list, sort the verbs according to the level of agreement they show with the original writer, i.e., are they used to show tentative, neutral or strong agreement?**

	tentative	neutral	strong
research activity			
writing activity			

7.4 Some verbs can only be used with a direct object, e.g., _analyzed the data_, while others can be used in a reporting structure, e.g., _suggested that +_ report. Some verbs can be used in both these structures, e.g., _observe animal behaviour; observe that animals sometimes behave strangely_.

For each of the verbs in the list, say how it can be used. Check your answers in a dictionary.

Investigating language patterns for showing viewpoint

Writers can show in their review how sure they are about the truth of the findings and conclusions in the sources they refer to and how strongly they agree with their claims. The main patterns are shown below, but there are many variations. These usually depend on how close the writers view the source: close to their research, close to their view or close to the current state of knowledge.

Reporting research activity: what other writers *found* or *showed*

generalizing findings from one study (*found* + present simple)	*Huang et al. (2006) <u>found</u> that Chinese drivers <u>are</u> more aggressive than drivers in the USA …*
showing research activity (present perfect + source at end of sentence)	*… there <u>has been</u> an increasing amount of research on the technical aspects of ADAS development coming from China (Gong et al., 2008; Zhao et al., 2008; Wu et al., 2008) …*
locating findings within a single study (*showed* + past simple)	*A study by Xie and Parker (2002) <u>showed</u> that these aggressive violations significantly <u>contributed</u> to traffic accidents in China.*

Reporting thinking and writing activity: what other writers *claim*, *argue*, *suggest* or *note*

showing a conclusion is close to the writer's view (present simple)	*He <u>claims</u> that the extreme difference in the rate of fatalities between countries <u>suggests</u> that culture <u>has</u> an important influence on driving behaviour …*
showing agreement with a conclusion that was tentative in the source (*As* + present tense + *might*)	*<u>As</u> Lindgren et al., (2008) <u>note</u>, an ADAS that is of great value to drivers in one country <u>might be</u> of less value to those in another.*
showing a tentative conclusion in one study (past simple + *may*)	*[Xie and Parker] <u>speculated</u> that this deliberate behaviour <u>may be</u> a result of culturally specific norms …*

Task 8 Reporting conclusions from Lindgren et al. to show viewpoint

Below are some conclusions taken from the paper by Lindgren et al. (2008).

Report these findings so you could include them in a review. Decide whether you want to use a direct or indirect form of reporting (refer to Section 2) and be careful to include quotation marks if you copy the writers' words. Try to use different reporting styles and reporting verbs to show your viewpoint towards the ideas.

a The Chinese drivers in this study were fairly positive towards the introduction of ADASs into Chinese car design.

b People in China tend to follow social norms of driver behaviour, rather than following traffic regulations.

c Expectations of proper driving behaviour are similar in Sweden and China.

d If ADASs do not take cultural differences into account with respect to driving, they may not be accepted.

Self study

The choice of reporting styles and reporting verbs varies a great deal depending on your research field. Look again at the paper you found for self study in Section 3. Find more examples of different reporting verbs. Do the writers report research activity or thinking and writing activity? Which tense is used to report the ideas?

Section 5 Writing clearly and logically

What the university expects:
- effective communication – present complex ideas in response to the needs and expectations of an audience

Contexts:
- written reports for study and work

Aims:
- to understand how to link general and specific ideas
- to understand how to link familiar and new ideas
- to understand how moves in a text create links between ideas

Key words & phrases

write clearly and logically
exactly
cohesion
explicitly
conjunctions
implicitly

University lecturers want their students to write clearly and logically, but they expect students to find out for themselves exactly what this means. It mainly involves understanding and meeting the expectations of academic readers about the way ideas are linked between sentences, within paragraphs and across whole texts. This linking, known as *cohesion*, can be shown *explicitly* with conjunctions or *implicitly* in the position of ideas.

Task 1 Looking back in a text to make links between ideas

1.1 Read the paragraph above and find words which refer back to the ideas listed below. One is given as an example. What kinds of words are used to make these links?

university lecturers	a *their*	b _____
students	c _____	
write clearly and logically	d _____	e _____
the way ideas are linked	f _____	

1.2 Look at the starting points of the sentences in the paragraph. These show the development of the topic. How does the topic change in sentences 2 and 3? Where does the new topic come from?

1.3 Where are new ideas placed in these sentences?

1.4 In the paragraph, which ideas are general and which are specific?

Study smart: linking ideas in a paragraph

Ideas in a paragraph are linked in three main ways:

1 They develop from general to specific in order to explain a concept to a reader in more detail:
write clearly and logically ➡ *the way ideas are linked … across whole texts*

2 They flow from one sentence to another so that new information at the end of one sentence can become familiar information at the beginning of the next:

topic	**new information**

They expect students to find out for themselves <u>exactly what this means</u>.

topic	**new information**

<u>It</u> mainly involves understanding … <u>the way ideas are linked …</u>

3 Pronouns and general nouns refer back to noun phrases. They can be used to repackage, i.e., summarize, ideas briefly at the beginning of a following sentence: *university lecturers* ➡ *they*
the way ideas are linked ➡ *this linking*

Task 2 Identifying links in a text

Below is an extract from the discussion section of the paper by Lindgren et al. (2008). Because they have read previous sections of the paper, readers already know that this is a study about expectations of proper driving behaviour. Sentences are labelled a–h to help with the tasks.

2.1 **Complete the notes in the table below the extract to show the organization from familiar information (the topic) to new information. How does the topic develop from general to specific (in the subjects of the sentences)?**

a This study has shown that expectations of proper driving behaviour are similar in Sweden and China. b Participants in both countries found problems in illegal passing, vulnerable road users and speeding. c However, differences between the two driving cultures are evident from participants' views on how frequent these situations were and whether they felt stressed when they encountered them. d For example, both the Chinese and Swedish participants found pedestrians and cyclists to be the greatest problems. e What is interesting is that almost 70% of the Swedish participants found 'not stopping at crossings' to be a big problem, while no Chinese drivers gave this any thought. f To slow down the car and stop at a crossing can be inconvenient for the driver but, in most Western countries, this type of behaviour has developed from a simple traffic rule into a social norm of respecting pedestrians. g This is, however, the opposite of the situation in China. h There, pedestrians must look carefully before crossing the road, even though there is a regulation stating that drivers must slow down or stop when a pedestrian is crossing.

topic (sentence starting point)	new information
This study _____	expectations _____ in Sweden and China
Participants in _____ ___	_____ passing, _____ road users and speeding
_____ ___ between the two driving cultures	how _____ these driving problems were and whether participants felt _____
_____	_____ pedestrians and cyclists
Almost 70% of the _____ participants	_____ a big problem
… no _____ drivers	gave this any thought
_____	inconvenient
… this type of _____	_____ of respecting pedestrians
This	the _____ in China
There	pedestrians must look _____

2.2 **Where does the topic change in the paragraph? What is the new topic? Where does it come from?**

2.3 **How is the comparison of findings between Sweden and China shown, explicitly or implicitly?**

2.4 **In which sentence do the writers show that they think a finding is important? How do they do this?**

Task 3 Building noun phrases to summarize familiar ideas

Below is an extract from the conclusion of the paper by Lindgren et al. (2008). Some of the noun phrases at the beginnings of the sentences, which summarize familiar ideas, are missing. The words you need for each noun phrase are listed a–d below the text.

Decide where each noun phrase fits in the text and write it correctly. Use new ideas in the previous sentence to help you choose and write a correct noun phrase.

This study has provided insights into the Chinese driving culture, the key safety issues that Chinese drivers face, and their attitudes towards ADAS. **1** _____ shows that traffic rules and regulations are very similar in Sweden and China, but there are major differences in terms of driving culture and driver behaviour. **2** _____ concerns driver skills. In China, luxury sedans, small, inexpensive cars, trucks, mopeds and rickshaws all share the roads. **3** _____ are novice drivers not used to driving in heavy traffic amidst this wide range of vehicles (Zhang et al., 2006). Furthermore, Chinese drivers tend to trust their own driving skill, experience and capabilities, even though they lack driver training and an understanding of safe driving guidelines (Zhang et al., 2006). **4** With _____, traffic problems will no doubt increase even further.

a users many these of road
b skills novice own confident their drivers in and guidelines ignoring driving
c Swedish and comparison the drivers with Chinese
d issue major one

Task 4 Thinking critically about linking ideas in abstracts

Read the abstract below from the research report by Lindgren et al. (2008). The organization is different from the paragraphs in the report.

4.1 Does it develop from general to specific ideas?

4.2 Does the information flow from familiar to new ideas?

4.3 Are there pronouns or general nouns which repackage information at the beginning of sentences?

4.4 How are the ideas in this text really linked together?

Advanced Driver Assistance Systems are intended to reduce traffic accidents and fatalities. The design of these systems is usually based on research on driving in Western countries. However, with the increase in car ownership in countries such as China, there is a need to investigate how these systems should be designed for developing markets. This study aimed to discover the most common traffic problems facing Chinese drivers, how those problems differ from those in a country with a more developed driving culture (Sweden), and what consequences these differences will have for the design of Advanced Driver Assistance Systems. Results show that, even though Swedish and Chinese traffic rules and regulations are similar, driver behaviour is very different. The observed differences suggest that Advanced Driver Assistance Systems designed for roads in Sweden may not necessarily be suitable in other markets.

The purpose of an abstract is to highlight key parts of the report for researchers who might decide to refer to it in their own studies. It consists of a series of 'moves' which summarize very briefly the most interesting ideas in the report. Moves in a text are like moves in a game. They are intended to achieve the overall purpose of the text. The moves in the abstract by Lindgren et al. (2008) follow the structure of the report. Because an expert reader anticipates these moves, the text does not need to be linked as clearly and logically as the paragraphs in the report.

Task 5 Identifying moves in an abstract

Look back to the guidelines for writing reports in Section 3.

5.1 Read the abstract again and decide which section of the report each sentence summarizes.

5.2 One section is not included. Which one is this and why has it been left out?

Task 6 Writing a paragraph

Look back to Sections 3 and 4 to remind yourself of the ideas about driving culture in Sweden and China in the paper by Lindgren et al. (2008). Write a short paragraph to compare the driving culture in your country with that in either Sweden or China. If you come from China or Sweden, choose another country to compare with yours. Make sure your paragraph develops from general to specific ideas. Start your sentences with familiar information. Show the comparison with your country using both explicit and implicit links.

Self study

General nouns refer back to noun phrases. They can be used to 'repackage', i.e., summarize, ideas briefly at the beginning of a following sentence, e.g.,

the way ideas are linked	➡	this linking
driver behaviour is very different	➡	The observed differences suggest that

Find an abstract for a published paper in your field and find the general nouns. Be prepared to report back to the class.

Unit 3
Key concepts and tools

Section 1 The concept of autonomy

What the university expects:
- awareness of how knowledge is advanced

Contexts:
- independent study

Aims:
- to understand how a concept is explained academically
- to summarize an academic text that explains a concept
- to understand how to be an autonomous student

Discussion

What are the similarities and differences between a human and a robot?

Task 1 Reading and thinking critically

1.1 In this definition of a robot from Unit 1, Section 4, what does the term *autonomously* mean?

Robotics has been defined as, 'the science which studies the intelligent connection between perception and action'[1]. A robot is thus a machine that can interact intelligently with its environment in order to perform physical tasks autonomously […]

1.2 What link does this definition of a robot make between *intelligence* and *autonomy*?

1.3 What else can be described as *autonomous*?

autonomous

1 **autonomous (adjective)**

an autonomous state, region, or organization is independent and has the power to govern itself

Scotland is an autonomous state in terms of its education, health and legal systems.

2 **autonomous (adjective)**

an autonomous person is independent and able to make their own decisions

synonyms: independent, self-directing, free, self-sufficient, self-reliant, voluntary, self-supporting, emancipated, by choice

Students who study because they are interested rather than to satisfy a teacher will develop as autonomous learners.

[1] Siciliano, B., & Khatib, O. (Eds.). (2008). *Springer handbook of robotics*. Berlin: Springer (pp. 2–3).

Task 2 Investigating grammar patterns

2.1 **Make a word family for *autonomous*. Find collocations in the dictionary entries on page 54 (there are five).**

2.2 **What word appears most frequently as a prefix in the synonyms in entry 2? Why?**

Task 3 Writing negative definitions

Entry 2 gives a positive definition of an autonomous person (what an autonomous person <u>is</u>).

3.1 **Write a negative definition of an autonomous person (what an autonomous person <u>is not</u>).**

3.2 **Support your definition by giving some examples of what an autonomous (independent) student does <u>not</u> do.**

Task 4 Preparing to read

Xiaohua is studying on the Foundation Programme at Gateway University. Her EAP teacher has recommended a book that compares studying at school with studying at university. The students in her EAP class are reading the book to explore some of the important concepts that they need to understand before they begin their university courses. They are taking turns to present each chapter as a basis for a weekly seminar. Xiaohua has to read the chapter about autonomy and write a short summary for a seminar discussion at her next EAP class.

The chapter is called *Autonomy and independent learning*. Before you read the chapter, list some ideas you expect it to cover.

Task 5 Reading for content overview

5.1 Read the following extract quickly to find out if it contains any of the ideas on the list you made in Task 4.

5.2 Find and highlight the main ideas in the text.

5.3 What information does the text contain that you did not predict?

Chapter 9 Autonomy and independent learning

Sue Argent

9.1 What universities expect

A high level of student autonomy is one of the clearest requirements for successful English-medium academic study, as this lecturer's comment illustrates: 'My students are great – they study really hard – now I want them to study smart'. His first year undergraduate class of international students were well-motivated high-flyers with excellent high school exam grades and prepared to study long hours. Yet they lacked the ability to study smart. This chapter looks at the main component of studying smart: learner autonomy.

EAP students need to develop learner autonomy for two reasons. First they need to be independent learners in order to learn their degree subjects successfully. They also need to be independent learners in order to continue to learn English throughout their university studies, because their EAP class may be the last English class they will have. Jordan (1997) and Field (2007) are among several authors who stress the need for EAP students to continue language learning after leaving language instruction.

9.2 What student autonomy means

Autonomous learners make their own decisions about learning, instead of depending on others, for example, a teacher, to tell them what to do. The development of learner autonomy has been described as:

'a process that enables learners to recognize and address their own needs, to choose and apply their own learning strategies or styles eventually leading to the effective management of learning.' Penaflorida (2002)

Autonomy for an EAP student must involve self-direction, the ability to see and use wisely opportunities for learning in the various situations in which they function. This autonomy needs to be applied both in learning about the content and approaches of their subject discipline and also in learning its language.

Self-direction may be an unfamiliar concept for students who have just left high school. At university, students have to find and use sources of information without a teacher, perhaps after a high school career in which teachers selected and processed information for them. They have to organize their study activities for themselves when they may have previously worked within a highly structured timetable that allowed very little free choice or free time. They have to work on collaborative projects with new colleagues, writing group reports and making joint presentations when they may have experienced only individual work and assessment in school. These are challenges that are shared by all students when moving from high school to university. For international students, the challenge is often made greater by the move from the educational culture of one country to that of another.

A further challenge is the need to continue the language learning process beyond any EAP courses available. Without the help of a language teacher, a student has to take

Key words & phrases

a high level of

English-medium

illustrates

study smart

well-motivated

high-flyers

lacked

the main component of

to address needs

to apply learning strategies

effective management

self-direction

highly structured

collaborative projects

joint presentations

take responsibility for

responsibility for learning how to communicate competently in his or her specialist field, i.e., how to function as a member of the appropriate discourse community. The ability to continue independently learning the language of the target academic and professional community must be a key goal for every EAP student. Autonomy for an EAP student means self-direction, taking responsibility and independent learning in all aspects of study at university, including language learning.

9.3 Student autonomy, study competence and study skills

The two aspects of autonomy in EAP – autonomy for academic study and autonomy for continued language learning – share an underlying capacity. Waters and Waters (1995) offer the most useful term, referring to a general, underlying capacity for study as study competence.

It is important to distinguish this deeper-level study competence from the more surface-level study skills, i.e., the knowledge and techniques which students can be trained to use for effective study. These include skills such as time management, proofreading, making notes and the conventions of referencing. Most EAP courses incorporate this type of work. Study skills are a useful part of any student's repertoire, but they can only be used outside the EAP classroom if students develop the underlying study competence.

9.4 The elements of study competence

There are several elements which are important in study competence. A student with study competence is:

1 self-aware, or knows about self as a learner
2 willing to find out things
3 willing to tolerate uncertainty
4 able to self-evaluate
5 realistic in setting manageable goals
6 willing to experiment with new methods and materials
7 actively involved in the learning process
8 organized in terms of time and resources inside and outside the classroom
9 self-confident
10 able to monitor own learning
11 a critical thinker

These elements fall into three groups based on three core competencies: being active in learning, taking risks in learning and reflecting on learning. These core competencies form three dimensions of study competence:

passive ➡ active

risk-averse ➡ risk-comfortable

unreflective ➡ reflective

It is important to think about where you are now on each of these dimensions.

References:

Field, J. (2007). Looking outwards, not inwards. *ELT Journal, 61*(1), pages 30–38.
Jordan, R. R. (1997). *English for Academic Purposes: A guide and resource book for teachers.* Cambridge: Cambridge University Press.
Penaflorida, A. H. (2002). *Nontraditional forms of assessment and response to student writing: A step toward learner autonomy.* In J. C. Richards & W. A. Renandya (Eds.), *Methodology in language teaching: An anthology of current practice* (p. 346). Cambridge: Cambridge University Press.
Waters, M., & Waters, A. (1995). *Study tasks in English.* Cambridge: Cambridge University Press.

Source: Argent, S. (2013). *From high school to university: A handbook for EAP students.* Summerford: Gateway University Press.

Key words & phrases

specialist field
discourse community
target
underlying capacity
study competence
deeper-level study
surface-level study
techniques
incorporate
repertoire
elements
self-aware
to tolerate
to self-evaluate
manageable
self-confident
to monitor
dimensions

Task 6 Reading carefully to understand the explanation of a concept

The author's main purpose is to explain the concept of autonomy to EAP students.

Put the following sections in the correct order to make an outline of the extract and show the steps in the author's explanation.

a Definitions relating to autonomy

b Analysis of autonomy into three groups of components

c Comparison between study skills and study competence

d Comparison between school and university

e A justification for developing autonomy

Study smart: explaining a key concept

There are several moves in explaining a concept academically. They do not have to be in the same order, but explaining an academic concept usually involves:

1. at least one main definition
2. reasons why the concept is important for the writer's purpose and intended reader
3. ways in which the concept is related to other (also defined) concepts, for example, similarities and differences, causes and effects, developmental or hierarchical relationships
4. analysis of the concept into components or types
5. examples in which the concept is applied in a familiar context

Task 7 Reading critically to identify moves in a text

7.1 Which sections of the extract show each of the above moves?

7.2 What is the purpose of the references section?

Investigating language: contrastive definitions

A term can be defined by contrasting it with another similar term, e.g., *point source pollution is the pollution of a watercourse from a single outlet, such as a factory pipe, while non-point source (NPS) pollution is the pollution of a watercourse from rain water runoff over a wide area, for example, nitrates from agricultural land.*
Purpose: Contrastive definitions are useful in showing specific and important distinctions between two terms when these distinctions might not be very obvious.

Task 8 Writing contrastive definitions

8.1 What is the main difference between *study skills* and *study competence*?

8.2 Use this difference to write contrastive definitions of *study skills* and *study competence*.

A running definition of a term is a brief explanation or synonym, often found right next to the term inside brackets or commas, for example, *Next, the source code (the computer program) is written.* Running definitions are used to provide a quick explanation that helps the reader or listener to understand a term without having to process a full definition. This could be because the writer expects the reader to know the full definition already and is just giving a quick reminder, or it could be because a more detailed definition will come later, after further exploration.

Task 9 Investigating language

Find an example of a running definition in the extract.

Khalid uses this definition of *robotics*:

Robotics has been defined as 'the science which studies the intelligent connection between perception and action' (Siciliano & Khatib, 2008, pp. 2–3).

The term *robot* is not explicitly defined, but the definition can be understood if you read the extract carefully and think critically, which is what Khalid did to establish his definition:

A robot is thus a machine that can interact intelligently with its environment in order to perform physical tasks autonomously.

Writers use *explicit* definitions when their purpose is to clarify a concept. *Implicit* definitions may not be part of the writer's purpose and so they have to be constructed by the reader. A reader constructs an explicit definition to fit with his or her own purpose for reading.

Task 10 Writing explicit and implicit definitions

10.1 **Write an explicit definition of *autonomy* using the implicit definition in Penaflorida's explanation of developing autonomy in section 9.2 of the extract.**

10.2 **Write an explicit definition of *plagiarism* using this implicit definition from a university website:**

You must adequately acknowledge the source of your information in your writing, otherwise you may be accused of plagiarism. Even if you do not copy information word for word (for example, if you change some words and move them around), without proper citation this is still considered to be plagiarism.

Task 11 Understanding the concept of autonomy

11.1 Put the elements of study competence listed in section 9.4 of the extract into the following three groups: active, risk comfortable, reflective. Some elements may fit more than one category. Discuss your choices with other students.

11.2 Which elements are your strengths and which are your weaknesses? Use the three dimensions to evaluate yourself critically as a learner. Write about 150 words, including specific examples, to justify your evaluation.

Discussion

In section 9.2 of the extract about autonomy, the writer refers to the challenges when moving from high school to university, and from the educational culture of one country to that of another. Discuss some examples of this from your own experience.

Task 12 Writing a summary

Read the extract about autonomy again carefully. Using your outline from Task 6 as a framework, write a summary of the text in about 200 words. Try to write without referring back to the source. The summary should be suitable for Xiaohua to hand out to her classmates at the beginning of her seminar.

Self study

Find explanations of the concept of plagiarism on university websites. Identify the moves in one of these explanations. Bring a printout to share at the next class.

Section 2 Tools for researching vocabulary

Although universities provide a considerable amount of support for students, you will be expected to work much more independently of teaching staff than you were at school. Basic IT skills are assumed, and you will have to find and use a large number of tools yourself. Students can do a great deal to help each other understand how to use these tools.

Matt is a first-year student studying for a BSc in Building and Estate Management. Unlike Chen and Maysoun, he did not study on the pre-sessional English course. As a result, he is struggling with writing his assignments. The writing teacher, Jenifer, has been helping him. Xiaohua finds him working on his laptop in the coffee shop.

Task 1 Listening for the main idea: a problem

🔊T08 Listen to the first part of the conversation.

1.1 Why was it correct for Chen to use the word *malicious,* but not for Matt?

1.2 What do you think Xiaohua will say to help him?

1.3 Can you suggest a word that Matt could use instead of *malicious*?

Task 2 Listening for the main idea: a solution

🔊T09 Listen to the second part of the conversation.

2.1 Matt and Xiaohua have very different ideas about good words to use in academic writing. What are they?

2.2 What resource does Matt use to check collocations? What resource does Xiaohua use?

Task 3 Reading carefully to understand the explanation of a tool

Xiaohua shows Matt the handout that she was given in her EAP class about researching vocabulary in context.

Researching vocabulary in context

Introduction

GATEWAY UNIVERSITY

1 When you are studying at university, you need to know not only what words mean but also how they are used in different contexts. You may have heard that to really know how to use vocabulary you have to read hundreds of books. This sounds an impossible task, but computers can help you to do very quickly something similar to reading hundreds of books.

2 To research vocabulary in context, you can use a tool called a 'concordancer'. A concordancer is a search engine; a computer application that can search a large amount of electronically stored text to find words and phrases that you specify in a search query as a 'search string'. This very large collection of texts is called a 'corpus' and is used for studying language. Some concordancing tools are freely available on the Internet for students and teachers to research the vocabulary that you find in your reading or want to use in your writing.

3 The most familiar application that searches for words and phrases is Google, a search engine that searches all the texts on the World Wide Web. However, because many of the texts on the World Wide Web belong to commercial websites that are trying to sell something, it gives a biased view of how language is used. It is better to use a search engine that can search the style that you are trying to learn from, for example, an academic corpus.

4 The first website we are going to look at, BYU-BNC, uses the British National Corpus (BNC) of over 100 million words. In the address bar, type in this URL: http://corpus.byu.edu/bnc/

Key words & phrases

vocabulary in context
a concordancer
a search engine
a computer application
electronically stored
a search query
a search string
a corpus
commercial websites
a biased view
an academic corpus

3.1 Identify the following sections in the handout and write the number of the paragraph in which each one appears.

a definitions of key terms ____
b explanation of how the tool is used ____
c comparison/evaluation ____
d a justification for using the tool ____

3.2 Answer these questions about the handout.

a What three key terms are defined?
b What familiar example is used to explain the tool?
c How useful is this example for researching academic vocabulary? Give reasons for your answer.

There are several moves in explaining a key tool. They do not have to be in the same order, but explaining a key tool usually involves:

1. at least one main definition
2. reasons why the tool is important
3. ways in which the tool is related to other tools, for example, similarities and differences, advantages and disadvantages
4. analysis of the tool into components or types and/or explanation of how it is used
5. examples in which the tool is used in a familiar context

Task 4 Listening to follow instructions and record results

When Matt has finished reading the handout, Xiaohua shows him how to carry out search queries.

⊙T10 Listen to Xiaohua's instructions in the third part of the conversation. While you listen, look at the screenshots.

Screenshot A

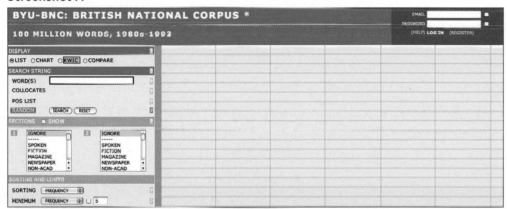

Screenshot B

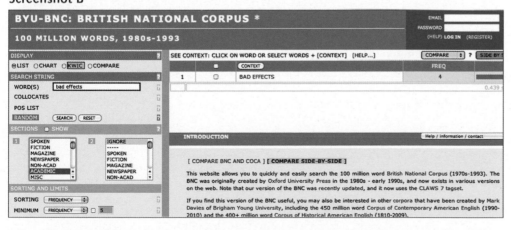

4.1 On screenshot A, find and circle the places where they click or type to set up the concordance search. Number these places to show the order in which Xiaohua gives her instructions.

4.2 On screenshot B, find and circle the location of the choice for the academic corpus and circle the frequency figure for 'bad effects'.

4.3 The table shows the results of a concordance search for negative adjectives that form collocations with *effects*, together with frequencies in the academic corpus.

Complete the table with the six collocations that Xiaohua and Matt research.

search words	frequency in academic corpus (per 100 million words)
_____ effects	0
undesirable effects	2
disastrous effects	3
_____ effects	4
devastating effects	5
serious effects	7
_____ effects	12
_____ effects	12
_____ effects	13
deleterious effects	15
toxic effects	16
damaging effects	16
_____ effects	75

4.4 What should Matt do to get some examples of the collocation *adverse effects* in context?

Task 5 Thinking critically

5.1 Do you think Matt has chosen a suitable word?

5.2 Can you account for the difference in frequency between *toxic* and *adverse*?

5.3 In the table in Task 4, check the frequency of the collocation you suggested in Task 1.3.

Discussion

What is a 'resource'? Without using a dictionary, try to define the term *resource*. Make a list of the resources that you use for researching English vocabulary.

Task 6 Comparing word meanings: *tools, sources, resources*

Study the dictionary entries for three commonly confused academic words[2].

> **tool**
>
> **tool** /tuːl/ noun [countable]
>
> 1. a piece of equipment, usually one that you hold in your hand, that is designed to do a particular type of work
>   *kitchen/gardening/dental tools; a set of tools*
> 2. something that you use in order to perform a job or to achieve an aim
>   *These sales forecasts are an extremely useful tool for management.*
>   *Words are essential tools for formulating and communicating thoughts.*

> **source**
>
> **source** /sɔːs/ noun [countable]
> 1. a person or place or thing that provides something that you need or want
>   *The sun is a source of light and heat.*
>   *The library is a source of information and advice.*
> 2. an author or text that provides information referred to by a new author or text
>   *The student failed because he did not include his sources in his essay.*
> 3. the cause of a problem or the place where it began
>   *The source of the infection could not be found.*
> 4. the beginning of a river or stream
>   *In the 19ᵗʰ century, explorers located the source of the Nile.*

> **resource**
>
> **resource** /rɪzɔːs/ noun [countable]
> 1. something that you can use to achieve something, especially in work or study
>   *The library is a key resource for research.*
> 2. money, workers or equipment used to run a business
>   *The human resources department*
> 3. naturally occurring things such as coal, trees and oil that are used by people
>   *The region is rich in mineral resources.*
> 4. the qualities and skills that someone has to deal with problems
>   *Students have to develop resources to cope with the challenges of doing research.*

6.1 Show one difference in meaning between *source* and *resource* by choosing the best words to complete the following sentences. Which word has a general meaning and which word is more specific?

   a A *source / resource* is a book or journal that you can use to study.

   b A *source / resource* is a book or journal that contains ideas that you could use in your texts.

6.2 In fact, the meaning of *resources* includes *tools* (a tool is a type of resource), so that they are interchangeable in many sentences.

   Show one difference in meaning between *resources* and *tools* by choosing the best words to complete the sentences below.

   a One of the university's most important *resources / tools* is the library.

   b Many management *resources / tools* are known by their acronyms, for example SMART objectives.

   c Useful computer programs for analyzing research data are often referred to as *resources / tools*.

6.3 Think about your own language. Do you have different words to express these meanings?

---

[2] Tool, source, resource. (2013). In *macmillandictionary.com*. Retrieved from http://www.macmillandictionary.com/

Concordancers are particularly helpful tools for finding out how words that seem very similar in meaning, for example, *tools*, *sources* and *resources*, are used in real texts. Concordance lines show the key words in context, so they add to your knowledge of the meanings of the words by showing differences in their collocations.

Task 7 Understanding concordance lines (KWIC)

7.1 **Study these concordance lines from the BYU-BNC (academic) corpus[3]. Can you see any differences in how the key words *tool(s)*, *resource(s)* and *source(s)* are used in academic texts? Discuss your ideas with a partner.**

7.2 **Find some adjective–noun, noun–noun and noun–preposition collocations for the key words.**

context	key word	context
approach to statistical analysis is to use one of a range of	tools	to test for "significance" as a means of indicating
nequate planning will lead to failure - however good the	tools	and techniques used in the database project. The
widely felt effect has been the perfecting of traditional	tools	of research_, data-collections, concordances
orderings may exist. While the computer is an obvious	tool	for handling and organizing large quantities of data
and providing the designer with a set of very powerful	tools	. The most useful tool is interference checking.
identification of equivalence or near-equivalence is a	tool	of analysis which sharpens one's awareness of
researchers to be knowledgeable about bibliographical	sources	and, sadly, how few social science undergraduates
visual cortex of monkeys, there are a number of indirect	sources	of evidence to support this position.
".PRIMARY AND SECONDARY SOURCES. Primary	sources	provide data gathered at first hand; that is to say
may decide to replace passive structures in the	source	text with stylistically more acceptable alternative
Below Average Income -- DSS, 1990b). Other data	sources	, most notably the small-scale studies, identify house
operation must therefore indicate three locations, two	source	locations for the two operands, and a destination
nsidered individually: population, non-renewable natural	resources	cultivated land and agricultural capital, industrial cap
Public -- pollution of air and land; depletion of scarce	resources	; increased tax bill (because of corporate tax avoid
towards repair grants was apparent but a shortage of	resources	has led to a cutback. However, as much of this stock
which assistance is offered and the arrangements and	resources	for meeting those needs. Stage 2: determining the
are employed by policemen and women as the main	resource	for accomplishing police work, and their relevance
programs in subject areas which will be held as a library	resource	. Objective 3 Information retrieval should be

[3] Brigham Young University. (2013). *British National Corpus*. Retrieved from http://corpus.byu.edu/bnc/

Task 8 Selecting key words in context

Write *tool(s)*, *source(s)* or *resource(s)* as appropriate in the 'key word' column to complete these concordance lines. What helped you to identify the key word?

	context	key word	context
1	ignoring court rulings. To quote an anonymous		: " The first rule in running prisons has always
2	lculators. The word processor is a very powerful		for the transfer of thought from brain to paper;
3	ciated with making precise calculations of actual		needs and costs, and reflects the use of weighte
4	map. A map is both a repository of facts and a		for drawing inferences. The first of these propert
5	rvices, there may well be better uses for scarce		. Capital investment is rarely a solution to comp
6	s from satellite imagery represent an important		of data, particularly in third-world countries.
7	use of its indexes and bibliographical reference		are an important part of the skill-learning aspect
8	each hour of the day and day of the year for all		of pollution. In practice, only approximate figure
9	avour to explore and exploit Antarctica's natural		for their own benefit. There is a similar situation
10	for young teenage mothers it is their lack of		, rather than their race, which most structures
11	assic techniques. These molecules, the ultimate		of information about what is going on at a specif
12	nformation technology is an extremely powerful		. It opens up opportunities to supply a wide vari

Discussion

What are the advantages and disadvantages of different resources and tools for researching vocabulary?

Self study

Choose another pair or group of words with similar meanings which you would like to clarify. Research the differences in meaning in order to explain them to other students. Use a concordancer if you have access to the Internet.

Section 3 Key concepts and tools

What the university expects:
- awareness of how knowledge is advanced

Contexts:
- understanding key concepts for study and work

Aims:
- to understand why academic writers define terms
- to identify the components of definitions
- to identify the moves in explaining terms

Discussion

What will you spend most time learning on your university course? Make a list and compare your list with another group.

Task 1 Reading quickly for the main idea

1.1 **Read this extract from Xiaohua's book quickly to find the answer to the discussion question.**

1.2 **Does this answer agree with yours?**

> *'Most of your time at university will be spent studying the concepts and tools of your field.'* A lecturer in Environmental Studies

Understanding the key concepts and tools of a subject discipline is the main purpose of both undergraduate and postgraduate study. Key concepts in a field are the ideas that have been most useful in taking the academics in that field forward, in making new discoveries and in explaining observations. They are carefully worked out and described in published papers. They may become referred to as models and theories, such as 'the greenhouse effect' or 'price elasticity'. They are often based on analogies or metaphors, as these examples show. They are known and used by all the experts in the field. The term 'tools', on the other hand, refers to anything designed for a specific purpose or task. Tools can range in complexity from lists of criteria to statistical methods and software packages. When a key concept or tool is explained in academic texts and lectures, definitions are central to the explanation.

Source: Argent, S. (2013). *From high school to university: A handbook for EAP students.* Summerford: Gateway University Press.

Key words & phrases

taking ... forward

making discoveries

theories

elasticity

analogies

metaphors

complexity

statistical methods

software packages

central to

Task 2 Reading critically

2.1 **Find definitions in the extract of the terms that the lecturer mentions.**

2.2 **Find examples used to explain the terms.**

2.3 **Find four terms that need to be explained more fully in order to understand academic concepts more clearly.**

Discussion

Why do academic writers need to define terms for concepts and tools? Can you think of a reason why definitions of the same term might be different in different academic texts by the same writer?

One important reason for defining terms is to label specific ideas, e.g., 'advanced driver assistance systems'. Frequently, these are shortened using acronyms (words made from the first letters) such as ADAS, so that they can be easily recognized and referred to by people who use them. The PIE cycle, SMART objectives and the GROW technique are management tools labelled in this way. They become part of the jargon of the discipline. The defining feature of many terms such as these, especially tools, is their function or purpose.

Investigating language: functional definitions

A term can be defined by its purpose or function, using a purpose statement or prepositional phrase, e.g., *A concordancer is a computer application for finding key words and phrases in context.*
Purpose: Writers use functional definitions to define something when they want to focus on its use or purpose.

Investigating language: formal definitions

A definition with its special feature in a relative clause is sometimes known as a *formal definition*:
Key concepts in a field are the ideas that have been most useful in taking the academics in that field forward, in making new discoveries and in explaining observations.

Sometimes the relative pronoun is dropped:
The term 'tools', on the other hand, refers to anything designed for a specific purpose or task.
Purpose: Formal definitions are used to define fully and precisely what a term means because the relative clause can contain a lot of specific detail about the key defining features.

Task 3 Defining by purpose or function

3.1 Complete this definition with a purpose statement.

Active safety systems, also known as Advanced Driver Assistance Systems (ADASs), are a type of independent electronic system designed _____

_____

3.2 Complete these prepositional phrases to reconstruct the definitions from Unit 2.

a The PIE cycle is a process for _____

_____

b The GROW model is a technique for _____

_____

c The SMART acronym refers to a set of criteria for _____

_____

Task 4 Recognizing definitions

4.1 What are the different types of definition explored so far in this unit?

4.2 What are the key components of a full definition (i.e., not a running definition)?
Find a full definition in one of the texts in this unit that shows the components.

Investigating grammar patterns: the key components of definitions

A definition tells the reader exactly what something is. This requires three components:
the term, its class and its specific feature.

term	class	specific feature
mobile robot localization	processes	for determining a mobile robot's position
concordancer	computer application	that can search a large amount of electronically stored text to find words and phrases

Verbs can be used to link the term to its class, e.g., *is/are, refers to, known as*.
The class is a general noun in a noun phrase.
The rest of the noun phrase is the special feature expressed as a relative clause, a purpose
statement or prepositional phrase.

formal definition

term + verb + noun phrase which includes a relative clause	*A concordance is … a computer application that can search a large amount of electronically stored text …*

functional definition

term + verb + noun phrase which includes a prepositional phrase / purpose statement	*'Mobile robot localization' refers to the processes for determining a mobile robot's position.*

For better information flow within a text, for example, to position new information at the end of a sentence and
familiar information at the beginning, the term (underlined in these examples) can be put at the beginning or
end of the definition. In the first example, the second sentence starts with a noun phrase summary of familiar
information given in the first sentence (see highlighting) and ends with the term used for this information, a
corpus.
1. A concordancer is a search engine, a computer application that can search a large amount of electronically
   stored text to find words and phrases … This very large collection of texts is called a corpus …
2. The processes for determining a mobile robot's position are known as 'mobile robot localization'.

Task 5 Writing definitions

term	class	specific features
a corpus	texts	stored electronically … for studying language

5.1 From the components in the first row of the table, write a formal definition
of a corpus using a relative clause.

5.2 Think of four definitions for terms that you know and write the components in the correct columns in the table.

5.3 Exchange with another student and write out in full the four new definitions from the table.

> **Study smart:** assumed general nouns in definitions
>
> In some definitions, the class is not stated in a separate noun phrase because the writer assumes that the reader can recover it from the context, or the class is included in the term itself and the writer does not want to repeat it. You have to think critically to infer the class. In this definition, 'Capital expenditure involves acquiring or improving fixed assets for the future benefit of the company.', the class is *expenditure*, but is included in the term and so is not repeated.

Task 6 Thinking critically: inferring class in a definition

6.1 What is the class in each of these definitions?

a Static testing involves inspection and analysis of the program code and its supporting documentation, whereas dynamic testing involves running the program to ensure that the input–output mappings are correct.

b Primary succession occurs when plants become established on land which has not previously been inhabited and where no soil exists.

c Horizontal teams consist of groups of employees of the same level of command.

d Procedural programming is when each step of what you want the computer to do is spelt out and commands are used to update data in the program.

e An individual is said to be in energy balance when the energy they obtain from food over a period of time is equal to the energy they expend over the same period.

6.2 Find and highlight the key word or phrase that links the term to its specific feature.

Task 7 Reading critically: distinguishing description and definition

The key words and phrases you identified in Task 6.2 can be used to simply describe as well as to define.

Which of each pair of statements below is a definition and which is simply a description?

a **1** The use of IT was said to be bringing in the paperless office.
   2 A matrix which is symmetric about the centre point of its array is said to be centrosymmetric.

b **1** Technological obsolescence means that information rapidly becomes unreadable. Punch card readers are already being sorted by archivists.
   2 e-Marketing means marketing using the Internet.

c **1** Rainout occurs when material is incorporated into cloud water droplets or ice crystals which eventually grow to sufficient size to overcome gravity and fall to the ground. Washout occurs when material below the cloud is swept out by rain or snow as it falls.
   2 Coral bleaching occurs when coral reefs are stressed, for example, by increasing temperatures.

d **1** Current expenditure consists of those items that recur regularly: expenditure on wages and salaries is the most typical example.
   2 The board of directors consists of six members.

Task 8 Understanding text organization in explanations of key tools

Khalid is writing about mobile robot localization – how robots know where they are. One of the key tools that robots use is GPS. Here are the ideas that he wrote down to explain GPS in a few sentences.

8.1 **In what order should he write them to make a clear paragraph? Explain why you chose this order.**

a Although GPS has revolutionized many aspects of government and business activity, it has some limitations.

b The main components of the system are the space segment, the user segment and the control segment.

c The system was developed in the 1960s and 70s by the US military, but is now available for general use.

d In dead zones, a less accurate method called 'dead reckoning' may have to be incorporated into the GPS calculation.

e Satellite signals may sometimes fail to reach a receiver in dead zones, for example, near mountains.

f The Global Positioning System is a satellite-based navigation tool for finding precise positions on the Earth's surface.

g The space segment consists of the satellites in MEO (Medium Earth orbit) that send out signals to the user segment.

h The user segment comprises all the devices that receive signals from the satellites.

i The control segment consists of the ground stations that control the satellites.

Key words & phrases
has revolutionized
segment
dead zones
dead reckoning
be incorporated
satellite
navigation
orbit

8.2 **Identify the following moves in your version of Khalid's explanation of GPS. Write the letter for the sentence, or sentences, that show each move.**

functional definition _____

list of components _____

description of components _____

history _____

evaluation _____

Task 9 Writing definitions

From memory, write definitions of a concordancer, a robot, GPS, an independent learner and the PIE cycle. Check your answers with another student.

Self study

Find two terms that are used for study or research in your field. They can be concepts or tools. Prepare to explain them to other students.

Section 4 From metaphors to models

What the university expects:
- a spirit of enquiry – respond flexibly and positively to unfamiliar situations

Contexts:
- studying and working in new contexts

Aims:
- to explore a key academic concept as it is applied in different fields
- to make notes selectively in a long lecture
- to understand a lecturer's purposes from language cues

Discussion

What strategies can be used when you have to learn from long, difficult lectures? Make a list.

Task 1 Preparing to listen

Universities hold some cross-disciplinary lectures to cover important concepts and tools that cross discipline boundaries. An important type of analytical tool used in many different research fields is computer modelling. Khalid, Dimitri and Maysoun all need to use computer models for their research and so they decide to go to the lecture series together and share their notes. The first lecture in the series is an introduction to the topic of mathematical models.

1.1 **How do you think models are used in research? Compare your ideas with another group.**

1.2 **The lecturer gives the students a handout before the lecture starts to help them to make notes. Study the handout on pages 74–75 and try to predict some of the lecture content.**

1.3 **How does the handout make you feel? Discuss with other students.**

Study smart: preparation and review strategies for listening to lectures

Lectures often contain concepts that are difficult to understand, but there are strategies to help you.
1. Use any information you can to prepare for the lecture, for example, the lecture handout.
2. Take notes on the handout to supplement it: don't rewrite what is already there.
3. Keep listening and looking for definitions. These are often repeated in different ways.
4. Listen for points where the lecturer summarizes what he/she has said. Sometimes the summary will be from the last lecture in preparation for linking to the new material in this lecture.
5. Keep focused on your purpose so that you take notes only on information that is relevant, e.g., on the lecturer's examples that relate to your field or your experience.
6. Keep focused on the lecturer's purpose.
7. Keep calm and don't worry about sections you do not understand.
8. Do not waste time looking up words in a dictionary during the lecture because you will miss key information.
9. Check your notes with other students straight after the lecture and look for any additional material the lecturer puts on the relevant website/virtual learning environment (VLE).
10. Check any key terms that you don't understand in relevant books and other reference material after the lecture.

Task 2 Making notes while listening

2.1 🔘 T11 **Listen to the lecture on mathematical models.**

2.2 Maysoun could not go to the first lecture because her son was ill.
You are writing a short summary for her. Make notes on the handout including any examples that are useful for her field.

2.3 **Work with another student to check and improve your notes.**

2.4 **Look at the lecture transcript on pages 293–295 to clarify your understanding and record of the lecture. Highlight the key information given in the lecture and use it to check your notes.**

---

1. Mathematical models

Definition:

Used for:

---

2. Mathematical models

Purposes:

---

3. Mathematical models

Exponential growth curve

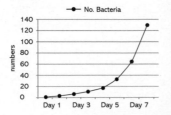

Equation:

4. Mathematical models
Dividing bacteria

5. Mathematical models
Geometric growth:

Examples: Moore's law

6. Mathematical models
Logistic growth curve

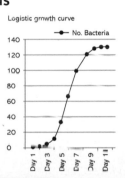

7. Mathematical models
Limiting factors for exponential growth:

8. Mathematical models
Mathematical models include:

Mathematical models change:

Basic process:

Task 3 Understanding a lecturer's purposes

3.1   How does the lecturer classify mathematical models?

3.2   Identify the lecturer's purposes, choosing from the following options. Then write them in the appropriate places on the transcript.

    a   to make sure everyone is at the right lecture

    b   to explain where to get information about the lecture

    c   to show what he thinks the students might know

    d   to explain his aims for the lecture series

    e   to show he's going to start the key information for the lecture

    f   to add a famous example that will interest the students

    g   to make the students feel less worried and anxious

    h   to give a familiar example that the students might know to help them to understand

    i   to summarize the explanation so far

3.3   Highlight any key language that signals these purposes. Were there any cues in the way the lecturer paused or used his voice?

3.4   Find a definition of mathematical models and two reformulations of the original definition. What is different about the second reformulation?

3.5   Find three running definitions.

Task 4 Thinking critically

Answer these questions about the lecture from memory. Refer to the transcript to check your answers.

a   Why does the lecturer give such a wide range of examples in the lecture?

b   The lecturer thinks that business students are likely to know the metaphors *stock market crashes*, *credit crunch* and *price squeeze*. Do these metaphors refer to positive or negative events?

c   Do researchers measure anything in your subject discipline? Give examples of these key variables or choose another discipline and suggest examples of key variables.

d   Think of examples of how the exponential growth in computer memory has impacted on products that we buy today compared with products ten or twenty years ago.

e   In the chess board example, how many grains of rice would be on the seventh square?

f   What could be the limiting factors in human population growth?

Task 5 Writing a summary

Write a summary of the lecture for Maysoun from your notes. Write about 250 words.

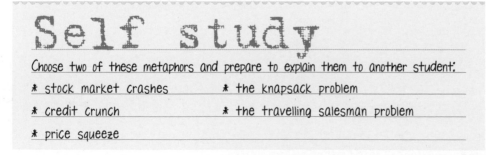

Self study

Choose two of these metaphors and prepare to explain them to another student:

* stock market crashes   * the knapsack problem

* credit crunch   * the travelling salesman problem

* price squeeze

Section 5 Concepts and tools that cross disciplines

What the university expects:
- a spirit of enquiry – pursue knowledge for its own sake

Contexts:
- studying and working in new contexts

Aims:
- to explore some key general academic concepts
- to use an index to find definitions
- to review types of definitions

All students at university experience times when they are confused or uncertain in their understanding of a new concept they meet. It is important to stay calm and find resources to research the concept.

Maysoun reads the notes that Khalid and Matt wrote for her. She feels worried and wants to have a deeper understanding of the words *concept, theory, model* and *metaphor*, but her dictionary gives only brief definitions. Her husband, Omar, is doing a PhD in Education and he recommends one of his books. Its purpose is to help Social Science postgraduate students in their studies, and Omar says that it gives very clear definitions of these concepts. She turns to the index to find the information she needs and notes the relevant page numbers, together with the reference details for the book.

Index

certainty, 81–89	mental map for exploring	task-driven reading, 10–11
concepts, 72–73	the literature	theoretical aim, 176
conclusion (component of	components of, 81	theories, 76–77
argument)	definition of, 70	tools for thinking, 71–79,
definition of, 71, 174	key, 71	91, 105
identification of, 35	metaphors, 75–76	
conclusion (of dissertation)	methodological aim, 176	
structure of, 182–184	models, 76–77	

Task 1 Using an index to locate key information

1.1 **Write the numbers of the pages where Maysoun will find the information she needs.**

Ref: Wallace, M., & Wray, A. (2010). *Critical reading and writing for postgraduates*. London: Sage.
concept _____ theory _____ model _____ metaphor _____

1.2 **How do you know whether an item might be just mentioned in the book or is covered in depth? Give examples.**

1.3 **One important term seems to be defined in more than one section of the book. What term is it and can you explain why it appears twice in the index?**

1.4 **Find the page numbers for any information that might be useful for your own studies and explain your choice to another student.**

Task 2 Reading critically

What can you infer (guess) from the page numbers for Maysoun's search terms?

Task 3 Reading quickly for the main idea

Read Texts A–C from Maysoun's book quickly to decide what words they explain and complete the three headings for each of the texts.

> **Key definitions**
>
> **A. What are _____?**
>
> Ideas like 'education' are concepts. The word (or term) education is used as the bridge between the abstract concept 'education' in the minds of the author and the reader. Using the term to refer to the concept, we can write about how we classify, interpret, describe, explain and evaluate aspects of the social world. One concept will be defined in relation to other concepts, so 'education' might be defined in relation to other concepts like 'instruction', 'creativity', 'training' or 'skill formation'.
>
> **B. What are _____?**
>
> A metaphor is a way of describing one unfamiliar or complex phenomenon in terms of another, more familiar or simpler one. The characteristics of something familiar and easy to understand are used to explore, by analogy, the nature of the more difficult phenomenon … A metaphor maps onto the concept that it describes, but not exactly. There are aspects of the concept that lie outside the bounds of the metaphor and also aspects of the metaphor that lie outside the bounds of the concept.
>
> **C. What are _____?**
>
> The terms 'theory' and 'model' refer to explanatory and often evaluative accounts of one or more aspects of the … world, incorporating a bundle of related concepts defined in a particular way.
>
> Theories and models may or may not be informed by research or practical experience.
>
> Theories are widely viewed as a coherent system of connected concepts … They may be used to interpret and explain what has happened and to predict what will happen.
>
> Models generally entail a small bundle of concepts and their relationships to each other. They tend to refer to a specific aspect of a phenomenon, which may form part of a broader theory. It is common, therefore, to see a specific phenomenon being modelled on the basis of the predictions or prescriptions of a more general theory.

Key words & phrases

- abstract concept
- classify
- interpret
- in relation to
- creativity
- phenomenon
- explore
- by analogy
- the nature of
- maps onto
- lie outside the bounds of
- theory
- model
- accounts of
- incorporating
- a bundle of
- be informed by
- a coherent system of
- entail
- a broader theory
- being modelled on

Source: Extracts adapted from Wallace, M., & Wray, A. (2011). *Critical reading and writing for postgraduates.* London: Sage.

Task 4 Reading critically to apply general ideas to specific examples

4.1 Below are examples of the terms explained in Texts A, B and C. Read A, B and C again carefully and for each example decide whether the word or phrase that is being explained refers to a concept, a metaphor, a theory, or a model.

4.2 Underline the terms and suggest an academic discipline that would use these terms. The first has been done for you. Note that there are extra spaces in d, f and h where the terms have been removed.

   a Waters and Waters offer the most useful term, referring to a general, underlying capacity for study as <u>study competence.</u>
      concept: used in education

   b The term *tropical rainforest* refers to the biome or ecosystem that has developed as a result of the climate and geography of the tropical areas of the world.

      _____ : used in _____

c Volatility in the market appears to be a meteor shower rather than a heat wave. In other words, news in the New York market can predict volatility in the Tokyo market several hours later and does not remain a localized factor.

_____: used in _____

d Global climate _____ are used to simulate a range of possible climate scenarios in the future.

_____: used in _____

e Moves in a text are like moves in a game. They are intended to achieve the overall purpose of the text.

_____: used in _____

f Special relativity _____ fits observations of elementary particles and their interactions, whereas general relativity _____ solves problems in explaining astrophysical events.

_____: used in _____

g In 1859, Darwin published his book _On the Origin of Species_, which explained evolution in terms of a process called natural selection.

_____: used in _____

h A simple mathematical _____ that you probably already know is the normal curve.

_____: used in _____

Task 5 Reading quickly for the main idea

5.1 Read Text D quickly to determine the purpose of the text. Choose from the following purposes:

a to explain the best type of definition
b to explain a possible problem in writing about concepts
c to explain how concepts can be employed in your writing
d to clarify the meaning of the term 'concept'

5.2 Read the text again quickly to find two phrases that show the answer to Task 5.1.

D. What are concepts?

It follows that the extent to which concepts can be successfully shared by an author and a reader depends on the extent to which they both interpret the term in the same way. Suppose an author states an opinion about a concept (e.g., adult education is of little benefit to the economy) and the reader disagrees with it. This could be for one of at least three reasons:

1 The author and reader understand[4] differently what the term refers to (e.g., 'adult education' means evening classes in flower arranging, versus 'adult education' means mature student access to full time university study).

2 They have different conceptualizations of the underlying phenomenon (e.g., adult education is largely about giving retired people access to pastimes, versus adult education is an opportunity to make up for previously missed opportunities).

3 The reader does not share the author's view about the concept (e.g., adult education is expensive and makes no difference to employability, versus all education is beneficial, because it stimulates the individual to make life-changing decisions).

Key words & phrases

the extent to which

depends on

interpret

adult education

flower arranging

versus

conceptualizations

phenomenon

retired people

pastimes

make up for

share the view

employability

beneficial

stimulates

life-changing decisions

---

[4] A more usual phrase might be _The author and reader each have a different understanding of ..._

If no one has the monopoly on the definition of concepts, there is great potential for confusion. This will result in a failure to communicate, one major reason why authors may not convince a reader about an issue that seems obvious to them. In order to see things through the author's eyes, the reader needs to find a way of working out what the author means by the terms used. What authors can do to help the reader is to offer an explicit 'stipulative definition' of the main concepts they are dealing with. In this way, readers can see where their own understanding is different and also make a deliberate, if temporary, change to their own conceptualization, so as to see things through the eyes of the author.

Just as you, as a reader, need authors to define their key concepts, as a writer, you risk confusing your readers unless you give a stipulative definition of the key concepts that you employ.

Source: Extract adapted from Wallace, M., & Wray, A. (2011). *Critical reading and writing for postgraduates.* London: Sage.

Key words & phrases

has the monopoly on

great potential for

through the author's eyes

a stipulative definition

Task 6 Reading carefully to follow an argument

Read Text D again carefully and complete this summary of the argument using the words in the box.

opportunity	confused	concepts	arguments
viewpoint	communicate	stipulative	reader

In order to **(a)** _____ clearly, an author has to establish with a **(b)** _____ a shared

understanding of any key **(c)** _____ in the text. If this is not achieved, the reader is

likely to be **(d)** _____ and remain unconvinced by the author's **(e)** _____.

An important method of sharing understanding is to give the reader **(f)** _____ definitions.

This gives the reader the **(g)** _____, even if only temporarily, to change their

(h) _____ and see things through the author's eyes.

Investigating language: stipulative definitions

Stipulative definitions (also known as 'working' definitions) tell you what something means in a particular context. Expressions to limit the scope of use (e.g., *in this chapter/context*) may be used, together with the modal verb *will/shall* or a verb which expresses intention, such as *propose* or *suggest*. The restricted context may just mean the context of a specific book or research report, or it might mean a field of study such as behavioural science or network theory. Stipulative definitions are used to ensure that the reader and writer share an understanding of a concept in order to explore it further or evaluate it.

Task 7 Reading critically to apply general ideas to specific examples

7.1 Read Text D again carefully and apply the information to the definitions opposite to identify which are stipulative.

7.2 Underline any word or phrase that indicates a stipulative definition.

7.3 Identify one contrastive and one negative definition.

a The term *tropical rainforest* refers to the biome or ecosystem that has developed as a result of the climate and geography of the tropical areas of the world.

b For behavioural scientists, a group consists of two or more people interacting interdependently to achieve common goals.

c A robot is a machine that can interact intelligently with its environment in order to perform physical tasks.

d A key in this context is taken in its widest definition – an artificial system for identifying animals or plants; the term *key* should not be restricted to the dichotomous kind.

e Change blindness is the lack of awareness of changing features of a scene, while inattentional blindness refers to the lack of conscious perception of conspicuous objects in a scene, when attention is directed elsewhere.

f Noise in this context means the unwanted products of the imaging system. Landsat images are scanned on a line-by-line basis, and this line-scanning process often leads to the production of horizontal striping effects on the resulting image.

g A good is either labour-intensive (meaning that relatively more labour than capital is required in the production process) or is capital-intensive (where the requirement for capital in production is higher than the requirement for labour).

h I propose a working definition of what it might mean to make a choice: a choice would involve reflection (in the present), memory (of the past) and imagination (of possible futures).

i In network theory, a network is an array of points connected by a line. Hubs are points with many connections. Networks are robust, but robustness requires hubs.

j Static testing involves inspection and analysis of the program code and its supporting documentation, whereas dynamic testing involves running the program to ensure that the input–output mappings are correct.

Task 8 Writing a summary of an argument

Imagine a student friend has e-mailed you to ask why academic writers need to use stipulative definitions. Read Extract D again carefully and then close the book, and in your own words write a summary of the argument for stipulative definitions. Write around 100 words.

Self study

Write an explanation of a concept or tool in your field. Use the moves you have learnt about in this unit and any appropriate types of definition. Your text should be suitable for a poster presentation for high school students who are preparing to apply for undergraduate courses in your subject discipline. Any sources you use should be properly referenced. Write about 500 words.

Unit 4
Resources for research

Section 1 Exploring the concept of research

What the university expects:
- a spirit of enquiry – pursue knowledge for its own sake

Contexts:
- directed search for information for study and work

Aims:
- to understand what doing research involves
- to understand a metaphor used to talk about research
- to demonstrate understanding by explaining the concept of research to other students

The library is a vital resource at university and students need to spend a large amount of time there. The librarians often encourage students to use their services by running informal seminars. Maysoun has found a flyer about a library seminar called *Starting out on your research journey*. She persuades Khalid, Dimitri and Guy to go with her to the library seminar to find out more about research.

Discussion

Read the flyer below, advertising the informal library seminars. Who is this seminar for – undergraduate or postgraduate students? Why are the librarians leading a seminar about research? Can you answer 'yes' to any of the questions? Look at the aims of the seminar. How do you think the librarians will help Maysoun get started on her research? Compare your ideas with another student.

Starting out on your research journey

GATEWAY UNIVERSITY

- Do you know what research involves?
- Do you understand how research is done in your field?
- Do you know how to get started on your own research project?

The first in a series of informal seminars with subject librarians to be held in the coffee bar at the Postgraduate Centre on 25th January at 12:30 p.m. Subject librarians for Environmental Sciences, Computer Science and Business Studies will be available for an informal discussion and Q&A session.

We aim to:
- demystify the research process
- answer your questions about getting started on your research
- encourage you to consult your subject librarian about your research project

Seminars last about 45 minutes. You are welcome to bring your lunch.

Key words & phrases

your research project
seminars
subject librarians
a Q&A session
to demystify
to consult
are welcome to

Task 1 Listening to understand the purpose of the seminar

1.1   ⊙T12 **Listen to the first part of the seminar. In their introductions, which students say they are already thinking about their research? Who thinks research is not relevant to them yet?**

1.2   **What contrast does the librarian make later to explain the concept of research more clearly?**

Task 2 Understanding how research is different from journalism

2.1   **Complete the table to show how journalism and research differ according to the subject librarian. Listen again if you need to.**

	journalism	research
starting point	a _____	b _____
questions	c describe: _____	d explain: _____
main content	e _____	f _____
planning	g _____	h systematic: _____
other differences	i _____	j contributes to theory and adds knowledge

2.2   **Why does the subject librarian discuss only the differences between journalism and research? Can you think of any similarities between them?**

Task 3 Thinking critically: identifying types of research

3.1 Below are the introductions from the report guidelines you studied in Unit 2, Section 3 on pages 36 and 37. How many different kinds of research are described in these two introductions?

3.2 What is the goal of each type of research?

3.3 What data is collected in each of these types?

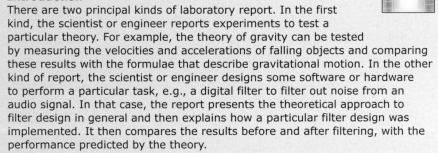

Department of Computer Science

Guidelines for writing laboratory reports
Introduction
There are two principal kinds of laboratory report. In the first kind, the scientist or engineer reports experiments to test a particular theory. For example, the theory of gravity can be tested by measuring the velocities and accelerations of falling objects and comparing these results with the formulae that describe gravitational motion. In the other kind of report, the scientist or engineer designs some software or hardware to perform a particular task, e.g., a digital filter to filter out noise from an audio signal. In that case, the report presents the theoretical approach to filter design in general and then explains how a particular filter design was implemented. It then compares the results before and after filtering, with the performance predicted by the theory.

School of Management

Guidelines for writing business reports
Introduction
A business report records the analysis of a business problem and recommended solutions. The analysis is intended to establish and interpret the facts which relate to the problem and to persuade a reader, e.g., a manager, to accept and implement the recommendations.

Task 4 Evaluating how much you understand

4.1 Look back to the questions in the flyer. Which ones can you answer now?

4.2 Which of the five students in the seminar has similar ideas about research to your ideas?

4.3 Do you still have other questions about research? Make a list and compare with another student.

Task 5 Listening critically for answers to your questions

5.1 ⊙T13 Listen to the next part of the seminar to see if your questions are answered.

5.2 What further comparison do the librarians make to explain the concept of research more clearly?

5.3 What questions do the students in the seminar still have about research? Do the librarians provide satisfactory answers?

Study smart: using metaphors to understand new concepts

Metaphors are used widely in all academic subjects to explain new and abstract concepts. The metaphor compares the new concept to a familiar one which shares similar features. This enables students to link what they already know to what is new in order to start exploring the new concept.

Task 6 Understanding a metaphor for research

6.1 In the seminar, the librarians used a metaphor to explain to the students what doing research is like.

Complete the sentences to show the metaphor that the librarians used for this comparison:

a Doing research is like _____

b To begin research, you need to _____

c By reading what other researchers have done, you can _____

6.2 Find the parts of the transcript on pages 298–301 that relate to journeys, and make a mind map of words connected to journeys that are used by the librarians, e.g., *destination, path.*

Task 7 Understanding the concept of research

7.1 Below are some assumptions about what is involved in research.

Write T (true) or F (false) next to each statement to show which assumptions are true and which are false according to the subject librarians. Listen to the complete seminar again if you need to.

a Research is only for postgraduate students. ☐

b Undergraduate students study the findings of research in their field. ☐

c You start research by finding data. ☐

d You start research by finding a problem or puzzle. ☐

e You start with a goal and plan how to achieve the goal. ☐

f You start by reading what other researchers have done. ☐

g You have to do something completely new. ☐

h You have to build on what other researchers have done. ☐

i You have to be prepared to explore unexpected findings. ☐

j You only really understand what research involves once you begin your research journey. ☐

7.2 **Explain to another student why the false statements are false.**

Task 8 Thinking critically about the research seminar

8.1 **Why is it appropriate for the subject specialist librarians to be running this research seminar and not lecturers from the departments?**

8.2 Khalid identified one way in which research is not like a journey: if a journey starts with a problem, you run away from the problem, but with research you run towards the problem.

Can you think of other limits to this metaphor? Which other aspects of a real journey are different from a research journey? Discuss with other students.

Task 9 Making a record of ideas from the seminar

Carmen, Victor and Paula want to record the ideas that came up during the seminar so other students can benefit from them. They decide to write some frequently asked questions (FAQs) to put on the library website.

Prepare answers to their questions which will help other students to understand what research involves.

What is research?
How is research different from journalism?
Do undergraduate students do research?
How do I start to do research?
Do I have to do something new that no-one has done before?
How can I be sure that no-one has done my research before?

Self study

Find out about a key piece of research in your field and explain it to another student. Alternatively, you could choose a well-known figure in your field, e.g., Rachel Carson, Amartya Sen, Steve Jobs, and explain their research to a partner.

Section 2 Tools for searching online

What the university expects:
* an awareness of how knowledge is advanced – develop criteria for evaluating information

Contexts:
* learning to use new tools, processes and systems

Aims:
* to understand how to search effectively for sources online
* to understand how to evaluate sources for relevance and quality
* to transform and re-present information from the lecture

Gateway University Library also offers practical talks on how to search online databases effectively and to evaluate sources.

Discussion

What tools, e.g., search engines, do you use to search on the Internet? How do you do your search? Do you type complete questions or just individual words? Do you know how to use advanced search options or Boolean operators to narrow or broaden a search?

Task 1 Listening to learn how to search effectively online

1.1 In his lecture about online resources, the librarian compares two online search tools: Google and the Web of Science. He shows both search pages on a screen during his talk.

Before you listen, look at the search pages below and on page 88, and discuss with a partner how you think they are used to search for sources online.

1.2 ⓝT14 **As you listen, choose the correct Boolean operator or symbol to match the everyday words in Google's advanced search, labelled a–d. Choose from AND, OR, NOT or inverted commas "_".**

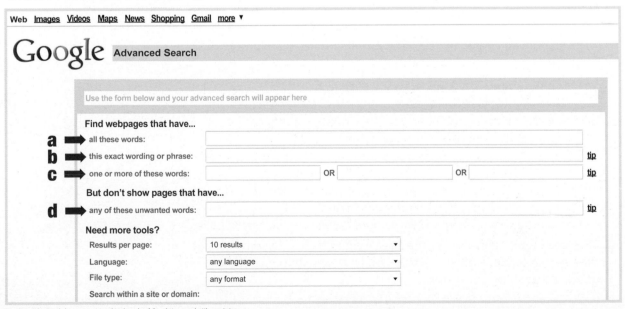

Google and the Google logo are registered trademarks of Google Inc., used with permission.

1.3 The librarian describes the layout and functions of the Web of Science search page.

As you listen, say how each function labelled a–f helps to broaden or narrow a search.

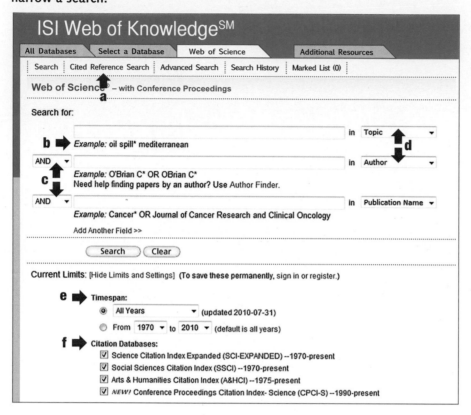

Task 2 Thinking critically about the librarian's talk

2.1 **Why does the librarian tell a joke at the start of his talk?**

2.2 The librarian discusses three search tools.

Which one does he discuss first? Why?

2.3 **Which ones does he consider to be more appropriate for research? Which specific aspects of these tools make them more appropriate for research?**

Task 3 Choosing suitable search terms

3.1 The students try some searches using Google Scholar. Below are the topics they are interested in researching.

Maysoun: I want to find out what the impact of climate change will be on water resources in Syria.

Dimitri: I'm interested in the recent financial crisis – in Europe, not the East-Asian one – and how to manage it.

Khalid: I'd like to know more about the design of software for advanced driver assistance systems.

Guy: I'm thinking about taking a gap year[1] and working as a volunteer on a project in the developing world.

Make a note of the keywords they should type into the search boxes.

3.2 **For each topic, say whether the search could be narrowed by connecting the search terms, e.g., with AND, OR, NOT or within inverted commas "_". Give a reason for your answer.**

---

[1] A gap year is a year away from normal study or work to do something else. Often, students take a gap year before starting university, but it can be taken at any time. Students sometimes look for voluntary work related to their field of study.

3.3 For any of the topics, say whether the search could be narrowed in other ways, e.g., by limiting the dates.

Once their search terms are sufficiently narrow to return a manageable number of results, the students have to select the sources that will be most useful for them to read. In his talk, the librarian referred to a number of criteria used to select the content to include in online databases. The same criteria can be used to evaluate the quality of sources.

> **Study smart:** a checklist for evaluating the quality of academic sources
>
> **Date:** Is the source up to date? (The time frame varies depending on the field.)
>
> **Author:** Is the author a recognized expert in his or her field? Have his/her articles been cited by a lot of other authors?
>
> **Publisher:** If an article, does it appear in an important and reputable journal? If a book, is it from a publisher who specializes in this field?
>
> **Quality:** Has the information been peer reviewed, i.e., checked by other experts?
>
> General criteria to evaluate the quality of webpages:
>
> **Purpose:** Why was the page put on the web? Is it selling products or services or ideas?
>
> **Viewpoint:** Does it include a variety of different viewpoints?

Task 4 Using a checklist to evaluate the quality of sources

4.1 Guy did a web search using the search term *gap year*. Below are four different websites which come up in his search results.

Who put these pages on the web and for what purpose? Which page is academic? Which one offers impartial help and support? Which two are selling products or services?

4.2 Which websites do you think Guy found in Google and which in Google Scholar? Give reasons for your answers.

4.3 How many of the questions from the quality checklist can you answer for each of these pages?

4.4 Which websites could Guy use for advice about gap years and which could he use for an essay about working on volunteer projects in the developing world?

4.5 Look at the results to find other more academic search terms that he could use to find sources.

Gap year, adventure travel & volunteer work abroad.
www.realgap.co.uk Specialists in gap-years, career breaks & adventure travel holidays. Realgap Experience are experts in providing rewarding gap-year jobs and volunteer projects in over 35 countries around the world.

GAPYEAR.COM – Ideas, Volunteering, Backpacking & Travel Mates
www.gapyear.com Gap-year guides, advice, suggestions and help. … Ski and snowboard training video: Fast Track your instructor dreams to get the training, certification, instructor job and winter season you want.

Welcome to Ethical Volunteering
www.ethicalvolunteering.org 1 Mar 2007 … This site offers advice & information for people who are interested in international volunteering and want to make sure that what they do is of value to themselves and the people they work with.

'Doing development': the gap year, volunteer-tourists and a popular practice of development
K Simpson – Journal of International Development, 2004
www3.interscience.wiley.com/109086586/abstract Abstract: Over the last ten years, the gap year has become a popular and publicly recognized phenonomenon. One of the most visible forms of this phenomenon has been the emergence of 'third world' volunteer-tourism programmes … Cited by 52 - Related articles.

Task 5 Selecting relevant sources from the search results

5.1 Maysoun used the search string 'climate change and water resources' in Google Scholar. Below is the first page of her search results.

Use the Study smart quality checklist on page 89 to decide which source is probably most relevant for Maysoun's research. Which source is likely to be least relevant?

5.2 **Explain to another student where on the page you found the information to make your evaluation.**

5.3 **What other information might these sources contain which could help Maysoun to locate more articles that are relevant for her research topic?**

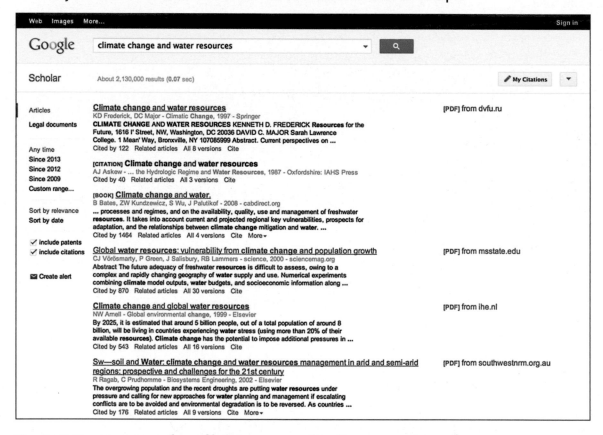

Task 6 Reviewing the effectiveness of online search tools

6.1 Work with a partner to discuss how Google Scholar and the Web of Science are similar to, and different from, Google. Listen to the librarian's talk again if you want to for more ideas. Which resource is more reliable for ensuring the quality of an article or a journal? Which resource is more reliable for finding articles written in languages other than English?

6.2 Make notes in a table to compare Google, Google Scholar and the Web of Science, using ideas from the talk or criteria from the checklist as the features for your comparison, for example:

- variety and type of information
- quality of information
- method of refining a search
- links to other pages or articles
- information about authors or publishers

6.3 **Summarize your discussion and present it to your classmates.**

Section 3 Reviewing the language of comparison and contrast

What the university expects:
- effective communication – present complex ideas in response to the needs and expectations of an audience

Contexts:
- written communication for study and work

Aims:
- to evaluate your ability to compare and contrast ideas
- to extend your range of language patterns for comparison and contrast

At university, students are expected to read the ideas of other writers and use them as the starting point for their own research. They can do this by categorizing ideas from different sources to determine to what extent they are similar or different and whether they match students' own experiences. Students are required to evaluate ideas using appropriate criteria, which enables them to show their viewpoint. These purposes are achieved by comparing and contrasting ideas.

Discussion

Work in a group to answer the following questions to find out what you already know:
- How should you take notes or organize ideas in order to categorize or evaluate them by comparing and contrasting?
- How can you show the basis for your comparison or contrast?
- How should you organize your writing to make the comparisons and contrasts clear to a reader?
- How can you show your viewpoint, e.g., whether you think something is an advantage or a disadvantage?
- How many different grammatical structures can you use to compare and contrast? Make a list.

Task 1 Writing an e-mail to demonstrate you can compare and contrast

The librarians' seminar and talk has changed Khalid's ideas. He now realizes that he should start thinking about research as soon as possible. He wants to share this new insight with his friend Mohammed, who is studying for a master's degree in Media Studies. He sends Mohammed an e-mail to tell him about the seminar and, in particular, the contrast between journalism and research.

Using the table below that you completed on page 83, write the e-mail that Khalid sends to Mohammed. Think carefully about what is familiar to Mohammed (journalism) and what might be new (research), so that you structure the e-mail to explain the new concept in terms of the familiar one. Use a wide variety of sentence patterns in your writing.

	journalism	research
similarities	both seek information; both have to be reported for impact	
starting point	events, news, problems	problems and puzzles
questions	describe: *what, when, where, who*	explain: *how, why*
main content	stories	data
planning	no control: respond to events	systematic: requires goal and plan
other differences	no theory or body of knowledge	test theory and add to knowledge

To:	m.salem@dodgson.ac.uk
From:	k.othmani@gateway.ac.uk
Subject:	Learning about research

Hi Mohammed,

Yesterday, I went to a really interesting seminar about research, which was run by librarians here. My friend, Maysoun, persuaded me to go to it and I'm sure glad she did because it changed the way I think about research. The librarians wanted to explain the concept of research to us and what it involves, so they compared it to something we already know about – journalism …

Investigating grammar patterns for comparison and contrast

When writers want to explain a new idea (research) in terms of something familiar (journalism), or to evaluate items and choose the best one, they compare the items to show how they are both similar and different. Writers contrast by showing only how items are different. Their purposes can be to define a concept by saying what it is not, or to correct mistaken assumptions, or to show the opposite side of an argument.

Patterns for similarity

A + verb + *the same as* + B A and B + verb + *the same* + noun phrase	*Guy's views about research are the same as Peter's [views].* *Different researchers in a field review the same key studies.*
A *is like* B A *is similar to* B	*Research is like a journey [because you have a destination].* *Google is similar to other search engines.*
Both A *and* B + verb phrase	*Both Google Scholar and the Web of Science list academic articles.*
They both + verb phrase	*They both give results which link articles together.*
noun phrase + *have in common*	*Cited reference searching shows all the citations which different articles have in common.*
clause + *and* + *so does/do* + noun phrase	*A journey has stages and so does research.*

Patterns for difference

A + *is not the same as* + B	*Journalism is not the same as research.*
A + *is different from* + B	*Undergraduate research is different from postgraduate research.*

Writers can show their viewpoint, i.e., whether they see something as an advantage or disadvantage, by choosing adjectives which are positive (e.g., *deep*) or negative (e.g., *hard*) in the grammar patterns below.

adjective/adverb + ~er + *than*	*Research goes deeper than journalism.* (advantage) *'How' and 'why' questions are harder to answer.* (disadvantage)
more/less + adjective/adverb/noun (+ *than*)	*This helps you to read in a more focused way.* (advantage) *Sources in Google are less academic than sources in Google Scholar.* (disadvantage)

Linking words and phrases which show relationships between ideas through grammatical links

clause + *whereas* + clause	*Anyone can put anything online, whereas not everything gets into the databases.*
clause + *but* + clause	*You don't need to use Boolean operators to search in Google, but you will see them when you search the Web of Science.*
some ... but others ...	*Some papers are listed in both Google Scholar and the Web of Science, but others only appear in Google Scholar.*
not only/simply ... but also	*The ranking is determined not only by the number of links from other pages, but also by the journal which published the articles.*
instead of + noun phrase	*Instead of everyday words [to show the type of search], we have Boolean operators.*
rather than + noun phrase	*The search finds pages [with any one of the terms you enter] rather than only pages [with all of them].*

Note that although they can be used in either position, *instead of* tends to be used at the beginning of sentences, while *rather than* is more common in the middle of sentences.

Signpost words and phrases which show relationships between ideas, but do not make grammatical links

However	*Google searches in a similar way to other search engines. However, it uses a PageRank algorithm to rank or sort the pages it finds in a special way.*
In contrast	*Google uses everyday words to describe the search string. In contrast, the Web of Science uses Boolean operators.*
on the other hand	*Research has to relate to theory. Journalism, on the other hand, reports a series of unconnected events in the real world.*

Task 2 Assessing your use of grammar patterns for comparison and contrast

2.1 Study the patterns for comparison and contrast on pages 92–93, and highlight in your completed e-mail any patterns that you have used. Compare with other students: who has used the widest variety of patterns?

2.2 Check your e-mail using this checklist of questions:

- Did you say how journalism and research are similar before showing how they are different?
- Did you compare the two items feature by feature, or did you list all the features of each item?
- Do your sentences start with what is familiar (journalism) and move to what is new (research)?
- How many sentence patterns for comparison and contrast did you use compared to the model?
- Did you use these sentence patterns accurately?

2.3 Choose some of the comparisons in your e-mail and redraft them using a different pattern.

Investigating grammar patterns for comparison which also show cause and effect

The relative size or quality of two items can be shown in the construction *the more … the more …* The relationship between the two comparisons is cause and effect. The pattern could be rewritten using a conditional structure, e.g., *If a search term is more general, it will return a larger number of hits.*

the more/less + adjective + noun phrase + *the* adjective(~er) + noun phrase	*The more general the search term, the larger the number of hits.*
the more/less + adjective + noun phrase + *the more/less/fewer* + noun phrase	*The more specific the search term, the fewer hits <u>you find</u>*.*
the more/less/fewer + noun phrase + *the* adjective(~er) + noun phrase	*The more links <u>a page has</u>*, the higher its ranking.*
the more + clause + *the more/less/fewer* + noun phrase	*The more Google expands, the more resources <u>it can provide</u>*.*
the more + clause + *the more*/adjective (~er) + clause	*The more you read, the clearer your ideas about research become.*

* **Note:** the reduced relative clauses in these noun phrases are <u>underlined</u>.

Task 3 Practising grammar patterns for comparison which also show cause and effect

3.1 Match the two halves of the sentences below to make sentences about searching the Internet using Google.

a The more specialized the Google application …   **1** … the lower it is ranked by the PageRank algorithm.

b The more precise the search term …   **2** … the more academic its content.

c The more keywords the search term contains …   **3** … the more relevant the information.

d The more Google expands …   **4** … the more users have found it useful.

e The fewer links to a page …   **5** … the smaller the number of hits.

f The more links a page has …   **6** … the more successful it becomes.

3.2 Use this pattern to redraft these conditional sentences, which give advice to new researchers. Make sure you maintain the sequence of given and new, cause and effect in your paraphrase.

  a Problem: I don't feel comfortable using the library.
      Advice: If you use the library often, you will feel more comfortable there.

  b Problem: I'm very slow searching the online databases.
      Advice: If you are familiar with the online databases, you will be able to search faster.

  c Problem: I don't know how to get going with my research.
      Advice: If you are clear about your starting point, it is easier to plan your research.

  d Problem: I can't find a gap in my research field that I can fill.
      Advice: If you read a lot of articles in your field, it is easier to find a gap in the research which you can fill.

  e Problem: I'm worried that someone else has done my research before me.
      Advice: If you are aware of the state of the art in your field, you can be more certain that your research has not been done before.

  f Problem: I want my research to make a significant contribution.
      Advice: If you have a lot of experience as a researcher, you are more likely to do research which moves the field forward considerably.

Task 4 Using the language of comparison and contrast to evaluate online search tools

In Section 2, Task 6, you made notes in a table to compare the effectiveness of Google, Google Scholar and the Web of Science for finding sources. You may have used some of the following features for your evaluation:
- variety and type of information
- quality of information
- method of refining a search
- links to other pages or articles
- information about authors or publishers

Use your table to write the answer to the following frequently asked question (FAQ), to be published on the library website for students to read:
Which online search tool is better for finding reliable information for an essay: Google, Google Scholar or the Web of Science?

Think carefully about what is familiar to your readers (students like you) and what might be new, so that you structure the answer to explain the new concept in terms of the familiar one. Use a wider variety of sentence patterns in your writing than you did for the e-mail you wrote in Task 1.

Self study

Compare two concepts in your field of study in order to explain their similarities and differences to someone who is not familiar with the concepts, e.g., vowels and consonants (linguistics).

Section 4 Surveying sources

Discussion

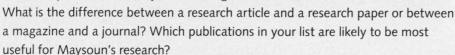

Work with a partner to make a list of the different types of academic publications that you know, e.g., book, research article. What is the difference between a research article and a research paper or between a magazine and a journal? Which publications in your list are likely to be most useful for Maysoun's research?

Task 1 Surveying a list of references

Maysoun has now collected a list of books, research papers and other sources in order to begin reading around her topic and to decide which aspect she would like to focus on.

1.1 **Survey her list opposite quickly to find:**

    a The number of books and published papers or articles.

    b The names of four companies which publish books in this field. Where are they located?

1.2 Professor Nigel Arnell is an important researcher in this field.

    Are any of his publications listed?

1.3 Every year, a report is published on the Earth's water resources.

    Who is the main author of the report for 2008–2009?

1.4 **Which source focuses on sustainability? Which sources examine future challenges?**

1.5 **Do any of these sources mention Syria specifically?**

1 Abdulla, F. A., & Al-Omari, A. S. (2008). The impact of climate change on the monthly runoff of a semi-arid catchment: Case study Zarqa river basin (Jordan). *Journal of Applied Biological Sciences, 2*(1), 43–50.

2 Arnell, N. (1996). *Global warming, river flows and water resources.* Oxford: Wiley. 551.48 ARN

3 Bou-Zeid, E. R., & El-Fadel, M. (2002). Climate change and water resources in Lebanon and the Middle East. *Journal of Water Resources Planning and Management, 128*(5), 343–355.

4 Evans, J. P. (2009). 21st century climate change in the Middle East. *Climatic Change, 92*(3–4), 417–432.

5 Gleick, P. H., Cooley, H., & Palaniappan, M. (2009). *The world's water 2008–2009: The biennial report on freshwater resources.* Washington: Island Press. 333.91 GLE

6 Hreiche, A., Bocquillon, C., Najem, W., & Dandach, D. (2005). The potential impact of future climate change on Lebanese river basin hydrology using scenarios. In T. Wagener *et al.* (Eds.), *Regional Hydrological Impacts of Climatic Change,* 103–110. Conference proceedings from International Association of Hydrological Science.

7 Mauser, W. (2009). *Water resources: Efficient, sustainable and equitable use.* London: Haus Publishing. 331.91 MAU

8 Nawaz, N. R. (2001). *Climate change and water resources: Impacts and uncertainties.* (Unpublished PhD thesis). Summerford: Gateway University Press.

9 Ragab, R., & Prudhomme, C. (2002). Climate change and water resources management in arid and semi-arid regions: Prospective and challenges for the 21st century. *Biosystems Engineering, 81*(1), 3–34.

10 Rind, D., Rosenzweig, C., & Goldberg, R. (1992). Modelling the hydrological cycle in assessments of climate change. *Nature, 358*(6382), 119–122.

11 Sexton, R. (1990). *Perspectives on the Middle East water crisis: Analysing freshwater problems in Jordan and Israel.* ODI/TWMI irrigation management report 90/3f. 627.5 ODI Zereini, F., & Hötzl, H. (Eds.). (2008). *Climatic changes and water resources in the Middle East and North Africa.* Berlin: Springer.

12 Zereini, F. & Hötzl, H. (Eds.). (2008). *Climatic changes and water resources in the Middle East and North Africa.* Berlin: Springer.

Key words & phrases

monthly runoff

semi-arid catchment

basin

a biennial report

hydrology

scenarios

conference proceedings

equitable

uncertainties

a PhD thesis

arid

prospective

modelling

assessments

perspectives

crisis

Task 2 Identifying different types of publications

This task helps you to recognize the clues you used to complete Task 1.

2.1 **Which types of publications has Maysoun found? Write the numbers of the sources next to each type of publication. Highlight in each reference the word, or words, which show the type of publication.**

books: _____

student research projects: _____

papers from a conference: _____

articles in research journals: _____

reports from international organizations: _____

2.2 **What determines the order in which the items are listed in a references list?**

2.3 **How is the layout and use of italics different for a reference to a book compared to an article?**

2.4 **Look at the titles which contain a colon: How is information different before and after the colon?**

Task 3 Reading critically to evaluate sources

3.1 Which sources give a general overview and which seem to be about more specific topics? What clues did you find in the references to help you answer?

3.2 Which sources seem a little out of date? Why do you think Maysoun has included these sources?

3.3 Which sources should Maysoun read first? Give reasons for your answers.

Task 4 Categorizing sources

Maysoun found some of her sources in Gateway University Library, so in her references list she inserted their Dewey Decimal numbers (underlined in her list) which indicate the topic focus of the book and where it can be found in the library. Below is an extract from the Dewey Decimal System[2] which shows three different categories in the system.

4.1 Study the titles of the four books with Dewey numbers. Decide the possible Dewey category and hence the focus of the other sources in Maysoun's list. Highlight in each title the word, or words, which helped you decide.

> **331** Land economics – managing, i.e., sharing, natural resources such as water
> **551** Hydrology – studying the movement of water
> **627** Hydraulic engineering – managing, i.e., planning, the movement of water

4.2 Why might it be useful for Maysoun to categorize her sources in this way?

Task 5 Identifying the research method in the title of an article

Four of the articles in Maysoun's list contain phrases in their titles which show the research method, i.e., how the research was carried out. The research methods are listed in the table below, together with brief definitions.

5.1 Match each method to its definition. Can you explain in more detail what each method involves?

research method	definition	in-text reference for article
1 analyzing problems	a a detailed study of a single individual or organization or event	
2 case study	b the use of mathematical language to describe the behaviour of a system in order to make predictions about it	
3 modelling	c the use of hypothetical (possible) situations to explore potential future outcomes	
4 scenarios	d establishing and interpreting facts on which to base recommendations	

[2] The Dewey Decimal System is one way to classify books so they can be easily stored and retrieved in a library. It is a numerical system based on ten general categories, each divided into ten more specific topics.

5.2 Identify the four articles by underlining the phrases in their titles which show the research methods. Then complete the table with the short reference that would be used to refer to the source in the text of a literature review, e.g., *Arnell, 1996.*

5.3 Why did these authors decide to include the research method in the title of their articles?

Task 6 Investigating grammar patterns for noun phrases in titles

6.1 The titles of research articles and journals contain the shortest possible summary of the topic or research area. These are expressed using noun phrases. Typical structures for noun phrases are shown below.

Find an example of each structure from the titles in Maysoun's list.

noun phrase structures	examples
noun + noun/adjective + noun + noun	
adjective + doing noun/doing noun + noun	
noun + noun + prepositional phrase*	
the + noun + *of* + noun + prepositional phrase*	

* prepositional phrase = preposition + noun phrase

6.2 The following noun phrases are taken from the titles in the list of references.

Rearrange the words to restore the original noun phrase. Think about the combined search terms which Maysoun used to find her sources to help you decide which words are collocations.

a change climatic

b engineering biosystems

c efficient use and equitable sustainable

d freshwater on the biennial resources report

e [the] regional climatic impacts of hydrological change

f [the] journal of resources planning and water management

g hydrological assessments in the cycle of climate modelling change

h climatic and North Africa resources in water changes and the Middle East

Self study

List the sources you found in your search in the Self study on page 91 using the correct order and layout so that a reader would find it easy to survey your sources. Compare the format of your list with Maysoun's to check that you included all the necessary information. Survey your list to decide if your sources are general or specific. Which sources will you choose to read first? Which sources should be read together?

Section 5 Using abstracts to select and compare sources

Key words & phrases

to read up about
climate modelling
complexity
limitations
to simulate
climate scenarios
circulation models
meteorology

Maysoun has decided to read up about climate modelling, in which computers are used to create mathematical models of the climate. These models cannot fully match the complexity of the climate system because of limitations in computer power. Their accuracy is tested by running them from points in the past and comparing their predictions with actual past measurements of surface temperature. The models represent the past climate reasonably accurately, which gives confidence in their ability to simulate future climate scenarios. Global climate models – sometimes also called general circulation models (GCMs) – are usually produced by meteorology centres such as the Hadley Centre in the UK or the Max Planck Institute in Germany. Maysoun is interested in researching how these GCMs can be applied to predict local hydrological processes within a region or a country such as Syria.

Discussion

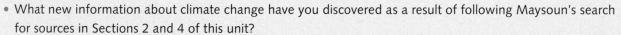

Answer the following questions to evaluate your initial understanding.
- What do you know about climate change, its causes and predictions for the future climate? Compare your knowledge with another student and with your class.
- What new information about climate change have you discovered as a result of following Maysoun's search for sources in Sections 2 and 4 of this unit?
- You are going to read the abstracts from articles that are very specific to Maysoun's research topic, so you may not understand them completely. Can you accept less than 100 per cent comprehension?

Task 1 Using the abstract to understand the purpose of an article

1.1 Opposite is a set of statements which describe the type and purpose of each article.

Read the article abstracts on pages 102–103, which are listed in order of first author family name. Match each statement a–f on page 101 to an article, and write the in-text reference for the article in the space provided. Give reasons for your answers.

1.2 Statements a–f are listed in the order that Maysoun chose to read the articles.

Why did she choose this order? Look at the document type of each abstract to help you answer.

a A review which critically evaluates the inconsistency of predictions from a number of models about the impact of climate change on water circulation.

b A paper which gives an overview of the current state of knowledge at the time it was published by comparing predictions for the Middle East from one GCM to actual measurements of rainfall and temperature.

c A review which analyzes and compares the results from a number of well-established GCMs in order to provide general predictions about climate change in the Middle East.

d An article which uses GCMs to give an overview of the possible impact of different climate change scenarios on countries in the Middle East and then considers one country in more detail in terms of two water resource indicators.

e A paper which uses a rainfall model to predict changes in the hydrologic cycle as a consequence of climate change, in particular changes in the type and timing of water flows.

f An article which uses scenarios with a variety of temperature and rainfall settings to predict the water balance in a particular location and compare with recorded measurements.

Abstract 1

Fayez A. Abdulla and Abbas S. Al-Omari

In this paper, the long-term hydrological responses of a semi-arid basin to climate changes were analyzed. This basin is the Zarqa River (Jordan). The climate changes were imposed with twelve hypothetical scenarios. Two of these scenarios were based on the predictions of the Hadley and MPI general circulation models (GCMs). The other ten scenarios are incremental scenarios associated with temperature increases by $+2^0C$ and $+4^0C$ and changes in rainfall of 0%, +10%, +20%, -10%, and -20%. These scenarios were the basis for observing causal relationships among runoff, air temperature, and rainfall, using the SFB water balance model developed by Boughton (1984). This model performed well for the Zarqa River for which the average monthly runoff from the model compared well to the observed average runoff. Both sets of climate change scenarios resulted in decreases in monthly runoff.

Document type: article

Key words: climate change, rainfall-runoff modelling, incremental scenarios

Source: Abdulla, F. A., & Al-Omari, A. S. (2008). The impact of climate change on the monthly runoff of a semi-arid catchment: Case study Zarqa river basin (Jordan). *Journal of Applied Biological Sciences*, 2(1), 43–50.

Key words & phrases

long-term
responses
were imposed
hypothetical
incremental
associated with
the basis for
causal relationships
the average

Abstract 2

E. R. Bou-Zeid and M. El-Fadel

While the extent of human-induced global warming is inconclusive, the vulnerability of natural systems to rapid changes in climate patterns is regarded as one of the most challenging issues in recent years. Water resources are a main component of natural systems that might be affected by climate change. This paper characterizes water resources in several Middle Eastern countries and presents regional climate predictions for various scenarios using general circulation models (GCMs). The country of Lebanon is selected as a case study for an in-depth investigation, with potential impacts on the water budget and soil moisture as indicators.

Document type: article

Key words: climate change; water resources; water balance; Middle East

Source: Bou-Zeid, E. R., & El-Fadel, M. (2002). Climate change and water resources in Lebanon and the Middle East. *Journal of Water Resources Planning and Management*, 128(5), 343–355.

Key words & phrases

human-induced
inconclusive
vulnerability
challenging issues
natural systems
characterizes
an in-depth investigation
water budget
soil moisture
indicators

Abstract 3

Jason P. Evans

This study examined the performance and future predictions for the Middle East produced by 18 global climate models (GCMs) participating in the Intergovernmental Panel on Climate Change (IPCC) Fourth Assessment Report. The models predict an overall temperature increase of 1.4 degrees by mid-century, increasing to almost 4 degrees by late-century for the Middle East. In terms of rainfall, the southernmost portion of the area experiences a small increase in rainfall. However, the largest change is a decrease in rainfall that occurs in an area covering the Eastern Mediterranean, Turkey, Syria, Northern Iraq, Northeastern Iran and the Caucasus caused by a decrease in storm activity over the Eastern Mediterranean. Other changes that are likely to impact the region include a decrease of over 170,000 square km in viable agricultural land by late-century, increases in the length of the dry season that reduces the length of time for grazing, and changes in the timing of the maximum rainfall in Northern Iran that will impact the growing season, forcing changes in crop strategy or even crop types.

Document type: review and meta-analysis

Key words: surface-temperature change; global rainfall; air temperature

Source: Evans, J. P. (2009). 21st century climate change in the Middle East. *Climatic Change*, 92(3–4), 417–432.

Key words & phrases

participating in
mid-century
southernmost
the portion
experiences
occurs
storm activity
to impact the region
viable
grazing
growing season
forcing changes
crop
strategy
review
meta-analysis

Abstract 4

Antoine Hreiche, Claude Bocquillon, Wajdi Najem and Diala Dandach

The significance of predicted climatic changes is still uncertain. The hydrological consequences of climatic changes on Lebanese catchments are analysed by means of different scenarios of rainfall variability and temperature increase. The conceptual rainfall–runoff model MEDOR is used to estimate change in runoff by simulation of six scenarios. These test the response to the duration of rainy events, their frequency, and the duration of the rainy season. This climate–runoff model is used to determine the impact of a temperature increase of 2 degrees on the flow characteristics of a watershed affected by seasonal snow cover. The modifications of the hydrological regimes are significant: droughts are predicted to occur 15 days to one month earlier; snowmelt floods are often replaced by rainfall floods; and the peak flow occurs two months earlier. These changes could have a great impact on water resources management in the future.

Document type: conference paper

Key words: climate change; simulations; streamflow impact; snow; Mediterranean

Key words & phrases

rainfall variability
conceptual
to estimate
the rainy season
to determine
watershed
modifications
snowmelt floods
the peak flow

Source: Hreiche, A., Bocquillon, C., Najem, W., & Dandach, D. (2005). The potential impact of future climate change on Lebanese river basin hydrology using scenarios. In T. Wagener *et al.* (Eds.), *Regional Hydrological Impacts of Climatic Change,* 103–110. Conference proceedings from International Association of Hydrological Science.

Abstract 5

Ragab Ragab and Christel Prudhomme

The increasing population and recent droughts are putting water resources under pressure. As countries are using their water resources with growing intensity, poor rainfall increasingly leads to national water crises. Global warming could cause further changes and uncertainty. The UK Hadley Centre's global climate model (GCM) was run to simulate the global climate according to scenarios of greenhouse gas emissions. Runs of the model were analysed for the 2050s. Outputs from the model provide estimations of climate variables, such as rainfall and temperature. These results, which are assumed to be representative of future climatic conditions, are compared to mean monthly values for the current climate and expressed in terms of percentage change. The results suggest that, for the dry season (April–September), by the 2050s, North Africa and some parts of Egypt, Saudi Arabia, Iran, Syria, Jordan and Israel, are expected to have reduced rainfall amounts of 20–25% less than the present mean values. This decrease in rainfall is accompanied by a temperature rise in those areas of between 2 and 2.75°C.

Document type: keynote paper presented to 2nd World Water Forum (2000)

Key words: climate change; water resources

Key words & phrases

putting … under pressure
growing intensity
greenhouse gas emissions
outputs
provide estimations
climate variables
assumed to be
    representative of
are compared to
mean values
expressed in terms of
percentage change
is accompanied by
keynote paper

Source: Ragab, R., & Prudhomme, C. (2002). Climate change and water resources management in arid and semi-arid regions: Prospective and challenges for the 21st century. *Biosystems Engineering, 81*(1), 3–34.

Abstract 6

David Rind, Cynthia Rosenzweig and Richard Goldberg

Climate change caused by increasing atmospheric concentrations of greenhouse gases may have important effects on water circulation and availability and thus on agriculture, forestry and river flow, with significant economic consequences. A variety of models are being used to evaluate hydrological effects, but their hydrological responses to global warming are often inconsistent. Improved understanding of basic hydrological processes is needed if we are to assess the impact of future climate change.

Document type: review

Key words: climate change; water circulation; models; hydrological processes

Key words & phrases

economic consequences
inconsistent

Source: Rind, D., Rosenzweig, C., & Goldberg, R. (1992). Modelling the hydrological cycle in assessments of climate change. *Nature, 358*(6382), 119–122.

Task 2 Reading for an overview

2.1 Read Abstracts 3, 5 and 6 from Task 1 and highlight in them the key points which Maysoun decided to record in her notes below.

> (Rind et al., 1992) ↑ greenhouse gas concentrations → changes T, rainfall → timing storms, flooding, droughts
> (Ragab & Prudhomme, 2002) Hadley Centre GCM simulate future (2050) climate scenarios variable = concentration GH gases; results T ↑ 2.0–2.75°C; rainfall ↓ 20%–25% in dry season for most Middle East countries
> (Evans, 2009) meta-analysis 18 GCMs in IPCC 4th report; results T ↑ 1.4°C 2050 and 4.0°C 2100; rainfall ↑ in south, ↓ most Middle East (↓ storm activity Eastern Mediterranean) → less farmland 2100

2.2 Use her notes in 2.1 to complete Maysoun's brief summary of the main ideas in these papers.

As a result of increases in _____, climate variables such as _____ are expected to _____. This in turn is predicted to lead to changes in the _____ of hydrological processes such as _____, _____ and _____ (_____ et al., 1992). The _____ global climate model was run with varying concentrations of _____ in order to _____ a range of future climate _____ in the Middle East and compare predictions of _____ and _____ in the mid-21st century with present mean values (_____, 2002). Seven years later, a _____ of results from the _____ included in the _____ was carried out (_____, 2009). Results from these two papers are broadly in agreement. Evans predicted a mean temperature increase for the Middle East of _____ by 2050, quite a lot less than the previous mean value of _____, but by the end of the 21st century, the temperature is expected to rise by _____. Both papers predict a _____ in most Middle East countries.

Task 3 Thinking critically about information in the abstracts

3.1 Do you think the complete versions of these sources will provide specific information about changes in local hydrological processes in Syria as a result of global changes in the climate? Give reasons for your answer.

3.2 Compare Abstracts 3 and 5 to find information which is given in one abstract, but not the other.

3.3 What does Maysoun have to do now to find this missing information?

Task 4 Checking your understanding of the impact of climate change on local hydrology

In order to understand Maysoun's topic more deeply, you need to try to express the ideas from the abstracts in your own words. This will show how your understanding has developed.

4.1 Global climate models are used to simulate a range of possible climate scenarios in the future.

What variables are put into the models to produce the different scenarios?

4.2 What indicators (i.e., features of the local hydrology) do researchers report to show the likely regional effects of different climate scenarios?

4.3 How do researchers check whether their predictions for these future scenarios are likely to be accurate?

4.4 Have you noticed any changes in any features of the local hydrology of your region or country?

Task 5 Making notes to compare predictions about impacts on local hydrology

Re-read Abstracts 1, 2 and 4, then add notes to the table in order to compare the authors' scenarios and predictions.

sources	date	location	models	variables/indicators	predictions
Bou-Zeid & El-Fadel	2002				regional predictions
Hreiche et al.	2005				timing: earlier droughts and floods type: rainfall not snowmelt floods ➡ earlier peak flows
Abdulla & Al-Omari	2008				runoff predicted by model similar to actual runoff decreased monthly runoff

Task 6 Using your notes to write a summary

Write a summary of the information in the table which will help Maysoun to remember the key points.

Study smart: locating and surveying sources

In order to search for, survey and evaluate sources effectively, Maysoun followed these steps:

1. Specify a topic and identify key words and phrases to use in a search.
2. Connect search terms to narrow the search and return a manageable number of results.
3. Use the results to find additional keywords to further refine or extend a search.
4. Use citation searching to find related articles which refer to each other.
5. Survey the search results using the quality checklist to select the most reliable.
6. Identify the type of source, e.g., book, article, and decide which sources are general or specific.
7. Group sources by relevant features, e.g., topic or research method.
8. Read the abstracts of review or keynote articles to get a general understanding.
9. Read the abstracts of specific articles to gain a more in-depth understanding.
10. Make notes and brief summaries in order to compare and interpret the information.

Task 7 Thinking critically about what you understand now

7.1 Look back to your answers to Task 1 where you assessed how much you knew about climate change. How has your understanding changed as a result of working with Maysoun's abstracts?

7.2 Were you able to accept less than 100 per cent comprehension, but still gain a better understanding?

Self study

Select six of the most relevant sources from the list you made for the Self study task in Section 4. List the abstracts (in the correct order for references), together with the full bibliographic reference, the document type and any key words. Survey your list to decide if your sources are general or specific. Complete steps 8–10 of the Study smart checklist for your abstracts.

Unit 5

Speaking for yourself

Section 1 Learning from experience

What the university expects:
- critical reflection – analyze and evaluate problems and solutions

Contexts:
- job interviews, literature reviews, reflective commentaries

Aims:
- to understand problem solving as knowledge building
- to understand how problem narratives are organized
- to categorize problems and solutions from different perspectives

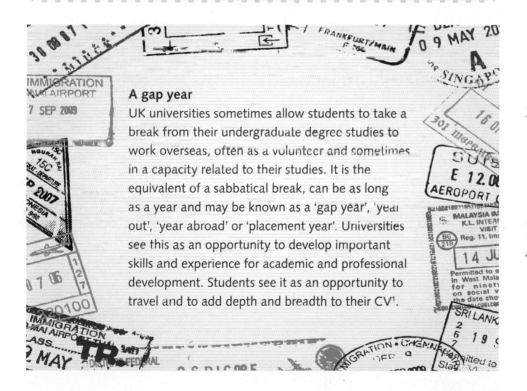

A gap year

UK universities sometimes allow students to take a break from their undergraduate degree studies to work overseas, often as a volunteer and sometimes in a capacity related to their studies. It is the equivalent of a sabbatical break, can be as long as a year and may be known as a 'gap year', 'year out', 'year abroad' or 'placement year'. Universities see this as an opportunity to develop important skills and experience for academic and professional development. Students see it as an opportunity to travel and to add depth and breadth to their CV[1].

Key words & phrases

take a break

in a capacity

a sabbatical break

a placement

depth and breadth

CV

Discussion

- What are the benefits of leaving home to live and work in another country?
- What problems do you think someone from the UK might face living and working in your country? Make a list.

[1]resumé in US English

Task 1 Listening critically to identify problems and their causes

Key words & phrases

non-governmental organization (NGO)

rural communities

puts … in contact with

Guy is thinking seriously about a gap year in Africa working for a non-governmental organization (NGO) that helps rural communities to develop co-operatives. He has some worries about going to live and work in another country, so Chen puts him in contact with Nick, his EAP teacher, who has experience of living abroad. Nick invites them to meet some of the other EAP teachers because they all have experience of living and working in other countries.

1.1 ⊕T15 Listen to the five teachers talking about their experiences in different parts of the world. Make notes to answer the following questions, so that later you can give an oral summary of the problem in each story and suggest solutions.

    a What did the speakers say to prepare the listener for their story?

    b What problems did they experience?

    c How did the problems arise?

1.2 Share your notes with other students so that you can add information that you missed.

Task 2 Discussing a problem to identify solutions

2.1 Work in groups and take it in turns to each choose one of the teachers' problems to summarize orally. After listening to the summary, the other members of the group suggest possible solutions to the problem. Work through all five problem stories in this way, making a note of your group's solutions.

2.2 Compare your solutions in a class discussion.

Task 3 Listening critically to compare solutions

3.1 ⊕T16 Listen to the next part of the conversation, in which the teachers explain their actual solutions (in each case, there could be more than one solution). Add the solutions to your notes, together with each teacher's evaluation.

3.2 Compare the teachers' solutions with your group's suggestions. How were your solutions similar or different?

3.3 This unit is called *Speaking for yourself.*
Which solutions show the importance of speaking for yourself?

3.4 How did the teachers feel about the solutions? How do you know? Try to recall their exact words and then check the transcript on pages 302.
Did Chen and Guy have any views on the solutions?

3.5 Which teacher reported a positive learning outcome, i.e., learning something useful as a result of the experience?

Task 4 Understanding the structure of a problem story

Key words & phrases

narratives

unfold

moves

orientate

make a link

4.1 Experiences are shared through narratives, or stories, which unfold in typical stages or moves. Pam uses six moves to construct her story clearly for her listeners.

Put these moves from both parts of the conversation into a more suitable order and match them to her narrative. One has been done for you.

a Problem: to describe the problem or problems.

b Situation: to explain the relevant background or context with the reasons why the problem occurred.

c Orientation: to orientate (prepare) your listeners by indicating that a narrative is about to begin and to make a link with a previous narrative.

d Learning outcome: to explain what you learnt from the experience.

e Evaluation: to evaluate the solution(s) or show your point of view.

f Solution: to explain one or more solutions.

Pam's story	moves
1. Well … My first teaching job was in Africa, too.	
2. It was a lot different from what they told us to expect in the orientation sessions. For a start, the university was still being built … I remember I had to teach speaking skills one afternoon each week and my class was timetabled in a temporary classroom, with a tin roof – you know, metal. Well, every afternoon we had a tropical rainstorm – not just a shower, big heavy drops, a real downpour. I didn't know what to do – I was a new teacher and I thought I was supposed to cope.	
3. On a tin roof, the noise is deafening: <u>no way</u> could we hear each other. It was impossible. I was too embarrassed to complain.	
4. The other teachers knew the problem with rain, of course, and I got a lot of help from them. After the first week, they kindly offered to swap classrooms with me when they could. Fortunately, we got a lovely new classroom complete with language lab and aircon the following term.	f, e
5. … the experience taught me to speak up on behalf of my students as well as myself and not be afraid to discuss with other teachers any problems I'm having.	

4.2 Identify moves a, b, c, e and f in the other teachers' stories.

4.3 The problem usually comes after the orientation and situation, but not always. **Which teacher stated the problem at the beginning of the problem narrative?**

4.4 These moves can be headings for organizing notes on a problem text. **Review the notes you made in Task 1 and organize them according to these moves. If you need to, listen again to complete them.**

The first step in solving a problem is to analyze it. Analysis involves looking at the problem in different ways in order to categorize it, i.e., to decide what type of problem it is.

How you categorize reflects your understanding, viewpoint or purpose. For example, problems can be analyzed from the point of view of difficulty, time or complexity: they can be easy or difficult to solve, long term or short term, simple or complex. In the teachers' stories, the problems can also be classified as relating to teaching or living conditions or in terms of their causes: the physical location, language, culture or the system (rules of the institution). Viewing a problem in different ways can help to solve it.

Task 5 Thinking critically: analyzing problems

5.1 **In groups, analyze the teachers' problems using the categories listed in the Study smart box.**

Pam's problem: a noisy classroom

Nick's problem: a student complaint

Heather's problem: communication difficulties/culture shock

Neal's problem: students texting in an exam

Kate's problem: accusing students of cheating

5.2 **In the same way, analyze the problems you listed in your discussion at the beginning of the lesson, i.e., problems someone from the UK might face in living and working in your country.**

In your discussion at the beginning of the lesson, you probably decided that problems are important: we learn from and through them, and the learning is both permanent and iterative, i.e., solving one problem enables you to start at a more advanced point when solving the next problem. Like Pam, the other teachers also learnt from their problems. A critical listener can work out some of what they learnt from the evidence in their stories. This type of critical thinking is called making inferences, from the verb to infer.

Key words & phrases

permanent

iterative

making inferences

Task 6 Listening critically: making inferences

6.1 **◉T16 Listen to the second part of the conversation again. Infer what each speaker learnt and write the learning outcome. The first one has been done for you.**

a Pam's problem: a noisy classroom

The experience taught me to speak up on behalf of my students as well as myself and not be afraid to discuss with other teachers any problems I'm having.

b Nick's problem: a student complaint

c Heather's problem: communication difficulties/culture shock

d Neal's problem: students texting in an exam

e Kate's problem: accusing students of cheating

6.2 **Check your answer by matching the speaker and problem with the list of learning outcomes that your teacher gives you.**

Task 7 Telling problem stories

7.1 Prepare a short presentation to report one of the problem stories from the teachers' discussion, including the solution and what they learnt from their experience. You should add your own evaluation of the solution.

7.1 Listen to each others' presentations and ask about anything you do not understand.

Task 8 Writing guidelines for working overseas

8.1 The learning outcomes from Task 6 can be adapted into guidelines suitable for Guy's intended gap year work.

Study the example and note the changes from the teacher's learning outcome to general guidelines.

learning outcomes	guidelines for Guy
Pam: ... *the experience taught me to speak up on behalf of my students as well as myself and not to be afraid to discuss with other teachers any problems I'm having.*	Be prepared to speak up on behalf of the people you are responsible for, such as trainees and workers. Don't be afraid to discuss with colleagues any problems you experience.

8.2 Adapt the learning outcomes from Task 6 in the same way to write a short set of general guidelines suitable for Guy. Put the guidelines into a logical order to write an e-mail to Guy. Write a short introduction and advice with specific examples. Write 300–500 words.

8.3 Write an e-mail to a UK friend who is going to live and work in your country. Write a short introduction and advice with specific examples. Write 300–500 words. Compare your guidelines with other students' and discuss any differences.

Self study

Prepare a short oral presentation with the title: *A problem I have faced.* Use what you learnt in this lesson to organize your ideas for the presentation. The language study in the next lessons will help you to express your ideas. You will make a 2/3-minute presentation on your problem in Section 5.

Section 2 Setting the right tone for enthusiasm and agreement

What the university expects:
- effective communication – listen and respond to the ideas of others

Contexts:
- seminars, discussions, meetings

Aims:
- to review how word and sentence stress contribute to a message
- to understand how to add emphasis to a message
- to show enthusiasm and agreement in discussions

Discussion

- How do you create a good impression in seminars, academic discussions or meetings?
- What impression does a person who remains silent create?

Task 1 Ear training

You are going to work on the stress patterns you've just listened to in the teachers' conversation and so you need to be able to listen very carefully to strings of language at normal speed. This is a warm-up exercise for your ears.

🔊T17 **Listen to a short extract from the first part of the conversation from Section 1 and try to write down exactly what Nick says. Ask for the recording to be replayed as often as you need.**

Investigating language patterns for speaking: word stress

English words have different numbers of syllables and different stress patterns. In each word, one syllable is stressed. This syllable is more prominent, i.e., it stands out and sounds a little louder than the other syllables. The stress pattern of a word is fixed, i.e., stays the same in normal speech, so listeners use it to help them recognize the word. It is important to get the stress pattern of the key words in your presentations correct, particularly key words in your subject area, so that people can understand you.

Task 2 Identifying word stress

2.1 In the box at the top of page 113 are 24 words from the listening texts in this unit.

> Put them into four groups according to where the main stress falls, i.e., on the first, second, third or fourth syllable. Note that only one of these is stressed on the fourth syllable and two of the words can be stressed on either the first or second syllable (according to whether UK or US stress).

> Ask your teacher to say aloud any words that you do not know.

Africa	confidential	data	engineering	experiences	explanation	information
university	themselves	interesting	Internet	online	perfect	question	recommendation
reputation	research	results	security	shampoo	situation	solution	stories	wonderful

2.2 How does your dictionary show stress and syllables in words?

2.3 Make similar groups of any key words that you are going to use in your presentation, *A problem I have faced.* Check their word stress and practise saying them aloud.

Investigating language patterns for speaking: sentence stress

Unlike word stress, sentence stress can change according to what the speaker wants the listener to pay attention to, which depends on the context. The table below shows some examples from the first part of the teachers' conversation. The word on which the sentence stress occurs is underlined, but the stressed syllable in that word is marked with the symbol '.

speaker wants listener to pay attention to	example
key information	Pam: '<u>My</u> first teaching job was in Africa, '<u>too</u>.
information to clarify who or what is being referred to	Neal: '<u>Where</u> are you going, Guy? '<u>What</u> are you hoping to '<u>do</u>?
a difference	Pam: … not just a '<u>shower</u>, big heavy '<u>drops</u> …

Task 3 Listening for sentence stress

3.1 ⊕T18 Listen to the examples from the table. Explain why the speakers chose to place stress on these particular words. You can look at the transcript of the teachers' problem stories on pages 300–302 for the context.

3.2 Stress each word in the following sentence in turn and discuss the difference in meaning:

I told him.

3.3 ⊕T19 Listen to these extracts from the teachers' problem stories and underline the words that are stressed. Use the stress mark ' to show where the stress falls in the word. You can look at the transcript of the teachers' problem stories on pages 300–302 for the context.

Pam: … the university was still being built. (stress three words)

Nick: … I told him you'd have some interesting stories about your experiences. (stress three words)

Heather: … your students or the experts? (stress two words)

Neal: … they weren't cheating for themselves, but they were helping their classmates. (stress three words)

Heather: I thought I had bought some shampoo, but it turned out to be something for cleaning the toilet! (stress three words)

Nick: Where did you learn to forge bank notes? (stress two words)

3.4 Practise reading the sentences with the same stress.

Task 4 Speaking for yourself

4.1 You can say: *'Where did you learn to forge 'bank notes?*

You can also say: *'Where did you learn to speak Chi'nese?*
'Where did you learn to use 'spreadsheets?

Think about your own subject area and the skills you need. Make more questions with this pattern: *'Where did you learn to ...?*

4.2 You can also say: *'How did you learn to 'type so 'fast?*
'How did you learn to 'speak so 'well?

Why would you ask questions with this pattern? Make more questions with this pattern to ask your classmates: *'How did you learn to ... so ...?*

4.3 You can say: *I 'thought I had bought some 'shampoo, but it turned out to be something for cleaning the 'toilet!*

You can also say: *I 'thought I'd won a million 'dollars, but it turned out to be a 'scam.*

Make more statements with this pattern: *I 'thought I ..., but it turned out to be ...*

Task 5 Listening carefully for sentence stress

5.1 ⊕T20 You are going to hear some extracts repeated from the library seminar in Unit 4, Section 1. In the extracts, the speakers are confirming these points to the students:

a Research involves problems.

b Research often starts with a problem or something you can't explain.

c You do research already – you just don't recognize it.

Listen carefully to their actual words. What do they actually say to confirm the three points? Why do they use this pattern?

5.2 ⊕T21 You are going to hear again two short extracts from Heather's problem story.

Write exactly what she says.

Investigating grammar patterns for confirming and contrasting: *do, did, does*

To confirm that something is true, speakers emphasize the verb phrase. They do this by placing stress on the auxiliary verb:
Sad to say, they 'are found in my country ...

But if there is no auxiliary, speakers (and writers) insert *do*:
But they 'do catch us foreigners out.

Emphatic *do* can be used to confirm something:
Research 'does involve problems, as Dimitri said.

Emphatic *do* can also be used to make contrasts. In the second sentence below, *did* is stressed:
... I really enjoyed bargaining in the market [...] I never 'did get used to the huge crowds of people everywhere, though.

Emphatic *do* can also be used after a concession (often with *but, although*):
Sad to say, they 'are found in my country, but easy to see, you know.
Yes, easy to see, but they 'do catch us foreigners out.

Task 6 Speaking for yourself

6.1 Contrasts

Work in groups and take it in turns to read out one of the statements. For each statement, the rest of the group should suggest a response that makes a contrast or concession using *but*. The first one has been done for you. Select the best suggestions and read them to the class, with suitable sentence stress.

a I am trying to lose weight.

But you do eat a lot of chocolate. (contrast)

But you do have to eat something. (concession)

b The professor doesn't have much money for his lab.

But _____

c He works hard at his studies.

But _____

d The launch has been delayed again.

But _____

e There isn't much time for me to finish this assignment.

But _____

f The instruments were checked carefully.

But _____

Use this pattern to make up more mini dialogues about your problems as students. Share them with the class.

6.2 *Although*

The linking word *although* collocates with *do*:

Although GPS is fairly reliable, it does have dead zones.

Here are some extracts from students' e-mails about life in the UK.

Complete these sentences with a suitable comment. The first one has been done for you. Select the best suggestions and read them to the class with correct sentence stress.

a Although our teachers are pretty smart, *they do make mistakes sometimes.*

b Although the weather is usually great, _____

_____.

c Although it is cold at night, _____

_____.

d Although food is expensive _____

_____.

e Although people here pay a lot of tax, _____

_____.

f Although the university can't provide your accommodation, _____

_____.

Make up your own sentences with this pattern and tell your classmates.

Investigating language patterns: tones and intonation

As well as stress, English speech uses intonation to show meaning. Intonation refers to the rise and fall of the pitch of the voice. All languages have intonation patterns, but in some, such as Chinese and Thai, they are pinned to individual words, whereas in others, such as English, they can change. Each distinct intonation pattern is a 'tone'.

A fall tone, which starts high, on a brief response can show that you agree or sympathize:

Yeah!

A rise–fall tone, which starts low, on a brief response can show your interest, enthusiasm or surprise:

Yeah

Task 7 Listening for tones

You are going to listen to some responses from the teachers' conversation.

7.1   ⊕T22 Listen to the first four, which show agreement. What tone is used?
Does the tone start high and fall ↘ or start low, rise and then fall? ↗

7.2   ⊕T22 Listen to the next five response, which show enthusiasm. What tone is used?
Does the tone start high and fall ↘ or start low, rise and then fall? ↗

Task 8 Speaking for yourself

8.1   **Work in pairs.**

Student 1: Choose a response from the transcript on pages 303–306 to say aloud to show agreement or enthusiasm.

Student 2: Give feedback by identifying agreement or enthusiasm in what Student 1 says.

Change roles.

8.2   **Work in pairs.**

Student 1: Suggest going somewhere (a shopping centre, a park, a party …).
Student 2: Respond, showing your enthusiasm.
Student 1: Suggest a time to meet.
Student 2: Agree.

Change roles and repeat Tasks 8.1 and 8.2.

8.3   Instead of using a rise–fall in response to Student 1's suggestion, Student 2 should now try to use a fall tone. How do you sound? How do you sound with a level tone?

Self study

* Listen to conversations on the bus or street, in the supermarket or on TV for tones showing agreement and enthusiasm.
* Check the word stress for ten key words in your subject area.
* Listen to someone telling a problem story and try to write some of their sentences with the stressed words underlined.

Section 3 Telling problem stories

Problems

Because problems provide opportunities for learning, they play an important role in university studies, and problem-solving skills are highly valued by employers[2]. Engineers and scientists, economists and entrepreneurs, and many academics and professionals devote much of their time to problem solving. Many university assignments in all subjects now involve reflective commentaries in which students report and reflect on problems and how they dealt with them. Knowing the moves, vocabulary and grammar patterns that feature in problem stories is essential if you are going to demonstrate your problem-solving ability in your writing and speaking at university.

Key words & phrases

play a role in

highly valued

entrepreneurs

devote time to

reflective commentaries

Discussion

- What problem-solving skills do you think you have?
- What problem-solving skills would you like to develop further?

Investigating grammar patterns for describing problems and solutions

Problems are frequently described using negative words and phrases. There are four main patterns:

patterns for problems	examples from the transcript
too + adjective/adverb + *to* + verb	I was <u>too embarrassed to complain</u>.
not + adjective/adverb	... one woman said she was<u>n't happy</u>.
negative prefixes	It was <u>impossible</u>.
words with a negative meaning	I felt <u>angry</u> and <u>confused</u>.

Solutions, on the other hand, tend to feature positive vocabulary items:

patterns for solutions	examples from the transcript
adjective/adverb with positive meaning	... a <u>lovely new</u> classroom ...
verb with positive meaning	... they <u>kindly offered</u> to swap ...
noun with positive meaning	... I got a lot of <u>help</u> from them.
signpost word with positive meaning	<u>Fortunately</u>, we got a lovely new classroom ...

Note: some words can be positive or negative depending on context, for example, *cheap*.

[2] Argent, S. (2013). *From high school to university: A handbook for EAP students.* Summerford: Gateway University Press

Task 1 Investigating grammar patterns for describing problems and solutions

1.1 Find more examples of positive and negative words and phrases in the transcript on pages 300–302.

1.2 Start a list of academic vocabulary that you have already encountered for describing problems and solutions. Divide the list into problem words and solution words. Add more to the list as you work through the unit.

Investigating grammar patterns for discussing the past

Problem stories, like many narratives, are often about the past and use the past simple to describe events, for example, *It rained every afternoon*. However, sometimes it is important to do more than just describe events – you need to speculate about them. Sometimes a speaker considers alternative courses of action, for example, *We could've given up and gone home*; sometimes a speaker makes an inference – filling a gap in what he/she knows – by guessing what happened when he/she was not there, for example, … *the International Officer might've said something to my classes*.

Note: In speaking, *have* is often shortened to *'ve* – /ə v/

Investigating grammar patterns for suggesting alternative solutions in the past

In a problem story, speakers need to explain possible solutions that they did not choose or that did not happen, i.e., what they *should have done*, *could have done* or *would have done*. They use the modal verbs *should*, *could* or *would* with a perfect infinitive (*have learnt*, *have gone*, *have given*) to explain them.

The choice of modal verb indicates viewpoint or stance: *should* shows that the speaker or writer is committed to or strongly recommends the solution; *could* shows that the speaker or writer only sees the solution as possible; *would* indicates that a solution is seen as probable. In all three patterns, the solution did not happen.

Note that in many speaking contexts, with the subject *you* it is better to avoid *should* and *should have*: *You should have* … can sound impolite because it is interpreted as giving strong advice, which may not be welcome. The other two patterns are more polite.

modal pattern	example	stance
should + perfect infinitive	*I 'should have learnt some of the 'language first* [but I did not]	strong recommendation
could + perfect infinitive	*We 'could have given 'up and gone 'home* [but we did not]	possible alternative solution
would + perfect infinitive	*A 'bit more infor'mation would have 'helped* [but I didn't have it]	probable alternative solution

Task 2 Thinking critically

2.1 Did you use these modal patterns when suggesting solutions in Task 2 on page 108? Check with your teacher.

2.2 Read the transcript on pages 300–302 of the two-part conversation about the teachers' problems, and suggest to each other more alternative solutions that were not chosen by the teachers. Choose a modal verb that shows your viewpoint, e.g., *Pam could've taught writing instead of speaking; Nick should've complained to the experts who ran his teacher training course.*

Task 3 Speaking for yourself

When explaining alternative solutions in the past, speakers stress the key information.

3.1 Highlight the sentence stress (marked by stress mark ') in the modal pattern examples in the table on page 118. Practise saying the examples aloud with these stress patterns.

3.2 In the context of Pam's problem of the noisy classroom, you can also say:

modal pattern A	modal pattern B	modal pattern C
She 'should've studied the 'climate first.	She 'could've 'stopped and complained to the di'rector.	A bit more 'confidence would have 'helped.

Notice the short forms *should've, could've, would've* and practise these sentences:

modal pattern A (context: failing an exam)	modal pattern B (context: rain on a football match)	modal pattern C (context: a weak essay)
He 'should've learnt some of the 'basics first.	We 'could've 'stopped and started a'gain.	A 'bit more dis'cussion would've 'helped.
I 'should've learnt some of the 'terms first.	They 'could've 'left and come back 'later.	A 'bit more 'data would've 'helped.
They 'should've read some of the cri'teria first.	He 'could've 'phoned and got the 'weather report.	A 'few more 'references would've 'helped.

3.3 Make more examples with the same modal patterns.

Task 4 Practising grammar patterns for explaining alternative solutions

Work in groups. Respond to these past problem situations with suitable suggestions using any of the stress patterns. The first one is given as an example. Compare your suggestions with another group.

a I failed my driving test.

Pattern A: You 'should've had a good night's 'sleep first.

Pattern B: Well, you 'could have 'cancelled and had some more 'lessons.

Pattern C: Yes, a bit more 'practice would've 'helped.

b We got lost in the city centre.

c I slipped on the icy path.

d The exam was too difficult for me.

e The library was too noisy for me.

f I lost my mobile phone on the bus.

Investigating grammar patterns for making inferences about the past

To make inferences about the past (to say what they think happened) in a problem story, speakers use *must, would, could, might* or *may* with a perfect infinitive. These modal verbs form two groups to show two levels of speaker confidence: high and medium.

Note that with *not*, *could* changes from medium to high level of confidence:

She could have complained (medium confidence).

She could not have complained (high confidence).

modal pattern	example	level of confidence
must or *would* + perfect infinitive	*They 'must've noticed my 'voice had got croaky …*	high (probable/likely)
could or *might* or *may* + perfect infinitive	*… the Inter'national Officer might've said something to my 'classes.*	medium (possible)
must or *would* or *could* + *not* + perfect infinitive	*Nick 'couldn't have known how the problem was 'growing.*	high (probable/likely)
might or *may* + *not* + perfect infinitive	*Nick might 'not have remembered everything the experts 'told him.*	medium (possible)

Task 5 Thinking critically: making inferences about the past

5.1 **Make more inferences about the people in the problem stories – what they thought and how they felt. Choose a modal verb that shows your level of confidence. e.g.,**
The shop assistant might have been worried about losing money from her pay.

5.2 **Discuss your inferences.**

Task 6 Speaking for yourself

When making inferences about the past, speakers stress the key information. Either the modal or *not* can be stressed.

6.1 **Highlight the sentence stress (marked by stress mark ') in the modal pattern examples above. Practise saying the examples aloud with these stress patterns.**

6.2 **In the context of Kate's problem of getting the grades wrong, you can also say:**

modal pattern A	modal pattern B	modal pattern C	modal pattern D
She 'must've worried about the 'consequences of the mistake.	The 'students might've complained to their 'parents.	She 'couldn't've known about the 'marking system.	She might 'not've remembered everything she'd been 'told.

Notice the short forms *must've*, *might've*, *couldn't've*, *might not've* and practise these sentences:

modal pattern A (context: a product price rise)	modal pattern B (context: no one came to the meeting)	modal pattern C (context: failing to get a place on a course)	modal pattern D (context: a failed assignment)
They 'must've noticed the 'sales had got better.	The 'secretary might've been called to the 'office.	We 'couldn't've known about the 'payment system.	He might 'not've understood the rules about 'plagiarism.
They 'must've realized the 'costs had got higher.	The 'students might've gone back to the 'conference.	They 'couldn't've filled in the 'form properly.	They might 'not've allowed enough time for the 'deadline.
They 'must've seen that the 'profits had dropped.	The pro'fessor might've stayed late in the 'library.	She 'couldn't've shown them her regi'stration card.	We might 'not've presented enough of the 'data.

6.3   Make more examples with the same modal patterns.

Task 7 Making inferences from case studies

7.1   Read the case study and discuss what happens, referring to the Discussion that follows.

A well-dressed Mexican pulled up in a taxi to the Palacio de Justicia in Lima, Peru. Armed guards were standing on the steps ascending to the building. The passenger paid and thanked the driver and opened the door of the cab, intent on the information he had come to get. As he leaned forward and put one foot onto the pavement, a cold rifle muzzle jabbed him in the temple and jerked his attention to matters at hand. The Peruvian guard holding the rifle shot two harsh words at him. The Mexican reddened, emerged from the taxi, and drew himself erect. With a sweep of his arm, he retorted three words: *¿Qué? ¿Nos conocemos?* (*What? Do we know each other?*) With a half bow, the guard lowered his rifle and courteously gestured the man up the steps, speaking in deferential tones.

Key words & phrases

ascending to
intent on
matters at hand
harsh
retorted
courteously
gestured
deferential tones
reaction
changed the attitude

Source: Novinger, T. (2001). *Intercultural Communication: A practical guide.* Austin: University of Texas Press, pp. 3–4.

Discussion

Categorize the possible causes of the problem in this case study in terms of language, culture or system. Infer what the guard with the gun said that caused this reaction from the Mexican, and what in the Mexican's behaviour and those three Spanish words instantly changed the Peruvian guard's attitude and behaviour?

7.2 **Read the case study and discuss what happens, referring to the Discussion that follows.**

When she was working in China, Heather shopped every week at a big supermarket 15 minutes' walk from the university campus. She usually returned by a pedicab³ operated by an elderly man. The fare was cheap and he took her right to her door. He was always smiling and friendly and tried to help her to learn a bit of Chinese.

One day he looked very distressed. He showed her a 20 yuan note (a large amount of money for him) and kept shaking his head.

When they got back to the university, she gave him 20 yuan in coins, as well as the one yuan fare, in exchange for the note. He was delighted. Some time later, she tried to spend the note in the local shop and attracted an angry crowd. One of her students told her it was a very obvious forgery and if the shop assistant had accepted it, it would have been deducted from her wages. Heather was really angry and avoided the pedicab driver for the next few weeks.

Weeks later, she was walking from the supermarket with a Chinese friend when the pedicab driver came running up shouting and laughing. The friend explained, 'He's saying what a very kind woman you are, that you helped him so much and he is so grateful, but he didn't see you for a long time. He wants you to travel for nothing from now on.'

Key words & phrases

fare
yuan
coins
attracted
very obvious
deducted from
wages
avoided

Discussion

Categorize the possible causes of the problem in this case study in terms of language, culture or system. Explain the behaviour of Heather and the driver.

Self study

Use the vocabulary and the grammar patterns you have learnt in this lesson in your presentation: *A problem I have faced.* Rehearse and record your presentation. Ask your teacher any questions you have, for example, about moves, grammar, vocabulary, stress or intonation in your presentation.

³ A small pedal-operated vehicle, serving as a taxi.

Section 4 Setting the right tone for listing and new information

What the university expects:
- effective communication – listen and respond to the ideas of others

Contexts:
- seminars, discussions, meetings

Aims:
- to hear and use tone patterns for listing
- to hear and use tone patterns for giving new information
- to understand the speaker's viewpoint from emphasizers

Task 1 Ear training

T23 Listen to a short extract from the first part of the conversation from Section 1 and try to write down exactly what Heather says. Ask for the recording to be replayed as often as you need.

Investigating language patterns: tone patterns

Tone units

In spoken English, words are grouped together into parcels of information known as *tone units* (shown here using ll). In his conversation with Guy, Neal uses two tone units to make two questions:

ll Where are you going, Guy? ll What are you hoping to do? ll

Each tone unit can have one, two or many syllables:

ll Great ll   ll of course ll   ll Wow ll   ll What a talented woman! ll

Timing

Each tone unit takes a similar length of time to say, so if a tone unit has many syllables, e.g., *What a talented woman!,* the speaker has to say them relatively quickly compared to a tone unit with only one or two syllables, e.g., *Wow!* This feature makes English very different from many other languages where syllables are evenly spaced in time.

English tones

There are five tones in English:

level →
rise ↗
fall ↘
rise–fall ↗↘
fall–rise ↘↗

Any word or phrase can be spoken with any of these tones. They do not have any meaning themselves, but in the shared context of the speaker and listener they make messages and viewpoints clearer. Remember that a fall tone starts high and a rise tone starts low. This will help you use the correct tone.

Task 2 Identifying tones

2.1 🎧T24 Listen to the speaker saying *so,* and say which tone is being used. Listen again and repeat.

2.2 Practise saying *yes, well* or *no* in pairs with the five different tones. Get your partner to identify your tones.

> **Investigating language patterns:** tones and stress
>
> Notice that when Nick says *What a talented woman!,* the tone begins on the last stressed syllable, which is the main stress, and continues to the end of the tone unit. Notice the starting point of the tone, high for a fall and low for a rise.
>
> ⟶
> What a 'talented woman!
> The stress means that the speaker wants to draw the listener's attention to *talented woman.*

Task 3 Listening for tones

3.1 🎧T25 Listen carefully to five extracts from the teachers' conversation. How many tone units are there in each extract?

3.2 Listen and mark the tone for each tone unit on the extracts. Choose from: fall, rise, and fall–rise. You can look at the full transcript on pages 300–302 for the context, if you need to.

Nick: This is Pam, Heather, Neal and Kate.

Heather: … things like spoons, plates, eggs.

Nick: I told him you'd have some interesting stories about your experiences.

Pam: My first teaching job was in Africa, too.

Pam: … not just a shower, big heavy drops.

Task 4 Speaking for yourself: giving complete lists

4.1 🎧T26 **Listen and repeat the lists.**

The tone pattern you heard is often used for lists that are complete. The rise tone tells the listener that there's more to come and the fall tone signals the end.

4.2 **Use the same tone pattern that Nick used to introduce Pam, Heather, Neal and Kate to introduce a group of your classmates. Make more lists with this tone pattern and say them aloud to each other.**

Task 5 Speaking for yourself: giving incomplete lists

5.1 🎧T27 **Listen and repeat the lists.**

The tone pattern you heard is often used for lists that are incomplete, for example, if you are giving examples.

5.2 **Use the same tone pattern to tell your classmates what kinds of things you like to eat. Make more lists with this tone pattern and say them aloud to each other.**

Task 6 Speaking for yourself: giving new information

6.1 A fall tone is also used when you are giving new information to your listeners – things that are new to the conversation or things that they do not know.

🎧T28 **Listen and repeat the sentence.**

Here the speaker thinks that all three tone units give new information for the listener. Notice the second and third tone units are very long in terms of syllables (eight). After *I told him*, the tone is level until you get to the stressed word *interesting*. The fall tone extends over the last four syllables in *experiences*.

6.2 **Read these in the same way.**
   a I 'told him you'd found some 'interesting data on the 'Internet.
   b I 'told him you'd got some 'interesting results in your re'search.
   c I 'told him you'd bought some 'new software for the de'partment

6.3 **Make more sentences with this tone pattern and say them aloud to each other.**

Showing a viewpoint using emphasizers
Words like *very*, *all* and *hardly* are important for showing the speaker's viewpoint and so they are often stressed.
Emphasizers are either maximizers – giving 'the glass is half full' viewpoint, e.g., *very*, *all* – or minimizers – giving 'the glass is half empty' viewpoint, e.g., *hardly*.
They are important in telling your problem story from your point of view.

Task 7 Noticing emphasizers

7.1 🎧T29 **Listen to these five extracts from the teachers' problem stories and write down any emphasizers that they use. Put them into two groups: maximizers and minimizers.**

7.2 **Practise reading the extracts aloud.**

7.3 **Think about how you could use emphasizers in your problem story.**

Task 8 Presenting a problem story

8.1 Neal tells Guy and Chen that problems are *good experience – part of 'life's rich pattern', as they say – and very useful for job interviews.*

How could telling a problem story be important in a job interview? Make a list of reasons.

8.2 Compare your reasons with the comments below on Gateway University's Student Careers website.

Gateway University's Student Careers
The ten most common interview questions

Question 4: 'Tell us about a problem you have solved.'

When interviewers ask this question, they want a specific example to show how you behaved when faced with a challenge. They want to assess how you would behave when dealing with challenges in their company if they employ you. They want to know:

- what skills you can use
- what kind of risks you are prepared to take
- how flexible you are
- how well you analyze problems and research solutions
- if you can evaluate possible solutions effectively
- if you can learn positive lessons, even from negative experiences

Be prepared to share a story where you faced a problem and succeeded.

8.3 The interviewer's reasons for asking this question provide a set of criteria for evaluating the interviewee.

In groups, choose one of the teacher's problems. Evaluate the teacher's story using these criteria, as if they were responding to the interview question *Tell us about a problem you have solved.*

Section 5 Setting the right tone for familiar and contrasting information

What the university expects:
• effective communication – listen and respond to the ideas of others

Contexts:
• seminars, discussions, meetings

Aims:
• to understand and use tone patterns for giving familiar information
• to understand and use tone patterns for contrasting information
• to use tone patterns for implicit cause–effect links

Task 1 Ear training

⊕T30 Listen to a short extract from the second part of the conversation from Section 1 and try to write down exactly what Nick says. Ask for the recording to be replayed as often as you need.

Task 2 Reviewing tone units and tones

⊕T31 Listen again to each of the teachers' story extracts that you heard in Section 4. How many tone units are there? What is the tone for each? Choose from: fall, rise and fall–rise. Listen as often as necessary. Read the transcript on page 304, if you need to.

Task 3 Speaking for yourself: including new information

3.1 ⊕T32 Listen to Pam explaining about her first job and repeat. In this example, *too* carries the fall tone signalling new information.

3.2 ⊕T33 Listen to two speakers talking and repeat.

3.3 Listen and repeat again, but this time add more information to each response, e.g., *Do you want to come with us?*

3.4 Prepare three prompts of your own. Student 1 should prompt Student 2, and Student 2 should give an extended response. Then change roles.

Task 4 Speaking for yourself: contrasting information

4.1 **T34 Listen to the teachers making contrasts and repeat.**

A fall–rise tone (e.g., on *shower* in the example below) is used for information that is not new for the listeners, for example, if something has been mentioned before in the conversation or is part of the shared context. In this case, Pam had just said *a tropical rainstorm*:

Well, every afternoon we had a tropical rainstorm – not just a 'shower, big heavy 'drops, a real downpour.

The context makes it clear that the first tone unit refers to expected information, and the second carries new contrasting information. To make the listener focus on this contrast, the speaker uses fall–rise followed by fall.

4.2 **Read this aloud to show the contrast:**

They 'weren't cheating for them'selves, but they were helping their 'classmates.

Make more contrasts using the same pattern:

They weren't … for themselves, but they were …

4.3 **Work in pairs to prepare a list of five questions for each other about opposites. Use this pattern:**

Do you prefer X or Y?
E.g., *Do you prefer rice or pasta/studying with music or in silence/sweet or salty popcorn?*

Ask the questions using the pattern for contrasting information. Remember to start high on the stressed syllables.

This pattern is common in the context of being able to offer your friends a choice.

4.4 **Try using a rise tone on the first tone unit.**
This time, remember to start low on the first stressed syllable. How does it sound different?

Investigating grammar for cause–effect links in speaking

In a problem story, the situation or background context contains the causes of the problem. In written text, cause–effect links are explicit and use a wide range of expressions. However, in spoken language, cause–effect links are often implicit and rely on the context and the juxtaposition of information, i.e., simply putting ideas together, sometimes with *and*, for the listener to infer what causes what:

No answer, no marks.
I was a new teacher and I thought I was supposed to cope.

For more explicit linking, speakers tend to use very simple cause–effect linking words such as *so, because, as, if*:

The university was still being built, so my class was timetabled in one of the temporary classrooms.

These types of linking are used particularly in informal conversation and sometimes in informal parts of lectures.

Key words & phrases

explicit

implicit

juxtaposition

Task 5 Identifying grammar for cause–effect links in speaking

5.1 Work in groups to find more examples of implicit and explicit cause–effect links in the transcript on pages 300–302.

5.2 Neal uses a more formal linking expression when he explains his solution to the exam problem.

Look at the second part of the conversation in the transcript on page 302. What is the linking expression he uses?

5.3 Implicit cause–effect links are short and so they are often used in advertising, or proverbs and sayings such as *No pain, no gain, No win, no fee, Give them an inch and they'll take a mile.*

Underline the words that are likely to be stressed in these examples.

Do you have a similar construction for these kinds of texts in your language?

Task 6 Speaking for yourself: implicit cause–effect links

6.1 ⊕T35 **Listen, identify the tone pattern and repeat.**

Short, implicit cause–effect links usually have two tone units: one for the cause or reason, and one for the effect or result. The cause is usually obvious from what has been said before. It is familiar information and has a rise tone.

6.2 Read these with the same tone pattern:

No answers, no marks.
No pain, no gain.
No win, no fee.
Buy one, get one free.
Give an inch and they'll take a mile.

It is also possible to use a fall–rise tone for the cause. Try this. What do you think is the difference?

Investigating grammar for cause–effect links

in speaking: comparatives in implicit cause–effect links

Speakers can also use comparative forms to make cause–effect links. In Unit 4, Section 3, you studied statements such as, *The more precise the search term, the smaller the number of hits*. When Neal talks about job interviews, he says:
The more experience you have, the more you have to say.

Task 7 Speaking for yourself: comparatives in implicit cause–effect links

7.1 Find two more examples of comparatives used to make cause–effect links in the transcript.

7.2 ⊕T36 Listen to these short, implicit cause–effect comments from the teachers' conversation and repeat.

7.3 ⊕T37 Listen carefully to more cause–effect comments and add them to the table beside the appropriate situation. You will hear each comment twice.

situation	cause–effect comment
1. buying a box of chocolates for an important family member	
2. comparing prices	
inviting people to a party	
3. solving a difficult problem	
4. being too ambitious	
5. a mechanical problem in a car	

7.4 Cover the table and work in pairs. Student 1: recall and report a situation from the table. Student 2: make a cause–effect comment in response.

7.5 Think of more short cause–effect comments appropriate for other situations, e.g., buying a TV, choosing a browser, selecting the size of a digital image.

Task 8 Making a short presentation

Present your problem story: *A problem I have faced.*
Listen to each other's presentations and then discuss the problem with each presenter.

Self study

One problem that all students face is exams. The next unit explores the issue of feedback on exams. You are going to write a report with the following title:

Critically examine the exam feedback systems you have experienced and outline an ideal system for giving university students feedback on their exam performance.

The report should be suitable for submission to a student–staff liaison committee which is going to discuss the issue in order to establish guidelines for departments across the university, and has asked for ideas from students. It should be 500–700 words.

Prepare for the unit by researching information, making notes and writing a plan for this report. Refer to steps 1–5 in Appendix 5g, which your teacher will provide, as your guide.

Unit 6

Cultures and systems

Section 1 Crossing cultures

What the university expects:
- a global and ethical understanding – respond sensitively in cross-cultural contexts; critical reflection – analyze and evaluate problems

Contexts:
- international settings and multicultural teams for work and study

Aims:
- to understand some basic features of intercultural communication
- to apply these to specific contexts at university
- to offer advice and solutions

Discussion

What do you think you will be doing four years from now? Ten years from now?

International students who become English-speaking global academics or professionals can expect to be involved in travel, teamworking and international projects. As they cross cultures, moving away from what is understood, familiar and comfortable, they will experience difficulties, but the precise causes of the problems may be hidden. The ability to analyze such experiences objectively can help to avoid some problems and to solve others more quickly. It is important to develop intercultural problem-solving skills in order to function effectively in a global context.

Key words & phrases

cross cultures
experience difficulties
the precise causes
objectively
intercultural
problem-solving skills
to function effectively
to cross cultural boundaries
intercultural communication
cross-cultural communication
cultural intelligence
a necessity
working across cultures

Task 1 Searching for information and surveying sources

1.1 Guy is looking for practical information to help him to cross cultural boundaries and work overseas.

What key words could he use for his search?

1.2 In the library, Guy found a book:

a Novinger, T. (2001). *Intercultural Communication: A practical guide*. Austin: University of Texas Press.

Using Google, he also found two websites.

b The University of Queensland. (2007). *Cross-cultural communication*. Retrieved from http://www.uq.edu.au/tutors/cross-cultural-communication

c Communicaid. (2011). *Cultural intelligence: A necessity for working effectively across cultures*. Retrieved from http://blog.communicaid.com/cross-cultural-training/cultural-intelligence-a-necessity-for-working-effectively-across-cultures/

From the titles and URLs, what can you infer about the quality of these sources and their suitability for helping Guy to understand how to work with people from cultures that are different from his own? You can use the checklist on page 89.

Task 2 Reading carefully to evaluate and report

2.1 Read Extracts A–C from the sources in Task 1. Working in groups of three, choose one of the sources and evaluate it against the other two. First, discuss the criteria you need in order to evaluate them. Use these criteria to make a table which you can complete to compare the sources. Decide which extract is the most useful for Guy and why.

2.2 Identify a key metaphor used in each extract. How does each metaphor help the writers to explain their points?

2.3 Use your comparison table to present your evaluation to another group. Decide how you are going to present the information: are you going to consider each extract in turn, or consider each feature in turn?

Listeners should ask questions about anything they do not understand.

One listener should be chosen to listen for language for recommending: *he should, he needs/it's better, it's got more* + positive vocabulary; and for rejecting: *It's not, it's too* + negative vocabulary. Report back to the group on their use of this language.

Key words & phrases

expanding
shrinking
on a daily basis
an obstacle
a hurdle
to navigate
estimate
nonverbally
the waking hours
has drilled into us
is conditioned
from birth
speak up
keep quiet
facial expressions
meet with approval
provoke
a reprimand
gestures
acceptable
table utensils
fashion
manner
tone of voice
to employ
posture
is censured
is praised
make eye contact
countless
consciously
interacting socially
internalized
a subconscious level
deviations from
prescribed
cultural norms
an artifice
apply a framework
target culture

Extract A

Preface

Tracy Novinger

In our world of expanding technology and shrinking geography, people of different cultures have increasing frequency of contact and need for effective communication on a daily basis. Speaking a different language is an obvious obstacle to intercultural communication, but a greater and more difficult hurdle is to 'speak' a different culture. Even though we may learn the words, the grammar, and the recognizable pronunciation of a language, we may still not know how to navigate around the greater obstacles to communication that are presented by cultural difference.

Communication specialists estimate that from two-thirds to three-fourths of our communication takes place non-verbally through behaviour. All behaviour is communication, and since we cannot not behave, we cannot not communicate. During all of the waking hours that we spend with other human beings we 'speak' volumes through the behaviour our culture has drilled into us.

Each of us is conditioned by our culture from birth. We learn when to speak up and when to keep quiet. We learn that some facial expressions meet with approval and others provoke a reprimand. We are taught which gestures are acceptable and which are not, and whether we can publicly unwrap a gift; we learn where to put our hands at a meal, whether or not we can make noise with our mouth when we eat, which table utensils to use or not use, and in what fashion we may use them. We learn how to address people in a manner approved by our culture, what tone of voice to employ, what posture is censured and what is praised, when and how to make eye contact and for how long, and countless other things that would be impossible to remember consciously and use all at the same time when interacting socially. This communicative behaviour is learned so well that it becomes internalized at a subconscious level. We are primarily aware of deviations from our prescribed cultural norms, and we tend to negatively evaluate any such deviations.

Since we learn our cultural behaviour in units, it is a useful artifice to compare cultural differences in units. To learn to communicate across cultures more quickly and more effectively, we can apply a framework of categories of potential obstacles (cultural units) to our own and to a target culture.

Part I of this book addresses the need for successful communication across cultures and defines what constitutes a culture. Next, an original taxonomy of potential intercultural communication obstacles is constructed from the literature of communication, anthropology, psychology, sociology, business, and current events, as well as from interviews with persons of multicultural backgrounds. The categories are explained, and many are illustrated with anecdotes.

Part II applies the framework of obstacles outlined in Part I to the differences in cultural units of the United States and Mexico. This application demonstrates how these cultural differences create misunderstanding and ineffectual communication in commonly occurring business and social situations.

Part III prescribes an effective approach to intercultural communication between any two cultures, using the framework of potential obstacles to efficiently obtain results. We can act consciously to transcend the rules with which our culture grips us.

Source: Novinger, T. (2001). *Intercultural Communication: A practical guide*. Austin: University of Texas Press. pp. ix–x

Key words & phrases

addresses the need for
constitutes
a taxonomy
anthropology
the literature
current events
multicultural
anecdotes
ineffectual
to transcend
grips

Extract B

The University of Queensland

Universities are enriched by students and staff from many nations and of many cultures.

Different cultures have different 'rules' that influence things like how we behave, how we speak, what we value, our concepts of time, interpersonal space, and even humour.

Each of us interprets a situation through our own cultural 'lens'.

Intercultural communication involves understanding others and making yourself understood by others.

To communicate effectively with people from other cultures you need to:

- be aware of the possibility of cultural difference
- acknowledge and respect difference
- strive to understand.

Ideas for better cross-cultural communication include:

- Speak clearly, at normal pace, normal volume, with no colloquialisms (e.g., *hang on a tick*) or double negatives (e.g., *not bad*).
- Use short sentences.
- Provide instructions in a clear sequence.
- Summarize.
- Check understanding – ask questions which require more than a 'yes' or 'no' answer.
- Demonstrate if possible.
- Write instructions down if necessary.
- Make procedures very clear.
- Be aware of non-verbal signals.

Be patient – non-English speakers may have to translate what you've said into their home language and then try to convert their response back into English.

A Cultural Diversity and Inclusive Practice Toolkit with Theory into Practice Strategy Folios (TIPS) is available.

The Teaching and Learning Tips consist of:

- Teaching Offshore
- Small Groups
- Designing Culturally Inclusive Environments
- Inclusive Practices for Managing Controversial Issues

More information on Equity and Diversity can be found on the Equity Office website.

Source: The University of Queensland. (2007). *Cross-cultural communication*. Retrieved from http://www.uq.edu.au/tutors/cross-cultural-communication

Key words & phrases

are enriched
interpersonal space
humour
lens
acknowledge
respect
strive to
colloquialisms
non-verbal signals
cultural diversity
inclusive practices
strategy
folios
offshore
controversial issues
equity and diversity

Extract C

| 🏠 | Communicaid | Cross Cultural Training | Contact Us | | Search | 🔍 |

Doing business with colleagues, clients and partners from around the globe is now commonplace for many professionals. While some of us frequently travel abroad to do business with colleagues in a different cultural background on a daily basis, others are communicating with international counterparts by phone, e-mail or other virtual platforms. Working effectively across cultures, whether face-to-face or virtually, requires a high level of cultural intelligence.

Cultural intelligence has been defined in many ways over the years, but in simple terms it is the ability to interact confidently and effectively with people from different cultural backgrounds on a social and professional level.

Cultural intelligence requires being aware of your own culture as well as cultural differences in the way that others behave and think. Many individuals, though not all, who have extensive experience travelling and working with other cultures often become "global chameleons" and develop a high level of cultural intelligence. Through experience, intercultural training initiatives and cross-cultural interactions, global chameleons are people who have learned to effectively adapt their behaviour and attitudes instinctively when working across cultures.

According to Joo-Seng Tan, Director of the Centre for Cultural Intelligence at the Nanyang Business School in Singapore, there are three key steps to developing cultural intelligence:

1. Think about culture

2. Be motivated to change your behaviour

3. Act in an appropriate way

Although these three steps seem pretty straight forward, they require a specific set of cross-cultural skills and attitudes which can be difficult to develop on your own. Most of us simply lack the knowledge to do so and, as we all know, motivating yourself can be quite hard too. Participating in a cross-cultural awareness course like Working Effectively across Cultures can help you work through these three steps and others to develop the level of cultural intelligence you require in your unique international role.

Experienced cross-cultural experts will not only tell you more about different cultural values, such as how attitudes to time, tasks or risk might impact your working relationships, but they will also help you to reflect about your own cultural identity to increase your self-awareness. By sharing with you anecdotes and first hand experiences and discussing your own, they will help you to identify differences and similarities between cultures so that you start to understand how to respond appropriately in each cultural context.

Cultural intelligence is important for anyone working across cultures, but it is particularly beneficial for international managers and global business leaders. Culturally intelligent managers are able to see how their employees behave in different cultural settings and understand what they expect. Culturally intelligent managers have the ability, as Tan suggests, to "create a new mental framework for understanding what they experience", which allows them to consider how working practices and communication styles could be different when working across cultures. A high level of cultural intelligence helps them to create a positive environment, harness team members' skills and develop high performing teams that will deliver the best results when working across cultures.

© Communicaid Group Ltd. 2011

Key words & phrases

clients
partners
commonplace
abroad
counterparts
virtual platforms
face-to-face
over the years
in simple terms
different cultural backgrounds
on a professional level
have extensive experience
global chameleons
training initiatives
instinctively
pretty
unique
cultural values
cultural identity
self-awareness
first hand experiences
a positive environment
harness skills
deliver results

Source: Communicaid. (2011). *Cultural intelligence: A necessity for working effectively across cultures.* Retrieved from http://blog.communicaid.com/cross-cultural-training/cultural-intelligence-a-necessity-for-working-effectively-across-cultures/

Task 3 Thinking critically: discussion

In Unit 5, you listened to teachers reporting problems caused by the following types of factors in the background situation:
- difficult physical conditions
- misunderstandings arising from language difficulties
- embarrassing moments caused by lack of cultural knowledge
- misunderstandings caused by not knowing the systems used

Have you experienced any problems in these categories during your EAP course? Make a note of them and explain them to another student.

Task 4 Analyzing problems and offering advice

The following scenarios are examples of common problems for international students. They all arise from lack of knowledge. Do they need more knowledge about language, culture or systems?

4.1 **⊕T38 Listen to the conversation for Scenario 1.**

Scenario 1: A brief conversation between an administrative officer helping students to register and an accounting student, Student A.

In groups, discuss how you would explain the problem to the student, and how you would offer advice to both the student and the administrative officer.

4.2 **Read Scenarios 2 to 4 carefully and, in groups, discuss how you would explain the problem and offer advice to each student.**

Scenario 2: Student B e-mails a friend:
This week, I am supposed to start a group project which means working with some other students. They had a meeting, but I didn't go. I think I'll just do the project by myself.

Scenario 3: Student C has failed an assignment, but her tutor, Mary, is very friendly and Student C is sure that when she explains how hard she worked on the assignment, Mary will improve the grade.

Scenario 4: Student D complains to a friend about one of the lecturers:
I have been going to his office every day to find him, but he is never there, even though I leave notes saying I'm looking for him.

Task 5 A case study: avoiding problems and seeing solutions – Sofia's problem

5.1 **Read the case study and answer the questions a–e on page 136.**

Sofia Meyer was a postgraduate student who found herself struggling to follow lectures and produce coursework in her first term of an engineering course at a UK university. She knew that her problem was the standard of her English, so discussed the issue with her supervisor in the first term exam week. He suggested she enrol on the next in-sessional EAP course, and gave her the name of the tutor who ran it – Ms Joan Pollock. Sofia went straight to the tutor's office, where she found her surrounded by piles of exam scripts.

Sofia said: *I am a student from [country]. I would like to tell you about my situation so that you can give me some advice.*

a If you were Sofia, what would you have done or said? Why?

b Sofia was upset because the tutor seemed angry and abrupt. She came away feeling confused about what the tutor had said and not sure what to do next. How appropriate is this?

c She went back to her supervisor who advised her to e-mail the EAP tutor. What would you do? Why?

5.2 **In groups, compare your answers and decide what aspects of intercultural communication – language, culture or system – caused the problems. Report your ideas to the class.**

Task 6 Writing

Write Sofia's e-mail to the EAP tutor.

Self study

a Guy does not have enough money to fund himself for a gap year abroad, but he can apply to a range of organizations for grants. First, he has to write a proposal and he wants to include a personal statement showing intercultural awareness and the ability to respond sensitively in a cross-cultural context.

Read the leaflet *The ethical volunteering guide* provided by your teacher, also downloadable from www.ethicalvolunteering.org/index.html. Write a brief e-mail to Guy to bring this leaflet to his attention. Write 150–200 words.

  * Explain the author, purpose and intended reader.
  * Summarize the main ideas.
  * Evaluate how useful the resource is for Guy.

Send the e-mail to your teacher for feedback.

b Write a personal statement about yourself, giving evidence of your intercultural awareness and your ability to respond sensitively in a cross-cultural context. Identify ways in which you would like to develop further.

Write 150–200 words.

Send the statement to your teacher for feedback.

Key words & phrases

to fund himself

grants

a proposal

ethical volunteering

Section 2 Negotiating the system: brick walls and gatekeepers

What the university expects:
- autonomy – set goals and direct your own learning; effective communication – take a stance and negotiate with others

Contexts:
- finding a way through bureaucratic systems

Aims:
- to identify the sources of problems in bureaucratic systems at university
- to recognize and use strategies for negotiating solutions
- to review key language patterns for negotiating solutions

Discussion

What does the term *negotiation* mean? What do the metaphors 'brick walls' and 'gatekeepers' refer to in the section title and the introduction below? Why are patience, diplomacy and persistence important qualities in negotiators? What other qualities are important?

Key words & phrases

gatekeepers
encounter problems
embedded in
facing a brick wall
negotiate
bureaucratic procedures
patience
diplomacy
persistence

Life at university is not always easy and students sometimes encounter problems. The first step in dealing with any problem is to identify its source. When the cause of a problem is embedded in the systems and procedures of the university, students can feel powerless, as though they are facing a brick wall. One option is to negotiate (find a way) around the obstacle, or find a gateway through the bureaucratic procedures to achieve the goal. This requires patience, diplomacy and persistence, because the route is controlled by gatekeepers.

Task 1 Describing problems and considering solutions

1.1 In Unit 1, three students were interested in moving because of problems with their accommodation.

What were their accommodation problems? Could they have solved their problems without moving accommodation? How?

1.2 In groups, identify any problems with the accommodation, facilities and courses in your school. Are any of them caused by bureaucracy?

Make a list as a class.

Task 2 Listening critically

> **A case study: dealing with systems and gatekeepers – Guy's problem**
> Guy is planning his second semester timetable for Business Studies. Gateway University encourages cross-disciplinary study and Guy has discovered that the Department of Agriculture is offering a module about co-operatives and development. He wants to study this module, but he is not sure how to register for it.

Work in groups. Listen to three conversations as Guy tries to negotiate a way to study this module. At the end of each negotiation, use the questions (a–e) to evaluate his progress and suggest what he should do next.

a What is Guy's aim?

b Does he achieve it?

c What did he get right (in terms of language, culture or system)?

d What did he get wrong (in terms of language, culture or system)?

e What should he do next?

2.1 Guy catches his tutor, Dr Malik, at the end of a lecture to ask him about the module he wants to study.

⊙**T39 Listen to their conversation.**

2.2 Guy telephones the administrative officer for the Department of Agriculture, Margaret Ellis.

⊙**T40 Listen to their conversation.**

2.3 Guy e-mails Dr Malik, who suggests that he goes to see the Business Studies administrative officer for undergraduate programmes, who might be able to sort things out.

⊙**T41 Listen to their conversation.**

Task 3 Writing

Read Dr Carbrook's webpage. In the same groups, brainstorm, plan and write Guy's e-mail to her.

Dr Alice Carbrook

Current position:
Research Professor, International Co-operative Research Foundation

E-mail:
A.Carbrook@cf.ac.uk

About me

After graduating from Bangor University in 1989, I taught in agricultural colleges in Zambia and Uganda. Back in the UK, I gained a PhD. My dissertation was in agricultural economics and development and involved research into the needs of small-scale co-operatives in Africa. I have been employed as an advisor to several NGOs operating on the continent of Africa, as well as lecturing in the UK and USA.

I have worked for the ICRF since 2009, supporting research in co-operatives and international development with a focus on agricultural trade, co-operative governance and localized training. I lecture for the foundation at various universities and also supervize research students.

Research interests: effectiveness of local training; education for sustainability; large-scale economics of small-scale projects.

Selected publications:

Carbrook, A. (1998). *Co-operative movements in Africa: Fifty years of development*. Manchester: Rochdale House.

Carbrook, A. (Ed.). (2006). *New approaches to fair trade*. Proceedings from *Summerford Co-operative Conference 2005*. Summerford: Gateway University Press.

Carbrook, A., Holland, S., & Jeffrey, J. (2008). *Co-operative development in Africa: A guide to principles and practice*. London: Luccombe Press.

Carbrook, A. (2011). *Groping in the dark or turning on the light: Co-operative initiatives and international aid*. In J. R. Dyson (Ed.), *Current issues in the economics of aid*. Summerford: Gateway University Press.

Key words & phrases

current position

with a focus on

governance

sustainability

large-scale

small-scale

Task 4 Reading critically

Read Dr Carbrook's response and evaluate Guy's success in negotiating his way through the system.

To:	g.evans5@gwu.ac.uk
From:	a.carbrook@gwu.ac.uk
Subject:	Ag. co-op lectures

Dear Guy,

Thank you for getting in touch, and thank you for your interest in my work.

I'm sorry that you have had such a hard time trying to access my lectures. Actually, I'm teaching a similar course for the Adult Education programme at Summerford College on Tuesday and Thursday evenings. It's not as detailed and technical as the one I'm doing for the Agriculture students at Gateway University, but that might be better for you. It starts next week. I think it's about £90 for the five-week course. Could you manage that? I think there are still places.

You mentioned that you are planning to work with an NGO in Africa. Have you got fixed up yet? I'm looking for an assistant to help me this summer. I'm going to Malawi in June to do some training, so the local farmers can keep their own accounts, manage their logistics and so on. I'm attaching a job spec and an application form, in case you are interested.

Best wishes,
Alice

Key words & phrases

getting in touch

a hard time

got fixed up

logistics

job spec

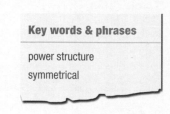

Investigating language patterns for negotiating

An important aspect of getting things done in a bureaucracy is the recognition that the power structure is not symmetrical; the gatekeeper has more power than the student. A student therefore needs to use good negotiating strategies, including a variety of diplomatic language patterns that will influence the gatekeeper to help. Gatekeepers, on the other hand, may well use strategies for avoiding action.

Key words & phrases

power structure

symmetrical

Task 5 Analyzing strategies for negotiating solutions

5.1 Read the transcripts on pages 305–306 of Guy's three negotiations and highlight the points where Guy demonstrates negotiating strategies to persuade the gatekeepers to help, for example, where he acknowledges that gatekeepers are busy.

5.2 Work in groups to complete the table of Guy's negotiating strategies by adding examples of the language he uses. For example, to acknowledge that Dr Malik is busy, Guy says, *Sorry ... Have you got time?*

Guy's key language patterns:

strategy	strategic language examples
to acknowledge that gatekeepers are busy	
to acknowledge/calm gatekeeper's feelings	
to acknowledge the quality of their information/help	
to signal he understands their message	
to check by summarizing their message	
to ask for information, a favour or permission	
to ask for help directly	
to show his own feelings	
to show appreciation for help	
to keep open the possibility of further negotiation	

5.3 In the same way, complete the table for gatekeepers' strategies and language.

Gatekeeper's language patterns:

strategy	strategic language examples
to try to avoid or end the negotiation	
to avoid taking any action	
to suggest actions for Guy to take	
to check information	
to gain thinking time	
to show sympathy	

5.4 What negotiating strategies and language patterns do you use? Add more language examples from your own experience to both tables.

Task 6 Negotiating

In groups of three, negotiate an outcome using one of the role-play scenarios on the role-play cards that the teacher provides. Have a student, a gatekeeper and an observer. Study and prepare your roles.

Work through three different scenarios and change roles each time.

Evaluate the success of the student in each scenario, for example, in terms of diplomacy and persistence. Share with the rest of the class.

Task 7 Writing/Speaking

Choose one of the scenarios you have rehearsed. Think about how you would approach the gatekeeper to arrange the initial meeting. Write an e-mail to the gatekeeper or leave a voice message to set the meeting up.

Self study

Identify strategies and vocabulary that you would use in your own language and culture for dealing with Guy's problem. How do they differ from the ones presented here?

Section 3 Setting the right tone for negotiating the system

What the university expects:
• effective communication – take a stance and negotiate with others

Contexts:
• accessing university support services

Aims:
• to understand and use tones for being diplomatic
• to understand and use tones for being assertive
• to understand stress pattern choices

Discussion

Knowing which words and phrases might persuade gatekeepers to take some action is important, but it is not the complete picture. Negotiators often start a sentence by apologizing, using the word *sorry*. In groups, try saying the word *sorry* in as many different ways as possible and decide what impression they give of the speaker's attitude. How is the effect achieved?

Key words & phrases

take some action
the complete picture
give an impression
achieve the effect

Investigating language patterns: intonation patterns with *sorry*

The intonation pattern on the word *sorry* carries key information about the speaker's intention and attitude. The range of possibilities can only be narrowed by context, including the information that follows the word *sorry*. However, in general:

1. A level tone on *sorry* can make the speaker sound bored, disengaged or insincere.
2. A fall tone on *sorry* can sound assertive or dismissive, implying that the speaker expects no further discussion.
3. A rise tone on the word *sorry* is generally used in two ways – to indicate communication breakdown (e.g., to ask for repetition or further information) or to assert control over the interaction, for example, to interrupt, redirect or even leave the discussion.
4. A fall–rise tone on *sorry* sounds more diplomatic, sensitive and sincere.
5. A rise–fall tone on *sorry* indicates surprise or irony (insincerity).

Task 1 Listening critically for the speaker's attitude: *sorry*

The speakers used the word *sorry* several times in the three negotiations.

1.1　⊙T42 **Listen to some short extracts from the conversations again and categorize the impression each speaker gives as diplomatic or assertive. Choose from:**

> diplomatic　　　assertive/dismissive　　　assertive/controlling

What tone is used on the word *sorry* in each case? Choose from:

> fall　　　rise　　　fall–rise

speaker	impression	tone on *sorry*	any other features that help create the impression
Guy			context: Guy is interrupting a teacher in a hurry and asking a favour
Dr Malik			gives an explanation
Margaret Ellis			said very quickly, stress on '*not* and '*problem*
Jeremy Bailey			adds a comment using the same tone pattern

1.2　**What is the difference in purpose between a fall–rise tone in a gatekeeper such as Jeremy Bailey and a fall–rise tone in a student such as Guy?**

Task 2 Listening critically for the speaker's attitude: requests and responses

2.1　⊙T43 **Part 1 Listen to these pairs of requests from the negotiations in Section 2. Which sounds more diplomatic and which sounds more assertive to the listener? What is the difference in tone? Listen as often as necessary. Read the transcript on page 311 as you listen, if you need to.**

2.2　⊙T43 **Part 2 Listen to these pairs of responses from the negotiations in Section 2. Which sounds more diplomatic and which sounds more assertive and unsympathetic to the listener? What is the difference in tone? Listen as often as necessary. Read the transcript as you listen, if you need to.**

Task 3 Speaking for yourself: using diplomatic and assertive tones

3.1 🎧T44 **Listen again to the requests and responses and repeat them with the correct tones.**

3.2 **In pairs, read the requests and responses in the transcript on page 307 and practise the fall–rise tone for being diplomatic and sensitive. Listen to each other and give feedback on how diplomatic and sensitive you sound. Now make assertive requests and responses with a fall tone.**

> **Study smart:** choosing the impression you want to give
>
> A fall–rise tone shows diplomacy when making a request and sensitivity to the listener when responding to a request. Along with suitable information, this tone can make a gatekeeper seem more sympathetic. A fall tone in the same contexts can sound too assertive or insensitive. If you speak assertively when you are making a request, it can sound more like an order. If a problem or negative word, such as *not, can't* or *wrong* is stressed, the effect can be very assertive. Here are two ways a customer can respond to a market trader who has given the wrong change:
>
> *You gave me the 'wrong 'change.* (assertive)   *You gave me the wrong 'change.* (more diplomatic)

Task 4 Speaking for yourself: avoiding negative stress

Practise being diplomatic by avoiding negative stress.

4.1 🎧T45 **Part 1 Listen and repeat the customer's responses.**

4.2 🎧T45 **Part 2 Listen to these gatekeepers' responses again and repeat them.**

4.3 **In pairs, practise pointing out these problems diplomatically. Introduce your comment diplomatically with *Sorry* or *I'm afraid*. Give each other feedback on how diplomatic you sound.**

   a You gave me the wrong form.
   b This isn't my assignment.
   c You sent me the wrong attachment.
   d You deleted my e-mail.
   e You forgot my tutorial.
   f You missed the appointment.

4.3 **Make up some more examples of your own and try them out on each other.**

> **Study smart:** pointing out mistakes diplomatically
>
> Sometimes gatekeepers are directly responsible for a problem and you may have to point this out. However, pointing out a powerful person's mistakes is a difficult part of negotiating. It helps to be indirect, e.g., *I think there could be a problem* is better than *You made a mistake*. You need negative language to present a problem, but if you stress the negative words it is heard as a criticism, which is counterproductive. When you need help from a gatekeeper, avoid stressing negative words. You need to use a fall tone because you are giving new information, but you can introduce the comment with a diplomatic phrase such as *I'm sorry* or *Excuse me*, using the diplomatic fall–rise tone. However, you always have a choice in the impression you give and you may feel that sometimes you need to be assertive.

Key words & phrases

are directly responsible for

pointing out

counterproductive

Task 5 Speaking for yourself: diplomatic requests

In Section 2, Task 5, you listed some ways to make a diplomatic request, i.e., ask for information, a favour or permission.

In pairs, make up a short conversation, for example, ask for help with writing an e-mail, ask to make a call on a mobile phone or ask for advice about your computer.

> Student 1: Make a diplomatic request. Add some reasons to justify your request.
> Student 2: Respond sensitively.

Change roles.

Task 6 Speaking for yourself: negotiating

In groups of three, work through more scenarios from Section 2, Task 7, but this time work on using appropriate stress and intonation patterns.

Run three different scenarios and change roles each time.

The observer should evaluate the success of the students in each scenario in terms of preparation, diplomacy and persistence, and the language used. Share your evaluation with the rest of the class.

Section 4 Presenting a case for change: Part 1

What the university expects:
- autonomy – set goals and direct your own learning; a spirit of enquiry – persist in efforts to secure answers

Contexts:
- seminars, discussions, meetings

Aims:
- to understand the roles and responsibilities of students in the wider context of the university community
- to identify strategies for making effective contributions in meetings
- to understand and practise strategies for being assertive

Meetings

Most problems with university bureaucracy are solved by individual students negotiating their way around obstacles or through bureaucratic procedures. Sometimes, however, it is important to work together to take issue with and try to change the systems that create obstacles; in other words, to dismantle the brick wall. In this situation, a group, or groups, of stakeholders hold meetings to agree on any actions to be taken. Often, changes have to be made through the university's structure of committees, which hold regular meetings. Meetings at university have an agenda to give them a framework and items for the agenda are called for in advance. The stakeholders at the meeting decide what action to take on items. Their decisions are recorded formally in the minutes as actions to be taken by named individuals. Most of the work is actually done outside the meeting by these named individuals and usually involves researching issues and producing reports.

Key words & phrases

to take issue with
to dismantle
stakeholders
hold meetings
committees
an agenda
a framework
items
the minutes

Discussion

Discuss your experience of meetings. Have you ever contributed to a meeting? What makes a contribution to a meeting effective? In groups, make a list of these criteria and share with the class.

Chen's presentation

The students at Gateway University campaigned through the Student Union last semester for better feedback on exams. Chen is involved in the campaign. He has been elected as the student representative for the Department of Maths and Computer Science and he has to research the issue in order to give a presentation to the School of Physical Sciences student–staff liaison committee on behalf of the students in his department.

Task 1 Preparing to listen

1.1 Look at the meeting agenda. What stakeholders might be at the meeting and what roles will they have?

1.2 Which agenda item is Chen's presentation? Chen's task was to research and report on what feedback on exams is given in other departments and other universities. How do you think he did this research?

AGENDA
School of Physical Sciences Student–Staff Liaison Committee
Meeting to be held on Monday 18th March 2013 at 2:15 p.m. in AT G13.

1 Welcome and apologies.

2 Approval of minutes from meeting held Monday 4th Feb 2013.

3 Matters arising from previous meeting.

    3.1 Item 3.3: update from Chair on print quota.

    3.2 Item 11.1: update from class reps on first-year experience.

4 Organization and management of modules and courses (i.e., timetabling and communication).

    4.1 Discussion on *What staff expect of students*, a draft paper.

5 Academic advice and support.

    5.1 Report from Maths and Computer Science (exam feedback).

6 Teaching delivery and content (use of VLE, AV, etc.).

    6.1 Access across departments.

7 Societies:

    Maths Society – update on Graduation Ball.

    Computer Science Society – poster competition.

8 Any other business.

9 Date of next meeting.

Task 2 Listening critically to follow the argument

As you listen to the four parts of the meeting, make notes for an article in *News 4 U*, the International Students' Association newsletter.

2.1　🎧T46 Listen to Part 1 of the meeting. Chen is making the case for what kinds of changes? Suggest solutions to the problem he raises at the end of Part 1.

2.2　🎧T47 Listen to Part 2 of the meeting and suggest solutions to the problem he raises at the end of Part 2.

2.3　🎧T48 Listen to Part 3 of the meeting and suggest solutions to the problem he raises at the end of Part 3.

2.4　🎧T49 Listen to Part 4 of the meeting. What further problems are covered in the meeting?

2.5　Share your notes with another student.

Task 3 Evaluating the discussion

3.1　In pairs, outline the context of Chen's presentation at the meeting, i.e., who are the main stakeholders in the issue, and what is the background and purpose of the presentation.

3.2　What are the responsibilities of the five participants who speak in the meeting?

　　Now listen again, if you wish, and use the list of criteria from your earlier discussion about effective contributions to answer the following questions.

3.3　How effective is Chen's presentation? Give specific examples of what he does to make it effective. Work with other students to make a checklist of recommendations specifically for presenting a case in a meeting.

3.4　Do you think the meeting goes smoothly? What kinds of contributions are made by other participants?

Study smart: strategic moves in effective group discussions

There are many conventions for effective group discussions. Their purpose is to allow members of the group to contribute to the negotiation, but also to help the discussion to go smoothly and to keep everyone focused on the group aims. The conventions are observed by strategic moves – moves designed to achieve the meeting aims. These include inviting someone to speak, directing the flow of discussion, interrupting a speaker to get more information or to present a different viewpoint. Each strategic move is achieved through strategic language – language that is to some extent dependent on the context of the meeting and on participants' roles.

Task 4 Understanding strategic moves in meetings

4.1 In pairs, find examples of the strategic moves described in the Study smart, as well as any others, in the transcript on pages 312–314. Underline the language used by speakers to make each strategic move.

The list below provides examples of strategic language used by members of the committee as they negotiate a shared understanding of the issue and what they want to achieve.

4.2 Complete the table with a strategic move (a–i) to describe each set of examples of strategic language. The first one has been done for you.

a value a contribution
b move the discussion back to the issue
c interrupt the speaker for clarification
d agree a course of action
e encourage someone to speak
f ask for a speaker's view on a specific point
g disagree directly on a point
h confirm another speaker's point by adding to it
i accept a point made by another speaker

strategic language examples	strategic move
1. Chair (Nabil): … *you put this item on the agenda – would you like to speak about it?* Chair: *What did you find out, Chen?* Chair: *What was the best practice you found, then? Who's doing it right?*	*e*
2. Chair: *Good idea./Good point.*	
3. Chair: *Could I just ask …?* Dr Michaelson: *Sorry, but I'm just curious. I thought …* Student A: *You mean …?*	
4. Student B: Yes, *I'm interested in what you said, Chen, about markers' comments …* *What do you think?*	
5. Dr Michaelson: *Not really – the opposite.* Dr Michaelson: *Yes, but … there are a lot of practical problems …*	
6. Chen: *Anyway … but sorry, that's not the point. The point is this …* Chen: *But, to go back to your question about …* Student B: *Could you tell us about your third group of points?*	
7. Dr Michaelson: *So that's quite a difference between high school and university.* Dr Michaelson: *Yes, you mean marking criteria …* Dr Michaelson: *Yes, it's a university policy.*	
8. Chen: *Yes, true.* Chen: *Yes, I see.*	
9. All: *Yes, agreed.*	

Interruptions

Many international students are culturally programmed not to interrupt. However, effective contributions are often made through interruptions (as in the third set of examples in the table on page 147). Sometimes they have to be made by the interrupter talking over (i.e., at the same time as) the first speaker. This is acceptable in less formal contexts and can be a useful strategy. However, such interruptions usually start with diplomatic phrases such as *Sorry* and *Could I just ... ?*

Disagreement

Similarly, many international students find it difficult to disagree directly when speaking with another person. English speakers feel the same way in everyday conversations. However, disagreement is inevitable in academic discussion (as in the fifth set of examples). Even so, English speakers almost never use *I disagree* or *I don't agree*; they prefer a more diplomatic indication of their attitude. In spoken English, *Yes, but* is twenty times more frequent than *I don't agree* or *I disagree*, and *Not really* is also much more frequent[1].

Orientation

It is always helpful in a meeting, lecture or presentation to ask questions in two parts. The first part, orientation, is to identify the topic, and the second is to ask the specific question. This is particularly important if some time has passed since the topic was last discussed (as in the fourth example). It is diplomatic because the orientation helps the person questioned to recall quickly what has already been said.

Key words & phrases

culturally programmed

talking over

inevitable

indication of

orientation

Task 5 Listening for sentence stress

⊕T50 Listen to this extract from Chen's presentation and underline the words that he stresses.

Obviously, exam technique and essay technique are very different things, and we've particularly had student feedback saying that it's changed the way they have approached exams, it's changed the way they revise, it's changed the way they write in exams and it's meant that they have got a clear idea of what we're looking for.[2]

Task 6 Listening for strategic tones

The tones that a speaker chooses to use can support his/her strategy.

⊕T51 Listen to seven examples from the meeting and identify the tones that are used on the stressed words (underlined), then complete the table at the top of page 149.

[1] Brigham Young University. (2013.) *British National Corpus.* Retrieved from http://corpus.byu.edu/bnc

[2] Thomas, N. (2007). *Feedback on exams: Written sheets in History.* University of Nottingham. Retrieved October 24, 2012, from http://www.nottingham.ac.uk/pesl/resources/assessment/feedback610

strategy	example	tones used
1. give new information	*I thought that <u>e'xam</u> scripts were covered by '<u>data</u> protection.*	
2. start the discussion	*'<u>Chen</u>, you put this item on the <u>a'genda</u> – would you like to '<u>speak</u> about it?*	
3. disagree diplomatically	*Not '<u>really</u> …*	
4. check information	*You mean they are <u>confi'dential</u>? No one is allowed to '<u>see</u> them?*	
5. move the discussion back to the issue	*… but '<u>sorry</u>, that's not the '<u>point</u>. The point is '<u>this</u> …*	
6. offer alternatives	*… do we want Gateway to have '<u>best</u> practice or '<u>worst</u> practice?*	
7. show surprise	*'<u>Yeah</u>! How did you '<u>know</u>?*	

Task 7 Speaking assertively

Chen sounds assertive when he moves the discussion back to the main issue.

7.1 **⊙T52 Listen and repeat what Chen says with the same tone pattern.**

7.2 **In pairs, practise being assertive. Put the prompts a–e into the framework given to make your assertion. The first one has been done for you.**

But, sorry, that's not the _____. The _____ is this: do we want _____ to _____ or _____?

a point / Gateway / best practice / worst practice
   But, sorry, that's not the <u>point</u>. The <u>point</u> is this: do we want <u>Gateway</u> to have <u>best practice</u> or <u>worst practice</u>?

b issue / company / profit / loss

c question / project / success / failure

d problem / funds / effectively / wastefully

e choice / meeting / stability / change

7.3 **Make up some more assertions to practise.**

Task 8 Writing

Use your notes from Chen's presentation to write an article for *News 4 U*, the International Students' Association newsletter. Write 150–200 words.

Self study

Think about situations where you would like to be more assertive or more diplomatic in discussions than you feel you are at present – perhaps this has emerged in your role plays in Sections 2 and 3. How will you change in the desired direction? Be ready to share your ideas with other students.

Section 5 Presenting a case for change: Part 2

Discussion

What different types of meetings do students have to participate in at university? Which require an agenda and minutes? What are their purposes?

Task 1 Writing

1.1 Read the minutes opposite. What are the main differences between the minutes and an article in *News 4 U?*

1.2 Write minutes for Chen's item at the student–staff liaison committee using your notes from Section 4, Task 2.1.

Task 2 Preparing for a meeting

2.1 Chen's presentation was successful because he researched and prepared well, as you did for your own written report about exam feedback systems.

How did this help you to follow the arguments raised at the meeting and to note the main points for the minutes? Discuss in groups.

2.2 Prepare to hold a meeting to discuss issues such as feedback on exams and/or the problems you would like to address in your own school or university. Write an agenda. Choose a student to chair the meeting, another to take the minutes, and a main speaker for each item on the agenda. Take some time to prepare for each item and consider what you want to do with the minutes after the meeting.

Task 3 Speaking

Hold your meeting, ensuring it is run smoothly and properly minuted.

Task 4 Thinking critically: reviewing your role

Write some comments on how well you participated in the meeting, in particular with respect to your own goals.

Write similar comments about the other people at your meeting.

Minutes of meeting held Monday 18th March 2013:

1. Apologies received from A. G. Bell, Maria Agnesi, Liu Hui, Jamshid AlKashi.
2. Minutes from meeting held Monday 4th Feb 2013 approved by Dr Michaelson, seconded by Helen Winters.
3. Matters arising from previous meeting.
    Item 3.3: Chair reported that the print quotas are to be reviewed across the university.
    Item 11.1: update from class reps on first-year experience.
    Action: Carried over until next meeting
4. Organization and management of modules and courses (i.e., timetabling and communication).
4.1 Discussion on *What staff expect of students,* a draft paper. The committee discussed the previously circulated draft paper, noting previous wording of an earlier Study skills leaflet.
    The main points were as follows:
    The document is helpful but few would read it, so it would be best to publish it on VISION.
    In comparison to the Study skills leaflet, the language is harder for students to understand.
    Action: Chair to report to LTSC on 25/10/13.
5. Academic advice and support.
5.1 Report on exam feedback from Chen Zhi Qiang (Maths and Computer Science).

Section 1 Understanding ethical thinking

What the university expects:
- a global and ethical understanding – respond sensitively in cross-cultural contexts

Contexts:
- multicultural groups and teams for study and work

Aims:
- to explore ethical thinking
- to investigate what you already know about making ethical decisions
- to investigate language for discussing ethical choices and their consequences

The university requires all students (both undergraduates and postgraduates) to submit proposals for their research projects to an ethics committee, which will evaluate their research design against ethical standards for conducting research. Maysoun's supervisor, Dr Charles, advises her to attend a series of lectures intended to help students understand the concept of ethics and ethical research. Maysoun is upset about this extra commitment when she already has a lot on her plate at university as well as at home. However, Dr Charles reassures her that she will quickly grasp the concept because she makes ethical choices in her life all the time without realizing. Dr Charles gives Maysoun a handout from a module on ethics and suggests she looks at some of the exercises to prepare for the first lecture.

Key words & phrases

ethical thinking
to submit a proposal
an ethics committee
evaluate against
ethical standards
conducting research
commitment
a lot on her plate
reassures
grasp the concept
ethics

Introducing ethical thinking in science

Ethics is about the moral decisions we have to make about the way we behave towards other people. We are often confronted with a number of possible courses of action and we have to choose the best one. Before we make a decision, we usually create scenarios – virtual or unreal situations – in our minds and imagine responding in one way or another. We are effectively entering a virtual world where we can try things out to see how they might work or what the consequences might be. After we have conducted this thought experiment, we then return to the real world and make our decision. This ability to think in a virtual or hypothetical space is one of the features that distinguishes humans from other primates.

GATEWAY UNIVERSITY

Key words & phrases

a course of action
are confronted with
unreal situations
a virtual world
a thought experiment
the real world
a hypothetical space
primates
to leave a tip
a market trader
looks smart
even if
a cash machine
an offside offence

Test your ethical thinking with these questions:

1. If you enjoy a meal in a restaurant, is it acceptable not to leave a tip?
2. If a market trader gives too much change, do you tell him and return the money?
3. If your friend asked for your opinion about her new dress, would you say it looks smart, even if you don't think so?
4. If you saw someone use a cash machine but forget to take the money, would you return the money to them?
5. If you found money in a cash machine near a bank, would you return the money to the bank?
6. If you use the work of other writers in your essay, do you have to acknowledge the source with a reference?
7. If you were a player in a football team and the referee failed to see an offside offence by a member of your team, would you tell the referee?

Your answers to these questions and how difficult you found each one will tell you a lot about the moral standards you live by.

Discussion

Answer the questions in the handout and try to think of a reason for each answer. Were some questions easier to answer than others? Why? Compare your ideas in pairs and as a class. What differences do you find?

Task 1 Investigating grammar patterns for events and responses

1.1 Below are sets of statements which you might have used in your discussion of ethical thinking.

Study the sets of statements, paying particular attention to the first part of each statement – the *if*-clause. This signals that the event described in each set is not real. Decide which of the events is more or less likely to happen in the real world.

1.2 **Study the sets of statements again, this time paying particular attention to the second part of each statement. This imagines one possible response to each unreal event. Choose the statement that is different in some way from the other two and give reasons for your choice.**

1.3 **Which statement in each set is closest to your view? Compare with other students.**

a **1** If I enjoy a meal in a restaurant, I always leave a tip.
   2 If I enjoy a meal in a restaurant, I might leave a tip.
   3 If I don't enjoy a meal in a restaurant, I don't leave a tip.

b **1** If a market trader gives me too much change, I might not tell him and keep the money.
   2 If a market trader gives me too much change, I won't tell him and keep the money.
   3 If a market trader gives me too much change, I will tell him and return the money.

c **1** If I saw someone forget to take money from a cash machine, I would return the money to them.
   2 If I saw someone forget to take money from a cash machine, I might return the money to them.
   3 If I saw someone forget to take money from a cash machine, I might not return the money to them.

d **1** If I found money in a cash machine near a bank, I would return the money to the bank.
   2 If I found money in a cash machine near a bank, I would not return the money to the bank.
   3 If I found money in a cash machine near a bank, I might not return the money to the bank.

e **1** If I use the work of other writers in my essay, I have to acknowledge the source with a reference.
   2 If I use the work of other writers in my essay, I should acknowledge the source with a reference.
   3 If I use the work of other writers in my essay, I must acknowledge the source with a reference.

Investigating grammar patterns for events and responses

Choosing between competing options involves entering an unreal or virtual world in order to speculate about different events and possible responses to each one. Speakers and writers can signal they are entering unreality using signpost expressions, such as *if*, *unless* or *even if*. They can emphasize the distance from the real and present world using the past tense or modal verbs.

Events can be linked to their responses in two-part sentences, often called conditional sentences. The verbs in each part can take a variety of forms depending on the speaker/writer's viewpoint. There are two key questions:

1. How likely is the event to happen in the real world?
2. How certain is the response? (How strong is the cause-and-effect link between event and response?)

Event is viewed as probable (likely to happen) (present verb)	Link between event and response is strong (present verb or modal *will*)
If I <u>enjoy</u> a meal in a restaurant, …	*… I always <u>leave</u> a tip.*
If a market trader <u>gives</u> me too much change, …	*… I <u>will tell</u> him and return the money.*
	Link between event and response is weak (modal *might*)
	… I <u>might leave</u> a tip.
	… I <u>might not tell</u> him and keep the money.
Event is viewed as possible (less likely to happen) (past verb)	Link between event and response is strong (modal *would*, i.e., past form of *will*)
If I <u>saw</u> someone forget to take money from a cash machine, …	*… I <u>would return</u> the money to them.*
If I <u>found</u> money in a cash machine near a bank, …	*… I <u>would return</u> the money to the bank.*
	Link between event and response is weak (modal *might*)
	… I <u>might return</u> the money to them.
	… I <u>might not return</u> the money to the bank.

Rules and regulations can also be expressed using these structures:

Event is expected to happen (present verb)	Link to a regulation which is obligatory (modal *have to*)
If I <u>use</u> the work of other writers in my essay, …	*… I <u>have to acknowledge</u> the source with a reference.*
	Link to a regulation which writer wants to emphasize (modal *must*) … *you <u>must acknowledge</u> the source with a reference.*

Task 2 Choosing to express events and responses differently

2.1 Your teacher will display some statements collected from your discussion of the ethical questions.

Work in pairs or small groups to answer these two questions. According to the speaker:

a how likely is the event to happen in the real world?

b how certain is the response? (How strong is the cause-and-effect link between event and response?)

2.2 **Do you think the levels of likelihood and certainty are appropriate? Change some of your statements to make them more or less likely and more or less certain. Compare with other groups.**

Task 3 Investigating cultural differences through case studies

3.1 Work with other students from your country, if possible. Choose one of the case studies below and brainstorm some conventions that might be different between your country and the UK. Think about the possible responses to these different conventions for someone who wants to travel to the UK to study or work. What advice would you give?

3.2 Write a short report (for students or professionals going to the UK from your country) to explain the likely consequences if they do not pay attention to the different conventions in relation to gift giving or copyright.

3.3 Give your report to another group who will comment on the language you have chosen to express events, responses and likely consequences.

Case study 1: Gift giving

All cultures value giving gifts to friends and relatives, teachers or professional colleagues, but there are different cultural conventions relating to the type of gift that is appropriate, who can accept gifts and what people should do when they receive a gift. For example, when you receive a gift in the UK, it is considered polite to open it immediately, to thank the giver, and to comment enthusiastically on the high quality of the gift. However, teachers and professionals do not normally expect to receive gifts from their students or clients and might refuse to accept very expensive gifts because these might look like bribes.

Case study 2: Copyright

All cultures have rules about the ownership of new inventions and original ideas, but there are different cultural conventions relating to how these can be shared. In the UK, there are patent laws to ensure that an inventor has exclusive rights to make money from a new product, and copyright laws to allow artists, musicians and writers sole ownership of their artistic creations. Thus it is illegal to sell fake goods which look like famous brands and it is also illegal to download and share music from the Internet without paying for it. Similarly, academic papers are considered to be the intellectual property of their authors. Although it is possible to copy the author's words from the paper, this copying must be indicated clearly and the owner of the words must be identified using a reference.

Key words & phrases
professional colleagues
cultural conventions
it is considered to be
enthusiastically
bribes
patent laws
exclusive rights
copyright laws
sole ownership
intellectual property
inverted commas

Self study

The first lecture in the series on research ethics will be an introduction to the concept of ethics. Students who want to attend are asked to prepare for the lecture by downloading and studying the presentation slides, which are posted on the university intranet. The slides are shown on the following page in Section 2. Study them carefully and try to answer the questions in Slides 1 and 4. Where could you go to find out more about this subject?

Section 2 A lecture on ethics

What the university expects:
- a global and ethical understanding – demonstrate a high level of ethical commitment

Contexts:
- situations in study and work which require ethical decisions

Aims:
- to understand the concept of ethics
- to plan and adapt note-making strategies during lectures
- to demonstrate understanding by focused summarizing

Discussion

Work in groups to review your understanding of ethical thinking. Can you answer the questions in Slides 1 and 4? Can you think of examples of ethical dilemmas and consequences? How is ethical thinking relevant to you right now?

1 Introduction to ethics – overview

- What is *ethics*?
- Understanding ethical choices
- Understanding ethical consequences
- Applying standards to decide and evaluate
- Why is ethics important in research?
- Case studies for discussion

2 What is ethics?

- 'The branch of philosophy concerned with the evaluation of human conduct' (Blackburn, 1996)
- '*Morality* is the right or wrong (or otherwise) of an action, a way of life or a decision, while *ethics* is the study of such standards as we use or propose to judge such things' (Newall, 2005)
- Ethical standards different from laws

3 Ethics is about:

- competing moral choices
- consequences of making those choices
- standards to decide and evaluate choices

4 Understanding ethical dilemmas

- Is it OK to lie?
- Situations when lying might be OK
- Consequences of lying in those situations
- Behave towards others as you want them to behave towards you

5 Understanding ethical consequences

- Example from robotics
  - Privacy
- Social interaction and dependency

6 Applying ethical standards

- Robots are tools, not people
- Ethics applies to designers, not robots
- Five ethical rules for designers of robots

7 Why is ethics important in research?

- Ensure integrity and quality in research
  - Add new knowledge to discipline
  - Produce accurate results
  - Poor quality research ➔ harm
  - Wastes time and money

8 Case study questions

- What is the problem or issue?
- What is the relevant information?
- What are the different options and choices?
- What are the consequences of the choices?
- Are there any ethical codes or rules to apply?

9 References

Blackburn, S. (2008). *Oxford dictionary of philosophy* (2nd ed.). Oxford: Oxford University Press.

Boddy, J. et al. (n.d.). *The research ethics guidebook*. Retrieved from http://www. ethicsguidebook.ac.uk/

Calo, M. R. (2011). *Privacy and robots*. Retrieved from http://www.youtube.com/ watch?v=uX4iOGJBcZU

10 References (cont'd)

Newall, P. (2005). Ethics. *The Galilean Library*. Retrieved from http://www.galilean -library.org/site/index.php/page/index.html/_/ essays/introducingphilosophy/11-ethics-r27

Singer, P. (2011). *Practical ethics* (3rd ed.). Cambridge: Cambridge University Press.

Winfield, A. (2011). Roboethics for Humans. *New Scientist*, *210*(2811). Retrieved from http://www. newscientist.com//issue/2811

Task 1 Listening critically to plan your approach

1.1 ⓈT53 Listen to the introduction to the lecture. Why is Irina Pavlenko a suitable lecturer to explain research ethics to students? Which groups of students is her lecture useful for? How do you expect the content of her talk to be similar to or different from her slides?

1.2 According to the lecturer, which aspect of her talk will best help her listeners to understand the concept of ethics? What notes should students take in order to remember her explanations?

1.3 Think of a possible framework – layout and headings – for your notes. Compare with other students.

Task 2 Recording key information from the lecture

2.1 ⓈT54 Listen to the remainder of the lecture and follow the presentation slides. Take additional notes on the lecturer's main points and the examples she uses to illustrate and explain those points. Use the layout and headings you specified in Task 1, but be prepared to adapt them if necessary.

2.2 Compare your headings and your notes with other students. Do you agree on the main points and the examples?

2.3 Did you copy any ideas from the presentation slides in your notes? Is this a good strategy?

2.4 In groups, choose either the example about votes for women or the example about social robots and add more detail under your headings so you can make a presentation of this example. Listen again or refer to the presentation slides and the transcript on page 311–312, if you need to.

2.5 Did you need to adapt your note-taking framework as the lecture proceeded or later when you added more detail?

Study smart: understanding the lecturer's purpose and planning your approach

A lecturer's purpose, particularly at postgraduate level, is not simply to give information. Most lecturers will make a number of key points, illustrated with examples, in order to explain theoretical concepts and link them to practical, real situations. Lecturers then expect students to do some follow-up reading, using the sources provided, to enhance their understanding. Students can show they understand by applying the new concepts to real or hypothetical case studies.

It is important to plan and be prepared to adapt your note-taking strategy during lectures, for example, by changing headings or using a different layout. The overview slide usually gives the structure for the lecture and there may be a handout you can use for your notes. You should pay attention to examples and include them in your notes because they will help you to apply the concepts in new contexts.

Investigating grammar patterns for situations or events and their consequences

Before we make ethical decisions, we assess competing options by speculating about future situations or events and their likely consequences. Sometimes, however, we want to report ethical decisions and consequences in the past. We do this in order to contrast the consequences of options which were <u>not</u> chosen with what actually happened or to reflect on hypothetical past consequences.

The more unlikely the speaker views the situation or event, the further back into the past it is placed.

Situation viewed as likely in the future	Link between situation and consequence is strong
(present verb)	(modal *can*)
If robots become common in our homes, …	*… [then] they can be used to collect information about us which we might want to keep private.*
Event viewed as likely in the past	Link to past consequence is strong
(past verb)	(modal *would*, i.e., past form of *will*)
[Men generally thought that] if women <u>were given</u> the vote, …	*… this <u>would change</u> the relationship between men and women …*
Event did not happen in the past	Link to hypothetical consequence in the past is strong
(past perfect verb)	(modal *would* + perfect infinitive)
If these people <u>had been discovered</u>, …	*… the Nazis <u>would have killed</u> both the Jews and their protectors.*

Task 3 Investigating grammar patterns from the lecture

3.1   Look at the transcript of the lecture on pages 311–312 to find other examples of conditional structures which refer to speculation about past or present options and their consequences.

3.2   For each example, say how likely the situation or event is, or was, to occur and how certain the consequence is or was.

3.3   The known consequences of actual choices can be evaluated using other structures which link cause and effect. Find three examples in the transcript.

3.4   The conditional structure can also be used for other purposes, such as giving instructions or signposting parts of the lecture. Find examples used for these purposes in the lecture.

Task 4 Thinking critically about the lecturer's choice of grammar patterns

4.1   Look at the following sentence taken from the lecture. It has a similar structure to a conditional with a different link word: *when*. Why has the lecturer chosen to present this information in this way?

When women did not have the right to vote, society considered them to be inferior to men.

4.2   Could you disagree with this statement? Why?/Why not?

4.3   Look at the following argument taken from the lecture. Can you think of reasons why the underlined final sentence is presented in this order and not with the event (*if*-clause) first? Think about its connection back to the subject of the first sentence.

Another consequence we need to consider is robots as social actors, employed to care for vulnerable people such as the elderly or disabled or children. On the face of it, this seems like a good idea. Robots do not get tired and they have endless patience. They can even be programmed to express human emotions. Indeed, people are more likely to accept care from robots if these machines look and behave like humans, at least to some extent.

4.4   How do the structure and the choice of language in this paragraph show that it is an argument?

Task 5 Summarizing key information from the lecture to demonstrate understanding

5.1   Present your group's analysis of one of the lecturer's examples, which you prepared in Task 2.4.

5.2   As you listen to the presentations, be prepared to challenge the analysis of the events and consequences.

Self study

With your group, choose one of the case studies shown in Section 5 and arrange to meet outside class to discuss your case study. Prepare a presentation of the case to be given to your class for discussion at a later stage. You will need to consult the references given at the end of each case to obtain more information for your discussion.

Section 3 What is scholarship?

What the university expects:
- a global and ethical understanding – demonstrate a high level of ethical commitment and take responsibility for your actions

Contexts:
- situations in which the work of other writers is used and acknowledged

Aims:
- to understand the concepts of *scholarship* and *unfair means*
- to read critically and ask sceptical questions about a website
- to evaluate the website using a student code of practice
- to write an e-mail advising a student about options and consequences

The university expects students to be able to manage their workload and meet deadlines, but this can be difficult for some students. Chen receives an e-mail from his friend Matt who is struggling with writing assignments for his Building and Estate Management course. Matt has sent Chen a link to a website which he thinks can solve his problems, so Chen decides to take a look at it.

To:	z.q.chen@gwu.ac.uk	
From:	y.z.cao@gwu.ac.uk	
Subject:	situation very bad	

Hi Chen,
Long time no contact you – sorry 4 that! I got a lot of pressure right now 'cos too many assignments. Still my writing is bad and no time to go to writing centre see Jenifer. Plus not possible to do what she says 'cos not enough time to learn all that stuff before my assignment due. I wish I studied on pre-sessional like you and Maysoun. You know I have to work hard make my parents proud. I so worried to let them down after pay so much money. But I think I found solution. My friend sent me link for www.AllMyOwn.com where can get essay on any topic. This can be answer to my problems – what do you think? Maybe can see you 4 coffee soon?
Matt

Discussion

What problems does Matt have? Why does he have these problems? How do you think the website he has found can solve his problems? Are there any ethical issues he should consider?

Task 1 Reading critically to understand the purpose of the website

1.1 Study the website to decide exactly what product or service it is selling. Find evidence for your answer.

1.2 Look at the images and the URL of the site. How do these contribute to the message?

1.3 Look carefully at the language used to describe the product or service, particularly the use of pronouns such as *we* and *your*. Can you find any evidence of an intention to mislead customers?

1.4 Who runs the company AllMyOwn.com? Is English their first or second language? How do you know and does this matter?

AllMyOwn.com
Achieve the grades you deserve

| About us | Services | FAQs | Prices | Order now |

Under pressure from university assignments?
Feeling stressed and out of control?

We can help with a wide selection of bespoke essays. Let our highly skilled team of experts craft your academic essay tailed to your personal requirements. No matter the subject of your essay, we can provide support to achieve your winning grades. We also supply proofreading services. Let us convert your draft essay to 1st Class academic standard. Contact us now for a quotation – we respond in 24 hours with competitive prices.

About us

AllMyOwn.com is a registered company which offers academic consultancy services to students. We have helped many thousands of students to gain 1st Class grades through consulting our expert writers. Our experts are qualified to MA standard and can write high quality essays in a few hours. We believe in operating against ethical standards of honesty, trust and integrity.

Honesty
We will not sell your essay to other clients or third parties. We deplore plagiarism. All our essays are checked by latest plagiarism software such as Turnitin®.
We guarantee your money back if plagiarism is detected in an essay.

Trust
We fully comply with the 1998 Data Protection Act. Your personal details are strictly confidential. Your university cannot find out if you used our service.

Integrity
Our success depends on our reputation in providing custom essay writing services. We hold our ethos very dear to us and believe that these are sound basis to continue our business success.

Services
Essay is the most popular mode of assessment by universities. However, universities now have few resources to give individual help to students. Yet they still demand students to pay attention to critical evaluation, balanced argument, structure and coherence in essays. Our highly skilled writers have many years' experience and understand the academic requirements. Using our essays can help you to meet these requirements.

Our editing service can raise your draft essay to 1st Class standard. We can redraft and add new paragraphs to improve your argument. We can add new references to support your points. Our experts can ensure that your essay fully complies with the academic conventions of referencing so you cannot be accused of plagiarism.

Key words & phrases

out of control

bespoke

craft your essay

tailored to

a quotation

a registered company

consultancy services

third parties

deplore

plagiarism software

Turnitin®

guarantee

comply with

strictly confidential

critical evaluation

balanced argument

coherence

be accused of plagiarism

Task 2 Responding sceptically to claims on the website

2.1 As Chen reads the first paragraph from the *About us* section of AllMyOwn.com, he asks some sceptical questions. These questions will help him to decide if the website is trying to mislead him.

Can you answer Chen's questions?

a *AllMyOwn.com is a registered company …*
Why does being a registered company matter?

b *… which offers academic consultancy services to students.*
Why do they say *consultancy services* here when they talked about essays in the introduction? What are they actually selling?

c *We have helped many thousands of students …*
Why is the number of students mentioned?

d *… to gain 1st Class grades through consulting our expert writers.*
What do the experts actually do? How do they help students?

e *Our experts are qualified to MA standard …*
Why is the experts' level of qualification relevant?

f *Our experts … write high quality essays in a few hours.*
Why is the speed at which they can write relevant? What is the implied link in meaning between this sentence and *We have helped*?

g *We believe in operating against ethical standards of honesty, trust and integrity.*
Shouldn't this be *operating according to* ethical standards? What does *operating against* ethical standards mean?

2.2 Read the statements under the headings *Honesty, Trust* and *Integrity* and write some sceptical questions like Chen's about these statements. Give your questions to another student to answer.

2.3 What reasons does the website give to justify students' use of its products and services? Are these valid reasons?

Task 3 Reading critically to find inconsistencies in the website

3.1 Study the second part of the website on page 164 to find information which is inconsistent with claims made in the first part.

3.2 Do you agree with the answers to the FAQs? How would you answer these questions?

3.3 Study the terms and conditions carefully. How do these suggest that the products and services on the website should actually be used?

3.4 Do you think it is appropriate for Matt to use AllMyOwn.com as a solution to his problem? Give reasons for your answer based on your answers in Tasks 3.1–3.3.

AllMyOwn.com
Achieve the grades
you deserve

| About us | Services | FAQs | Prices | Order now |

Frequently asked questions

Is buying an essay cheating?

Nowadays, universities have few resources to support students who benefit from individual attention. Class sizes are too many and tutors can be absent or unwilling. Especially students who English is not their first language can find difficult to understand assignments' requirement.

Using an essay written by our experts is same benefit as having a private meeting with a tutor to discuss essay question. Not only does a model show structure and preferred style of academic essays but also it provides further ideas to ensure scholarly authority of the work.

If you use model in the correct way, you are not cheating by buying our essays.

Is using an editing service cheating?

Many universities request students to have their essays proofread before submission in order to remove spelling, grammar and punctuation mistakes which prevent easy reading of the paper. If English is not your first language, you may also have problems with correct vocabulary and formal style. Because tutors ask you to check these aspects of your essay, it is not cheating to ask an editor service to do this.

Terms and conditions

1. AllMyOwn.com Ltd. retains copyright of all the products supplied to you. By placing an order, you agree that you will not re-sell the product or attempt to obtain other unauthorised benefits.

2. We strongly recommend that you conform to your university regulations on intellectual property rights. We are not responsible for any unauthorised and illegal use of a paper. Once you receive the paper you commissioned, the decision to use it in a particular way is completely yours.

3. The academic standard suggested by AllMyOwn.com Ltd. for the paper you commissioned is not intended to guarantee any degree standard, grade or marks as assessed by your university.

4. By placing an order you agree not to submit, in part or full, any paper supplied by AllMyOwn.com Ltd. to any educational institution in the UK or abroad as your own work.

5. The recommended use of our service is to consider it a scholarly piece of work of the kind found in academic journals or books. You may only use it as an example for your own essay or research. If we suspect abuse of our service at any stage of the order process, we reserve the right to cancel your order.

Key words & phrases

cheating

individual attention

scholarly

retains copyright

unauthorised benefits

strongly recommend

in part or full

reserve the right

to cancel

Task 4 Evaluating the claims on the website against the code of practice

Gateway University publishes a code of practice to help students to understand and follow the ethical principles of good scholarship. Each student receives a copy of the code, and there is a lecture at the beginning of each year during induction week to explain the concept of scholarship and to emphasize the importance of compliance with the principles outlined in the code. In addition, students are required to sign a declaration on the front cover of their assignments to say that the work is all their own. Chen consults his copy of the code and compares it with the claims on AllMyOwn.com.

4.1 **Study the definitions of *scholarship* and *unfair means* in the code of practice opposite. If Matt uses the products and services of AllMyOwn.com, can he be accused of using unfair means? Give reasons for your answer.**

4.2 According to the code, which specific aspects of the products and services offered by AllMyOwn.com should Matt <u>not</u> use?

4.3 Are there any products or services from the website that would be ethical?

Student Code of Practice for Scholarship

Introduction

The purpose of this code of practice is to provide students at Gateway University with a clear definition of the concept of *scholarship* and its opposite term – *unfair means* – so that students understand the culture and values of the academic community they are joining and what type of behaviour is expected of them.

Definitions

Scholarship is the set of behaviours expected of you by the academic community in relation to the use and creation of ideas and knowledge within that community. You have joined the university to understand ideas in your field more deeply and to benefit from the research and thinking of experts. You learn by reading and thinking about their ideas and then by selecting and applying these ideas in your own work. In doing this, you demonstrate that you have acquired the skills and attributes of a graduate and you understand what constitutes good practice in your field. One important aspect of good practice is respect for intellectual property rights, which means that you must show if you have used ideas that do not belong to you. Scholarship involves being honest, trustworthy and accurate in your use of the work of other people.

Unfair means is unethical behaviour in which you set out deliberately to cheat or steal the work of other students or of experts in your field in order to gain an unfair advantage. Using unfair means undermines the integrity of your work. It is regarded extremely seriously within the academic community and there are severe penalties if you are found out. Aspects of unfair means include *plagiarism*, *submitting commissioned work* and *collusion*.

Plagiarism involves stealing the work of other scholars, including experts or other students, and presenting this as if it is your own work.

- You are plagiarizing if you cut sentences, paragraphs or whole texts from the Internet or other sources and paste them into your own work so that it is not clear what is from a source and what is your own.

- You are plagiarizing if you take substantial amounts of texts from the Internet or other sources and produce a close paraphrase of them, e.g., by using synonyms.

- You are plagiarizing if you do not use correct referencing conventions to show that the sections you included belong to another writer.

Submitting commissioned work involves buying an essay or other work from the Internet or from another student and submitting it as your own work. It is also a form of plagiarism because exchanging money for an essay you have not written but intend to use is unethical and shows a clear intention to deceive the university staff.

Collusion occurs when two or more people collaborate on a piece of work which each of them then submits as their own for individual assessment. You are often required to work in teams to submit team assignments. This is not collusion because your assessment specifies that you should work together. If your assessment requires an individual piece of work, then it must be all your own work.

Penalties for using unfair means

If you are discovered to have used unfair means in your work, you will be asked to attend an academic misconduct board. You will be notified of this meeting one week in advance and you will be sent evidence, for example a Turnitin® report showing that you have used sources unethically in your work. You can make a written statement about this evidence and your actions prior to the board meeting. During the meeting, you will be asked how you constructed your work and if you agree that you used unfair means. You can explain the extenuating circumstances – other events which have happened in your life – which caused you to behave unethically and the board will take these into account. You can find more information on the university website about the penalties which will apply.

www.gateway.edu/registry/discipline

Key words & phrases

scholarship

unfair means

the academic community

have joined the university

acquired skills

attributes

good practice

unethical behaviour

deliberately

to gain an unfair advantage

severe penalties

are found out

a close paraphrase

an intention to deceive

an academic misconduct board

to be notified

a written statement

extenuating circumstances

Task 5 Evaluating extenuating circumstances

5.1 Below are some written statements produced by students who were accused of using unfair means.

What extenuating circumstances do they list which caused them to behave unethically?

5.2 **Evaluate these statements against the code of practice in Task 4 to decide if the accusations against the students are reasonable.**

5.3 **Which students did not know the correct behaviour and which students had the deliberate intention to cheat?**

5.4 **What advice would you give to each student? Discuss in groups.**

a When I made notes for my essay, I forgot to record exactly which source I found the information in and I didn't have time to go back and look, so I thought I could just include all the sources in my bibliography and not bother with references in the text. I didn't think it was such a big deal.

b I broke up with my girlfriend last week so I was too stressed to spend time on my essay until the deadline and then I realized that there was not enough time so I just found a text on the Internet and summarized it. I couldn't tell my tutor because a relationship is a very personal thing so I can only talk to my friends about it.

c I arrived late for the university programme because my visa didn't arrive on time so I miss the induction and I didn't know I am not allowed to copy. In my undergraduate degree we studied creative writing and the lecturer he encouraged us to copy the style of other writers to improve our own style.

d My English level is not so good and I don't really catch the meaning in a text. Not possible for me to write my own words because way to write too informal and don't have enough words. I pick up some words from parts of the text and put them together and find some synonyms in my dictionary hope lecturer will catch my meaning.

Task 6 Writing an e-mail to offer warning and advice

6.1 Write the e-mail that Chen sends to Matt to make him aware what AllMyOwn.com is really selling and to warn him about the consequences of using their products and services. Use information from the code of practice to explain what will happen to Matt if he is found out. Suggest a different course of action to help him to cope with the pressure he is under.

✉	To:	y.z.cao@gwu.ac.uk
	From:	z.q.chen@gwu.ac.uk
	Subject:	RE: situation very bad

Hi Matt,

_____

_____

_____

Would be good to meet for coffee. Tell me when and where.
Chen

6.2 Exchange your e-mail with another student and give each other feedback. Check that they have used their own words and referenced correctly if they have copied word for word from the code of practice.

Self study

Look on some university websites to see if you can find information or similar codes of practice about scholarship and unfair means. What are the penalties for not following good practice? How does the university deal with cases of cheating?

Section 4 An academic misconduct hearing

What the university expects:
- a global and ethical understanding – demonstrate a high level of ethical commitment and take responsibility for your actions

Contexts:
- disciplinary procedures

Aims:
- to understand what counts as evidence of plagiarism
- to understand the procedure for disciplinary action
- to demonstrate understanding of the seriousness of academic misconduct

The university deals with cheating and unethical behaviour by calling students to attend an academic misconduct board, where they are asked to explain their actions. Chen helped Matt to understand that buying an essay was unethical and persuaded him to speak to his academic tutor about his problems. However, some other students in Matt's department have been accused of using unfair means in their assignments and have been called to attend the academic misconduct board. One week before the meeting, they receive a letter which contains the evidence of plagiarism that the committee will consider.

The main evidence in plagiarism cases comes from Turnitin®, which is a service for checking the originality of student work; in other words, how much is copied from another source, such as academic publications, online encyclopedias and news agencies, and how much is their own work. The Turnitin website explains how the service works[1]:

Key words & phrases

originality

online encyclopedias

news agencies

Home

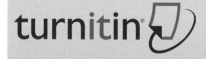

Turnitin uses a plagiarism prevention technology for analyzing called OriginalityCheck® to compare a student paper's text to a vast database of 30+ billion current and archived webpages, over 300+ million papers in a student paper repository, and 120,000+ professional, academic and commercial journals and publications. The software is regularly updated with new content acquired through a robust web crawler, student paper submissions, and new partnerships. Comparison of newly submitted papers against these databases helps to prevent copying and pasting from a variety of sources as well as recycling of text from other students' papers from previous classes or institutions.

Turnitin shows how much of the student's paper matches content from our databases so instructors can quickly understand how much of the paper is unoriginal.

Key words & phrases

plagiarism prevention

archived

repository

robust

a web crawler

submissions

partnerships

comparison against

---

[1] *Turnitin FAQ.* (2013). Retrieved from http://www.turnitin.com/en_us/products/faqs

Task 1 Understanding the Turnitin service

1.1 Read the information about Turnitin. What is the purpose of the service?

1.2 Put the following statements in order to show the process of producing an originality report:

    a OriginalityCheck® compiles a list of all the matches between assignment and other texts.

    b Turnitin produces an originality report with sections of text linked to matching sources.

    c The lecturer or student submits an assignment in electronic form to the Turnitin website.

    d OriginalityCheck® technology compares the student's assignment with texts in its database.

1.3 Why do you think the service is called Turnitin? Look in a dictionary to find the meaning of the verb *to turn* (something or somebody) *in*.

1.4 Discuss in groups how the Turnitin service can provide evidence of plagiarism.

1.5 The technology finds all examples of matching text. Can you think of any instances when matching text would <u>not</u> be evidence of plagiarism?

1.6 Do you think Turnitin would be able to detect whether an essay had been bought from a 'cheat' website such as AllMyOwn.com?

Study smart: providing evidence of scholarship and avoiding plagiarism

At university, you are expected to show that you have read widely in your subject. You can show this most easily by including the ideas of other writers in your essays and reports, together with a short reference in the text and a full bibliographic reference at the end. If you copy the ideas of other writers but you do not show that you have copied (using inverted commas) and you fail to acknowledge the source, your lecturer assumes that you believe the ideas are your own. You can then be accused of plagiarism. The university considers plagiarism to be a serious offence as it is a form of cheating.

Discussion

You are going to listen to the meeting of a school academic misconduct board. This is a formal meeting, similar in some respects to a court of law, where evidence is produced and students are able to defend their actions. Discuss with other students what you think will happen at this board meeting. How do you think the student who has been called to this meeting feels?

Task 2 Listening to understand the procedure for dealing with cheating

2.1 T55 Listen to the Academic Misconduct Board meeting. How many cases is the board going to consider? What type of academic misconduct will be under discussion?

2.2 **Number the steps in the process for considering each case in the correct order.**

   ___ **a** The student is asked to explain any extenuating circumstances which caused him to cheat.

   ___ **b** The board members discuss the student's comments, make a decision and decide on a penalty.

   ___ **c** The student is asked to come into the meeting and is introduced to the board members.

   ___ **d** The student is able to ask questions of the board members.

   ___ **e** The board members read and discuss the case and the evidence of cheating.

   ___ **f** The student has an opportunity to admit that he cheated and to apologize.

   ___ **g** The student is asked to explain how he constructed his essay.

2.3 **How does the student sound, for example, relaxed or frightened? How do the board members sound?**

2.4 **When does the student find out the decision of the board and what he has to do?**

Task 3 Listening to understand the procedure for weighing the evidence and deciding on a penalty

3.1 ⊕T55 **Listen again, if you need to, in order to list the four different types of evidence which the board members mention. Which is evidence of cheating or evidence of extenuating circumstances?**

3.2 **How did Dr Ojukwu try to ensure that students would not cheat in his assignment?**

3.3 **Does the student admit that he cheated? How might this help his case? What extenuating circumstances does he give?**

3.4 **Study the definitions of the three types of misconduct mentioned and the penalties that the board can impose. Label each type of misconduct with the terms used by Dr Sanders.**

   a _____ occurs if a student copies material and provides a reference, but fails to show that it is a quote. They must resubmit the assignment. This penalty may be applied only when it is a first offence for a student in the first year and it is clear that the student did not understand the conventions for using the work of other writers.

   b _____ occurs if most of the work comes from sources which are referenced and there is little evidence of the student's own work, for example, if the student has paraphrased too closely. The student must resubmit the assessments for the whole module and these are capped so they cannot be any higher than the original mark awarded.

   c _____ occurs if a student copies material and fails to show it is a quote or to provide any reference at all so that it appears that the work is presented as his or her own. The student must resubmit the assessments for this module and another module which was previously completed successfully. These are capped so they cannot be any higher than the original mark awarded.

Task 4 Listening to understand the procedure of the university

The diagram below shows the university procedure for consideration of academic misconduct offences.

4.1 ⊚T55 **Listen again or read the transcript on pages 312–314 and select information to complete the diagram.**

4.2 **Which points in the diagram offer options which lead to different pathways? How Is this shown in the diagram? How does Dr Sanders explain these options during the hearing?**

4.3 **Work in pairs to decide how you would explain this procedure to a first-year student from another country who had just joined the university. How would you make this student understand the seriousness of cheating?**

Procedure for consideration of academic misconduct offences:

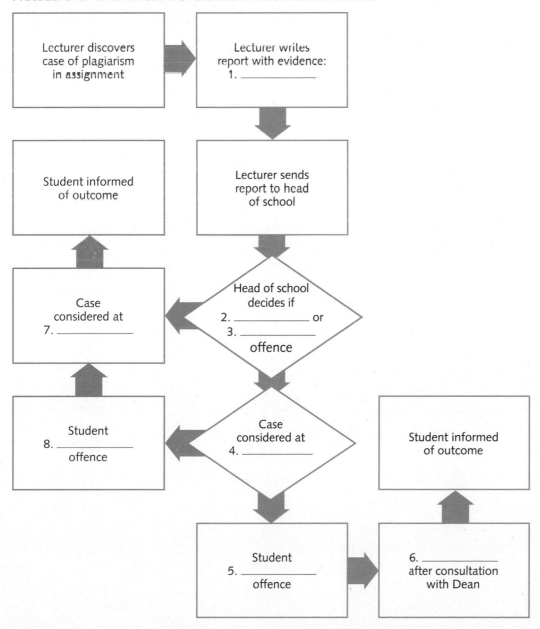

Investigating grammar patterns for describing processes and procedures

A process is a set of steps to produce something, e.g., a Turnitin report. A procedure is a set of steps to arrive at a decision, e.g., about academic misconduct. It is a process with options which may lead to different pathways. Conditional structures are used to present different options and their pathways.

Option (present verb)	Link to logical next step in pathway (present verb)
… if there are any major cases we cannot resolve here, …	… these go to the University Discipline Committee.
Option (present verb) … if he continues to deny wrongdoing and we cannot get him to admit to using unfair means, …	Link to possible next step in pathway (modal verb) … we may have to refer him higher up to the University Discipline Committee.

Task 5 Making a record and acting on the board's decision

Opposite is the incident report form for academic misconduct (IRFAM).

5.1 Study the form and decide if an employer could ever find out that a student had cheated. Give reasons for your answer. How do you think an employer would view an applicant who had cheated in an assignment?

5.2 Complete the form by adding details of the student's explanation and extenuating circumstances, together with details of the board members' discussion, their findings, their decision and the penalty.

5.3 Write a formal letter to the student explaining the decision and the reasons for it.

Self study

Select a source that you want to use for an assignment and make notes from the relevant sections. Record the bibliographic details for your source. Include ideas from the source in your assignment in a way that respects the intellectual property of the original author so that you cannot be accused of plagiarism.

Incident report form for academic misconduct (IRFAM)

For use by academic staff and heads of department

Please complete all relevant sections

Member of staff reporting incident	Dr Noah Ojukwu	School/Section	Built Environment
Student name	Student X	Male/Female	Male
Registration number	GW00038429	Programme and year of study	Construction Management Year 1

Details of incident

Coursework assignment for Construction Management module plagiarized from source material given to student in class and from government website on health and safety in construction. Evidence of plagiarism in Turnitin report (attached).

Evidence including Turnitin report in cases of plagiarism	✓	Copy of relevant code of practice given to student	✓

Classification of case (decided by head of school)	Category B or minor offence ✓	Category A or major offence	Appeal against decision in Category A or B case

Consideration of category B offence	Details of student explanation and extenuating circumstances	Details of findings, decision and penalty

Signature of convenor		Date
Signature of Dean		Date

For office use only	Letter received	Added to student record	Other

Section 5 Discussing ethical case studies

At university, students develop ethical, social, cultural and environmental sensitivity largely through researching case studies, which are usually drawn from the real world. At the end of her lecture on ethics, Dr Pavlenko handed out some case studies for the following week. She asked the students to choose one case to research and discuss during the week so that they could present the results of their discussion and respond to critical comments.

Task 1 Preparing and presenting the case

1.1 Choose and read one of the case studies on pages 175–177 (or others your teacher gives you). Work in groups to search for more information relating to it, using the references given and any others you find.

1.2 Analyze the case using the questions provided and try to agree on an ethical course of action.

1.3 Present your case to your classmates and respond to their critical comments and suggestions.

1.4 Prepare a written report of your case which explains the ethical options and consequences. Use a similar structure for your report to the one you wrote in Unit 6. Show clearly which option you prefer.

Case study 1: The Lewis wind farm

The Scottish Government has put in place a climate change policy to reduce reliance on unsustainable fossil fuels and to increase the amount of energy generated from renewable sources such as wind farms. It aims to meet 50 per cent of electricity demand from renewables by 2020. In response to this policy, the Lewis Wind Power company applied to develop a large onshore wind farm to the west of Stornoway, on the Isle of Lewis, in 2011.

The site chosen for the development is part of a large area of peat bog – spongy ground composed of water and rotting vegetation which is unable to decompose completely. Peat bogs cannot support farming and although the peat was traditionally cut and dried for fuel, it is a fossil fuel energy source so its use as a fuel is discouraged. The Lewis peat bog is an area of natural beauty, rich in insect and plant life and home to many endangered species of birds such as golden eagles, red throated divers and merlins. Other species such as whooping swans migrate there to nest and rear their young. Part of the proposed location for the wind farm is on a Special Protection Area for birds, which gives legal protection to their habitats and nesting sites. The Royal Society for the Protection of Birds (RSPB) initially objected to the wind farm proposal on the grounds that significant numbers of birds would be killed as a result of colliding with wind turbines or overhead power lines and others would be displaced from habitats and nesting sites by the need to build roads and dig channels for underground cables. The RSPB later withdrew its objection when the company agreed to reduce the number of wind turbines on the site. In addition, peat bogs are an important carbon store, preventing the carbon in the rotting vegetation from returning to the atmosphere as carbon dioxide. If they are disturbed, especially if water drains into the underground channels, they will dry out and may catch fire, thus releasing more carbon dioxide. The Lewis Wind Power company claims that the development will create jobs for local people in an area which currently has high rates of unemployment.

Questions

- What is at issue here?
- What are the opposing positions?
- What are the different options and choices?
- What are the consequences of choosing each option?
- Can you reach some kind of consensus about allowing the development to proceed?

References

RSPB. (2008). *Save the Lewis peatlands*. Retrieved from http://www.rspb.org.uk/supporting/campaigns/lewis/index.aspx
Stornoway Wind Farm. (2010). Retrieved from http://www.stornowaywind.com/
The Scottish Government. (2010). *Lewis wind farm*. Retrieved from http://www.scotland.gov.uk/News/Releases/2010/01/14095411

Key words & phrases

unsustainable
renewable sources
wind farms
renewables
the site
a peat bog
spongy
rotting
to decompose
area of natural beauty
rich in
home to
endangered species
Special Protection Area
on the grounds that
to collide with
wind turbines
overhead power lines
underground cables

Case study 2: Providing care for the elderly with uBot-5

The number of elderly people of retirement age is expected to reach 16 million in the UK and 77 million in the USA over the next 20 to 30 years. At the same time, the number of potential carers is expected to decline. Medical and community care services are likely to be put under severe pressure as a result of these changes and policymakers are already investigating alternative care arrangements for this group. Two main problems for older people are the need for care after an accident or illness, and feelings of loneliness or isolation, which can lead to depression.

One option, developed by researchers at the University of Massachusetts, Amherst, is a robotic assistant, uBot-5, which is designed to care for elderly people in their homes or in hospitals. The uBot-5 is a mobile platform balanced on two wheels. It has the mechanical equivalent of a spinal cord and two arms, which it can use to push itself back to a vertical position if it falls over. It can perform a variety of tasks, carrying loads of up to one kilogram or moving objects out of the way. It can even throw a ball while remaining balanced on its wheels. The uBot-5 monitors its environment through a variety of sensors, including a webcam and a microphone. There is a touch-sensitive

Key words & phrases

elderly people
retirement age
community care
under pressure
policymakers
care arrangements
loneliness
depression
the equivalent of
to push itself
monitors
sensors
touch-sensitive

LCD display that allows a person to interact with the robot directly or to connect to a remote family member or medical service provider. The robot is clearly not human, but it can recognize human activity in its environment and can also demonstrate human actions which a doctor might ask a patient to perform, such as raising its arms. It can recognize inactivity and alert emergency services, for example, if a patient has had a fall.

Other researchers at the University of Southern California are developing software to enable social robots such as uBot-5 to interact with people who have had strokes or developed Alzheimer's disease in order to encourage their physical and mental recovery. The robots are programmed to coach the patients, motivating them to carry out rehabilitation tasks. The machine learning software enables the robot to monitor the reactions of a patient and gradually adapt to their mood, for example, praising them more often to keep them working on a task. The ultimate goal is to perfect a robot who can empathize with patients while providing care. However, there is a danger that robots might become so responsive to the patient's mood that people might come to trust the robots more than real people.

Analysis

Evaluate the design of robots such as the uBot-5 against the ethical standards for roboticists (listed below) devised by the UK Research Councils.

- Robots should be designed and operated to comply with the law, including privacy.
- Robots are products: they should be designed to be safe and secure.
- Robots are manufactured artefacts: the illusion of emotions and intent should not be used to exploit vulnerable users.
- It should be possible to find out who is responsible for any robot.

What would roboticists have to do to ensure that robots like the uBot-5 would not harm people?

References

Axelrod, B. (2011, February 16). The Next Big Thing! Service oriented architectures. *Robot Magazine*. Retrieved from http://www.botmag.com/index.php/service-oriented-architectures-two-leading-systems-mrds-and-vos-point-to-the-future-of-robotics EPSRC. (n.d.). *Principles of robotics. Regulating robots in the real world*. Retrieved from http://www.epsrc.ac.uk/research/ourportfolio/themes/engineering/activities/Pages/principlesofrobotics.aspx

Groopman, J. (2009, November 2). Robots that care. *The New Yorker*. Retrieved from http://www.newyorker.com/reporting/2009/11/02/091102fa_fact_groopman?currentPage=all

The Laboratory for Perceptual Robotics. (n.d.). *uBot-5*. Retrieved from http://www-robotics.cs.umass.edu/index.php/Robots/UBot-5 University of Massachusetts Amherst. (2008, April 21). New robots can provide elder care for aging baby boomers. *ScienceDaily*. Retrieved from http://www.sciencedaily.com/releases/2008/04/080416212725.htm

Key words & phrases

medical service provider
alert
strokes
Alzheimer's disease
rehabilitation
machine learning
adapt to
praising
the ultimate goal
to perfect
empathize

Case study 3: Gift giving and whistleblowing

Mr Forbes is a town planner who works for a local government planning department with responsibility for development control. This involves assessing proposals from private individuals who want to build new houses or extend existing houses, and also assessing proposals from companies who want to start up or extend their operations. Mr Forbes works in an historic city where many of the buildings are listed, which means they have been placed on a statutory list of buildings of special architectural or historical interest. These buildings cannot be altered or extended significantly and must retain their original features. The owner has a statutory obligation to maintain the building and can be prosecuted for failing to do so. Mr Forbes writes reports for his manager, Mr Wheeler, who presents these for consideration by elected councillors at the Planning Committee. Mr Forbes and Mr Wheeler have considerable knowledge of the planning laws so they offer impartial advice to the elected councillors, who must consider each proposal in relation to the housing and employment needs of the local community.

Mr Forbes has worked on a proposal from Ezylife Property Developers to turn an historic hotel in the centre of the city into luxury apartments. The hotel has many original features and although the proposal will retain the original external features, many of the internal features will be damaged or destroyed by the development. Mr Forbes decided

Key words & phrases

a town planner
development control
assessing proposals
a statutory list
original features
a statutory obligation
can be prosecuted
offer impartial advice
elected councillors
property developers

to write a report which recommends refusing planning permission on the grounds that the development will significantly alter the historic features of the building. He discussed this with Mr Wheeler who appeared to agree with his assessment. The report was presented to the Planning Committee the following month.

Mr Wheeler is friendly with the owner of Ezylife Property Developers, Tim Crispin, as they were school friends and they regularly play golf and socialize together. In Mr Forbes' opinion, Mr Wheeler spends too much time with Tim Crispin. Mr Forbes especially resents the long lunches the two men often have together in expensive restaurants, leaving Mr Forbes and his colleagues to deal with telephone enquiries from the public on planning issues. One day, Mr Wheeler mentions in passing that he has recently joined Tim Crispin's golf club, which surprises Mr Forbes because the fees for this golf club are very expensive and Mr Wheeler has a wife and two children to support.

Mr Forbes is even more surprised the following month when he reads the minutes of the Planning Committee and discovers that Ezylife Property Developers have been given permission to proceed with the development of the historic hotel against the advice in his report. While it is not uncommon for the Planning Committee to decide against the advice of the planning officers, this case seems to be a clear-cut contravention of the law on listed buildings. Mr Forbes is not sure what to do.

Questions
- What is the problem according to Mr Forbes?
- Does he have enough evidence of unethical behaviour?
- What are the different options for him to disclose this behaviour?
- Is it in the public interest for this behaviour to be disclosed?
- How do Mr Forbes' personal feelings complicate the issue?
- What are the consequences for him personally of blowing the whistle?

References
GOV.UK. (2013, June 6). *Whilstleblowing*. Retrieved from http://www.gov.uk/whistleblowing
Historic Scotland. (n.d.). *What is listing?* Retrieved from http://www.historic-scotland.gov.uk/index/heritage/historicandlistedbuildings/listing.htm

Key words & phrases
on the grounds that

socialize

to proceed with

not uncommon

against the advice

clear-cut

a contravention of

listed buildings

to disclose

blowing the whistle

Self study

Look on the Internet to find examples of ethical case studies related to your discipline. Analyze one of the cases using the ethical questions you learnt in this unit, or appropriate standards or guidelines. Write a report of your ethical case study, recommending a course of action. Follow the guidelines for reports that you studied in Units 2 and 6.

Unit 8

Critical reading and academic argument

Section 1 A point of view

What the university expects:
- awareness of how knowledge is advanced – tolerate temporary and conditional viewpoints; consider opposing positions

Contexts:
- responding to the question, *To what extent?*

Aims:
- to understand and work with temporary viewpoints
- to recognize and analyze stance
- to show nuanced endorsement of claims

International study and global professional practice both involve developing sensitivity to different ways of doing things and giving serious consideration to different points of view. In Unit 5, for example, Kate was surprised to learn that giving a grade zero to a student meant an accusation of cheating, and Nick discovered that his students wanted to hear him talk much more than his expert teacher trainers back in the UK wanted him to. They both adapted their behaviour to align with their new situations.

Key words & phrases

sensitivity to
giving serious consideration to
an accusation
to align with

Discussion

Think of your personal responses to these questions and then discuss them in a group. Be prepared to report to the class.
- What are the most striking differences in ways of doing things that you have noticed in your new place of study?
- What different points of view are you aware of?
- Have you changed your own point of view on anything? In what way? Is it a permanent or temporary change?
- How easily can you adapt or align yourself, and do you think you should?

Task 1 Listening for places on a map

1.1 Find your home country on the world map and show it to another student.

1.2 Guy is walking back to his flat with Mauricio, a postgraduate that he met at the International Students' Association. They have both been to an evening class at Summerford College on *Co-operative societies as an instrument of change in the developing world*.

⦿T56 **Listen to their conversation and locate the countries they mention on the world map.**

Discussion

- How did you feel about using this map? How is the world presented in maps in your country?
- Do you usually turn maps in the direction you are travelling in order to follow them?

Task 2 Understanding viewpoint

Look at the two images of the moon. Which is more familiar to you? Explain where you need to be to see the other image.

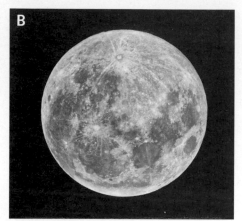

Study smart: viewpoints

What you see depends on where you stand. It can be hard to put yourself in someone else's shoes or to see things through their eyes. Many cultures have metaphors similar to these. In academic argument, an understanding of another's viewpoint is important for two main reasons:
* to identify the opposing arguments of various stakeholders that you need to counter to maintain your position;
* to help you to reassess and even modify or realign your own position.

Task 3 Thinking critically: inferring points of view

Working in groups, identify different stakeholders in the following issues and discuss their possible viewpoints. Compare your answers with another group.

a Companies in the UK are being urged to organize their pay structures so that the pay differential between the highest and lowest paid is not greater than a factor of 20.

b When unemployment is high, older workers could be encouraged to retire early to open up job opportunities for younger people.

c Wealthy members of a community should pay a considerably higher percentage of their income in tax than other taxpayers.

d Developed countries need to give aid to developing countries, even if the donor country's GDP is increasing more slowly than the recipient country's GDP.

e Global climate change is a serious global problem that requires co-operation between developed and developing nations.

f Books, films and music should be freely available to download from the Internet.

g Many countries now ban smoking in all public and commercial premises. Some are considering extending the smoking ban to private vehicles.

Study smart: carefully taking a stance in academic argument

Making a claim is an essential move in an argument. A claim is a stated viewpoint. The term *stance* means the extent to which you endorse, or give your support to, a claim. Your stance is where you stand on the line of agreement or disagreement with a claim. It refers to your position.

agree   disagree

endorse the claim   reject the claim

However, taking a stance in an academic argument is rarely as simple as agreeing or disagreeing with a claim. An academic writer has to think through many aspects of the claim. The endorsement or rejection is usually nuanced, which means that it is expressed with caution, limits and conditions. In academic argument, a stance is always defended or supported, using reasons, evidence and examples, and it is easier to defend a claim from a counterargument if it has been carefully expressed in this way.

Key words & phrases

making a claim

move

stance

the extent to which

endorse

taking a stance

to think through

is nuanced

is defended

a counterargument

Task 4 Taking a nuanced stance using limits and conditions

Consider the claim *Smoking is dangerous.* Think about the limits and conditions that could apply to the claim and work with another student to express the claim more cautiously. Compare your new claim with others in the class.

Task 5 Reading critically to identify and analyze stance

In the following statements (a–d), four academic writers take a similar stance to each other in relation to smoking in private vehicles.

5.1 In what ways are their stances subtly different? Which two are most similar?

a Smoking is a danger not only to the health of smokers, but also to others in the vehicle who have to inhale their smoke.

b Clearly, smoking is a danger not only to the health of smokers, but also to others in the vehicle who have to inhale their smoke.

c There is a widely held view that smoking is a danger not only to the health of smokers, but also to others in the vehicle who have to inhale their smoke.

d Smoking is a danger not only to the health of smokers, but also possibly to others in the vehicle who have to inhale their smoke.

5.2 What words or phrases express the differences? Highlight them and suggest alternative expressions that maintain the subtle differences between the stances taken.

....

ACCESS EAP: Frameworks • Unit 8 • Section 1   181

Viewpoints on machine translation

Chen is revising for an exam in Computer Science by looking through some past exam papers. He comes across this question and decides to try to answer it: *To what extent can machines replace humans in translating from one language to another?*

To answer the question, Chen brainstorms what he knows about machine translation and works out a provisional stance. Then he reads some texts to find more information to clarify, modify and support his stance.

Discussion

- Do you ever use software to translate information from one language to another?
- How effective is it?
- How much do you know about how machine translation software works?

Task 6 Endorsing a claim

6.1   Discuss with another student your own stance in relation to the claim
      Machines can never replace humans in translating from one language to another.

6.2   This claim is very strong. You would probably prefer to endorse a more nuanced claim.

      Think about what limits and conditions you want to apply and rewrite it as a claim you feel more able to endorse. Compare with your partner.

Task 7 Reading critically

7.1   Work in a group to read one of the three texts on pages 183 and 184, and decide what stance is taken by the following in relation to the claim in Task 6.1:
      - ALPAC
      - academic blogger
      - academic writer
      - EAMT

7.2   Work with your group to make notes from the text you read on:
      - support for the claim
      - reasons for rejecting it

7.3   Examine the claim you wrote in Task 6.2 and modify it, if you wish, now you have read the texts.

Source A: academic writer

Francis G. Keenan

Despite considerable funding, the results of these 'first generation' MT systems were far from encouraging. Frequently, the results were so error-prone that it took more effort to correct the translation than it actually did to manually translate the text. There were a number of reasons for the lack of success. One must first consider the computers available at the time, which were roughly equivalent in power to an average modern programmable calculator. Also, the translation process amounted to little more than looking up words in bilingual dictionaries. Obviously, such methods are far from sufficient (an apocryphal example of the problems that arose involves the translation of the sentence 'The spirit is willing but the flesh is weak' into Russian and then back-translated to English as 'The vodka is strong but the meat is rotten'). Some syntactic knowledge was utilised in these early systems, but it tended to be ad hoc and pre-dated current work on formal linguistic theory. The 1966 ALPAC[1] committee report on machine translation systems concluded that human translation was superior in terms of speed, accuracy and cost.

Source: Keenan, F. G. (1992). *Large vocabulary syntactic analysis for text recognition.* Unpublished PhD thesis, Nottingham Trent University, Nottingham.

Key words & phrases

first generation
far from
error-prone
manually
a number of
amounted to little more than
ad hoc

Source B: European Association for Machine Translation (EAMT)

Adapted from European Association for Machine Translation

Machine translation (MT) is the application of computers to the task of translating texts from one natural language to another. One of the very earliest pursuits in computer science, MT has proved to be an elusive goal, but today a number of systems are available which produce output which, if not perfect, is of sufficient quality to be useful in a number of specific domains.

In recent years, translation software packages which are designed primarily as an aid for the human translator in the production of translations, rather than a standalone 'black box', have become popular within professional translation organizations. These programs, referred to as computer-aided translation (CAT), use a variety of linguistic tools to improve the productivity of translators, particularly when translating highly repetitive texts, such as technical documentation. Another viable application for MT is content scanning; that is, using a translation system simply to obtain a rough draft so as to be able to get the general gist of a text.

Human language is enormously complex, and translation between languages is certainly not just a matter of replacing the words. Texts where the style and nuance of the language is especially important are a challenge even for professional translators. So we should not be surprised that the inherent limitations of the current generation of translation programs mean that they are less able to translate some kinds of texts. Users of MT programs should be aware of these limitations when they judge the translation. In particular, round-trip translation (where a text is translated into a foreign language and back into your own language) is a very bad way to judge whether the translation is any good. It may be good fun, but it won't tell you much about the translation quality: a bad round-trip does not mean the outward journey was bad; and a good round-trip might mask a meaningless word-for-word translation.

Source: Adapted from European Association for Machine Translation. (n.d.). *What is machine translation?* Retrieved on February 29, 2012, from www.eamt.org/mt.php

Key words & phrases

pursuits
proved to be
an elusive goal
specific domains
standalone
a black box
highly repetitive
viable application
general gist
inherent limitations
might mask
word-for-word translation

[1] Automatic Language Processing Advisory Committee, a group of seven scientists convened by the US government in 1964.

Source C: academic blogger
How good is machine translation?
Online discussion forum

Obviously, no machine can translate from one language to another with total reliability. However, machine translation (MT) has seen enormous developments since the ALPAC report in 1966, which severely constrained funding for research and development for the following decade. Computing power now allows the application of highly sophisticated statistical analysis and provides rich corpora of examples for some target languages. In addition to using probability, programs can be taught to use context, word order and grammar in the translation process. Many designers of translation tools now employ a machine learning algorithm, which means that this kind of translation will probably improve along with developments in machine learning.

Despite MT's clear inferiority to human translation, computers have established a firm foothold in several roles. Computer software is often used as a tool by professional translators (computer aided translation or CAT). CAT can both reduce the workload of many translation tasks and speed up the process, particularly for highly predictable text such as technical manuals. MT can also prove cost-effective by providing a rough draft for the reader to get the general topic and main ideas of a text.

The Internet makes hundreds of billions of pages of text available to a global readership and their need for translation may well ensure the continued development of MT, although this is a hugely challenging task. One of the most exciting developments for web translation is Duolingo, developed by Luis von Ahn and his team, the inventor of CAPTCHA. People sign up to Duolingo and learn a new language for free by translating sentences from real web texts, for example, Wikipedia. The resulting translations from hundreds of learners are combined to decide the best version. A very good translation of a text can thus be built up.

Key words & phrases

total reliability
funding
research and development
statistical analysis
probability
inferiority
a firm foothold
highly predictable

Source: Text summarized from a discussion thread online. Retrieved February 29, 2012, from http://forums.xkcd.com/viewtopic.php?f=25&t=39131

Task 8 Summarizing reading

8.1   Work in groups of three and each read a different text. Using only your notes and without referring to the texts, take it in turns to present a brief oral summary of what your text has to say in relation to the claim. Whilst listening, the other two students should work together to write down the summary, again without referring to the texts. Each group will eventually have summaries of these three sources.

Task 9 Thinking critically

Read the texts again, if you need to, in order to answer these questions:

9.1   What is *round-trip translation*? Suggest a better test for translation than *round-trip translation* and support your claim.

9.2   What problems will the Duolingo project have to solve in order to successfully translate web texts, for example, Wikipedia?

Academic writers present claims to the reader for consideration. Writers can nuance their endorsement by choosing from three different types of endorsement of a claim: strength, e.g., *true, definitely true*; caution, *perhaps true*; or distance, *thought to be true by others*.

1 Strength

To endorse a claim, it simply has to be stated; it is not necessary to preface the claim with *in my opinion* or *I think*. While *in my opinion*, *in my view* or *I think* are relatively rare in academic writing, expressions such as *it is clear that*, *clearly* and *obviously* are commonly used to endorse claims more strongly. These expressions can also act as argument signals by establishing the claim firmly if the claim is about to be hedged, extended or defended against a counterargument.

2 Caution

A claim can be made more cautiously by stating limits or conditions, and by adding a word of caution such as *possibly*, *some* or *may* (sometimes called *hedging* because it protects the claim, like a hedge round a field). The aim of hedging is to make reasonable claims that can be academically debated, rather than extreme, excessive claims that are easily refuted (proved wrong).

3 Distance

Endorsement of a claim can also be nuanced by attributing the claim to others as 'a widely held view' (sometimes called *distancing*). Distancing can be used to avoid commitment or to strengthen the writer's endorsement, depending on who the 'others' are. For example, properly referenced academic sources strengthen the writer's endorsement.

Task 10 Investigating language for strengthening, hedging and distancing

10.1 Read the statements in Task 5.1 and the three texts on machine translation again, and identify any strengthening, hedging and distancing language for nuanced endorsement.

10.2 Identify more language for nuanced endorsement from your own vocabulary knowledge.

Task 11 Timed writing

Without referring again to the reading texts, write a brief answer to the following exam question: *To what extent can machines replace humans in translating from one language to another?*

Give each other feedback on nuanced stance.

Self study

* Find a text in your field in which a writer discusses an important issue. Find examples of the different types of endorsement that the writer uses, and any hedging and distancing. Bring them to the next class to discuss.

* In Unit 4, Section 2, you chose a topic that interested you, completing the sentence *I want to find out about ...* In the six sources you selected, find claims on which the writers take a stance and note the strength of endorsement, any hedging and distancing. Be ready to share them in the next class.

Section 2 Reasonable scepticism[2]: how to be a critical reader

What the university expects:
• critical reflection – analyze and evaluate claims and evidence; evaluate critically the quality and impact of the work of others

Contexts:
• reading for research and for written communication for study and work

Aims:
• to understand how to read critically for a writing purpose
• to analyze argument structure
• to evaluate assumptions in arguments

Discussion

• As a class, discuss the question *How much time should I spend studying each week at university?* Read the university guidelines on page 187.
• Is the Gateway University answer surprising?

---

[2] The term 'reasonable scepticism' is borrowed with permission from Wallace, M., & Wray, A. (2011). *Critical reading and writing for postgraduates.* London: Sage.

Task 1 Reflecting on personal goals

How much time do you spend studying each week? Divide your study time into being taught by a teacher and working on your own. What do you mostly do when you are working on your own? What changes will you need to make before you align with the university's expectations?

Prospective students: FAQs

How much time should I spend studying each week?

One important difference between school and university is not the total amount of time spent learning, but the amount of time spent learning independently. Undergraduates are timetabled to spend only about ten per cent of their time being taught directly by their specialist lecturers and tutors in classes, tutorials and lectures. The figure varies slightly between subject disciplines and even between courses in the same department, but ten per cent is a good guide[3]. The implication of this is that you can expect to spend around 90 per cent of your time in independent study, and much of that time you will spend reading in your subject area and preparing for assignments and exams. Postgraduate students can expect an even higher figure than 90 per cent.

It is useful to think of yourself while at university as doing a full time job. UK workers in full-time jobs put in an average of 40 hours every week[4]. Of course, many professionals, for example, managers, teachers and those who own their own businesses, work longer hours. As a highly motivated student who wants to be successful, you will align yourself closer to this group. How many hours a week do you expect to invest in learning independently?

Discussion

'At university, you are expected not just to work hard, but to work intelligently on your own. A significant component of this personal academic study is critical reading' (Argent, 2013). With a partner, write a list to complete this statement as fully as you can:
At university, a critical reader is someone who _____
Compare your lists in larger groups and make a checklist.

[3] University of Exeter. Retrieved from http://as.exeter.ac.uk/support/development/taughtstudents/skillse-resources
[4] European Foundation for the Improvement of Living and Working Conditions (Eurofound). (2010). *Fifth European working conditions survey. European Union.* Retrieved March 30, 2012, from http://www.eurofound.europa.eu/publications/htmlfiles/ef1074.htm

Discussion

In addition to reading, you will also spend a substantial amount of time writing. Consider this claim:

To be an academic writer, you first have to be a critical reader.

To what extent do you personally think this claim is true? Decide on your own stance and give reasons to support it.

Task 2 Reading quickly for the writer's purpose

2.1   Read the following text quickly to identify what type of text it is and its overall purpose.

2.2   Discuss in pairs whether you should accept the ideas in the text at face value. What do you expect the author to do to persuade you to accept them?

2.3   From your discussions about critical reading, what specific information would you like to find in this text?

Chapter 6 Critical Reading

Sue Argent

6.1 Critical readers

At university, you are expected not just to work hard, but to work intelligently on your own. A significant component of this personal academic study is critical reading because academics read in order to write.

Since there is almost always a written outcome to any reading, critical readers will have a specific writing task in mind and a clear purpose when reading. A critical reader's purpose is often different from the author's purpose in writing the text, and so it is important to keep focused on your own purpose as you read. A critical reader will select information that relates specifically to this purpose and will interact with the author's ideas through carefully focused questions relevant to their own writing task. A critical reader will make notes on the answers that will help him or her to summarize and use the author's ideas for their own purpose – properly referenced, of course.

At the same time as they are noting the author's viewpoints on these questions, critical readers evaluate the author's arguments. Most academic texts are a complex of developing arguments, and each argument is a claim linked explicitly or implicitly to supporting evidence. Critical readers recognize the writer's overall purpose in presenting the arguments and understand how they are connected. They analyze and probe each argument, identifying any claims made, assessing the extent to which they are justified by the support and looking for unwarranted assumptions. They evaluate support for the claims by asking questions such as, 'Is there enough supporting information and is it appropriate?' Wallace and Wray (2011) label this reading approach as 'reasonable scepticism' and characterize it as 'being open minded and willing to be convinced, but only if authors can adequately back their claims' (p. 5).

Key words & phrases

properly referenced

a complex of

explicitly

implicitly

probe

unwarranted

assumptions

scepticism

open minded

The supporting information can take many different forms, depending on the field of study and the type of claim. Authors may support their claims by providing reasons, consequences or examples, or even by exploring an analogy. Support can also include mathematical derivations, diagrams, research data or authoritative sources, these sources appearing as supporting voices in the text. Exactly what 'reasonably sceptical' means also varies according to the type of text, the experience of the reader and even their academic discipline.

6.2 Reasonable scepticism

The extent to which a reader is able to use reasonable scepticism depends on the type of text, the reader's own experience and the subject discipline in which the text was written and published.

A critical reader is likely to be more sceptical when reading some types of text (genres) than others, depending on the purpose of the text and the intended reader. For example, a reader can reasonably be more sceptical about a newspaper article on climate change than a journal article written by an established researcher in the field, who is writing for other experts in the same field. However, this is a generalization and it is always legitimate to challenge academic research. The ability to deploy reasonable scepticism develops gradually. Students who are at the beginning of their academic studies have to concentrate on acquiring knowledge and competence. For example, a pre-university student using an introductory textbook will be mainly concerned with critical reading to understand the writer's ideas and to relate them to his or her own questions and experience. This student is likely to take the support for claims at face value, rather than try to evaluate it in any depth. A postgraduate student reading to produce a literature review is also ready to accept an author's claims, but should be able to use his or her own experience and knowledge to evaluate them much more rigorously.

Historically, all disciplines progress by reasonably sceptical questioning. However, some subject disciplines, for example, philosophy, history and literature, introduce a sceptical approach right from the beginning as a way of inducting students into the academic discipline. Here, the reasons for and the consequences of claims are often the object of sceptical evaluation. Science and technology, on the other hand, have a body of accepted knowledge which must be learnt to provide a sound basis from which to begin asking sceptical questions. In these disciplines, reasonable scepticism starts later in a student's academic development and is more commonly aimed at research methods, techniques and models.

6.3 Critical reading for writing

Wallace and Wray (2011) firmly link critical reading and academic writing: 'One person's writing is another person's reading' (p. 14). Being a critical reader helps you to write better in two ways. Firstly, good academic writers think about their potential critical readers as they write. This is not simply to anticipate criticism: academic writers want their arguments to be accepted and so they try to signal the argument components clearly and build a structure that is easy to follow. Arguing clearly is easier to do if you understand what a critical reader is looking for. Secondly, without a critical reading habit, a writer is much more likely to be dominated by the text he or she is reading, becoming a voiceless or even a plagiaristic writer. A critical reading habit helps you to develop your own voice as a writer. This is because it enables you to step back from the text you are reading, to engage with the author's ideas and to relate them to your own.

Reference: Wallace, M., & Wray, A. (2011). *Critical reading and writing for postgraduates*. London: Sage.

Source: Extract from Argent, S. (2013) *From high school to university: A handbook for EAP students*. Summerford: Gateway University Press

Key words & phrases
mathematical derivations
authoritative sources
legitimate
to deploy
rigorously
inducting into
the object of
a body of knowledge
a sound basis
firmly link
to anticipate
to signal
voiceless
plagiaristic
step back from
to engage with ideas

Task 3 Reading critically with focused questions

Read the text again carefully and make notes to answer these questions.

3.1 To what extent does your understanding of a critical reader align with the author's explanation?

3.2 What is 'reasonable scepticism' and how does it vary from one discipline to another?

3.3 What can you accept at face value in your own discipline and what are you expected to be reasonably sceptical about?

3.4 Think about the claim: *To be an academic writer, you first have to be a critical reader.* How does the writer's stance or supporting argument differ from yours? Are you convinced by her argument?

Task 4 Thinking critically about being sceptical

According to Wallace and Wray (2011), being 'reasonably sceptical' means 'being open minded and willing to be convinced, but only if authors can adequately back their claims'.

4.1 Discuss the following scenarios with a partner. Describe what would be a reasonably sceptical approach in each case. How much can the reader accept at face value and how much does he or she need to challenge? What additional information do you need to help you to decide?

  a A first-year undergraduate Computing Science student is reading a 'cheat' website[5].

  b A postgraduate Environmental Science student is reading a report on the Lewis Wind Power farm proposal[6] by a group of undergraduates in her tutor group.

  c To help her to write an essay, an EAP student is reading an article in a newspaper about healthy eating.

  d A final-year undergraduate Economics student is reading a journal article by his professor about sustainable global food supplies.

  e To help her to write an essay, an EAP student is reading an introductory textbook on nutrition.

  f A first-year undergraduate Business Studies student is reading a software company's website about its software applications for business.

  g A PhD student writing his dissertation on Public Health Policy is reading a blog on a website about the health benefits of fast-food restaurants.

4.2 How easy is it to be a reasonable sceptic at your level and in your discipline? Compare with students from other fields.

4.3 Look back at the machine translation argument texts in Section 1. Which sceptical evaluation proved to be accurate, but hindered progress in the field?

Task 5 Investigating argument structure and language

5.1 Identify the main claims in the text on pages 188–189. Note that claims can be part of a sentence and can also stretch across two sentences. What do you notice about their position in the paragraph? What kind of support is provided by the author?

[5] See Unit 7 pages 162–164.
[6] See Unit 7 page 175.

5.2 Identify any strengthening, hedging and distancing in the text on reading.

5.3 The author claims that writers 'try to signal the argument components clearly'. These include linking and signpost expressions, sometimes known as transition signals.

What argument signals can you find that the author herself uses?

Task 6 Writing an interpretive summary

When you write a summary of your reading, you have your own purpose, which is different from the authors' purposes. You interpret the source texts in order to answer your own questions.

6.1 Without referring again to the text, complete these sentences to make an interpretive summary in your own words to answer your focused questions in Task 3. Note any comparisons with your own views or with any other sources that you know.

   a Critical reading involves …

   b Reasonable scepticism is …

   c Reasonable scepticism varies according to …

   d Critical reading is important in academic writing because …

6.2 Consult the text to check your answer and add the correct reference.

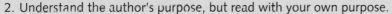

Study smart: critical reading procedure

In order to read critically for a writing purpose, follow these steps:

1. Clearly specify your purpose for reading a source – this could be an essay title, a research question or more specifically focused questions that form part of your research.
2. Understand the author's purpose, but read with your own purpose.
3. Select information that relates to your purpose.
4. Focus your reading through your questions.
5. Identify the author's claims and supporting evidence.
6. Evaluate the claims and supporting evidence using reasonable scepticism.
7. Compare claims with other sources and with your own stance.
8. Without looking at the source (so that you use your own words), make your own interpretive summary by writing the author's answers to your questions.
9. Note the reference details for the source.

Task 7 Reflecting on personal goals

Look back at Tasks 2–6 and identify which of them helped you to do each of the steps in the Study smart critical reading procedure. Use your performance on the tasks and the steps to assess the extent to which you are already a critical reader in your studies, and what you need to do to improve. Compare with other students.

Task 8 Analyzing the framework of an argument

Step 5 in the Study smart critical reading procedure is *identify the author's claims and supporting evidence.*

8.1 **Find the claim and the support in the following simple argument, and say what kind of support is provided. Identify argument signals or persuasive language which help you to do this.**

Studying English on a computer is cheaper than joining a class because there is so much free material on the Internet.

8.2 The following argument comes from Chen's presentation on exam feedback (page 148).

Find the main claim and say what kind of support is provided. What is the function of the first sentence? Identify argument signals or persuasive language which help you to do this.

Obviously, exam technique and essay technique are very different things. This means that students need feedback on exam performance as well as on coursework. At Nottingham University[7], students reported that feedback on their history exams has changed the way they have approached exams. It has changed the way they revise and the way they write in exams and it has meant that they now have a clear idea of what the examiners are looking for.

8.3 **Study the structure of this argument from section 6.3 of the text on page 189. The sentences are numbered. Find the main claim and the two supporting claims. What are the functions of the remaining five sentences? Identify argument signals or persuasive language which help you to do this.**

1. Wallace and Wray (2011) firmly link critical reading and academic writing: 'One person's writing is another person's reading' (p. 14). **2.** Being a critical reader helps you to write better in two ways. **3.** Firstly, good academic writers think about their potential critical readers as they write. **4.** This is not simply to anticipate criticism: academic writers want their arguments to be accepted and so they try to signal the argument components clearly and build a structure that is easy to follow. **5.** Arguing clearly is easier to do if you understand what a critical reader is looking for. **6.** Secondly, without a critical reading habit, a writer is more likely to be dominated by the text he or she is reading, becoming a voiceless or even a plagiaristic writer. **7.** A critical reading habit helps you to develop your own voice as a writer. **8.** This is because it enables you to step back from the text you are reading, to engage with the author's ideas and to relate them to your own.

8.4 The following argument from an early objection to the Lewis Wind Power wind farm proposal (page 175) contains a strongly endorsed claim and a counterclaim with weak or neutral endorsement[8].

Find these claims. Why is the counterclaim weakly endorsed? Explain the reason for its position in the paragraph.

The only benefit of the proposed wind farm is its potential contribution to carbon saving, but we do not have data that can be weighed against all the adverse impacts. However, the most telling argument against the development is that this is a Special Protection Area, designated to protect breeding populations of rare birds. The legal protection that such areas enjoy makes it strange that it should ever have been considered for a massive wind farm, whatever the effect on Scotland's economy.

Key words & phrases
weighed against
adverse impacts
telling argument
designated
legal protection
enjoy

---

[7] Thomas, N. (2007). *Feedback on exams: Written sheets in History.* University of Nottingham.
 Retrieved October 24, 2012, from http://www.nottingham.ac.uk/pesl/resources/assessment/feedback610/
[8] The RSPB has since withdrawn its objection following efforts by Lewis Wind Power to reduce the impact
 on rare bird species, but this argument still stands as a useful text for study.

Investigating argument structure and language: warranted and unwarranted assumptions

Within the framework of an argument, support is linked to the claim by information intended to justify the claim. This information may be *explicit*, i.e., stated in the text of the argument, or *implicit*, i.e., assumed. For example, in this argument it is explicit:

Despite considerable funding, the results of these 'first generation' MT systems were far from encouraging. Frequently, the results were so error-prone that it took more effort to correct the translation than it actually did to manually translate the text.

The framework of the argument is shown in this diagram:

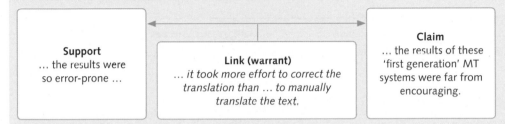

| **Support**
… the results were so error-prone … | **Link (warrant)**
… *it took more effort to correct the translation than … to manually translate the text.* | **Claim**
… the results of these 'first generation' MT systems were far from encouraging. |

If the link is acceptable, it is said to be *warranted*; if not, it is *unwarranted*. Do you think the link is warranted in this case?

Note: The construction *so … that* strengthens the link between claim and support. Compare it with just using *so* or *and* after *error-prone*.

Frequently, the link is implicit (assumed), as in this argument from the abstract of the ADAS report in Unit 2. The first sentence gives some background to the argument.

Advanced Driver Assistance Systems are intended to reduce traffic accidents and fatalities. The design of these systems is usually based on research on driving in Western countries. However, with the increase in car ownership in countries such as China, there is a need to investigate how these systems should be designed for developing markets.[9]

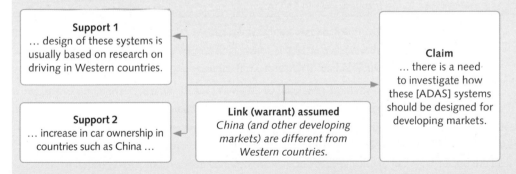

| **Support 1**
… design of these systems is usually based on research on driving in Western countries. | **Link (warrant) assumed**
China (and other developing markets) are different from Western countries. | **Claim**
… there is a need to investigate how these [ADAS] systems should be designed for developing markets. |
| **Support 2**
… increase in car ownership in countries such as China … | | |

As a critical reader, are you prepared to accept this assumption as warranted?

An assumption can be made by authors because it is part of the background knowledge that they share with their intended reader. It saves everyone precious writing and reading time if readers can make the mental jumps over the gap between support and claim. However, a critical reader needs to identify any assumptions in order to evaluate them. In fact, unwarranted assumptions are often the weakest component in the argument structure. Finding and challenging a hidden assumption in an argument is an essential strategy in critical reading.

[9] Lingdren, A., Chen, F., Jordan, P.W. & Zhang, H. (2008). Requirements for the design of Advanced Driver Assistance Systems:
The differences between Swedish and Chinese drivers. *International Journal of Design* 2 (2), 41–54.

Task 9 Identifying assumptions

9.1 What assumption is made every time a writer refers to 'Western countries'?

9.2 This one-sentence argument contains at least one implicit or hidden assumption that the reader has to make in order to link the claim and supporting reason.

Studying English on a computer is cheaper than joining a class because there is so much free material on the Internet.

Explain any assumptions that you can find. Are these assumptions warranted?

9.3 Find an assumption in the argument from Chen's presentation on page 192. Is it warranted?

Task 10 Reading critically to analyze and evaluate an argument

10.1 State the assumption linking the support to the claim in this argument from Unit 1. You can make an argument diagram to help you. Is the assumption warranted?

A professional e-mail has to be written with much more care than an e-mail to a friend and looks very different. At university, you will have to write professional e-mails to the staff, e.g., professors, lecturers and secretaries, and to other students and outside organizations … You should always think about your readers because they will evaluate you on the basis of how you write.

10.2 Two possible alternative assumptions could link the support to the claim in this argument from Unit 7.

Is either of them warranted? You can make an argument diagram to help you.

Essay is the most popular mode of assessment by universities. However, universities now have few resources to give individual help to students. Yet they still demand students pay attention to critical evaluation, balanced argument, structure and coherence in essays. Our highly skilled writers have many years' experience and understand the academic requirements. Using our essays can help you to meet these requirements.

10.3 The main claims in the arguments in Tasks 8 and 10, and in the Investigating argument structure and language examples, are placed sometimes before, sometimes in the middle and sometimes after their support.

Can you think of any reasons for these differences?

Study smart: argument structure

- Each argument must have at least one claim and some supporting information.
- Arguments can be any length, from one or two sentences to a complete PhD thesis.
- Longer arguments may have main claims, supporting claims and counterclaims. The longest arguments have an elaborate framework constructed from many shorter arguments.
- Writers generally build each argument within a paragraph structure.
- The argument is sometimes introduced and supported by a background claim linking with the previous paragraph (sometimes identified as a 'topic sentence'). Often a counterclaim is introduced first (signalled as a concession) so it can be dismissed before the claim which the writer endorses is presented.

- The main claim is the main idea of the paragraph and its position in the paragraph is determined by the author's need for clarity, cohesion and persuasive force.
- The supporting information can take a variety of forms: reasons, purposes or consequences; examples or analogies; mathematical derivations, diagrams, tables or graphs; research data or authoritative sources – other voices in the argument.
- The supporting information is linked to the claim by information that justifies or warrants the claim.
- The justification or warrant may be stated (explicit) or assumed (implicit).
- Assumed justification is often the weakest component in an argument's structure and therefore has critical importance.

Task 11 Timed writing from reading

11.1 Draft a brief answer to this question without looking back to the text about critical reading in Task 2.

How important is it to be a critical reader in order to write good academic arguments?

11.2 Re-read section 6.3 *Critical reading for writing* of the text on page 189 and correct your draft as necessary.

Task 12 Timed writing from discussion

12.1 Choose one issue from Section 1, Task 3 on page 180 and decide your viewpoint. Prepare a brief oral presentation explaining your stance on the issue.

12.2 Work in pairs. Present your stance to your partner, then change roles. You can challenge each other's stance.

12.3 Together, write a short argument about one of the claims, explaining and supporting your stance.

12.4 Exchange with another pair and read their argument critically. How convincing is it? Do they make any unwarranted assumptions? What further information do they need to include to make it more convincing?

Self study

* Find a text in your field in which a writer discusses an important issue. What type of supporting evidence does the writer present for any claims? Evaluate any assumptions made. Bring your ideas to the next class for discussion.

* In Unit 4, Section 2, you chose a topic that interested you, completing the sentence *I want to find out about ...*
Make your purpose more specific by writing a question, or questions, you would like to answer, and then use the critical reading procedure to read the six sources you selected at the end of Unit 4. Be prepared to report what you learnt in the next class.

Section 3 Writer's voice: reasonable persuasion

What the university expects:

• critical reflection – evaluate critically the quality and impact of your own and others' work; effective communication – take a stance and defend it

Contexts:

• reading and writing for assignments, dissertations and publication

Aims:

• to recognize voice in argument
• to review ways of being persuasive in academic texts
• to begin to develop a voice when writing from data and from sources

Discussion

Read the lecturers' comments about their students' writing in the speech bubbles below.

• How can a writer make the move from descriptive to persuasive writing?
• What do you think is meant by *voice* in the context of university writing?
• Explain the analogies of the pearls and the lemons.

'They don't signal the importance of the points they are making clearly enough. The writing is almost too descriptive and not persuasive enough.'

'When I give them lemons, I don't want lemons back – I want the juice.'

'When they write, they have no voice – they just string together other people's ideas like pearls in a necklace.'

Task 1 Reading to understand writer's voice

1.1 Compare your Discussion answers with the following explanation of writer's voice.

1.2 Use the information in the second paragraph to make your own checklist for writing with a clear voice.

7.2 Writer's voice

In high school English essays, your writing is expected to be creative and expressive; the information you are presenting is often less important than the way you express it – your voice. In contrast, writing about academic subjects at university demands absolutely accurate and precise information, a demand that can be so intimidating that students lose their voice.

Many students writing in their academic fields make the mistake of hiding completely behind other people's ideas and data. Such voiceless writers simply describe: they fail to relate ideas, e.g., by comparing and contrasting them; they fail to present the ideas and data as evidence for their own claims; they avoid making comments that evaluate or interpret the evidence. Rather like a string of pearls, their texts 'simply read as a string of quotations, devoid of the student's academic voice that "ties" the ideas together into a coherent argument' (University of Wollongong, 2006).

Reference: University of Wollongong. (2006). *Expressing your voice in academic writing*. Retrieved April 21, 2012, from http://unilearning.uow.edu.au/academic/4bi.html

Source: Extract from Argent, S. (2013). *From high school to university: A handbook for EAP students*. Summerford: Gateway University Press

Source: Extract from Argent, S. (2013). *From high school to university: A handbook for EAP students*. Summerford: Gateway University Press

Key words & phrases

creative

expressive

intimidating

devoid of

ties ideas together

a coherent argument

Study smart: writer's voice

All academic writing is argument. Academic writers do not simply describe; they want their readers to be persuaded by their arguments. They make claims and support them, refute (reject) counterclaims and use a range of strategies to show their stance in arguments and to signal the argument structure clearly, including:

* nuanced endorsement (strength, caution and distance)
* argument signals (e.g., *however, if, because*)
* the position of claims, counterclaims and their support

As a student academic writer, it is very important that your academic voice is strong and clear in your writing. Having a clear writer's voice involves arguing by:

* taking a nuanced stance
* selecting and reporting evidence (sources or data) critically
* interpreting evidence to support your stance
* choosing a persuasive structure for your argument
* integrating the evidence into your argument, with the appropriate signals
* using your own words

On her EAP course, Xiaohua is learning to make her own voice clear in her writing. She has been asked to write a critical evaluation of an important concept in her field and she has decided to compare open-source software and commercial software.

Discussion

- What software do you use for writing assignments and reports, examining data, browsing and communicating?
- What is the difference between open-source software (such as OpenOffice) and closed-source, commercial or proprietary software (such as Microsoft Office)?
- Which do you think is better and why?

Task 2 Reading to understand writer's stance

Xiaohua has been reading critically and has selected arguments from four different authors, which she thinks might suit her purpose (Step 3 in the Study smart critical reading procedure on page 191: *Select information that relates to your purpose*). Before she can use the ideas in her own writing, she needs to identify and evaluate the authors' claims and supporting evidence using reasonable scepticism (Steps 5 and 6).

2.1 Read the sources on pages 199–200 to answer the following questions.

a Which type of software do most authors prefer?

b What features of the software are discussed?

Xiaohua has decided that her main claim is: *Open-source software is better than commercial software.*

2.2 What stance on this claim is shown in each of the ten arguments? Write the correct numbers under each stance in the table.

Which arguments align with your own stance?

endorsement	neutral stance	rejection

2.3 In considering the differences between the two types of software, there is direct disagreement over which feature? Which arguments disagree on this and what are their stances?

2.4 Which author do you find most convincing and why?

Source A

Ben Pfaff and Ken David

Argument 1

The motivations of those in this new open-source community are to write quality software for themselves. Studies have found that those who perform creative work due to intrinsic motivations do better work than those who are promised rewards for performance. This applies to professional programmers as easily as to the studies' subject groups. Open-source programmers write what they do because they want to, so they produce better work.

Source: Pfaff, B., & David, K. (1998). *Society and open source. Why open source software is better for society than proprietary closed source software.* Retrieved October 10, 2012, from http://benpfaff.org/writings/anp/oss-is-better.html

Key words & phrases

intrinsic motivations

Source B

Super Web Group

Argument 2

One of the largest benefits of open-source software is that, for the most part, it is free. Also, open-source software has a long track record of being incredibly stable, even at launch, because so many more developers work on it. For this reason, it may also be more secure. Finally, open-source software typically comes with no license restrictions, meaning that it may be used in any way that the end user may wish.

Argument 3

Closed-source software also has an argument for being more secure. This is that fewer people see the code, so there is less opportunity for people to know about the most intimate hacks and weaknesses. Closed-source software also has a huge advantage – it is typically backed by a large company, which offers support and can ensure that updates will continue as scheduled.

Source: Super Web Group. (2010). *Are open source software tools better than commercial?* Retrieved March 19, 2012, from http://www.superwebgroup.com/are-open-source-software-tools-better-than-commercial/

Key words & phrases

a track record

at launch

licence restrictions

end user

hacks

updates

Source C

Seow Hiong Goh

Argument 4

It has been argued that open-source solutions, with their source code available for public scrutiny, are inherently more secure than commercial software solutions, whose source code is not published. On the other hand, it has also been argued that it is easier to find and exploit flaws in software whose source code is published. The debate in this area rages on. The truth of the matter is that the security of any technological product and implementation is not predetermined by the method of development or distribution. Some commercial products are less secure than their community-developed counterparts, just as some open-source products are less secure than their commercial counterparts. While the design of security features matters significantly, it is even more important how well the software is deployed, configured and maintained, including upgrading the products to fix flaws as they are discovered. These variables are contingent on the customer taking due care – not the licensing or development model.

Key words & phrases

public scrutiny

find flaws

the debate rages on

the truth of the matter

predetermined by

deployed

configured

upgrading

variables

contingent on

taking due care

Argument 5

Another argument in this area of security focuses on the assertion that there have been many more reported cases of security flaws in commercial software solutions compared to open-source solutions. Here, it should be borne in mind that the problems may be more prevalent and widespread as a result of the popularity of a platform or software, and not due to its design or the method of software development. The platform that is more commonly in use will be the platform that security attacks are more likely to be launched, as hackers arguably have a greater incentive to hit a larger target than a smaller one.

Security flaws are a result of a combination of factors, including the software design and implementation, as well as user behavior and usage, coupled with the skill and expertise of the user in installing, deploying and maintaining the software. Anecdotal experiences relating to the number of attacks borne by commercial platforms are not necessarily testimonies to the notion that open-source solutions are less vulnerable or that commercial software solutions are more vulnerable.

Source: Goh, S. H. (2004). *Open source vs commercial apps: The differences that matter II.* Retrieved March 19, 2012, from http://www.zdnet.com/open-source-vs-commercial-apps-the-differences-that-matter-ii-39195509.htm

Key words & phrases

the assertion that

it should be borne in mind

prevalent

arguably

a greater incentive

coupled with

anecdotal

not necessarily

testimonies to

vulnerable

Source D

Youssef Kassab

Argument 6

The open-source model offers 'better' software and encourages innovation. The developers contribute to open projects to gain reputation among their peers. Some of them gain money through donations from users or through support/maintenance or training contracts. Solutions using this model have lower cost and are perfect for start-ups and home users.

Argument 7

Cost, security and flexibility are the most important advantages. Open-source solutions, with their source code available for public scrutiny, are inherently more secure than commercial software solutions, whose source code is not published. Developers will find vulnerabilities in the code and fix them. Most of the open software has large active communities behind their development. They can be more secure than commercial software.

Argument 8

[The fact that] Those solutions are more flexible for customers compared to commercial software stems from the ability of a customer to examine the source code and make the necessary alterations to the code to effect changes in the behavior of the system desired by the customer. This also allows the technically-savvy customer to potentially identify any problems in the system and to make his own changes or fixes to the software to rectify the problem.

Argument 9

Bug fixes for those solutions come from a greater variety of sources. They may be developed through community effort and distributed through channels such as discussion groups. Such fixes may be iteratively refined and improved on by the community if the initial fixes do not correct the bug completely.

Argument 10

OpenOffice.org, Apache, and Linux are the most famous and most used solutions. They are widely used and well known for their stability compared to Microsoft commercial products. A recent research survey showed nearly 50% of businesses plan to use Linux for mission-critical systems by 2012, vs. just 18% in 2007.

Source: Kassab, Y. (2009). *Why is open source better than commercial software?* Retrieved March 19, 2012, from http://ezinearticles.com/?Why-is-Open-Source-Better-Than-Commercial-Software?&id=2895035

Key words & phrases

innovation

gain reputation

donations

start-ups

vulnerabilities

active communities

to effect changes

technically-savvy

to rectify the problem

bug fixes

iteratively refined

mission-critical systems

Task 3 Understanding the role of structure and signalling in showing writer's voice

3.1 Look back to Arguments 4 and 5 in Source C. Identify the claims which the author goes on to refute. What support does the writer put forward for these claims?

3.2 Highlight the signalling language which helped you to identify these claims.

3.3 Identify the claims which the author endorses.

3.4 Highlight the signalling or persuasive language which indicates this endorsement.

3.5 What underlying assumption do Arguments 4 and 5 question?

Task 4 Investigating language for expressing writer's voice

4.1 In the left-hand column of the table is part of Argument 2 with some words missing.

Compare it with the original text in the right-hand column to identify these words, and explain to a partner what effect they have.

version 1	version 2 (original)
One of the benefits of open-source software is that it is free. Open-source software has a track record of being stable at launch. More developers work on it. It is more secure.	One of the largest benefits of open-source software is that, for the most part, it is free. Also, open-source software has a long track record of being incredibly stable, even at launch, because so many more developers work on it. For this reason, it may also be more secure.

4.2 Find more examples of persuasive voice in Arguments 3, 4, 5, 6, 7, 9 and 10.

4.3 Which author reports statistical data to support a claim and how does this author influence the way you read the data?

Task 5 Developing your own voice in academic writing

5.1 Decide whether you endorse or reject the claim: *Open-source software is better than commercial software.* Form a group with other students who have the same stance as you.

5.2 In your groups, write a short text which endorses the opposite stance, i.e., if you decided open-source software is better, attempt to endorse the claim that commercial software is better. Support your claim using ideas from the sources with appropriate acknowledgement.

5.3 Add argument signals to your claim which show it is not really the one you endorse.

5.4 Now add the opposite claim that your group does endorse. Make your claim more convincing using supporting ideas and persuasive language. Show clearly with signalling language that this is the argument you endorse.

5.5 Give your argument to another group and evaluate their argument. How convincing do you find it?

Task 6 Reporting data persuasively to support claims

Two authors reported this data from a Gateway University study of local businesses. However, they each reported the same data to support a different claim.

	addressed training and skills requirements	integrated business and technology objectives	met their own success criteria
proportion of businesses in the study	39.2%	24.5%	15%

For each author, write the claim that answers the question: *How well are local businesses progressing?*

Reported data A: In the study, almost 40% of businesses addressed training and skills requirements, nearly 25% integrated business and technology objectives, and 15% met all their success criteria.
Claim A: _____

Reported data B: In the study, less than 40% fully addressed training and skills requirements, less than 25% properly integrated business and technology objectives, and only 15% met all their success criteria.
Claim B: _____

How did you make your decision? How do the writers show their different voices?

Study smart: using data to support a claim

Writers use moves when arguing from data. In Argument 10 of the software text on page 200, the author makes three moves in the final paragraph.

move	example
locating/identifying the data	*A recent research survey …*
making a claim about what the data show	*They are widely used and well known for their stability compared to Microsoft commercial products.*
reporting the data persuasively to support the claim	*… nearly 50% of businesses plan to use Linux for mission-critical systems by 2012, vs. just 18% in 2007.*

Task 7 Reporting data to support claims

Use the three moves described in the Study smart above to report data in the table opposite, taken from the ADAS report that you read in Unit 2. Write a short text to answer the research question:
Are there differences in how Swedish and Chinese drivers interpret possible incidents?

Two groups of drivers, one Swedish and one Chinese, were shown the same video of city driving in China, filmed using a camcorder in a car. They were asked to identify and comment on possible traffic safety problems as they watched.

Driver perceptions of city driving (adapted from ADAS report[10]):

	Swedish drivers	proportion	Chinese drivers	proportion
Problems identified	pedestrians	90%	speeding	80%
	bicyclists	80%	pedestrians	55%
	not stopping at crossing	70%	bicyclists	55%
	speeding	45%		
Is this a common situation in your country?	no	100%	yes	64%
Would you be stressed by encountering this problem?	yes	70%	no	59%

7.2   Work in pairs to compare the texts you have written. Do you agree with your partner's claims about the data? Has your partner used any persuasive language to report the data? Find parts of their text which are more or less persuasive. How could they make their claims more convincing?

7.3   Compare your texts with this extract from the authors' discussion. How similar is your argument to the authors'? In what ways do the authors take their argument further than simply reporting the data persuasively?

… after all had watched the videos, it was clear that major differences lie in their responses to the situations. This can be shown by summarizing participants' answers to how common they found different situations to be, and whether they felt stressed in these types of situations. This was the case in the city driving videos, where both the Chinese and Swedish participants found pedestrians and bicyclists to be the greatest problems. The interesting finding here is that almost 70% of the Swedish participants found 'not stopping at crossings' to be a big problem, while no Chinese drivers gave this any thought. To slow down the car and stop at a crossing can be inconvenient for the driver, but, in most Western countries, this type of behavior has developed from a simple traffic rule into a social norm of respecting pedestrians. This is, however, the opposite of the situation in China. There, pedestrians must take a very careful look before crossing the road, even though there is a regulation stating that drivers must slow down or stop when a pedestrian is crossing.

Key words & phrases

differences lie in
participants
felt stressed
no [person noun] gave this any thought
inconvenient
social norm
a regulation

Source: Lindgren, A., Chen, F., Jordan, P. W., & Zhang, H. (2008). Requirements for the design of Advanced Driver Assistance Systems: The differences between Swedish and Chinese drivers. *International Journal of Design, 2(2),* 49.

7.4   Find examples of persuasive language in the extract from the ADAS report discussion.

[10] Lindgren, A., Chen, F., Jordan, P. W., & Zhang, H. (2008). Requirements for the design of Advanced Driver Assistance Systems: The differences between Swedish and Chinese drivers. *International Journal of Design, 2(2),* 47.

Task 8 Identifying types of persuasive language

8.1 **What is your stance on this claim?**

It is better to live in the city than in the countryside.

8.2 **Consider the writers of these statements. Would they endorse or reject the claim, or be neutral? How do you know?**

a Life in the countryside is natural.

b Life in the countryside is primitive.

c Life in the city is interesting.

d Life in the city is stressful.

e Life in the countryside is simple.

f Life in the city is complex.

g He wasted three years living in the country.

h He spent three years living in the country.

i I have enjoyed three years of life in the countryside.

j I have suffered three years of life in the countryside.

k I have experienced three years of life in the city.

Task 9 Identifying voice through evaluative vocabulary

9.1 **Identify the persuasive language in these claims from academic texts. Change them to make the writer's voice less persuasive. Which version do you prefer?**

a This is a hugely challenging task.

b The programme design is too complex.

c Ecosystems may suffer from a lack of complexity.

d Some software is vulnerable to security problems.

9.2 **In these claims, which of the two words in italics is more persuasive? Why?**

a One of the most *exciting / interesting* developments for web translation is Duolingo.

b How many hours a week do you expect to *spend / invest in* learning independently?

c The legal protection that such areas *have / enjoy* makes it strange that [the Lewis Power wind farm proposal] should ever have been considered for a massive wind farm, whatever the effect on Scotland's economy.

d Without a critical reading habit, a writer is much more likely to be *dominated / influenced* by the text he or she is reading.

e Global climate change is a serious global *problem / threat* that requires co-operation between developed and developing nations.

f Computing power now allows the application of highly *sophisticated / complex* statistical analysis and provides a *large / rich* corpora of examples for some target languages.

g It is always *legitimate / acceptable* to *question / challenge* academic research.

h Students reported that feedback on their history exams has *improved / changed* the way they have approached exams.

i A postgraduate student reading to produce a literature review is also ready to accept an author's claims, but should be able to evaluate them much more *rigorously / carefully*.

j Although the Global Positioning System (GPS) has *revolutionized / changed* many aspects of government and business activity, it has some limitations.

k Universities now have few resources to give individual help to students. Yet they still *demand / ask* students to pay attention to critical evaluation, balanced argument, structure and coherence in essays.

l Assumed justification is often the weakest component in an argument's structure and therefore has *great / critical* importance.

9.3 Here are two versions of the same text from Source C on page 184. Which version shows the author's voice?

a Despite MT's inferiority to human translation, computers have established a foothold in several roles. Computer software is used as a tool by professional translators. CAT can reduce the workload of many translation tasks and speed up the process for predictable text such as technical manuals.

b Despite MT's clear inferiority to human translation, computers have established a firm foothold in several roles. Computer software is often used as a tool by professional translators. CAT can both reduce the workload of many translation tasks and speed up the process, particularly for highly predictable text such as technical manuals.

9.4 Underline the words that add persuasive force to the following statements. In each case, do they maximize or minimize?

a This is not simply to anticipate criticism.

b 'Reasonable scepticism' is 'being open minded and willing to be convinced, but only if authors can adequately back their claims' (Wallace & Wray, 2011).

c A postgraduate student reading to produce a literature review is also ready to accept an author's claims, but should be able to evaluate them much more rigorously.

d Although the Global Positioning System (GPS) has revolutionized many aspects of government and business activity, it has some limitations.

e However, universities now have few resources to give individual help to students.

f Our highly skilled writers have many years' experience and understand the academic requirements.

g 'Health is a state of complete physical, mental and social well-being, and not merely the absence of disease or infirmity' (WHO, 1946).

h According to the WHO definition of health, few people would be considered healthy for any reasonable period of time.

i An important assumption in science and engineering is the concept of a closed system. A closed system is one which is isolated completely from its surrounding environment. In practice, a closed system is never fully achievable.

j Few computer users have the ability to read source code.

Investigating language: persuasive language in writing

Academic writers report evidence critically. They use persuasive language to help their readers towards their preferred interpretation of the text:

- evaluative vocabulary such as *natural*, *enjoy* and *waste* (as in Task 8.2), particularly when presenting problems and solutions;
- intensifiers which add emphasis by maximizing (e.g., *almost*) or minimizing (e.g., *less than*), particularly when reporting data highlighting (e.g., *especially*) and particularly to draw the reader's attention to important points.

Persuasive language makes the writer's intended meaning clear and gives persuasive force to the writer's voice.

Task 10 Organizing and recording key vocabulary for persuading

Make a note of examples of persuasive language from this section. The table demonstrates one way of organizing the language.

evaluative vocabulary		intensifiers	
desirable (+ve*)	**undesirable (-ve*)**	**maximizers**	**minimizers**
natural	*primitive*	*almost*	*less than*
context-dependent evaluative vocabulary		**highlighters**	
simple / complex		*particularly*	

* +ve/-ve = positive/negative connotation

Investigating grammar patterns with *few* and *little*

The words *few* and *little* are frequent quantifiers in academic texts. Without an article, they are used as strong minimizers:
Few environmentalists support an expansion in coal-fired power generation.
Little research has been carried out on climate change impacts in this region.

However, with an article, they affirm occurrence or presence rather than minimize quantity. Because of this affirming function, *a few* and *a little* are often found associated with a concession clause:
Few environmentalists support an expansion in coal-fired power generation, but a few support nuclear power generation because of its negligible carbon emissions. Although little research has been carried out on climate change impacts in this region, a little information is emerging from studies in neighbouring areas.

Task 11 Practising grammar patterns with *few* and *little*

11.1 Complete these sentences with *few, a few, little* or *a little*.

a Comparatively _____ is known about the detailed floristic and vegetational history of these ecologically unique islands.

b The vast majority of the poorest children gained _____, if any, qualifications from their schooling.

c Carnivores are among the most socially complex mammals, although only _____ of them form sociable groups.

d Whilst a thorough understanding of Artificial Intelligence is not required, candidates should have _____ background knowledge since all are likely to meet it at one time or another.

e There is _____ doubt about the important standards that need to be covered in an electronic publishing course.

f Whilst most bryozoa require microscopic examination, _____ form colonies large and distinctive enough to be easily recognizable.

g In comparison to speech, automatic handwriting recognition has received _____ attention.

h One of the factors limiting our understanding is that, with _____ exceptions, we can never have a macroscopic single crystal to study.

i Moreover, the increasing emphasis on indirect taxation may have _____ impact on work incentives.

11.2 Find useful collocations for *few* and *little* in the examples.

Task 12 Adding writer's voice to student writing

These extracts from student assignments contain claims that show weak writer's voice.

Identify the weaknesses and rewrite the claims more persuasively, underlining the persuasive language that you use.

a Gathering information about the pollution produced might be important for each company to reduce its polluting environment.

b Mobile ad-hoc wireless networks do not depend on extraneous hardware. Compared with regular mobile networks, ad-hoc networks have many features.

c The research on driver behaviour in China seems little.

d A wide range of research is being carried out to develop intelligent systems which can predict, analyze and express emotions. Applying machine learning algorithms to recognize emotions is quite relevant as these algorithms are also based on the concept of cognitive procedures, i.e., learning from experience or examples.

Task 13 Writing from sources

Using sources you have read in this unit, work in pairs to write a short answer to each of the following questions. Each question reflects a different purpose from the author's, so you need to select and use only information that is relevant to the question. This means that you can refer to the sources, but you will have to write in your own words.

One useful strategy for doing this is to tell your partner what your argument is, and for them to write it down so you can work on it together to improve it.

Your answer should consist of a suitably nuanced claim with appropriate support. Reference your sources correctly.

a How can a translation from one language into another be evaluated?

b What reading strategies can help to make a writer produce better academic arguments?

c How well is the Chinese car market served by designers of Advanced Driver Assistance Systems?

d Should businesses that need their data to be very secure use commercial or open-source software?

Self study

* Look critically through some of your own academic writing on your EAP course. Does it show writer's voice? Is it too descriptive? Have you produced just a string of quotations?

* Find a text in your field containing some data. Study the way that the author uses data to make claims and support them. Find examples of any of the key argument language you have studied so far in the unit. Have your data and text ready for discussion in Section 5, Arguing from data.

* Make your own interpretive summaries of the six sources you have read for the Self study task at the end of Section 2. Note the reference details for the sources.

Section 4 Arguing from sources: assignments

What the university expects:
- awareness of how knowledge is advanced – develop criteria for evaluating knowledge; effective communication – take a stance and defend it

Contexts:
- writing literature reviews for assignments, dissertations and publication

Aims:
- to understand assignment tasks that require argument
- to develop a framework for activating writer's voice
- to use sources to write argument texts

Academic writers argue about how to interpret theories and concepts, how to conduct research and how to solve problems. They present arguments in order to move the discussion forward – to add something new to the discussion. They never simply repeat the arguments of other writers; instead they redefine, analyze, critically compare and evaluate. These aspects of academic competence are an important part of your training as a student and are often reflected in the wording of your assignment titles. However, as a quick search through university websites will demonstrate, the terminology of assignment and essay titles is far from clear.

Discussion

What do you think is meant by these terms from assignment titles and what are the essential differences between them?

> define   explain   discuss   outline   analyze   evaluate   critically

What other words occur frequently in your assignment titles? What can you do if you are not sure what to do for an assignment?

Study smart: assignment and essay titles

An essential step in writing assignments is to understand the title.
Ask yourself:
- What is the topic?
- What are the specific aspects of the topic that need to be covered?
- What is the task? In other words, what are you being asked to do in relation to the topic?

Lecturers use key words in the title to try to signal what they want you to do. You can use a glossary to help you to understand these, but if you are not sure about a title, you can always ask your lecturer for advice.

Task 1 Understanding essay and assignment titles

Write each term next to its meaning in the table to make a glossary.

define   explain   discuss*   outline   analyze   evaluate/assess   critically

term	meaning
1.	Give the main points, show the basic structure.
2.	Show clearly why and how something happens. For example, say what factors contribute to an effect or outcome, say what steps are needed in a process and why, say how things are classified and compared.
3.	Show how successful, valuable or important something is. The criteria used in your evaluation should be explained and justified.
4.	Give the exact meaning of a term; say how different or similar it is to related terms. You can contrast unfamiliar terms with more familiar terms and give examples to make the meaning clear.
5.	Break something down, for example, a concept, theory or procedure, into its component parts, and then consider how the main components relate to each other and to the outside world. Examine it from different perspectives and note, for example, the factors affecting it and the possible consequences of any changes.
6.	To answer a question in this way, you have to note undesirable features, mistakes or weaknesses of the subject of the question, as well as favourable and desirable aspects. You must also clearly indicate your basis for these judgements – undesirable in terms of what? Undesirable for whom? In what context? Why?
7.	Give the most important aspects of the topic, subject or question, along with any implications or consequences. Try to identify any inherent problems and possible solutions.

*Discuss should be assumed to include *critically*.

Study smart: activating your writer's voice

Writer's voice begins before reading. It starts with understanding what the essay or assignment title means. The next stage is sometimes referred to as *brainstorming* and is followed by developing a framework for reading.

Brainstorm:

1. Think carefully about the essay title to generate lots of ideas. Write them down.
2. Organize the ideas around the instruction in the title (e.g., *define*, *analyze*, *evaluate*).
3. Develop a provisional point of view – this can be modified later and any reasons for the changes will be useful in the argument.

Develop a framework for reading:

4. Draft a provisional answer or outline.
5. Note any problems that could arise.
6. Note any questions that will need an answer when you read critically.

These steps mean that you approach your reading as a critical reader with focused questions. You will not be dominated by the texts you read. You have a framework for your reading and writing and the framework supports your writer's voice, even if you modify your ideas as you read and write.

Task 2 Planning a student assignment with writer's voice

Mauricio, like many research students in UK universities, takes responsibility for a small tutorial group of undergraduate students in his department, the School of Health. He is supporting a first-year undergraduate group which has been set the following assignment:

Critically evaluate definitions of health as a concept for health professionals.
(400–500 words)

Mauricio gave his tutor group the following short reading list:

Assignment 1: Definitions of health

Here is your reading list:

Awofeso, N. (2005). Re-defining 'health'. Commentary on editorial by Üstün and Jakob. *Bulletin of the World Health Organization*. Retrieved from http://www.who.int/bulletin/bulletin_board/83/ustun11051/en/

Naidoo, J., & Wills, J. (2000). *Health promotion: Foundations for practice* (2nd ed.). (p. 5). London: Baillière Tindall & Royal College of Nursing.

WHO. (1946). *Preamble to the Constitution of the World Health Organization* as adopted by the International Health Conference, New York, 19–22 June 1946; signed on 22 July 1946 by the representatives of 61 States (Official Records of the World Health Organization, no. 2, p. 100) and entered into force on 7 April 1948. Retrieved from http://whqlibdoc.who.int/hist/official_records/constitution.pdf

Yach, D. (1998). Health and illness: The definition of the World Health Organization. *Ethik in der Medizin, 10*(5), S7–S13. Retrieved from http://www.medizin-ethik.ch/publik/health_illness.htm

Follow the advice that he has given them as if you were preparing to write the assignment yourself. Before you read any of the sources, prepare a framework structure for your answer.

- Analyze the essay title to make sure you understand what is expected.
- Think why the concept is important and how it is measured.
- Think of any problems with defining the concept.
- Think what further information you need.
- Draft an answer and make organized notes.
- Write some focused questions for your critical reading.

Task 3 Reading sources critically

Read the relevant parts of the source texts opposite critically with your focused questions, and map the ideas from the different sources onto your prepared framework.

Niyi Awofeso

Critics argue that the WHO definition of health is utopian, inflexible, and unrealistic, and that including the word 'complete' in the definition makes it highly unlikely that anyone would be healthy for a reasonable period of time.

The words 'health' and 'happiness' designate distinct life experiences, whose relationship is neither fixed nor constant. Failure to distinguish happiness from health implies that any disturbance in happiness, however minimal, may come to be perceived as a health problem.

Jennie Naidoo and Jane Wills, p. 5

Health is a broad concept which can embody a huge range of meanings, from the narrowly technical to the all-embracing moral or philosophical. The word 'health' is derived from the Old English word for heal (*hael*) which means 'whole', signalling that health concerns the whole person and his or her integrity, soundness, or well-being.

Health has two common meanings in everyday use, one negative and one positive. The negative definition of health is the absence of disease or illness. This is the meaning of health within the Western scientific medical model, which is explored in detail later on in this chapter. The positive definition of health is a state of well-being, interpreted by the World Health Organization in its constitution as 'a state of complete physical, mental and social well-being, [sic] not merely the absence of [sic] infirmity' (WHO, 1946).

WHO, p. 1

Health is a state of complete physical, mental and social well-being, and not merely the absence of disease or infirmity.

Derek Yach

Over the decades, there have been many criticisms of the definition of health and of the shorthand version of 'health as a human right'. Some considered the definition too inclusive and thought it should focus rather on the physical domain of health, the rationale being that health and its achievement was best left to health professionals and to the application of specific health and medical interventions. There are others who felt the definition excluded important dimensions, such as the spiritual and ethical dimensions of health. I will return to this later.

The third concern was that many felt that it was unrealistic to believe that all could be healthy. Protagonists of this view point out that there are genetic impediments to the attainment of health by all; that there are limits to the availability of resources available to ensure that all can attain the highest level of health; and that our scientific knowledge remains incomplete with regard to the true determinants of health and effectiveness of interventions.

The physical dimension of health could be measured in terms of life expectancy, the infant mortality rate and other relatively objective measures. However, with advances in technology, particularly in the fields of imaging and genetic screening, we now recognize that almost all of the population either have an actual or potential predisposition to some future disease.

Task 4 Evaluating voice in student writing: a case study

Read the two student answers below and answer the following questions.

4.1 Which student has answered the question more effectively by moving the discussion forward, beyond the sources? Which student uses very little writer's voice?

4.2 How do the students show in their introduction that they are moving (or not moving) the discussion forward?

4.3 Mauricio told the group that he wanted to hear their own voices in their essays. His advice was:

a take a nuanced stance

b select and critically report evidence from the sources

c interpret evidence to support your stance

d choose a persuasive structure for your argument

e integrate the evidence into your argument, with the appropriate argument signals and using your own words

Justify your choices in Task 4.1 by evaluating the two student texts using Mauricio's criteria.

4.4 How close to plagiarism does the weaker student come? Check the definition on page 59.

Student A

A critical evaluation of the concept of *health*

The word 'health' comes from the much older word in English, i.e., *hael*, meaning heal or make whole (Naidoo & Wills, 2000). This suggests that the concept of health has historically involved the idea of being whole. A narrow definition of health as simply the absence of physical illness or disability of any kind is clearly inadequate because it does not take into account wider mental and social aspects of a person's health. Health professionals need a more comprehensive definition. In this essay, I will first explain the background and then evaluate definitions in terms of how well they cover aspects of health and how easily they can be used to provide valuable research information for improving health.

At a time of global concern over peace, human rights and human development, the World Health Organization (WHO) was formed in 1946, only a year after the United Nations. WHO immediately recognized the need for a comprehensive and practical definition of health with which health professionals could begin to do research and set internationally understood standards. In an important step, WHO officially defined health as 'a state of complete physical, mental and social well-being, and not merely the absence of disease or infirmity' (WHO, 1946, p. 1). Since then, there have been rapid advances in medical knowledge, together with global growth in communication, trade and travel. Debate about the definition has inevitably continued.

Both Yach (1998) and Afoweso (2005) report that the first WHO definition has been criticized for being both idealistic and unachievable. Afoweso (2005) identifies its failure to distinguish clearly between health and happiness and warns that any slight unhappiness could be seen as a health issue. The implication of this confusion is that health professionals could be distracted from basic health care.

In addition, Yach (1998) has pointed out that the definition fails to take account of the different physical potential of individuals. Modern genetics can now identify in individuals different risks and predispositions for developing all kinds of illnesses, such as diabetes, heart disease and cancers – not just the fully inherited conditions like cystic fibrosis. In fact, both Afoweso (2005) and Yach (1998) acknowledge the problem that, according to the WHO definition, few people would be considered healthy for any reasonable period of time. Yach goes on to suggest that technological advances such as imaging and genetic screening have the capacity to reveal developing or potential disease in most of the population (ibid.), i.e., even those who seem healthy.

In order to make progress in national and global health improvement, comparisons and trends in health are essential. Therefore, any definition of health has to be translatable into variables that can be measured. This implies physical measures such as infant mortality rates and life expectancy. However, with the WHO's broad definition, similar measurements for mental and social health are difficult to undertake. Nevertheless, it is important for health professionals to continue the debate.

Student B

A critical evaluation of the concept of *health*

As health professionals, we need to explain clearly what the term 'health' means. It is very important for our practice that we fully understand what we mean by the term. In this essay, I will trace some of the views of health that have been debated over the decades with many comments from the debate. I will conclude by suggesting the best definition.

The World Health Organization in 1946 defined health as 'a state of complete physical, mental and social well-being, and not merely the absence of disease or infirmity' (WHO, 1946, p. 1).

Yach (1998) mentions that there have been many criticisms of this definition of health since 1946. Yach (ibid.) points out that some consider the definition too wide and think it should focus on physical health, because achieving health is best done by health professionals with specific health and medical policies. He also says that there are others who feel the definition ignores other aspects of health.

The WHO definition could also be too unrealistic because 'there are genetic impediments to the attainment of health by all'; 'there are limits to the availability of resources available to ensure that all can attain the highest level of health'; and 'our scientific knowledge remains incomplete with regard to the true determinants of health and effectiveness of interventions' (Yach, 1998, pp. S5–S7).

Yach (1998) also points out that 'with advances in technology, particularly in the fields of imaging and genetic screening, we now recognize that almost all of the population either have an actual or potential predisposition to some future disease' (pp. S5–S7).

The word *health* is derived from the Old English word for heal *(hael)*, which means whole, signalling that health concerns the whole person and his or her integrity, soundness, or well-being (Naidoo & Wills, 2000, p. 5).

According to Naidoo and Wills (2000), there are two everyday meanings for health, one negative and one positive. They say that the WHO definition is the positive one and the negative one is part of the Western scientific medical model.

More recently, Afoweso (2005) also reports criticism that the WHO definition of health is flawed because it is 'utopian, inflexible, and unrealistic', and because 'including the word "complete" in the definition makes it highly unlikely that anyone would be healthy for a reasonable period of time'.

In my opinion, the definition should be narrower because the physical dimension of health could be measured in terms of life expectancy, the infant mortality rate and other relatively objective measures (Yach, 1998). This is not possible for the time being for other aspects of health and so health professionals should work within the Western scientific medical model.

Task 5 Thinking critically

In the concluding paragraph, Student A states that ... *any definition of health has to be translatable into variables that can be measured.* This process is known as 'operationalization'.

In the final paragraphs of the students' texts, find two ways that the concept of health can be operationalized. Suggest some other possible ways.

> **Study smart:** operationalizing a concept
>
> In order to argue effectively about a concept, academics need to ensure that they have a shared understanding of what the concept is. Sharing understanding is often achieved through a stipulative definition (see page 80). In order to research the concept empirically (in the real world), there has to be a further step – it has to be operationalized, i.e., expressed in terms of indicators or variables that can be observed or measured directly.

Task 6 Operationalizing a concept

Suggest how the following concepts could be operationalized for research purposes.

> happiness   pollution   product quality   success at university   poverty

> **Investigating key language for expressing writer's voice:** reporting sources
>
> In addition to nuanced endorsement of claims, argument signals, evaluative vocabulary and intensifiers, academic writers often express their voice in the way they report sources. They can show how a source relates to their own argument by evaluative reporting; for example, Student A used the verb *recognized* and then the evaluative adjective *important*:
> *WHO immediately recognized the need for a comprehensive and functional definition of health ... In an important step, WHO officially defined health as ...*
> Student B simply wrote in a neutral voice:
> *The World Health organization in 1946 defined health as ...*

Task 7 Investigating key language for reporting sources

Which of these writers evaluate the sources they are using and which report the information neutrally? How do you know?

a The trait theories failed to take account of the situation in which leadership was required.

b According to Naidoo and Wills (2000), there are two everyday meanings for *health* ...

c ... the results of these 'first generation' MT systems were far from encouraging.

d This approach was taken up in Computer Vision by Marr [19] and elaborated ...
   He also explained the link between the quantitative and qualitative descriptions.

e Protagonists of this view point out that there are genetic impediments to the attainment of health by all ...

f Holland (2010) appears to have ignored the possibility of a different explanation.

Task 8 Investigating key language for writer's voice

Explain, with examples, how the two students differ in:

a their use of argument signals.

b their use of persuasive language.

c the way they report information from sources.

Task 9 Thinking critically about assignment and essay titles

Guy has an assignment title for his Economics module: *Critically evaluate definitions of human development.*

In Computer Science, Chen has to: *Choose a digital device and critically analyze its carbon footprint.*

Discuss with a partner how Guy and Chen should proceed with their assignment titles. What information would you expect to find in a good answer?

Task 10 Generating ideas

Both assignments require definitions.

10.1 Work in a group to write a draft definition of either:

    a a carbon footprint

    or

    b human development

10.2 Why is the concept you have chosen important and how is it measured? Can you think of any problems associated with defining it? What further information do you need?

10.3 Report your definition and discussion to the class.

Task 11 Critically evaluate the concept of a carbon footprint

Chen decides to start his assignment by defining *carbon footprint*.

Write a critical evaluation of *carbon footprint* by following these steps.

11.1 Build your framework.

11.2 Read the source extracts on pages 216–218.

11.3 Write an answer in 300–400 words.

11.4 Peer review each other's texts, focusing on evidence of writer's voice.

Extract 1

Thomas Wiedmann and Jan Minx

The term 'carbon footprint' has become tremendously popular over the last few years and is now in widespread use across the media – at least in the United Kingdom. With climate change high up on the political and corporate agenda, carbon footprint calculations are in strong demand. Numerous approaches have been proposed to provide estimates, ranging from basic online calculators to sophisticated life-cycle analysis or input–output-based methods and tools. Despite its ubiquitous use, however, there is an apparent lack of academic definitions of what exactly a 'carbon footprint' is meant to be. The scientific literature is surprisingly void of clarifications, despite the fact that countless studies in energy and ecological economics that could have claimed to measure a 'carbon footprint' have been published over decades.

This report explores the apparent discrepancy between public and academic use of the term 'carbon footprint' and suggests a scientific definition based on commonly accepted accounting principles and modelling approaches. It addresses methodological question such as system boundaries, completeness, comprehensiveness, units and robustness of the indicator.

We propose the following definition of the term 'carbon footprint':

'The carbon footprint is a measure of the exclusive total amount of carbon dioxide emissions that is directly and indirectly caused by an activity or is accumulated over the life stages of a product.'

This includes activities of individuals, populations, governments, companies, organisations, processes, industry sectors, etc. Products include goods and services. In any case, all direct (on-site, internal) and indirect emissions (off-site, external, embodied, upstream, downstream) need to be taken into account. The definition provides some answers to the questions posed at the beginning. We include only CO_2 in the analysis, being well aware that there are other substances with greenhouse warming potential. However, many of those are either not based on carbon or are more difficult to quantify because of data availability. Methane could easily be included, but what information is gained from a partially aggregated indicator, that includes just two of a number of relevant greenhouse gases? A comprehensive greenhouse gas indicator should include all these gases and could, for example, be termed 'climate footprint'. In the case of 'carbon footprint', we opt for the most practical and clear solution and include only CO_2.

Key words & phrases
the media
high up on the agenda
in strong demand
ubiquitous
void of
countless studies
the discrepancy between
accounting principles
system boundaries
indicator
questions posed
opt for

Source: Wiedmann, T., & Minx, J. (2008). A definition of 'carbon footprint'. In C. C. Pertsova (Ed.), *Ecological economics research trends* (pp. 1–11). Hauppauge NY, USA: Nova Science Publishers. Retrieved October 3, 2012, from http://www.censa.org.uk/docs/ISA-UK_Report_07-01_carbon _footprint.pdf

Extract 2

Laurence A. Wright, Simon Kemp and Ian Williams

As the threat of climate change becomes more acute, so does the need for adequate measures of impact(s), management and mitigation. Although carbon footprints are increasingly being used by organizations in the public and private sectors, a number of challenges and questions need to be addressed; among them, what does the term 'carbon footprint' actually mean? The term needs a universally accepted definition before a consistent, accurate, comparable and transferable methodology can be developed. This article investigates the range of current definitions proposed for a carbon footprint in the context of inventoried emissions, applications, boundaries and limitations. We argue that to only account for CO_2 emissions would result in the omission of almost a third of GHGs[11] and a significant gap in their global management, whilst inclusion of all GHGs is very time-consuming and expensive, and should be considered only in system-specific life cycle-based assessments; this requires a separate definition, name and methodology. We suggest that as data collection for CO_2 and CH_4 emissions is relatively straightforward, these two carbon-based gases should be used in the determination of a carbon footprint. This should allow the carbon footprint to become a cost-effective, practical and repeatable metric that can be adopted by all types of organizations across the globe as a 'baseline' indicator. However, it is likely that a more comprehensive metric will be required in some circumstances and by some organizations, so we also propose further GHG inclusion for full life cycle assessment-based assessments; where complete data is obtainable it can be used to provide a 'climate footprint'. This name reflects the addition of noncarbon-based gases and encompasses the full range of gases used in the global political community's response in managing climate change. We conclude by considering lessons learnt with the proposal of sound and pragmatic definitions.

Carbon footprint: Measure of the total amount of CO_2 and CH_4 emissions of a defined population, system or activity, considering all relevant sources, sinks and storage within the spatial and temporal boundary of the population, system or activity of interest. Calculated as CO_2 equivalent using the relevant 100-year global warming potential.

Climate footprint: A measure of the total amount of CO_2, CH_4, nitrous oxide, hydrofluorocarbons, perfluorocarbons and sulfur hexafluoride emissions of a defined population, system or activity, considering all relevant sources, sinks and storage within the spatial and temporal boundary of the population, system or activity of interest. Calculated as CO_2 equivalent using the relevant 100-year global warming potential.

Key words & phrases
as …, so …
acute
mitigation
universally accepted
a metric
a baseline indicator
encompasses
lessons learnt
sound
pragmatic
sinks
spatial
temporal

Source: Wright, L. A., Kemp S., & Williams, I. (2011). 'Carbon footprinting': Towards a universally accepted definition. *Carbon Management*, 2(1), 61–72. Retrieved April 21, 2012, from http://www.future-science.com/doi/abs/10.4155/cmt.10.39

[11]greenhouse gases

Extract 3

Ian Williams, Simon Kemp, Jonathan Coello, David A. Turner and Laurence A. Wright

p. 55

The term 'carbon footprint' has been criticized in the past as a misnomer, given that it does not have a unit of area while the word 'footprint' suggests a form of land take [7]. However, there is already wide acceptance of the term 'footprint' as a measure of human environmental impact and, thus, the fact that the carbon footprint does not apply literally to an amount of land area is not a conceptual problem with the use of the term. Furthermore, the additional uncertainties introduced by converting to a unit of land take makes such a calculation step undesirable [4].

A multitude of definitions for the carbon footprint have been forwarded in both the academic press [3, 4, 8] and grey literature[12] [101, 102]. Some definitions include only CO_2 emissions [4], others include all GHGs [8], some involve all direct and indirect GHG emissions [3], while others stipulate that only direct fuel and energy use should be included [101]. To reduce confusion surrounding the definition of a carbon footprint, Wright et al. recently proposed a definition aimed at being practicable, requiring only relatively easily obtainable data, whilst still capturing the bulk of anthropogenic climate forcing [3]. For the purposes of this article, we adopt the definition for a carbon footprint as proposed by Wright et al. [3], as we believe it to be the most clear, pragmatic and accurate definition available.

p. 61

When calculating a carbon footprint, emissions of both CO_2 and CH_4 are [sic] accounted for. However, it is desirable to express a carbon footprint using a single meaningful unit rather than separate emissions quantities for each GHG [33]. The unit used for this purpose is CO_{2e}, which is based on a calculation of the GWP[13] of 1 kg of a GHG over a certain number of years and expressed as the amount of CO_2 that would cause the same effect if emitted to the atmosphere.

Source: Williams, I., Kemp, S. Coello, J. Turner, D.A., & Wright, L.A. (2012). A beginner's guide to carbon footprinting. *Carbon Management,* Special report, *3*(1), 55–67.

Key words & phrases

a misnomer
land take
wide acceptance
literally
a multitude of
practicable
capturing
the bulk of
anthropogenic
a meaningful unit

Self study

* Find some writing from sources in your field, for example, a literature review. Find examples showing writer's voice in using the sources and note the citation and referencing conventions. Bring your findings to the next class for discussion.
* Redraft your essay on the meaning of *carbon footprint* to strengthen your writer's voice.

[12] literature that is not from an academic source
[13] Global Warming Potential

Section 5 Arguing from data

Academic writers use statistical research data from other researchers to support their claims. They also use their own research data. Students in almost all disciplines have to use data in the form of statistics, tables, charts and graphs in their argument texts. Arguments about how academic concepts relate to the real world sooner or later draw on this type of data for support.

Task 1 Listening critically for claims

Chen and Guy are out running.

⊙T57 Listen to the first part of their friendly argument and make notes to answer the following questions.

a What implicit question are they trying to answer?

b How does the question change during the argument?

c What claims does each of the friends make? Are they supported or just opinions at this stage?

Task 2 Thinking critically about claims

Now answer the following questions. Listen again, if you need to.

a Who do you think is right about China and the USA?

b In what ways do you think, as Chen suggests, that the answer is not so simple?

c What data do they need and where can they find it?

d What type of units are the data likely to be measured in?

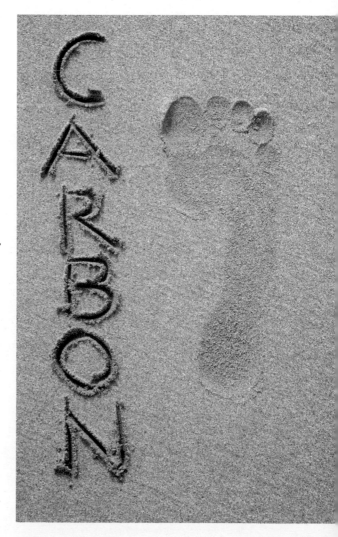

Task 3 Reading data critically

Read the table and decide whose argument it can be used to support.

CO_2 emissions and relative wealth by country (year indicates date of latest figures available):

country (from the top, HDI[4] bands are very high, high, medium, low)	CO_2 emissions in 2009 (million tonnes)	per capita CO_2 emissions in 2009 (tonnes)	per capita income in 2011 (2005 PPP$[15])
USA	5,425	17.67	43,071
UK	520	8.35	33,296
Russia	1,572	11.23	14,561
Brazil	420	2.11	10,162
China	7,711	5.83	7,476
India	1,602	1.38	3,468
Papua New Guinea	4.8	0.81	2,271
Yemen	22.9	1.0	2,213
Zimbabwe	10.6	0.93	376

Source: United Nations. (2011). *Human Development Statistical Annex*. Retrieved from http://hdr. undp.org/en/media/HDR_2011_EN_Tables.pdf (Full UN Human Development Reports (1990–2011) available at http://hdr.undp.org/en/)
Additional source: U.S. Energy Information Administration

Task 4 Listening for reported data

⊕T58 Listen to the second part of the friends' argument as they search for data to support their claims and look at the table above, which shows the data they found.

a Note any data that Guy and Chen report to support their claims.

b What other relevant questions are they beginning to identify?

Task 5 Thinking critically about data

5.1 Look again at the table. Does it give enough data to answer Guy's last question: *Who needs to change most and how?*

5.2 What other data would be helpful in seeing the bigger picture?

5.3 With another student, write some questions to focus their search for data.

---

[14] The Human Development Index or HDI is a summary measure for assessing long-term progress in three basic dimensions of human development. Each year, since 1990, the UN has published global rankings for human development. The most current report at the time of writing presents data for 187 countries.
[15] PPP=purchasing power parity – a term used in economics for the amount of money needed to buy the same items in two or more different countries. PPP$ enables quick comparisons between countries with different currencies.

ACCESS EAP: Frameworks • Unit 8 • Section 5

Task 6 Reading an argument from data critically

The 2011 Human Development Report is about development and the adverse repercussions of environment degradation.

Read this extract from Chapter 2 of the report *Patterns and trends in human development, equity and environmental indicators*.

6.1 **What is the difference between the authors' purpose in writing, and Chen and Guy's purpose in reading?**

6.2 **Does the report answer any of your focused questions from Task 5.3?**

6.3 The authors make the following statement near the beginning of the chapter: *We start by looking at patterns of carbon dioxide emissions over time …*

What variables appear to be associated with these patterns?

6.4 The authors state: *Some countries have advanced in both the HDI and environmental sustainability (those in the lower right quadrants of Figure 2.2) – an important point investigated below.*

Explain to another student why this observation is important for Guy's question: *Who needs to change most and how?* Suggest reasons for the observation.

Chapter 2:

Patterns and trends in human development, equity and environmental indicators

United Nations

Has progress come at the cost of environmental degradation?

We have drawn on a wealth of research and analysis to determine which indicators provide the best insights.

We start by looking at patterns of carbon dioxide emissions over time, a good if imperfect proxy for the environmental impacts of a country's economic activity on climate. Emissions per capita are much greater in very high HDI countries than in low, medium and high HDI countries combined, because of many more energy-intensive activities, such as driving cars, using air conditioning and relying on fossil fuel-based electricity[16]. Today, the average person in a very high HDI country accounts for more than four times the carbon dioxide emissions and about twice the emissions of the other important greenhouse gases (methane, nitrous oxide) as a person in a low, medium or high HDI country[17]. Compared with an average person living in a low HDI country, a person in a very high HDI country accounts for about 30 times the carbon dioxide emissions. For example, the average UK citizen accounts for as much greenhouse gas emissions in two months as a person in a low HDI country generates in a year. And the average Qatari – living in the country with the highest per capita greenhouse gas emissions – does so in only 10 days, although this figure reflects both consumption within the country and production that is consumed elsewhere, an issue we revisit below.

Of course, development has many dimensions. The HDI recognizes this by aggregating measures of three key dimensions – income, health and education. How do these dimensions interact with measures of environmental degradation?

The dimensions interact very differently with carbon dioxide emissions per capita: the association is positive and strong for income, still positive but weaker for the HDI and nonexistent for health and education (Figure 2.1). This result is of course intuitive: activities that emit carbon dioxide into the atmosphere are those linked to the production and distribution of goods. Carbon dioxide is emitted by factories and trucks, not by learning and vaccinations. These results also show the nonlinear relationship

Key words & phrases

equity
have drawn on
a wealth of
insights
a proxy for
aggregating
environmental degradation
the association
nonexistent
intuitive
the nonlinear relationship

---

[16] The ratio of per capita greenhouse gas emissions in very high to those in low, medium and high HDI countries was 3.7 in 1990 and 3.3 in 2005. Underlying the small drop in the ratio, total greenhouse gas emissions have grown much faster in developing countries, partly because of their faster population growth.

[17] The differences are 4.4 times for carbon dioxide emissions, 1.3 times for methane and 2.1 times for nitrous oxide.

between carbon dioxide emissions per capita and HDI components: there is practically no relation at low levels of human development, but a 'tipping point' appears to be reached beyond which a strong positive correlation between carbon dioxide emissions per capita and income is observed.

The correlation between some key measures of sustainability and national levels of development are well known. Less well known, and emerging from our analysis, is that growth in carbon dioxide emissions per capita is related to the speed of development. Countries with faster HDI improvements also experience a faster increase in carbon dioxide emissions per capita (Figure 2.2)[18]. Changes over time – not the snapshot relationship, which reflects cumulative effects – are the best guide to what to expect as a result of development today.

The bottom line: recent progress in the HDI has come at the cost of global warming. In countries advancing fastest in the HDI, carbon dioxide emissions per capita also grew faster. But these environmental costs come from economic growth, not broader gains in HDI, and the relationship is not fixed. Some countries have advanced in both the HDI and environmental sustainability (those in the lower right quadrants of (Figure 2.2) – an important point investigated below.

Key words & phrases

a tipping point

a correlation

sustainability

emerging

snapshot

cumulative effects

the best guide

the bottom line

has come at the cost of

quadrants

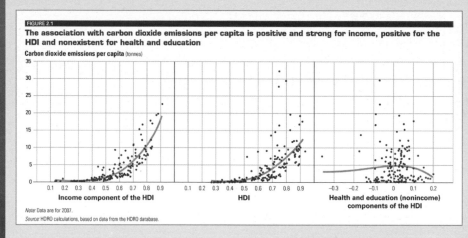

FIGURE 2.1

The association with carbon dioxide emissions per capita is positive and strong for income, positive for the HDI and nonexistent for health and education

Carbon dioxide emissions per capita (tonnes)

Income component of the HDI

HDI

Health and education (nonincome) components of the HDI

Note: Data are for 2007.
Source: HDRO calculations, based on data from the HDRO database.

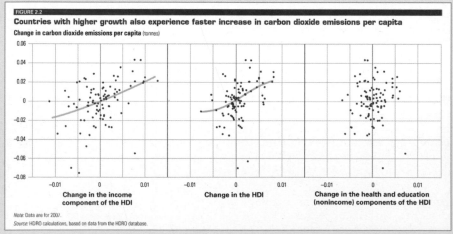

FIGURE 2.2

Countries with higher growth also experience faster increase in carbon dioxide emissions per capita

Change in carbon dioxide emissions per capita (tonnes)

Change in the income component of the HDI

Change in the HDI

Change in the health and education (nonincome) components of the HDI

Note: Data are for 2007.
Source: HDRO calculations, based on data from the HDRO database.

Source: United Nations. (2012). *Human Development Report 2011*. Retrieved April 26, 2012, from http://www.undp.prg/content/ham/undp/library/corporate/HDR/2011%20Global%20HDR/English/HDR_2011_EN_Chapter2.pdf

[18] The strong correlations between both the levels and changes in environmental impacts and the HDI also suggest that the link between these two phenomena has not changed much over time. This contrasts, for example, with life expectancy and income, where levels but not changes are correlated, indicating changes over time in the underlying processes. See 2010 HDR (UNDP–HDRO 2010; see inside back cover for a list of HDRs) and Georgiadis, Pineda and Rodriguez (2010).

Study smart: persuasive organization to support a claim

Arguing from data goes beyond reporting data to support a claim. When using data in argument, academic writers look critically behind and beyond the figures to interpret the data. They try to explain what the data means and what conclusions can be drawn to move forward the developing argument.

In an argument from data, authors generally use these four moves, shown here with examples from the fourth and final claim in the discussion extract from the UN report.

move	example
locating/identifying the data	... (those in the lower right quadrants of Figure 2.2) ...
making a claim about what the data show	... these environmental costs come from economic growth, not broader gains in HDI, and the relationship is not fixed.
reporting data persuasively to support the claim	Some countries have advanced in both the HDI and environmental sustainability ...
interpreting the data to support the argument	... an important point investigated below.

Task 7 Analyzing moves in an argument from data

Identify argument moves in the extract from the UN Human Development Report.

7.1 Identify the authors' three earlier claims (claim 2 comes with a subclaim). Then identify any data that they report to support each claim and any interpretation of the supporting data.

7.2 The relevant data come from a table (page 220) and from graphs (page 222).

In what way do these forms of data presentation differ? How does this difference affect the way the authors write?

7.3 What is the difference between the heading for the table and the headings for the graphs?

Task 8 Reading critically to interpret data

8.1 What could account for the very high per capita emissions in Qatar?

8.2 What warning do the authors give about the Qatar data and how does it relate to Chen's observation about making and selling a mobile phone to Guy?

Arguing from data begins in the same way as from text sources – with critical reading. Some steps relate to the way the data are researched and presented, as in Step 3 below. Otherwise, critically reading data follows the same steps as critically reading sources.

1. Have a clear purpose for reading the data – this could be an essay title, a research question or more specifically focused questions that form part of your research.
2. Understand the purpose for which the data are presented, but read with your own purpose.
3. Think about how the data have been collected and what the data actually represent.
4. Read the data using focused questions.
5. Be prepared to modify your questions as you learn more.
6. Select and label data that relate to your questions.
7. Report relevant data in suitably nuanced claims.
8. Support your claims with specific examples from the data.
9. Interpret the data by relating them to your argument framework.
10. Compare data from other sources.
11. Note the reference details for the data.

Investigating language for key functions in data reporting

Reporting data involves labelling the data, making numerical comparisons and reporting associations.

1 Labelling data

To report data accurately in text, writers label the data carefully using noun phrases. These are usually derived from the noun phrases that label the headings in tables or graphs and charts, for example, as in the second graph on page 222:

Change in carbon dioxide emissions per capita

Change in the health and education (nonincome) components of the HDI

These noun phrases can be long, to include more information the first time a data label is introduced, or short, to briefly remind the reader of information previously introduced.

2 Making numerical comparisons

Writers often estimate proportions or differences from the data to support their claims: *Today, the average person in a very high HDI country accounts for more than four times the carbon dioxide emissions ... as a person in a low, medium or high HDI country.*

3 Reporting associations within the data

Academic writers look for associations, or correlations, between variables because these can suggest direct or indirect causal relationships:

... the association is positive and strong for income, still positive but weaker for the HDI and nonexistent for health and education ...

Task 9 Identifying language for key functions in data reporting

9.1 **Labelling data**
In the text, find noun phrase labels derived from the graphs on page 222. Explain why some are shortened.

9.2 **Making numerical comparisons**
Find more examples of numerical comparisons in the text.

9.3 **Reporting associations within the data**
Find more examples in the text of associations between variables in the data. Note any useful collocations.

9.4 Write a report of some data from the table on page 220. Exchange your text with another student and give feedback on clear data labelling, numerical comparisons and associations between variables in the data.

Investigating language: persuasive organization in writing from data and sources

Just as academic writers use persuasive language to help their readers towards their preferred interpretation of text, they also use persuasive language to help their readers towards their preferred interpretation of data. Two useful organizing strategies are used in the extract from the UN report.

1 Contrasting for emphasis

For example: *Changes over time – not the snapshot relationship, which reflects cumulative effects – are the best guide to what to expect as a result of development today.*

Compare with: *Changes over time are the best guide to what to expect as a result of development today.*

2 Moving an adjective phrase to highlight data

An adverb–adjective collocation such as *particularly surprising*, which would normally follow the verb *be*, is moved to the beginning of the sentence to highlight and comment on data, with subject–verb inversion (the subject follows the verb).

Here is an example from a later section of Chapter 2 of the UN report:

Particularly striking were the changes in these countries [Arab States in 2010] relative to others at a similar HDI 40 years earlier. For instance, in 1970, Tunisia had a lower life expectancy than the Democratic Republic of the Congo and fewer children in school than Malawi. Yet, by 2010, Tunisia was in the high HDI category, with an average life expectancy of 74 years and most children enrolled through secondary school.

Compare with: *The changes in these countries, relative to others at a similar HDI 40 years earlier on, were particularly striking.*

A comparative adjective can be moved to the beginning of the sentence to emphasize a contrast with the previous sentence: *The correlation between some key measures of sustainability and national levels of development are well known. Less well known, and emerging from our analysis, is that growth in carbon dioxide emissions per capita is related to the speed of development.*

Compare with: *The correlation between some key measures of sustainability and national levels of development are well known. Something that is less well known is that growth in carbon dioxide emissions per capita is related to the speed of development.*

Task 10 Indentifying persuasive organization

10.1 Find two more examples of contrasting for emphasis, one in the third paragraph and one in the last paragraph of the extract on pages 221–222.

10.2 Suggest other adjective collocations that could be used in this way to highlight data.

Task 11 Identifying key features of arguing from data

Use the argument from data that you found for the Self study task in Section 3 to identify features you have studied in this section. Discuss your findings with the class.

Task 12 Timed writing: writing an argument from data

Use the table on page 220 to write an answer to the assignment title *Critically compare the carbon footprints of the BRIC countries*. Write 300–400 words.

Self study

* In class, agree an assignment title that is based on the United Nations Human Development Report 2011. Find the information you need and write an assignment answer that relates to your own country.

* What data will Chen have to find for his assignment *Choose a digital device and critically analyze its carbon footprint*, and how can he find it? He has chosen a mobile phone.

Section 1 Communicating research transparently: where is the evidence?

What the university expects:
- critical reflection – analyze and evaluate claims and evidence; an awareness of how knowledge is advanced – develop criteria for evaluating knowledge

Contexts:
- communicating research for study and work

Aims:
- to critically evaluate research claims reported in newspapers
- to understand how research evidence is used to support claims
- to understand how to evaluate the quality of research evidence

Discussion

Below are three headlines from newspapers which report the findings of research. Discuss the headlines with a partner and identify the strength of each claim. How sure is each author that the claim is true? Would you accept each claim as it is presented? What research evidence would you need to be convinced of the claim? What would researchers do to gather this evidence?

The heart drug with an unusual side-effect ... it could make you less RACIST [1]

The Telegraph

Mobile phone use and cancer linked [2]

SURPRISE STATUS UPDATE: MORE ADULTS LIKE FACEBOOK AND TWITTER THAN TEENAGERS [3]

[1] Bates, C. (2012, March 10). The heart drug with an unusual side effect ... it could make you less RACIST. *Mail Online*. Retrieved from http://www.dailymail.co.uk/health/article-2111600/Blood-pressure-drug-combats-racism-unusual-effect

[2] Fleming, N. (2007, August 30). Mobile phone use and cancer linked. *The Telegraph*. Retrieved from http://www.telegraph.co.uk/news/uknews/1561675/Mobile-phone-use-and-cancer-linked.html

[3] Thornhill, T. (2012, February 10). Suprise status update: More adults like Facebook and Twitter than teenagers. *Mail Online*. Retrieved from http://www.dailymail.co.uk/sciencetech/article-2099442/Surprise-status-update-More-adults-like-Facebook-Twitter-teenagers.html

Task 1 Evaluating evidence to support the strength of the claim

1.1 Now read the first part of each newspaper report, which gives more information about the study that produced each claim. Is the strength of claim in the headline the same as that in the report? Give evidence from each text for your answer.

1.2 Can you identify the research method in each report which provided evidence to support the claim?

1.3 In the report about racism, why do some words have inverted commas around them?

1.4 Do you now have enough information about the way each study was conducted and how findings were analyzed to be confident about the truth of each claim? If not, what other information would you need?

Surprise status update: More adults like Facebook and Twitter than teenagers

Facebook and Twitter are often thought of as sites teenagers are more interested in than adults, but it turns out that it's the grown-ups who are having a better time on them, according to a new survey.

A whopping 85 per cent of adults say that other people on the social networking sites (SNS) are mostly kind, with only 5 per cent saying that other people are mostly unkind. In comparison, 69 per cent of teenagers say that people on sites like Facebook and Twitter are mostly kind, with 20 per cent complaining that others are mostly unkind.

Mobile phone use and cancer linked

Fresh fears over the health hazards linked to using mobile phones have been raised after scientists found that handset radiation could trigger cell division. A study found that exposure to mobile phone signals for just five minutes stimulated human cells to split in two – a process that occurs naturally when tissue grows or rejuvenates, but that is also central to the development of cancer.

The heart drug with an unusual side-effect ... it could make you less RACIST

A common heart disease drug may have the unusual side-effect of combating racism, a new study suggests.

Volunteers given the beta blocker, used to lower heart rates, scored lower on a standard psychological test of 'implicit' racist attitudes.

They appeared to be less racially prejudiced at a subconscious level than another group treated with a 'dummy' placebo pill.

Scientists believe the discovery can be explained by the fact that racism is fundamentally founded on fear.

Propranolol acts both on nerve circuits that govern automatic functions such as heart rate, and the part of the brain involved in fear and emotional responses.

Task 2 Thinking critically about implications for the general population

2.1 Each newspaper report seems to imply that the findings of the studies could be true for the general population.

Read the headlines and the reports again carefully. What is each writer implying about the impact of the findings on ordinary people's lives? Is this justified on the basis of the information provided in the reports?

2.2 In the report about racism, what support is provided for the explanation in the sentence below?

Scientists believe the discovery can be explained by the fact that racism is fundamentally founded on fear.

2.3 Study the chart below from The Pew Research Center⁴, which carried out a study of social networking sites. What question did the researchers ask? How accurately does the newspaper report the findings? Look in particular at the underlined claims in the first sentence:

Facebook and Twitter are often thought of as <u>sites teenagers are more interested in than adults</u>, but it turns out that <u>it's the grown-ups who are having a better time on them</u> ...

Is the journalist justified in making these claims on the basis of answers to the survey question shown in the chart? What do you think his definition of an adult might be? What definition do the researchers use?

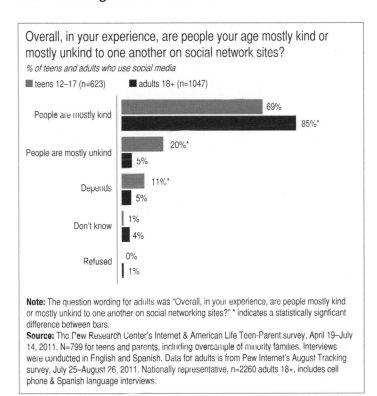

Overall, in your experience, are people your age mostly kind or mostly unkind to one another on social network sites?

% of teens and adults who use social media

■ teens 12–17 (n=623)   ■ adults 18+ (n=1047)

People are mostly kind	69% / 85%*
People are mostly unkind	20%* / 5%
Depends	11%* / 5%
Don't know	1% / 4%
Refused	0% / 1%

Note: The question wording for adults was "Overall, in your experience, are people mostly kind or mostly unkind to one another on social networking sites?" * indicates a statistically signficant difference between bars.
Source: The Pew Research Center's Internet & American Life Teen-Parent survey, April 19–July 14, 2011. N=799 for teens and parents, including oversample of minority families. Interviews were conducted in English and Spanish. Data for adults is from Pew Internet's August Tracking survey, July 25–August 26, 2011. Nationally representative, n=2260 adults 18+, includes cell phone & Spanish language interviews.

Study smart: supporting claims with evidence

Newspaper reports of research are sometimes misleading in order to make the research evidence seem more exciting or more widely applicable to the general population and thus more interesting to read. This is one reason why newspapers are less reliable sources for academic essays. Researchers are usually much more cautious in their claims and much more careful to support their claims with sound research evidence because they anticipate critical questions from their readers.

⁴ Lenhart, A., Madden, M., Smith, A., Purcell, K., Zickuhr, K. & Rainie, L. (2011). *Teens, kindness and cruelty on social network sites.* Retrieved from http://pewinternet.org/Reports/2011/Teens-and-social-media/Part-2/Section-1.aspx

Discussion

The Guardian newspaper publishes a regular column called *Bad Science*, written by Ben Goldacre, which evaluates research findings reported in newspapers and asks critical questions about the original research. Why do you think the column is called *Bad Science*? The article you are going to read next is called *Are mobile phones a health risk? There's no answer yet.* What do you expect the author to discuss?

Task 3 Reading quickly to understand the author's purpose

3.1 Read the article opposite quickly and decide which of the following statements shows the author's purpose.

   a to explain the limitations of scientific research

   b to calm people's fears about the risk of getting cancer from mobile phones

   c to understand the meaning of the words *possible* and *possibly* as used in the IARC report

   d to enable the general public to understand an evidence-based approach for evaluating claims

   e to explain how studies to identify links between cancer and mobile phone use were conducted

3.2 Where does the author indicate his purpose in writing the article?

Task 4 Reading carefully to understand the main points and assess your stance towards them

4.1 Before you read the article again, study the following claims and decide which ones you agree or disagree with. Discuss with a partner, giving reasons for your answers.

   a The readers of *The Guardian* are not especially interested in the risk of developing brain cancer.

   b The public tend to trust scientists because they seem to be authority figures.

   c It is irresponsible to publish claims from research without showing the evidence that supports them.

   d Assessing the research evidence about potential risks would enable people to make better lifestyle choices.

   e It is fairly easy to conduct research into heart disease or cancer.

   f People taking part in research on their health tend to have unreliable memories.

   g Research carried out over long periods of time is unlikely to give reliable results.

   h The risk of developing brain cancer as a result of using mobile phones is insignificant compared to other lifestyle risks.

4.2 These claims are summaries of the points Ben Goldacre made, but some of them are the opposite of his points.

Read the article again carefully to decide with which claims Ben Goldacre would agree or disagree. Find evidence in the text for your answers.

Work in pairs to compare your answers.

Are mobiles a health risk? There's no answer yet[5]

How can the public make an informed decision when there are so many variables?

Ben Goldacre

Mobile phones 'possibly' cause brain cancer, according to a report this week from the IARC (International Agency for Research on Cancer), part of the WHO (World Health Organization). The report has triggered over 3,000 news articles around the world. Like you, I'm not interested in marginal changes around small lifestyle risks for the risks themselves; but I am interested in the methodological issues they throw up.

First, transparency: science isn't about authoritative utterances from men in white coats, it's about showing your working. What does this report say? How do they reason around contradictory data? Nobody can answer those questions, because the report isn't available. Nobody you see writing confidently about it has read it. There is only a press release. Nobody at IARC even replied to my emails requesting more information.

This isn't just irritating. Phones are a potential risk exposure where people can make a personal choice. People want information. It's in the news right now. The word 'possibly' informs nobody. How can we put flesh on that with the research that is already published, and what are the limits of the research?

The crudest data you could look at is the overall rate of different brain cancers: this hasn't changed much over time, despite an increase in mobile phone use, but it's a crude measure, affected by lots of stuff.

Ideally, we'd look at individuals, to see if greater mobile use is correlated with brain cancer, but that can be tricky. These tumours are rare – about 10 cases in every 100,000 people each year – and that affects how you research them.

For common things, such as heart disease, you take a few thousand people and measure factors you think are relevant – smoking, diet, some blood tests – then wait a few years until they get the disease. This is a 'prospective cohort study', but they're less useful for studying rare tumours because you won't get enough cases appearing in your study group to spot an association with your potential cause.

For rare diseases, you do a 'retrospective case-control study': gather lots of cases, get a control group of people who don't have the rare disease, but are otherwise similar; then finally, see if your cases are more or less likely to report being exposed to mobile phones.

This sounds fine, but such studies are vulnerable to the frailties of memory. If someone has a tumour on the left of their head, say, and you ask, 'Which side did you mostly use your phone on 10 years ago?', they might unintentionally be more likely to remember 'the left'. In one study, 10 cases (but no controls) reported phone usage figures that overall worked out as more than 12 hours a day, which might be an exaggeration.

Then there are other problems, such as time course: it's possible that mobile phones might cause brain cancer but through exposure over 30 years, while we've only got data for 10 or 20 years, so the future risk may be unknowable right now (though, to be fair, exposures that cause peak problems after decades, such as asbestos, do still have measurable effects after only 10 years). And then, of course, phones change over time: 20 years ago phones had more powerful transmitters, for example. So we might get a false alarm, or false reassurance, by measuring the impact of irrelevant technology.

But lastly, as so often, there's the issue of a large increase in a small baseline risk. The absolute worst-case scenario, from the Interphone study, is this: it found phone use overall was associated with fewer tumours, which is odd. But very, very high phone use was associated with a 40% increase in tumours. If everyone used their phones that much – an extreme assumption – and the effect is true, this would still only take you from 10 cases in 100,000 people to 14 cases in 100,000 people.

So that's what 'possible' looks like. As I said, the risk is less interesting than the science behind it.

[5] Goldacre, B. (2011, June 4). Are mobiles a health risk? There's no answer yet. *The Guardian*. Retrieved from http://www.guardian.co.uk/commentisfree/2011/jun/04/bad-science-ben-goldacre-mobile-phone-health

Key words & phrases

- an informed decision
- marginal changes
- methodological issues
- transparency
- authoritative utterances
- reason around
- contradictory data
- a press release
- a potential risk exposure
- the limits of the research
- the overall rate
- a prospective cohort study
- a retrospective case-control study
- the frailties of memory
- unintentionally
- time course
- unknowable
- powerful transmitters
- a false alarm
- false reassurance
- a small baseline risk
- the worst case scenario

Task 5 Asking critical questions about research design

5.1 The article explains that research on the incidence of health problems such as heart disease and cancer can be carried out *prospectively* (looking forward) or *retrospectively* (looking back).

Use information from the article to complete the notes in the table to show the differences between these two methods.

	prospective cohort study	retrospective case-control study
What types of subjects are chosen for the study?		
At what point in the study are the variables identified?		
At what point in the study is the disease identified?		

5.2 Which of these research designs is used to study heart disease and which is used to study brain cancer? What determines the choice of research design?

5.3 What are the limitations of each research design for investigating the link between brain cancer and mobile phone use?

5.4 Which of these research designs moves from general to specific, using theory to formulate hypotheses prior to testing by data collection, and which moves from specific to general, collecting data and observing patterns in order to formulate tentative hypotheses which can later be tested?

5.5 How similar or different to these research designs are studies in your field? Does your field adopt a *deductive* approach, using theory to formulate hypotheses for testing, or an *inductive* approach, collecting data and looking for patterns and regularities, or a mixture of both these approaches? Compare your ideas with a student from a different discipline.

Study smart: critically evaluating research

Understanding how a study has been carried out enables a critical reader to assess the quality of research findings. In order to critically evaluate research, academic readers ask the following questions:

Transparency: Does the author provide enough information about the study methods to enable readers to evaluate the results?

Research design: Is the approach to data collection appropriate for what the researcher wants to find out? Does the data-collection method take account of all the variables?

Limitations: Will any limitations of the method affect the credibility of the results?

Interpretation: Are claims made by the researchers justified on the basis of their results? Is their use of statistics appropriate to the research design? How do they deal with contradictory results?

Task 6 Thinking critically about limitations

In his *Bad Science* article, Ben Goldacre listed some typical problems or limitations in research which produce unreliable results.

Find these in the article and say what kind of problem they represent, e.g., a problem in research design: sampling or measurement, or interpretation of findings.

Task 7 Noticing language: contrasting formal and informal features of the article

The Ben Goldacre article appeared in a newspaper, so it was written in a conversational style with a mixture of formal and informal language. A lecturer or supervisor speaking at university might also use this mixture of styles.

Find and highlight the following phrases (or versions of these phrases) in the article. For each one, try to find a more formal alternative expression, with the same meaning, that you could use for writing.

a to throw up [methodological issues]

b to show your working

c to put flesh on claims

d a crude measure

e lots of stuff

f to be tricky

g to spot [an association]

h this sounds fine

i figures that worked out as

j to be fair

Self study

You can assess the evidence linking mobile phone use with brain cancer for yourself. Listen to Ben Goldacre on the TED website: http://www.ted.com/talks/ben_goldacre_battling_bad_science.html Choose one of the research papers you selected in Unit 4 and apply framework for critically evaluating research in the Study smart on page 232. In particular, find where in the paper the author discusses limitations in sampling, measurement or interpretation of the data.

Section 2 Research across the disciplines: what counts as evidence?

What the university expects:
- an awareness of how knowledge is advanced

Contexts:
- collecting data for research

Aims:
- to understand approaches to research in different disciplines
- to identify a lecturer's stance towards the material he/she is presenting
- to take notes in order to apply ideas from the lecture to specific examples

Classifying approaches to research

Researchers[6] who study the history and philosophy of science have suggested that scientific disciplines can be categorized in terms of three broad dimensions: hard or soft, pure or applied, life or non-life. Examples of hard sciences are chemistry and physics. These disciplines carry out controlled experiments with precise measurements which enable researchers to develop theories with strong predictive power. In contrast, soft sciences such as sociology or politics are less quantifiable and more open to interpretation, making it much more difficult to isolate and control variables in a research context. The pure or applied dimension reflects the level of practical application of a discipline in the real world, with particle physics being more theoretical and engineering more applied. The third dimension reflects the degree to which living things are the focus of research.

Key words & phrases

hard sciences
controlled experiments
to develop theories
strong predictive power
soft sciences
less quantifiable
open to interpretation
to isolate and control variables

Discussion

What type of real-world problems is your discipline concerned with? What kinds of theoretical ideas from your discipline are used to explain what happens in the world? Where on the diagram below would you place your discipline? Compare your ideas with other students who are entering different disciplines to you.

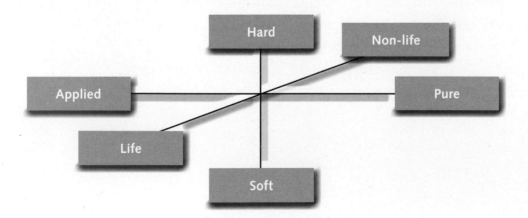

[6] Fanelli, D. (2010). 'Positive' results increase down the heirarchy of sciences. *PLoS ONE, 5*(4): e10068. DOI: 10.1371/journal.pone.0010068.

Task 1 Classifying approaches to research

1.1 Below is a bibliography of some of the books and papers that you have encountered already in this book.

Where on the diagram would you place them? Discuss with a partner, giving reasons for your answers.

1 Abdulla, F. A., & Al-Omari, A. S. (2008). The impact of climate change on the monthly runoff of a semi-arid catchment: Case study Zarqa river basin (Jordan). *Journal of Applied Biological Sciences*, 2(1), 43–50.

2 Lenhart, A., Madden, M., Smith, A., Purcell, K., Zickuhr, K., & Rainie, L. (2011). *Teens, kindness and cruelty on social network sites.* Retrieved from http://pewinternet.org/~/media//Files/Reports/2011/PIP_Teens_ Kindness_Cruelty_SNS_Report_Nov_2011_FINAL_110711.pdf

3 Lindgren, A., Chen, F., Jordan, P. W., & Zhang, H. (2008). Requirements for the design of Advanced Driver Assistance Systems: The differences between Swedish and Chinese drivers. *International Journal of Design*, 2(2), 41–54.

4 Rind, D., Rosenzweig, C., & Goldberg, R. (1992). Modelling the hydrological cycle in assessments of climate change. *Nature, 358*(6382), 119–122.

5 Terbeck, S., Kahane, G., McTavish, S., Savulescu, J., Cowen, P. J., & Hewstone, M. (2012). Propranolol reduces implicit negative racial bias. *Psychopharmacology, 22*(3), 419–424. Published online February 28, 2012. DOI: 10.1007/s00213-012-2657-5.

6 Tsai, W. M. (2009). *Robotics for hostile environments.* London: Roadhouse.

1.2 **What do you know about research in your own discipline? How do you think the approach to research design and data collection used in these papers is different from research in your discipline?**

1.3 **Do you think some disciplines produce higher-quality research than others? Can you explain why?**

1.4 There is a trend towards conducting multidisciplinary research in which concepts and methods from one discipline are applied to another.

What would be the challenges of this kind of research? Where on the diagram would you expect to find disciplines which could engage more easily in cross-discipline research projects?

Gateway University runs multidisciplinary training and support programmes in order to promote better links between different disciplines in the university, which in turn might lead to cross-disciplinary research projects. Lecturers from the Mathematics department deliver a lecture series to introduce concepts such as mathematical modelling and descriptive and inferential statistics. The Psychology department hosts seminars in which pairs of research-active staff from two different disciplines explore commonalities between their approaches to research. Students are actively encouraged to attend these seminars.

Key words & phrases

multidisciplinary

in turn

cross-disciplinary research projects

lecture series

inferential statistics

research-active

commonalities

actively encouraged

Task 2 Listening to identify the stance of the lecturer

2.1 ⦿T59 **Listen to the introduction to the lecture. What is the overall aim of the series of ten seminars? Why is this important according to the lecturer?**

2.2 **What is the lecturer's main thesis? Why is he an appropriate person to deliver this first lecture?**

2.3 **How do you think the lecture will be structured? What evidence do you think the lecturer will present to support his argument?**

2.4 **What is your viewpoint? Are you likely to agree or disagree with the lecturer's thesis? Compare your ideas with students from different disciplines. Are students from some disciplines more likely to agree with the lecturer's thesis than others? Can you use the diagram at the beginning of this section to explain why?**

Task 3 Thinking critically about direct and indirect measurement

In the next part, the lecturer is going to talk about indirect measurement, i.e., measuring something other than the concept of interest, but related to it in a specific way. This was introduced in Unit 8, Section 4 as follows:

In order to research the concept empirically (in the real world) … it has to be operationalized, i.e., expressed in terms of indicators or variables that can be observed or measured directly.

Work with other students to suggest ways to make the following indirect measurements:

3.1 **How can you measure the depth of water in a well?**

3.2 **How can you measure the distance between two far-away mountain peaks?**

3.3 **How can you measure the distance between two atoms in a crystal structure such as sugar or salt?**

3.4 **Look at the diagrams on the right, which the lecturer will refer to as examples of indirect measurement. What concepts do you think they measure indirectly?**

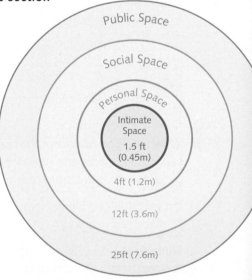

Public Space

Social Space

Personal Space

Intimate Space
1.5 ft
(0.45m)

4ft (1.2m)

12ft (3.6m)

25ft (7.6m)

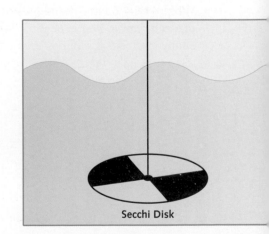

Secchi Disk

Task 4 Identifying the lecturer's main points and taking notes

4.1 ⊕T60 Listen to the lecture and take notes so that you can identify the points that the lecturer makes to persuade his audience to agree with his argument.

4.2 For each point, try to note the evidence the lecturer uses to support his point and make it more convincing.

4.3 In order to evaluate the lecturer's argument, you should try to relate what he claims to what you know about research in your own field. Go through your notes and add your own comment to each of the points you noted. Compare your notes with another student. To what extent do you agree with the lecturer's main thesis?

4.4 The lecturer gave three examples of the measurement of distance to operationalize concepts in the fields of physics, ecology and sociology.

Choose one example from a field that is different from your own and summarize what the lecturer said in your own words. Report your summary to the class.

Task 5 Applying ideas from the lecture to understand approaches to research

5.1 The lecturer said that deductive and inductive research approaches are related to one another in an iterative cycle.

Work with another student to draw a diagram which shows this iterative cycle of research. Indicate on your diagram where empirical data is collected, e.g., through observation or measurement, and how this links to theory and hypothesis formulation.

5.2 Now study the abstracts on pages 238–239. What kind of research approach – inductive or deductive – do they use? Find evidence in the abstract to support your answer.

Note: The key words and phrases for two of these extracts have already appeared in previous units.

5.3 How did the researchers operationalize the components of theory in their studies? What conditions did they set up or change and what variables did they measure?

5.4 How easy is it to operationalize the components of theory in your field? Compare your ideas with another student.

Abstract 1

Fayez A. Abdulla and Abbas S. Al-Omari

In this paper, the long-term hydrological responses of a semi-arid basin to climate changes were analyzed. This basin is the Zarqa River (Jordan). The climate changes were imposed with twelve hypothetical scenarios. Two of these scenarios were based on the predictions of the Hadley and MPI general circulation models (GCMs). The other ten scenarios are incremental scenarios associated with temperature increases by $+2^{0}C$ and $+4^{0}C$ and changes in rainfall of 0%, +10%, +20%, -10%, and -20%. These scenarios were the basis for observing causal relationships among runoff, air temperature, and rainfall, using the SFB water balance model developed by Boughton (1984). This model performed well for the Zarqa River for which the average monthly runoff from the model compared well to the observed average runoff. Both sets of climate change scenarios resulted in decreases in monthly runoff.

Source: Abdulla, F. A., & Al-Omari, A. S. (2008). The impact of climate change on the monthly runoff of a semi-arid catchment: Case study Zarqa river basin (Jordan). *Journal of Applied Biological Sciences*, 2(1), 43–50.

Abstract 2

Amanda Lenhart, Mary Madden, Aaron Smith, Kristen Purcell, Kathryn Zickuhr and Lee Rainie

Social media use has become so pervasive in the lives of American teens that having a presence on a social network site [such as Facebook or Twitter] is almost synonymous with being online. 95% of all teens aged 12–17 are now online and 80% of those online teens are users of social media sites. Many log on daily to their social network pages and these have become spaces where much of the social activity of teen life is echoed and amplified – in both good and bad ways.

We focused our attention in this research on social network sites because we wanted to understand the types of experiences teens are having there and how they are addressing negative behavior when they see it or experience it. As they navigate challenging social interactions online, who is influencing their sense of what it means to be a good or bad 'digital citizen'? How often do they intervene to stand up for others? How often do they join in the mean behavior? [...]

We asked teens the following question about what they see in social network spaces: 'Overall, in your experience, are people your age mostly *kind* or mostly *unkind* to one another on social network sites?'

Source: Lenhart, A., Madden, M., Smith, A., Purcell, K., Zickuhr, K., & Rainie, L. (2011). *Teens, kindness and cruelty on social network sites*. Retrieved from http://pewinternet.org/~/media//Files/Reports/2011/PIP_Teens_Kindness_Cruelty_SNS_Report_Nov_2011_FINAL_110711.pdf

Key words & phrases

pervasive
synonymous with
is echoed and amplified
focused attention
addressing negative behaviour
navigate interactions
digital citizen
intervene

Abstract 3

Anders Lindgren, Fang Chen, Patrick W. Jordan and Haixin Zhang

In order to decrease the amount of accidents or mitigate the consequences of them, today's vehicles are being equipped with Advanced Driver Assistance Systems. The functionality and design of these systems is almost entirely based on research related to the driving concerns in Western countries. However, with the rapid motorization in developing countries such as China, there is an increasing need to investigate how these systems should be designed for new and growing markets. In order to address this need, research was conducted to discover the most common traffic problems facing Chinese drivers, how those problems differ from those for drivers in a country with a more developed driving culture (Sweden), and what consequences these differences will have for the design of Advanced Driver Assistance Systems.

Source: Lindgren, A., Chen, F., Jordan, P. W., & Zhang, H. (2008). Requirements for the design of Advanced Driver Assistance Systems: The differences between Swedish and Chinese drivers. *International Journal of Design*, 2(2), 41–54.

Abstract 4

Sylvia Terbeck, Guy Kahane, Sarah McTavish, Julian Savulescu, Philip J. Cowen and Miles Hewstone

Implicit negative attitudes towards other races are important in certain kinds of prejudicial social behaviour. Emotional mechanisms are thought to be involved in mediating implicit 'outgroup' bias but there is little evidence concerning the underlying neurobiology. The aim of the present study was to examine the role of noradrenergic mechanisms in the generation of implicit racial attitudes.

In the present study we employed propranolol to test the hypothesis that emotional responses influenced by noradrenergic transmission play a mediating role in implicit but not explicit forms of prejudice. We predicted that ß-adrenoreceptor blockade should lead to a reduction in implicit racial attitudes, as measured by the IAT [implicit association test].

Key words & phrases

implicit attitudes
prejudicial behaviour
little evidence
play a mediating role

Source: Terbeck, S., Kahane, G., McTavish, S., Savulescu, J., Cowen, P. J., & Hewstone, M. (2012). Propranolol reduces implicit negative racial bias. *Psychopharmacology*, 22(3), 419–424. Published online February 28, 2012. DOI: 10.1007/s00213-012-2657-5.

Self study

Using the same paper you chose in Section 1, look more closely at the research method. What kind of research design is used — inductive or deductive? What variables can you identify? How did the researchers operationalize the components of theory in order to define variables which they could measure?

[7] *Noradrenergic* refers to the system responsible for the synthesis, storage, and release of the neurotransmitter noradrenalin. This chemical is released by the sympathetic nervous system and prepares the body for the 'fight or flight' reaction. It has been associated with brain functions such as memory, learning and emotions. The drug propranolol is known to block noradrenergic mechanisms. (Adapted from http://encyclopedia2.thefreedictionary.com/noradrenergic+system)

Section 3 Evaluating research: how good is the evidence?

What the university expects:
- critical reflection – analyze and evaluate claims and evidence; critically evaluate the quality and impact of others' work

Contexts:
- reading research papers

Aims:
- to understand how to evaluate the quality of research evidence
- to compare and evaluate the research designs in two studies with similar aims
- to interpret the findings from the studies in terms of your own experience
- to write a critical review of the studies which highlights a gap in the research

Discussion

Read the following opening sentences of two research reports on the topic of the globalization of education. Are you currently, or are you about to become, an internationally mobile student (IMS)? What other labels are used to refer to IMS in these extracts? Which label do you prefer and why? What are the advantages for you personally? What advantages are outlined in these extracts? Do you think there are any disadvantages? Would you regard yourself as an expert in this area?

There has been a substantial growth in the number of internationally mobile students (IMS) due to the internationalisation and globalisation of tertiary education. Many institutions, particularly those with business schools, have recruited increasingly large numbers of overseas students in their attempts to become more international.
(Kelly & Moogan, 2012)

International students constitute an important part of university life in the United Kingdom (UK). Most universities in the UK have a considerable fraction of their students from overseas and this has many advantages. It makes the university vibrant, enables contact, understanding, and shared experiences between students from different cultural and ethnic backgrounds, and allows university staff to broaden their knowledge about the education systems in different countries. (Lebcir et al., 2008)

In order to assess the quality of research evidence, you need to adopt a position of 'reasonable scepticism [...] being open minded and willing to be convinced but only if authors can adequately back their claims' (Wallace & Wray, 2011, p. 5). This is particularly important in research where new ideas are being put forward for debate. Reasonable scepticism requires a good understanding of the research field in terms of how concepts are operationalized, what methods are used and what kinds of results are produced. You also need to be able to question the findings based on your own experience. This requires you to read in detail the sections of a research report which deal with methods and results in order to critically evaluate the author's interpretation and to draw your own conclusions.

Task 1 Adopting a position of reasonable scepticism

Below are four claims adapted from the two research papers you are going to read. **Think about your own experience as you evaluate these claims. Would you accept each claim as it is presented? What research evidence would you need to be convinced of the claim? What would researchers do to gather this evidence?**

1 The transition period for IMS (the time taken to settle in to the new environment) continues beyond the end of the first semester and into the second semester.

2 IMS prefer examinations rather than coursework due to their prior higher education background, where rote learning is more common.

3 IMS who have previously studied in the UK can settle in faster and are better able to interpret communications from the tutor due to already knowing the 'rules'.

4 The ability of students to interact with others and their previous experience in teamwork is different depending on the country of origin.

Task 2 Understanding the purpose of the research

Read the abstract, the restatement of aims and the title on page 242 for each of the research papers. Which of the following questions can you answer using just the abstract?

2.1 What was the context for these studies? How similar or different are these contexts?

2.2 What did these researchers observe? This would be the dependent variable in these studies.

2.3 What factors – which might affect the dependent variable – do the researchers choose to study? Are these similar or different in each study?

2.4 Can you think of any other factors not mentioned in the abstracts which might have an effect? Think about your own personal experience if you are or have been an IMS in order to answer this.

2.5 What was the sample in each study?

2.6 How did the researchers operationalize the concepts they wanted to investigate? In other words, what methods did they use to collect, measure and analyze data?

2.7 Do the titles and abstracts provide all the information you need to answer these questions? If not, where do you have to look in each paper?

Abstract 1

Philip Kelly and Yvonne Moogan

The globalisation of higher education brings together learners and teachers from differing systems, creating a heterogeneous and diverse environment. Yet many higher education institutions typically rely on foreign students themselves to adapt to their new higher education environments. An investigation was undertaken as to whether traditional approaches are effective and efficient in meeting the needs of the internationally mobile student (IMS). Using data from the last ten years (1999 to 2009) from a post-1992 University in the North West of England an analysis of over 15,000 postgraduate assessments found a significant performance difference between home country students and internationally mobile students. Results found that home country students perform significantly better than international students, although the latter perform better in examinations than in coursework. However, there is a substantive improvement during the dissertation stage for both groups. Possible reasons for such variations in performance are explored.

Restatement of aim from the discussion: This study was undertaken to investigate the transition period for IMS, its consequences and impacts and was driven by questions about their performance.

Key words & phrases

- brings together
- heterogeneous
- was undertaken
- meeting the needs (of)
- using data from
- a significant difference between
- a substantive improvement

Source: Kelly, P., & Moogan, Y. (2012). Culture shock and higher education performance: Implications for teaching. *Higher Education Quarterly*, 66(1), 24–46.

Abstract 2

R. M. Lebcir, H. Wells and A. Bond

The aim of this study is to investigate the factors affecting the academic performance of international students in project management courses. To achieve this aim, a conceptual framework including three categories of factors: (i) Teaching Style, (ii) English Language and Communication and (iii) Assessment Methods was developed and empirically tested on a sample of international students from a British Post 92 University. The results suggest that the factors: level of details given in lectures, speed of lectures, academic Internet sources, English Language skills, group or individual assessment, the qualitative/quantitative content of assessment are important drivers of the academic performance of international students in project management.

Restatement of aim from the conclusion: The aim of this research is to investigate the factors affecting the academic performance of international students in project management.

Key words & phrases

- the factors affecting
- a conceptual framework
- empirically tested
- important drivers

Source: Lebcir, R. M., Wells, H., & Bond, A. (2008). Factors affecting academic performance of international students in project management courses: A case study from a British post-92 university. *International Journal of Project Management*, 26(3), 268–274.

ACCESS EAP: Frameworks • Unit 9 • Section 3

Task 3 Comparing the research designs

3.1 Now study the sections of each report where the authors say how they collected and analyzed data[7]. Complete the table to compare the two studies in greater detail.

aspect of research design	Kelly and Moogan (2012)	Lebcir et al. (2008)
research context		
aims		
independent variables which the researchers select or change		
dependent variable which the researchers measure		
reasons for selecting independent variables	available in Oracle Student System database	
sample size and type		
research design		
possible limitations according to the authors		

3.2 Which aspects of the studies are similar and which are different?

3.3 How have the researchers operationalized the concepts they want to study? In other words, what measurements did they make? How will they demonstrate a relationship between dependent and independent variables?

Empirical study

Phililp Kelly and Yvonne Moogan

A key aim of this quantitative study is to improve our understanding of the IMS transition period[8] and to explore possible causes of and practical responses to differences in performance between the IMS and home country students engaged in postgraduate level studies. The key independent variables of this study include student diversity characteristics (international, age and gender) and aspects of the education system (teaching and assessment methods) and the dependent variables (performance outcomes); intermediary variables include the duration and complexity of the transition period. […]

For this study, data was collected from the Oracle Student System database of information that integrates admissions, enrolment, assessment, progression and awards data for all students. This was then imported into a custom-built database used to manipulate and categorise and then export data for analysis in SPSS.

Data comprised of 2,159 Master of Business Administration (MBA) students enrolled at Liverpool Business School and registered during the last ten years (from 1999 to 2009). The MBA comprises two MBA programmes that share more than 60% commonality. There is an Executive MBA that attracts predominantly part-time mature home country students and an International MBA that attracts predominantly young students who are frequently international. […] Despite differing student entry points, both programmes include at least two identical modules in the second semester (strategic management and research methods), which are assessed via the same examination and course work respectively […]. In addition the dissertation module is identical on both programmes. The dissertation

Key words & phrases

quantitative study
independent variables
dependent variables
intermediary variables
was imported into
to manipulate
export data

---

[7] Note that in both these papers, aspects of the method appeared in the results section.
[8] Transition is defined in the article as 'international students face a transition (process of changing from one state to another) between their own culture and their new culture' (Kelly & Moogan, 2012, p. 25).

takes place in the third semester and the pass mark for all modules is 40%. [...] As some 15 credit modules (options) are the same on both programmes they are delivered by the same staff. In total, nearly 15,000 assessment items were completed by this sample and analysed by programme (Executive or International MBA).

The rationale for incorporating both programmes in the study was to increase the sample size of the home country students, for these are predominantly enrolled on the Executive MBA, whereas UK students enrolled on the International MBA are relatively small. [...] Ideally, a single multicultural cohort should be used for this type of investigation. However, this would not have provided sufficient data for meaningful analysis.

[...] Although this quantitative research is robust and substantial it is just a starting point to investigate student performance differentials and further research particularly in a qualitative direction is needed.

Key words & phrases

the rationale for

the sample size

robust

substantial

qualitative

Source: Kelly, P., & Moogan, Y. (2012). Culture shock and higher education performance: Implications for teaching. *Higher Education Quarterly*, *66*(1), 24–46.

3. Research methodology

R. M. Lebcir, H. Wells and A. Bond

[...] We are particularly interested in determining the factors which may affect international students' academic performance in project management modules.

To achieve this aim, we chose to design a questionnaire, which would include questions covering as comprehensively as possible the factors believed to impact international students' academic performance. [...] the questionnaire was informed by literature on teaching and learning of international students and the experience of the authors over a number of years as lecturers in the field of project management.

The questionnaire methodology was chosen for two reasons: it provides a consistent set of data from a large sample; and more significantly, by retaining anonymity, it allows students to express their concerns honestly, thus maximizing the quality and credibility of the data. The questionnaire was designed in a statement format to capture student opinion. The questionnaire included seventeen statements asking the student (the respondent) to rank the validity of each statement on a scale from one to five (1 = Strongly Disagree, 5 = Strongly Agree). The statements were grouped into the three categories defined earlier in the conceptual framework [in the literature review]: (i) Teaching Style, (ii) English Language and Communication, and (iii) Assessment Methods. [...] All of the questions on the questionnaire are of the opinion type.

The questionnaire was sent to international students who previously studied project management modules in a post-92 British University. These students come from a wide range of nationalities and satisfied the 'international students' definition presented earlier. The number of questionnaires sent was 300 from which we received 35 responses (Response rate 12%). Three questionnaires could not be used because of missing answers to some questions. Therefore, we could only use 32 questionnaires for this study. The research team was very disappointed with the response rate as this prevented it from the use of more sophisticated statistical analysis.

Key words & phrases

was informed by literature

questionnaire methodology

a consistent set of data

retaining anonymity

maximising the quality and credibility

to capture opinion

to rank on a scale

satisfied the definition

statistical analysis

4. Results

As mentioned earlier, our aim was to conduct a sophisticated statistical analysis of the questionnaire. However, to our chagrin, the number of replies to our questionnaire received at the time of preparing this paper was not enough to carry out this analysis. Therefore, we have been obliged to conduct a simple analysis in which we calculated some measures of central tendency and dispersion namely mean, median, and standard deviation of the scores associated with each statement in the questionnaire [37]. These measures are presented in Table 1.

The analysis of the results will focus on one category of factors at a time and is based on the values of the three measures presented in Table 1. A high value for the mean and/or the median indicates strong agreement with the statement in the questionnaire. A high value of the standard deviation indicates that individual scores are highly dispersed from the mean.

Key words & phrases

measures of central tendency and dispersion

mean

median

strong agreement

standard deviation

highly dispersed

Source: Lebcir, R. M., Wells, H., & Bond, A. (2008). Factors affecting academic performance of international students in project management courses: A case study from a British post-92 university. *International Journal of Project Management*, 26(3), 268–274.

Study smart: reliability, validity and credibility

In his *Bad Science* article on mobile phones, Ben Goldacre posed some key questions to assess the quality of research related to transparency, research design, limitations and interpretation of findings. The quality of research designs can be assessed in more detail in terms of three further aspects:

Reliability: Are the measures consistent and stable?

If the study was repeated, would the results be the same?

Validity: Have concepts been operationalized appropriately?

Do the measures reflect these concepts?

Are cause–effect relations between variables real?

Can findings be generalized to other contexts?

Credibility: Is the research trustworthy?

Is there sufficient detail about the method and its limitations?

How believable are the findings?

Task 4 Critically evaluating the research designs

4.1 **In both studies, the authors identify the method of sampling as a limitation of their study:**

Kelly and Morgan sampled year cohorts over a period of ten years, but said that 'Ideally, a single multicultural cohort should be used'.

Lebcir et al. sent 300 questionnaires and received only 35 back. They said this sample was not large enough to carry out a sophisticated statistical analysis.

What specific problems might be caused by the sampling method in each study? Think about variables in the sample which the researchers did not control or measure.

4.2 **Which study is likely to produce more reliable results? Why?**

4.3 **Which study is more precise in operationalizing the concepts to be measured?**

4.4 **To what extent do these studies uncover factors which could be changed to improve student performance?**

4.5 **Could the findings from either study be generalized to other contexts, e.g., other types of university?**

Task 5 Drawing conclusions from the findings of Kelly and Moogan (2012)

5.1 Study the table showing reported assessment scores, and the diagram from the results section of the paper showing differences in performance over time. What conclusions can you draw?

Note: M is the mean score (arithmetic average) and SD is the standard deviation (a measure of dispersion from the mean).

5.2 How would you explain these findings?

Reported assessment scores for home students and IMS for different assessment types:

assessment scores / student type	home country (UK) students		internationally mobile students (IMS)	
semester 1 coursework	M = 55.1	SD = 11.3	M = 45.1	SD = 12
overall coursework	M = 60	SD = 15.6	M = 47.4	SD = 14.8
examination	M = 54.4	SD = 13.7	M = 50.1	SD = 12.1

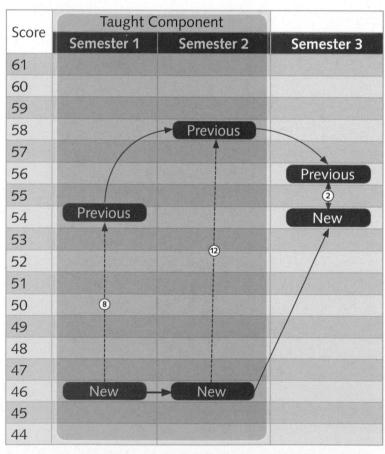

Figure 'Previous': international students with previous experience of studying in the UK (n=95). 'New': students new to the system of Higher Education in the UK (n=1843).

Task 6 Comparing your interpretation with that of the authors

6.1 Now study the extracts below from the results section where Kelly and Moogan interpret the findings. Underline in the text the claims they make to account for the findings.

6.2 What evidence do they give for their interpretations?

6.3 To what extent do you agree with their interpretation? Can you think of other explanations?

Results

Philip Kelly and Yvonne Moogan

Evidence of academic disadvantage and transition shock may be evident in the performance of students in their initial assessments. [...] There are three interesting observations: first, the IMS do not improve from semester one to semester two (but neither do the home country students); second, over the taught components of the master's degree, the IMS do not close the gap with the home country students; and third, both home country students and IMS improve in semester three, where the IMS close the gap. The gap between semester one and two should decrease if the IMS have adapted to the host education system and one assumes that there is no assessor bias. This may suggest that the transition period continues beyond the end of the first semester and into the second semester (and longer) whilst the IMS are still adapting. The largest increase in mean scores (especially for IMS) occurred in semester three when the independent learning (dissertation) took place and the differential for IMS / home country students narrowed to less than seven points. This may be due to more frequent and timely feedback whereby students use different skill sets in undertaking their own research and liaise with their supervisors independently throughout. [...]

As could have been predicted, the IMS preferred examinations to coursework during the taught component of the programme (although there is a marked improvement for the dissertation) and the gap with the home country students was much less for examination-based assessments. [...] IMS seem to prefer examinations rather than coursework (which may be due to their prior higher education background where rote learning is more common) as a means of achieving a successful outcome.

[...] The students who have previously studied in the UK seem to gain advantage in semester two which may be due to settling in faster and or being better equipped to interpret communications from the tutor due to already knowing the 'rules'.

Source: Kelly, P., & Moogan, Y. (2012). Culture shock and higher education performance: Implications for teaching. *Higher Education Quarterly*, 66(1), 24–46.

Key words & phrases

evidence of

evident in

close the gap

assessor bias

the differential narrowed

rote learning

a means of achieving

Task 7 Critically evaluating the findings and conclusions of Lebcir et al. (2008)

7.1 Lebcir et al. used a questionnaire with opinion statements for respondents to agree or disagree with, on a five-point scale. For each statement, the results from the 32 respondents are reported with the mean, median (middle value) and standard deviation (SD – a measure of variation from the mean).

Study the findings for two sets of statements, selected from the data, and the authors' interpretation of these. Can you find any inconsistencies in the way these findings are reported?

7.2 Why might the median be a better statistic to report the data than the mean? Is there another way to report the data that might show the results more clearly?

7.3 Identify the claims made to interpret these results. To what extent does the data support the claims?

7.4 Do you agree with the interpretation? Can you think of other explanations?

Teaching style and assessment methods
R. M. Lebcir, H. Wells and A. Bond

	mean	median	SD
1. The way the lecturer speaks is important in understanding the lecture.	3.69	4.00	1.01
2. The pace of delivery of the teaching is too slow.	2.00	2.00	0.82
3. The pace of delivery of the teaching is too fast.	2.25	2.50	1.00

The style of lecture presentation by lecturers appears to be a strong factor in helping students understand the subject. This indicates that students do rely heavily on their lecturers' skills in presenting and explaining lecture material. This finding is supported by the fact that the mean score to the opposite statements 'The pace of delivery of the teaching is too slow' and 'The pace of delivery of the teaching is too fast' are almost identical, although there is more agreement with the latter statement. These two statements clearly indicate that international students have different abilities and strengths, but they all rely on their lecturers' ability to deliver and explain the lecture material to understand the subject.

	mean	median	SD
15. I prefer to work in a teams for assignment work.	2.88	3.00	1.20
16. I prefer to work on my own for assignment work.	2.81	3.00	1.11

From results section: Opinions are also equally divided regarding the issue of working in group or individual assignments, although there is more bias towards preference of group assignments.

From discussion section: Regarding assignments, it is unclear from our results whether students prefer group or individual assignments. This may be explained by the fact that international students are not a homogenous group and, therefore, have different abilities and previous learning experiences. It is well known that the ability of students to interact with others and their previous experience in teamwork is different depending on the country of origin of the students and the subject they studied before coming to the UK.

Key words & phrases

a strong factor in
supported by the fact that
more agreement with
equally divided
bias towards
it is unclear from our results
explained by the fact that
it is well known

Source: Lebcir, R.M., Wells, H., & Bond, A. (2008). Factors affecting academic performance of international students in project management courses: A case study from a British post-92 university. *International Journal of Project Management, 26,* 268–274.

Task 8 Writing a summary of the research which indicates a gap

8.1 The authors of both these studies identified the limitations of their research in their conclusion:

The main limitations of this study concerned sampling. In some cases, the home country students and IMS were sometimes not in the same classroom, but in other cases they did share the same tutor. (Kelly & Moogan, 2012)

The most important [limitation] is our assumption that international students were a homogenous group whereas, in reality, they come from different regions of the world and, therefore, have different abilities, cultures, and learning experiences. (Lebcir et al., 2008)

Use your critical evaluation of the methods and results from these two studies to write a summary of this research which shows that a further study is required to answer the research question:
What factors affect the academic performance of internationally mobile students?

8.2 **Compare your summary with other students. Did you highlight the same limitations? Evaluate your summary using the Study smart checklist from Unit 8 on page 197 for writing from sources using your own voice. Did you:**

- take a nuanced stance?
- select and critically report evidence from these two papers?
- interpret evidence to support your stance?
- choose a persuasive structure for your argument?
- integrate the evidence into your argument, with the appropriate argument signals?
- use your own words?

8.3 **What does your summary need in order for it to function as a literature review for a new study?**

Self study

Using the research paper you selected in Section 1, study the way the author critically evaluates previous research, e.g., in the literature review, as the basis for his/her own studies. Use the quality checklists from Section 1 and this section to identify the type of critical evaluation the author uses to indicate that there is a gap in this area of research.

Section 4 The role of the literature review: linking theory to research design

What the university expects:

- an awareness of how knowledge is advanced; understand complex relationships between observations, evidence and theories

Contexts:

- writing literature reviews

Aims:

- to understand attempts to explain the world through frameworks of academic concepts
- to understand the purpose of a literature review in linking theory to research design
- to listen and take notes in order to align your viewpoint with what the university expects
- to apply concepts from a focus group discussion to case studies of student projects

Discussion

What is the connection between a *framework*, a *model* and a *theory*? How are these words used in your field? What collocations are typical in your field for these terms, e.g., *planning framework, business model, ecological theory*? How do they fit into the research process? What does it mean to link theory to practice? Compare your discussion with the FAQ below, which was posted in an online blog by the psychology lecturer, Robert Douglas, following his lecture on research across the disciplines.

Key words & phrases

the building blocks

preliminary

a meta-analysis

a conceptual model

under different conditions

high-level abstractions

BN Blogit Now

Posting   Settings   Layout   View blog

Create   Edit Posts   Moderate comments

Title: [   ]

FAQ: What is the connection between a *framework*, a *model* and a *theory*? How are these different from an approach?

In practice, these terms are sometimes used interchangeably. However, they are the building blocks of knowledge and are developed through the research process. Researchers might start with an inductive approach, observing or measuring a particular phenomenon in the natural or social world, e.g., the stars. A preliminary classification of aspects of the phenomenon which seem important is then specified within a framework, e.g., the astrological star signs. More evidence is collected to identify variables in the framework and to understand how they relate to one another. New studies test the framework by attempting to interpret findings within it and suggesting improvements. A meta-analysis of these studies might give rise to a conceptual model, a more general description of the phenomenon, which clarifies the relationships between variables. An example would be Kepler's mathematical equations to model planetary motion. Models enable researchers to simulate the phenomenon under different conditions in order to make predictions about it. The predictions are tested by comparing them with actual observations or measurements of the phenomenon in the real world. For example, the transits of Venus and Mercury allowed scientists to verify that Kepler's equations gave accurate predictions.

As the research field develops, theories emerge, e.g., Newton's theory of gravitation. These are high-level abstractions which combine sets of principles and definitions derived from the frameworks and models. They are the basis for deductive approaches to research, enabling the formulation of hypotheses that can be tested in new situations. This process of building frameworks, models and theories is often termed 'theorizing' and the components are sometimes referred to collectively as theory. Abstractions which form the basis for practical applications tend to be called approaches rather than theories or models and frameworks, e.g., an approach to research.

Task 1 Understanding examples of theories, models, frameworks and approaches

1.1 **Complete the brief definitions and descriptions below using the terms outlined in the FAQ:** *framework, model, theory* **or** *approach*. **For some answers, more than one answer may be possible.**

a Open source is a _____ for software development in which the source code for a particular application is made available for developers to download and improve. The open-source _____ offers 'better' software and encourages innovation. The developers contribute to open projects to gain reputation among their peers.

b A policy _____ is an organizational structure built on certain goals and principles on which to base decisions that influence development.

c Piaget's _____ of cognitive development attempts to explain the processes by which children come to know the world around them and develop cognitive and reasoning abilities as they mature.

d From the *Bad Science* article by Ben Goldacre, we derived a _____ of questions to help you to critically evaluate research papers.

e Meteorology centres such as the Hadley Centre in the UK or the Max Planck Institute in Germany have produced mathematical _____ of the climate which can be run on computers to simulate future climate scenarios.

f Many writers of course books for learning academic English use a syllabus of grammar items, e.g., *present simple, present perfect*, to structure their books. They believe that students need to understand grammar rules and produce accurate sentences in order to become more proficient. In this book, we use academic functions, e.g., *defining, arguing*, to structure the syllabus. We believe students first need to understand their purposes for using the language in order to progress. These approaches are based on different _____ of language learning. The syllabuses provide a _____ within which students can structure their learning and monitor their progress.

g Hazard analysis and critical control points, or HACCP (pronounced /ˈhæsʌp/), is a systematic preventive _____ to food safety and allergenic, chemical, and biological hazards in production processes that can cause the finished product to be unsafe, and designs measurements to reduce these risks to a safe level[9].

h An open systems _____ of teamwork (Ingram et al., 1997, p. 122) uses systems _____ to view teams as systems which 'take in resources (time, people, skills, problems) and transform them into outputs such as work, solutions and satisfactions'[10].

i Based on their review of the literature on teaching and learning, Lebcir et al. (2008) derived a _____ of factors which may affect international students' academic performance in project management modules and used this _____ to develop a questionnaire.

1.2 **Which frameworks, models or theories in your field are part of the common knowledge of the discipline and which are still being researched and developed? Compare with students from a similar discipline to yours.**

---

[9] Hazard analysis and critical control points. (n.d.). In *Wikipedia*. Retrieved May 31, 2013, from http://en.wikipedia.org/wiki/Hazard_analysis_and_critical_control_points

[10] Ingram, H., Teare, R., Scheuing, E., & Armistead, C. (1997). A systems model of effective teamwork. *The TQM Magazine*, 9(2), 118–127. Published by Emerald Group Publishing.

Task 2 Preparing to align your thinking with that of lecturers in the university

A teacher who co-ordinates the summer presessional course for international students at Gateway University is gathering information about approaches to research in different disciplines. She wants to make her course more relevant for students' needs on their future degrees so she is conducting focus group interviews with lecturers from different departments.

2.1   What kinds of questions do you think the pre-sessional co-ordinator will ask the lecturers in the focus group about research? Think about the lecture you listened to in Section 2 to help you formulate some questions.

2.2   In your view, should students on a pre-sessional course read research papers from their academic field and attempt to do some research? Explain your viewpoint to another student.

2.3   What kind of research project in your field could you complete in about six or eight weeks?

2.4   What would be the difficulties for students in designing research projects and for their teacher in supervising research projects for a mixed-discipline class on a presessional course?

Task 3 Listening critically to identify key points about research from the focus group

Work in a group with other students from similar disciplines to yours. Pay particular attention to ideas in the focus group discussion which relate to your discipline.

◉T61 Listen to the discussion and take notes so you can answer the following questions.

3.1   The interviewer asks the lecturers to introduce themselves.

Which disciplines are represented in the focus group? Are these disciplines hard or soft, pure or applied? Which ones deal with living or non-living samples?

3.2   What types of research projects can students do in each discipline? Note down any specific labels the lecturers give to projects or research. Which of these projects involve collecting data? What other type of project can students do?

3.3   How does a student choose a research topic in each of these fields?

3.4   What advice do these lecturers give to students about focusing their research topic? Why is this important, according to the lecturers?

3.5   The lecturers discuss the links between different parts of a research report.

What links do they expect students to make?

3.6   How do you think these lecturers would characterize a weak student?

3.7   Which types of projects are weak students advised to do? What are some of the problems weak students might have with this type of project?

3.8   What practical suggestions do the lecturers give Barbara Johnson about the projects that her students could do? Which of these projects could you do?

Task 4 Thinking critically about literature reviews

The lecturers talk about problems that students have understanding the purpose and structure of literature reviews, and how they relate to the other sections of the report.

4.1 **How does the literature review in a research report relate to frameworks, models or theories in a discipline? Compare the lecturers' comments with the FAQ on page 250 to help you answer.**

4.2 **Why is it important to critically evaluate findings from previous studies in the light of the frameworks, models or theories they were based on?**

4.3 **Where can researchers find critical evaluations of frameworks, models or theories to help with the critical evaluation in their own paper?**

4.4 You have studied the following research papers in earlier sections of this unit.

What frameworks, models or theories can you identify in these extracts? Look back to the abstracts on pages 238, 239 and 242 if you need to.

4.5 Readers often read the abstract and then the discussion or conclusions to get a flavour of the research before reading the whole paper.

Read the three extracts below and on page 254, and write some questions you would need these authors to answer in their literature review about their frameworks, models or theories in order to set the context for their research.

What kind of critical evaluation would you expect?

4.6 **Highlight expressions in the discussions or conclusions of each paper which show agreement with previous studies and indicate a link back to the literature review.**

Extract 1

Fayez A. Abdulla and Abbas S. Al-Omari

Aim: To use the Surface-Infiltration-Baseflow (SFB) water balance model developed by Boughton (1984) for observing causal relationships among runoff, air temperature and precipitation in twelve climate change scenarios.

Conclusions: The impact of the climate change on the monthly runoff of the Zarqa River basin (Jordan) was evaluated using the Surface-inFiltration-Baseflow (SFB) conceptual rainfall runoff mode, and application of climate change scenarios (GCMs and incremental scenarios). Seven years of meteorological and hydrological data were used for calibrating the model. […] The model performed well for the Zarqa River […]. The average monthly runoff compared well to the observed runoff.

Literature review questions:

_____

_____

_____

Source: Abdulla, F. A., & Al-Omari, A. S. (2008). The impact of climate change on the monthly runoff of a semi-arid catchment: Case study Zarqa river basin (Jordan). *Journal of Applied Biological Sciences*, 2(1), 43–50.

Extract 2

R. M. Lebcir, H. Wells and A. Bond

Aim: to investigate the factors affecting the academic performance of international students in project management courses in a British post-92 university.

Conclusions: The aim of this research is to investigate the factors affecting the academic performance of international students in project management. To this end, a framework was developed from the literature and tested empirically through an opinion-based questionnaire. Our objective is to identify, from international students' perspective, the factors affecting their performance so that possible corrective actions can be identified in order to improve the learning experience of these students and improve their performance. The results from the questionnaire regarding the explanatory factors impacting the academic performance of international students are in line with those described in other studies on the subject.

Literature review questions:

_____

_____

_____

Source: Lebcir, R. M., Wells, H., & Bond, A. (2008). Factors affecting academic performance of international students in project management courses: A case study from a British post-92 university. *International Journal of Project Management*, 26(3), 268–274.

Extract 3

Sylvia Terbeck, Guy Kahane, Sarah McTavish, Julian Savulescu, Philip J. Cowen and Miles Hewstone

Aim: In the present study we employed propranolol to test the hypothesis that emotional responses influenced by noradrenergic transmission play a mediating role in implicit but not explicit forms of prejudice. We predicted that ß-adrenoreceptor blockade should lead to a reduction in implicit racial attitudes, as measured by the IAT [implicit association test].

Discussion: The main finding of our study is that propranolol significantly reduced implicit but not explicit racial bias. This supports our hypothesis that noradrenaline-mediated emotional responses play a role in the generation of implicit negative racial attitudes, and supports prior theorising suggesting a greater affective component in implicit attitudes (Stanley et al., 2008).

Literature review questions:

_____

_____

_____

Source: Terbeck, S., Kahane, G., McTavish, S., Savulescu, J., Cowen, P. J., & Hewstone, M. (2012). Propranolol reduces implicit negative racial bias. *Psychopharmacology*, 22(3), 419–424. Published online February 28, 2012. DOI 10.1007/s00213-012-2657-5.

Study smart: writing a literature review

The author of a paper sets out the theoretical background to the research in a literature review. This is usually part of the introduction in a short research paper, e.g., Lindgren et al., but may be a separate chapter in a longer dissertation or thesis. The purpose is to:

- provide a convincing rationale for conducting the research
- define any concepts used to operationalize the components of theory
- outline frameworks or describe models which will form the basis for the data collection or analysis

Depending on the discipline and the level of maturity of the research area, the literature review will include some of the following:

- an overview of frameworks, models or theories showing their relevance to the research area
- a review of previous studies which highlights gaps in knowledge that the study seeks to fill
- a note of areas of disagreement among researchers about findings or their interpretation
- a justification for adopting a specific methodology or study design
- an evaluation or adaptation of existing data-collection methods

Which of these is more prominent and how they interrelate depends on the discipline, the research design and the research question. Research questions guide the selection of relevant literature and provide a plan for the structure of the literature review. They enable researchers to specify a purpose for their critical reading and frame the discussion of their findings. Research questions should:

- be focused – there is not enough time to 'solve the universe'
- enable a researcher to make a contribution to the field
- be worth answering to provide significant benefits or insights
- not be biased towards an answer which the researcher knows beforehand

Task 5 Formulating research questions to guide the selection of sources for literature reviews

Read the students' descriptions of research topics that interest them. They have only a general idea of the topic they want to research.

Christopher Steele:
I'm interested in online tools for teaching. I want to find out why physics students have difficulty learning about electricity. I want to design an online tool for teaching this concept.

Rowena Forbes:
My mum is going blind. She's got macular degeneration which gets worse as she gets older. She used to love visiting museums, but now she can't. I want to find out what museums can do for visually impaired people like my mum.

Wu Le:
When I graduate, I want to work in the petroleum industry in my country. For my project, I'm interested in microbial enhanced oil recovery. This involves injecting microorganisms into oil reservoirs to change the physical properties of the oil, making it more fluid and more easily extracted. This is a fairly new field of study, so I want to find out how much research has been done in this area.

Jasmin Kang:
I was working as a project manager before I started my degree. Teamworking is a really important aspect of project management, but it is very difficult to build effective teams. On our course, we have to do team assignments. I want to find out what my classmates think about learning in teams.

5.1 **What kind of research design would be appropriate for each topic? Choose from the following:**

case study   literature review   survey–interview   product design

5.2 **Write some questions that would help the students to focus their search for relevant sources.**

5.3 Now read these research questions which the students wrote at the beginning of their research:

Christopher Steele:	Do students have difficulty learning about physics?
Rowena Forbes:	What are facilities like for blind tourists who want to visit Summerford Museum?
Wu Le:	How can oil recovery be improved?
Jasmin Kang:	What do my classmates think about learning in teams?

Compare them with the questions you wrote in Task 5.2, referring to the criteria for research questions in the Study smart on page 255. Are your questions more or less focused than theirs? What problems can you see with these questions? Can you change them so that the research has the right focus for a 12-week project? You may need to write more than one question for each student.

Task 6 Deciding the structure of literature reviews

Below are the titles and aims for each of the students' projects, together with headings for sections in their literature reviews. The headings (a–f) are not in the correct order.

Reorder the headings so that the literature review provides a context and a convincing rationale for each study. Be prepared to justify your order.

A mechanical model of electricity for teaching students

Christopher Steele, University of Sheffield

Aims: to identify which concepts in electricity students find most problematic and to provide an IT-based tool to facilitate the communication of these concepts.

____ **a** Modelling the behaviour of electrons

____ **b** Student misunderstandings about electricity

____ **c** Design specifications for an online tool

____ **d** How new concepts are learnt

____ **e** Electricity in simple circuits

____ **f** Existing work on analogies of flow

Art and access: evaluating the museum experience for visually impaired people

Rowena Forbes, Gateway University

Aims: to identify the needs of people with visual impairment when visiting museums and relate these to policy documents on disability access in order to suggest criteria for the management of museums.

____ **a** Description of Summerford Museum

____ **b** Management of tourist destinations

____ **c** Problems for visually impaired people as tourists

____ **d** Definition of visual impairment

____ **e** Policies on access for disabled and visually impaired people

____ **f** Criteria for management of a tourist destination for visually impaired people

The mechanisms and application of microbial enhanced oil recovery

Wu Le, Heriot-Watt University

Aims: to review research on the use of Microbial EOR, to better understand the environmental limitations that affect its application and to consider the economic implications.

____ **a** Explanation of mechanisms for microbial EOR

____ **b** Efficiency and cost of oil recovery using microbial EOR

____ **c** Definition of enhanced oil recovery (EOR)

____ **d** Outline of variety of end products from microbial EOR

____ **e** Environmental constraints on the use of microbial EOR

____ **f** Research on the use of microorganisms for EOR

Learning in teams: a case study on a project management course

Jasmin Kang, Gateway University

Aims: to identify the factors that contribute to successful team learning on a master's degree course.

____ **a** Critical success factors for learning in teams

____ **b** Research on attributes of effective teamwork

____ **c** Barriers to team development

____ **d** Explanation of team development

____ **e** Definition of teams and teamworking

____ **f** Explanation of team-learning processes

Self study

Using the research paper you selected in Section 1, try to find research questions or research aims. In the literature review, identify headings used to structure the review. How well do these relate to the research questions? Can you see a clear link between the research questions, the literature review and the data collection and analysis? How do the research questions and the literature review link to arguments in the discussion or conclusion? Review each of the Self study activities you have carried out in this unit so that you are clear about how to critically evaluate a research paper.

Section 5 Critical reading of a research paper

What the university expects:
- critical reflection – analyze and evaluate claims and evidence; critically evaluate the quality and impact of others' work

Contexts:
- reading research papers

Aims:
- to review your understanding of how to evaluate the quality of research evidence
- to apply the framework for critical evaluation to a specific research paper

Discussion

Select one of the papers you have identified in the Self study activities in this book. Read the abstract carefully to decide which aspect of the study the authors believe is new and will build knowledge in the field, and explain your decision to other students. Give the abstract to another student to read and discuss your decision.

Study smart: framework for critically evaluating research

In this unit, we have derived the following framework for a critical evaluation of research. You can use this framework to evaluate your chosen paper and other research papers in your field.

Transparency:	Does the author provide enough information about the study methods to enable readers to evaluate the results?
Research design:	Is the approach to data collection appropriate for what the researcher wants to find out?
	Does the data-collection method take account of all the variables?
Reliability:	Are the measures consistent and stable?
	If the study was repeated, would the results be the same?
Validity:	Have concepts been operationalized appropriately?
	Do the measures reflect these concepts?
	Are cause–effect relations between variables real?
	Can findings be generalized to other contexts?
Credibility:	Is the research trustworthy?
	How believable are the findings?
Limitations:	Will any limitations of the method affect the credibility of the results?
Interpretation:	Are claims made by the researchers justified on the basis of their results?
	Is their use of statistics appropriate to the research design?
	How do they deal with contradictory results?

Task 1 Critically evaluating the research paper

Apply the framework for critically evaluating research to your chosen paper by answering the following.

a Find the main claims in the discussion section of your paper.

b What is the research context? How easy or difficult would it be to generalize findings to other contexts?

c What kind of research design is used – inductive or deductive?

d Can you identify a framework, model or theory on which the research design is based?

e Can you see a clear link between the research questions, the literature review and the data collection or analysis?

f How did the researchers operationalize the concepts to be measured in their studies?

g Can you identify independent variables which the researchers set up or changed or selected, and dependent variables which they measured?

h Do the researchers specify their sample type and size?

i Find where in the paper the authors discuss limitations in sampling, measurement or interpretation of the data. How do the authors think these limitations will affect the results?

j Look at the results, in particular how the authors interpret tables and graphs. Do you agree with the interpretation? Can you think of other explanations?

k How well are the research questions and the literature review linked to arguments in the discussion or conclusion?

l Using a citation search function, find other papers which refer to this one. Look in the introduction or discussion to find out how other authors have critically evaluated this paper.

Task 2 Writing a critical review of the research paper

Using your answers to the checklist in Task 1, write a critical review of your chosen paper, which identifies the limitations in the research design or data collection and challenges the interpretation of the results. You can use critical evaluations in other research articles to support your view.

Self study

You should now have enough information about the approach to research design, and the way it is communicated, to design and carry out your own research and write a report of your findings.

Section 1 Assessing readiness for university study

What the university expects:
- critical reflection – analyze and evaluate claims and evidence

Contexts:
- secure English language test (SELT) preparation

Aims:
- to understand how to align your competence to a standard framework
- to assess your current competence
- to understand how SELTs fit into preparation for study at university

Discussion

How do you know when you have an appropriate level of English for university study? How can you assess what you know and can do in English? What evidence of your English level do universities use to decide whether to admit you to a degree programme?

The Common European Framework of Reference for Languages (CEFR)

The CEFR 'describes in a comprehensive way what language learners have to learn to do in order to use a language for communication and what knowledge and skills they have to develop so as to be able to act effectively. The description also covers the cultural context in which language is set. The Framework also defines levels of proficiency which allow learners' progress to be measured at each stage of learning and on a life-long basis'[1].

The Home Office requires academic institutions in the UK to refer to the CEFR when accepting students onto degrees. Therefore, global language exams such as IELTS, TOEFL and PTE[2] Academic are now benchmarked to the CEFR.

Task 1 Understanding proficiency levels of the CEFR

1.1 According to the introduction above, what kind of competences in English are you required to learn for university study? Can you give examples from what you have learnt in this book?

1.2 Opposite are some can-do statements adapted from the CEFR for reading and writing at university.

   What differences can you find between the descriptors for levels C1, B2 and B1?

---

[1] Council of Europe. (2001). *Common European Framework of Reference.* Retrieved from http://www.coe.int/ t/dg4/linguistic/source/framework_en.pdf
[2] Pearson Test of English

1.3 For each skill, which level would be most appropriate for university study?

1.4 For each skill, decide which set of can-do statements best applies to you.

1.5 What evidence do you have for your claims about which statements best apply to you? Where does this evidence normally come from?

Reading

C1	I can understand a wide range of demanding, longer texts, whether or not they relate to my own field, provided I can reread difficult sections. I can identify finer points of detail including attitudes and implied – as well as stated – opinions. I can obtain information, ideas and opinions from highly specialized sources within my field. I can summarize long, demanding texts, commenting on and discussing contrasting points of view.
B2	I can understand the main ideas of complex texts on both concrete and abstract topics, including technical discussion in my field. I can understand specialized articles not related to my field, provided I can use a dictionary occasionally to confirm my interpretation of terminology. I can understand articles and reports concerned with contemporary problems in which the writers adopt particular stances or viewpoints. I can summarize extracts from texts containing opinions, argument and discussion or collate short pieces of information from several sources and summarize them for somebody else.
B1	I can understand the main points of clear standard texts on familiar topics regularly encountered in work, school, leisure, etc. I can read straightforward factual texts on subjects related to my field or my interests with a satisfactory level of comprehension. I can recognize the main argument or conclusions in clearly signalled argumentative texts, although I may not understand the details. I can paraphrase short written passages in a simple fashion, using the original text wording and ordering.

Writing

C1	I can produce clear, well-structured, detailed text on complex subjects, showing controlled use of organizational patterns, connectors and cohesive devices. I can underline the relevant salient issues, expanding and supporting points of view at some length with subsidiary points, reasons and relevant examples. I can write an essay or report which develops an argument systematically with appropriate highlighting of significant points and relevant supporting detail. I can evaluate different ideas or solutions to a problem.
B2	I can produce clear, detailed text on a wide range of subjects and explain a viewpoint on a topical issue giving the advantages and disadvantages of various options. I can write clear, detailed texts on a variety of subjects related to my field of interest, synthesizing and evaluating information and arguments from a number of sources. I can write an essay or report which develops an argument, giving reasons in support of or against a particular point of view and explaining the advantages and disadvantages of various options.
B1	I can produce simple connected text on topics of personal interest to me such as my experiences, dreams, hopes and ambitions and briefly give reasons and explanations for opinions and plans. I can write straightforward connected texts on a range of familiar subjects within my field of interest, by linking a series of shorter discrete elements into a linear sequence. I can write very brief reports using a standard conventional format in order to pass on routine factual information and state reasons for actions.

Task 2 Producing evidence to support your claims about your language competence

Many students choose one of the secure English language tests (SELTs) such as IELTS, TOEFL or PTE Academic as evidence to support the claim that they are ready to study in an English-medium institution. Below is a table which contrasts these three SELTs.

2.1 Compare the tasks in the table with the CEFR can-do statements in Task 1. To what extent do these tasks enable a student to provide evidence of their ability to study and complete university-level assessments in English? What other evidence could students provide?

2.2 Compare these reading and writing tasks with those that you have completed in this book. What key differences can you identify?

2.3 If you prepared for university study only by training to pass a SELT, what important attributes and skills might you be lacking?

	IELTS	TOEFL – iBT (Internet-based testing)	PTE Academic (Pearson Test of English Academic)
length	2 hours 45 mins + separate speaking test	4 hours + 10-min break	3 hours with optional break
medium	paper-based + audio	computer-based	computer-based
skills tested	reading, writing, listening, speaking tested separately	reading, writing, listening, speaking partly integrated and partly separate	reading, writing, listening, speaking partly integrated and partly separate
reading texts	three texts of around 800 words in an academic style, with 40 questions in total	between three and five texts of around 700 words in an academic style, with 12 to 14 questions per text	around five texts of between 80 and 300 words in an academic style, usually with one question per text
reading tasks	1. multiple choice questions or labelling diagrams or completing tables or matching features to elicit understanding of content 2. identifying paragraph purpose or matching headings to paragraphs to identify purpose and structure 3. identifying writer's viewpoint and also identifying implied meaning	1. comprehension questions to elicit understanding of content vocabulary, grammar and cohesive reference 2. prose summary and categorization questions to identify purpose and structure 3. inferencing questions to relate information across texts and identify implicit argument	1. multiple-choice questions to elicit understanding of content or tone 2. one-sentence summaries of main points or reordering paragraphs to identify structure 3. gap-filling questions to elicit understanding of vocabulary, grammar and cohesive reference
writing tasks	1. information transfer task relating narrowly to factual content of input diagram 2. discussion task developing a position in relation to a question or statement, ideas supported with evidence, and examples drawn from the candidates' own experience	1. integrated listening, reading and writing task, contrasting ideas from text and lecture input 2. discussion task developing a position in relation to a question or statement, ideas supported with evidence, and examples drawn from the candidates' own experience	1. summarizing task reducing a passage to one sentence 2. discussion task developing a position in relation to a question or statement, ideas supported with evidence, and examples drawn from the candidates' own experience
writing grading	graded by one examiner	graded by two examiners	graded by computer
reporting scales	1–9 bands	0–120 points	10–90 points

Task 3 Thinking critically about the attributes and skills required for university study

3.1 Below is an FAQ from a test preparation website.

According to this website, what are the limitations of SELTs? Are these limitations reasonable?

3.2 Look back to page 12 and reread the list of graduate attributes required for university-level study. **Which of these graduate attributes are SELTs designed to test?**

3.3 **According to this website, when might you acquire some of the other graduate attributes?**

FAQ: Why aren't the reading and writing tasks in SELTs more like university-level tasks?

SELTs are designed to test readiness for study at university in the English language and the ability to cope with the linguistic demands of that context immediately after entry. The content of SELTs is representative of the kinds of tasks and texts that students encounter at university. However, authentic examples of spoken or written language cannot be used because they contain references to discipline-specific or cultural content which may not be understood by all test takers. The implication of this is that reading and writing tasks in SELTs cannot simulate the type of university-level tasks which test takers will encounter in their studies. Preparation for SELTs cannot cover the whole range of university-level reading or writing competencies which students are likely to need; they will have to develop these during their course of study, often in ways that are specific to their particular academic discipline.

Discussion

How are SELTs such as IELTS, TOEFL or PTE different from exams at university? Which do you think is more difficult: passing a SELT or passing exams once you are at university?

Task 4 Comparing questions from SELTs with university exam questions

4.1 On page 264 are ten exam questions.

Which ones are from SELTs and which are from university subject exams? How do you know?

4.2 **Can you identify the disciplines from which the university subject exams are taken?**

4.3 **For each type of question, SELT or university subject, can you say what kind of knowledge it aims to test?**

4.4 **Which questions ask for a personal opinion and which ask for an evaluation of a topic?**

4.5 **How could you prepare to answer each type of question?**

a The graph below shows radio and television audiences throughout the day in 1992. Summarize the information by selecting and reporting the main features, and make comparisons where relevant.

b Explain, with the aid of a diagram, the difference between open-loop and closed-loop systems. Describe the advantages and disadvantages of each type of system with the use of an illustrative example (e.g., a temperature control system).

c The threat of nuclear weapons maintains world peace. Nuclear power provides cheap and clean energy. The benefits of nuclear technology far outweigh the disadvantages. To what extent do you agree or disagree?

d Most renewable energy resources have a much smaller energy density or power density than fossil fuels and are distributed over the Earth's surface. Discuss problems associated with this, and possible steps to overcome them. Provide examples to illustrate your points.

e Do you agree or disagree with the following statement? *Good teachers are more important to a child's development than good parents.* Use specific reasons and examples to support your answer.

f Evaluate the different ways in which project managers can enhance the knowledge, skills and competences of their employees.

g Using ideas and information gained from the industrial lectures in the course, write brief notes on three different roles that engineers and scientists can have when working in industry. Illustrate your answer with examples from the lectures.

h Tobacco, mainly in the form of cigarettes, is one of the most widely used drugs in the world. Over a billion adults legally smoke tobacco every day. The long-term health costs are high – for smokers themselves, and for the wider community in terms of health care costs and lost productivity. Do governments have a legitimate role to legislate to protect citizens from the harmful effects of their own decisions to smoke, or are such decisions up to the individual?

i Discuss how environmental valuation techniques might be used to assess the environmental impacts of wind farms.

j Discuss the importance of word of mouth as a marketing communications medium. Explain how a fashion retailer could generate positive word-of-mouth marketing using social media.

Task 5 Analyzing exam questions

5.1 Exam questions can be analyzed into three components: the topic, the specific aspects of the topic to be considered, and the functional language which tells you what to do.

Analyze the university subject exam questions in Task 4 using this framework.

5.2 In this book, you have learnt how to write with an academic voice by:
- making the subjects of your sentences concepts and not people
- taking a nuanced stance
- making claims supported with evidence

Choose one of the SELT discussion questions in Task 4 and use this framework to answer the question as you would expect an academic writer to answer it.

5.3 Work in pairs to exchange your writing and give each other feedback. Discuss the extent to which the framework helped you to answer the exam question.

Study smart: the different purposes of SELTs and subject exams

Questions in SELTs ask you to display your knowledge of language using whatever content on a given topic that you have at your disposal. The content is less important than the language. In contrast, university subject exams ask you to display your knowledge of content with whatever language you have available. The content is more important than the language, as long as the language is reasonably clear and accurate. At university, your knowledge of the subject can compensate for weakness in your ability to use language. You prepare for SELTS by improving your language to understand or communicate familiar content. You prepare for university subject exams by understanding and communicating new, specialist content.

Self study

If you are going to sit a SELT, in order to meet the entry requirements for the university where you want to study, you need to familiarize yourself with the exam format and try some practice tests to evaluate your performance. All this information is online; just search for the appropriate SELT.

Section 2 Teamwork in group projects

What the university expects:
- teamworking – encourage and advise others; contribute positively to teamwork and take on a variety of roles in a team

Contexts:
- projects for study and work which require collaboration

Aims:
- to understand the importance of teamwork in academic and professional life
- to analyze teamworking processes and competences
- to use key vocabulary for discussing group projects

Discussion

Talk briefly about your past experiences of working in groups or teams – in school or outside school. What did your group achieve and how did you feel?

Task 1 Working in a group to complete a task: the Marshmallow Challenge

1.1 Work in groups of four and agree on a name for your group. You have 18 minutes to complete the following task.

The Marshmallow Challenge
Build the tallest free-standing structure out of 20 strands of spaghetti, one yard of masking tape, one yard of string and one marshmallow. The marshmallow needs to be on top. You have 18 minutes.
Note: A 'yard' is just less than a metre in length.

1.2 Decide as a class which group achieved the best outcome and award a grade between 1 and 10 for each structure.

1.3 Now watch the TED talk by Tom Wujec at http://www.ted.com/talks/lang /en/tom_wujec_build_a_tower.html in which he explains the factors which affect team performance on this challenge. Make a note of his main points.

Task 2 Thinking critically to evaluate group performance

Write a personal evaluation of your group's performance on the Marshmallow Challenge using the questions below. Which of Tom Wujec's points applied to your group in this task? Compare your evaluation with the rest of your group.

a What went well and why?

b What went badly and why?

c What would improve performance next time?

Task 3 Thinking critically about groups and teams

In your groups, discuss the following questions and make a note of your ideas. Refer to Tom Wujec's points in your discussion.

3.1 What is the difference between a group and a team? How can a group turn into a team?

3.2 What makes one team more successful than another?

3.3 Why are teams important?

Task 4 Reading critically with focused questions

You are going to read an extract from the chapter about group work in *From high school to university: A handbook for EAP students* (Argent, 2013). The introduction contains the following statement:

… taught university courses at both postgraduate and undergraduate level will at some stage require students to collaborate on a project to produce an assessed piece of work.

4.1 Write a list of general questions about assessed group work at university that you would like answered. Compare your list with two or three other students and add further useful questions.

4.2 Find as many answers to your questions as you can in the extract on pages 268–269.

Chapter 10 Group work

Sue Argent

10.1 Group projects for assessment

A *group* is simply a number of people who have something in common, whereas a *team* is a group of people working together for a common purpose. Every student is expected to work with others throughout their time at university, not simply to co-operate to share resources such as set books or laboratory space and equipment, but at a much more profound level. For example, discussions during seminars are not just occasions to demonstrate learning, but opportunities to engage closely with and build on the ideas of others. In addition, taught university courses at both postgraduate and undergraduate level will at some stage require students to collaborate as a team on a project to produce an assessed piece of work. A group project simulates the challenges of working in a professional field. As one university website puts it:

The exercise … gives students experience of working against rigid deadlines, with a team of colleagues not of their own choosing, using externally prescribed tools to undertake a fixed project. This gives some idea of the problems encountered in normal professional practice[3].

The work for a group project usually involves a task of some complexity that requires an extended period of time to complete. The project may centre on a research question or the solution to a problem and may involve the library, laboratory or fieldwork. Alternatively, it could be a design project for a new device, system or service, or it could be a case study analysis. Whatever the nature of the project, there are outcomes (often referred to as *deliverables*) that can be assessed by the university, for example, a report, poster, presentation, product or service. Sometimes a combination of these is required and assessed.

The group project is the only form of assessment for many course modules, so your entire grade for the module may be based on the project. A group project may be assessed in a number of ways, but there is usually a group component and an individual component. In the group component, all members of the group achieve the same mark for the piece of work they jointly complete and submit. In addition to the required product or service, joint assessment can be for an oral presentation or a written report, and sometimes both of these. The individual component is most frequently a personal analysis and evaluation of the success of the project, with a reflective account of an individual's personal contribution to the project, using a diary format or a written evaluation. Often, and more problematically, the reflective commentary has to include an evaluation of each of the individual student's team mates and their contributions. Occasionally, an individual's performance is assessed through a group interview.

Clearly, a successful group project will gain high marks if the outcome of the project, the report, presentation or other product or service, is of high quality. However, groups do not always work together as successful teams, and good personal reflection, even on an otherwise unsuccessful project, can gain valuable marks for an individual student.

Key words & phrases
profound
to collaborate
rigid deadlines
not of their own choosing
prescribed
of some complexity
deliverables
a reflective account
problematically
the reflective commentary

[3] University of Cambridge. (2011). *Group Design Project 2011–2012: Project Briefing*. Retrieved June 26, 2012, from http://www.cl.cam.ac.uk/teaching/group-projects/StudentBriefing_1112.pdf

10.2 The benefits of group projects

There are many reasons for the inclusion of group projects as an important part of learning at university, not least because on leaving university, graduate professionals will find themselves regularly working as members of multidisciplinary, multinational teams on extensive, complex projects. Working effectively in this context demands a particular set of skills, knowledge and understanding that can never be learnt from working as an individual in isolation. Employers value these attributes and look for evidence of them in prospective employees. It is therefore essential for students to develop these attributes during their studies if they are to find work in their professional fields.

The opportunity to work in groups offers many benefits. Firstly, teams that work well can achieve much more than the same number of individuals working alone. This is because team members can provide complementary skills and knowledge, some of which a single individual may lack. The discussion and interaction within the team can provide innovative solutions to problems as they arise.

There is a whole range of benefits in terms of what participants learn. As a team member, you can develop your communicative and intercultural skills: for example, you will use your negotiating skills to be diplomatic and assertive as necessary. You can also learn how to take the initiative as a leader and how to support others effectively.

Perhaps most importantly, as a student you can learn a surprising amount about yourself because working in a team uncovers where your strengths and weaknesses really lie. For example, you may normally be shy but discover that you can take the lead when others become stressed and confused; you might feel that you talk too much but then find that others can 'bounce off' your ideas; you might find your sense of humour gives you a special talent for taking the stress out of situations.

Capturing all this in a reflective commentary will be invaluable when writing personal statements for a resumé, CV or job application.

Key words & phrases

complementary skills
innovative solutions
take the initiative
take the lead
bounce off your ideas

Source: Argent, S. (2013). *From high school to university: A handbook for EAP students*. Summerford: Gateway University Press.

Discussion

What do you think you would find most difficult in an assessed group project?

Task 5 Reading critically to evaluate group projects

A project brief is always provided to explain what the group has to do.

Work in groups with students from a similar discipline to yours. Together, read the four project briefs and answer the following questions. Compare your answers with other groups.

5.1 List the features that the briefs have in common. Why do you think these features are so important? Are there any differences?

5.2 How do these briefs differ from the Marshmallow Challenge at the beginning of this section?

5.3 How do they differ from work-based projects in the real world outside university?

5.4 Which one do you feel you could participate in? Why?

A. Tourism Management

> **Recruiting a new member of staff**
>
> Work in pairs to write a recruitment plan for a new member of staff. The plan must include 11 components including job description, person specification, equal opportunities considerations, job advertisement, letters to be sent to successful and unsuccessful candidates. *Joint assessment grade.*
>
> Role-play interviewing a candidate for the job for which you have written a recruitment plan. One of you should take the part of the interviewer, and the other the role of the candidate. *Individual assessment grade.*
>
> Individually, write a critical analysis of the whole process (3,000 words), including an evaluation of your partner's work and a self-reflective commentary. *Individual assessment grade.*

Key words & phrases

recruitment
person specification
equal opportunities
candidates
documentation

B. Information Technology

> **Creating a website for a client**
>
> Five clients have asked to participate in a project to produce a website for their company. They are a local children's playgroup, a new-start bed and breakfast business, a local parish council, a group of students starting a bicycle share scheme, and a lobby group objecting to plans to build an airport in Summerford. Read the full details of each client (supplied) and state your own preferences for a project client using the attached form.
>
> You will be assigned with four other students to a project, according to your preferences as much as possible. Together, you must plan and carry out the project to produce the website. You will need to gather the client's requirements, produce a design for the website, build, test and launch it.
>
> Deliverables:
>
> a The website.
>
> b A 3,000 to 5,000-word report of the project, including correspondence, meeting minutes and presentations to clients.
>
> c A personal online journal recording your reflections on the process and on the contributions of the other members of the team. This journal will be accessible only to you and your tutor.
>
> **Assessment:** You will be assessed by the client and tutors on the quality and functionality of the website and on your professional skills as a team. You will be assessed individually by tutors on the report and journal.

Key words & phrases

clients
preferences
be assigned to
launch
corresondence
functionality

C. Environmental Science

Producing a conservation management plan

1. Work together in groups of six to produce a conservation management plan. You will be allocated one of the five sites you visited last term. The plan must include a Phase 1 Habitat Survey to identify the habitats, key plant species and other important aspects of the site. Indicate any further species-specific surveys that might be necessary at a later date. Identify any likely stakeholders' interests. Assess the site's potential for recreational, educational or other community use and report any potential areas of conflict.
2. Arrange fact-finding meetings with stakeholders and minute these.
3. Deliverables: an information leaflet for visitors to the site; a presentation for a public meeting about your plan; a report to the local authority. These will be awarded a group grade.
4. Evaluate the contribution of each group member to the task (including yourself) in a self-reflective commentary. This will be awarded an individual grade.

Key words & phrases

be allocated

habitat survey

species

recreational use

fact-finding

local authority

be awarded

D. Computer Science

Software design and engineering

You will be assigned in groups of six to one of our clients. The group will design a solution to a problem identified by the client by producing a requirements specification and designing, implementing and testing a suitable system. You will be assessed jointly on the combined group product and individually on your own contribution.

Different deliverable documents are required:

- specification and project plan
- progress report on implementation and testing
- group report and personal reports

The group report should consider to what extent the project was successful, describe fully any lessons learnt by the team, and include a summary of the contribution by different team members in completing the system.

The personal report should be a brief personal review giving details of your individual contribution to the project. This should include a representative part of the work you contributed such as program code or documentation, as appropriate. You should include a section in which you assess the individual contributions made by each member of the group.

There will be a public presentation consisting of practical demonstrations and a seminar. The coordinators, clients and members of staff who attend the seminar will vote to award achievement prizes.

Key words & phrases

requirements specification

a representative part

program code

as appropriate

Source: University of Cambridge. (2011). *Group Design Project 2011–2012: Project Briefing*. Retrieved June 26, 2012, from http://www.cl.cam.ac.uk/teaching/group-projects/StudentBriefing_1112.pdf

Task 6 Thinking critically to analyze a complex task

6.1 **Work in groups of four to each analyze a different project brief.**

    a Brainstorm what the project involves in terms of activities, responsibilities and skills.

    b Identify any problems you think the students might experience.

    c The briefs are only outlines. Identify further information you need by drawing up a list of questions to e-mail to your tutor.

6.2 **Present your ideas to the rest of the class. The rest of the class should contribute suggestions and critically evaluate the group's analysis.**

Task 7 Thinking critically to predict content and create focused questions

Much research has been done into three key aspects of working in groups:
- the stages through which groups develop;
- the different roles which group members play during a group project;
- the skills and competencies that are needed for a successful project outcome.

7.1 **Work in three groups, each exploring one of these aspects. Brainstorm what you already know about the aspect you are considering. Make a list of focused questions with which to read critically.**

7.2 **Find as many answers to your questions as you can in the following extract.**

7.3 **Present what you have learnt to the class.**

Chapter 10 Group work (Continued)

10.3 The dynamics of teamwork

Research into how groups work has shown the importance of three aspects of teams: the phases through which a team typically passes as a task is undertaken, the roles adopted as people interact in a team, and the skills and abilities that are important for successful teamwork.

10.3.1 Group formation

Although there are several different models of the process of group formation, there is general agreement that groups evolve through different stages as they work on a task. What follows is a brief outline of the process. For more detail, consult the references at the end of the chapter.

There is generally an initial phase in which individuals need to form relationships. However long a group of students may have known each other, when they come together for a group project, they are a newly formed group and must bond to form a team. At this point, many enterprises such as businesses use team-building activities to enhance and speed up the process. Even if everyone wants to get on with the task, the main focus is on getting to know the other members of the group; any engagement with the task is superficial because team members prioritize harmony and deliberately avoid conflict.

Key words & phrases

engagement

superficial

harmony

Later comes a more difficult phase. A good working relationship involves pooling resources such as time, energy, knowledge, experience, skills and ideas. This kind of sharing requires trust between team members, which takes time to build and means taking risks. Groups always have to experience a stage of conflict since individuals have competing ideas about how to proceed and will try to promote their own views. Although essentially constructive, this second phase can be very distressing and uncomfortable, but little will be achieved until these conflicts are resolved. Personal agendas have to be set aside; strong personalities have to give way. Everyone has to see that they can only achieve success by being a team and trusting each other's judgement. If this phase is successful, the group identity begins to take shape because the members develop an understanding of their combined strengths and weaknesses. Ideally, they become more open to each other's ideas and no longer feel intimidated or threatened. As a result, they are truly free to explore and exploit the group's potential to complete the task and they bond as a team. The value of consciously and continually fostering this team feeling should not be underestimated.

The process is iterative. Even when the team has formed a set of good working relationships, there can be conflict later. Once the group has started work, each new phase of the project brings new challenges to threaten team cohesion and these have to be met by rebuilding trust. However, each cycle is easier and faster than before. The first recognition and resolution of conflict is a kind of template for managing later episodes.

10.3.2 Team member roles

Research by Meredith Belbin in the 1960s identified different roles in groups that are endeavouring to complete a task such as a project. Each role brings a different set of skills and way of approaching the task (see the table on page 274). Individual team members may have a preferred role, but generally people display role profiles, with several roles available to them. Generally speaking, a balanced group, i.e., a group whose members are able to play a range of roles at different times, works better. Given the opportunity and familiarity with the workforce, a manager will pick teams so that the individuals within it complement each other. However, this option is often not possible and is unlikely to be the case at university. Therefore, group members need to understand different team roles and be prepared to change and adapt their own role as necessary.

Anyone who emerges as a team leader has a special role, requiring energy and initiative, as well as a clear view of the project aims and the trust of the rest of the group. Different styles of leadership, particular strengths or very specific expertise, may be needed at different points in the project, and so the leader will change from time to time throughout the project for different components or aspects of the task.

Key words & phrases

pooling resources
competing ideas
how to proceed
to promote
personal agendas
set aside
group identity
to take shape
ideally
open to ideas
feel intimidated
exploit
bond as a team
fostering
underestimated
template
episodes
complement each other

The NINE Belbin Team Roles

Team role	Contribution	Allowable weaknesses
Plant	Creative, imaginative, free-thinking. Generates ideas and solves difficult problems.	Ignores incidentals. Too preoccupied to communicate effectively.
Resource Investigator	Outgoing, enthusiastic, communicative. Explores opportunities and develops contacts.	Over-optimistic. Loses interest once initial enthusiasm has passed.
Co-ordinator	Mature, confident, identifies talent. Clarifies goals. Delegates effectively.	Can be seen as manipulative. Offloads own share of the work.
Shaper	Challenging, dynamic, thrives on pressure. Has the drive and courage to overcome obstacles.	Prone to provocation. Offends people's feelings.
Monitor Evaluator	Sober, strategic and discerning. Sees all options and judges accurately.	Lacks drive and ability to inspire others. Can be overly critical.
Teamworker	Co-operative, perceptive and diplomatic. Listens and averts friction.	Indecisive in crunch situations. Avoids confrontation.
Implementer	Practical, reliable, efficient. Turns ideas into actions and organises work that needs to be done.	Somewhat inflexible. Slow to respond to new possibilities.
Completer Finisher	Painstaking, conscientious, anxious. Searches out errors. Polishes and perfects.	Inclined to worry unduly. Reluctant to delegate.
Specialist	Single-minded, self-starting, dedicated. Provides knowledge and skills in rare supply.	Contributes only on a narrow front. Dwells on technicalities.

Key words & phrases

incidentals
preoccupied
outgoing
develops contacts
talent
delegates
manipulative
offloads
dynamic
thrives on
drive
prone to
provocation
sober
discerning
to inspire
perceptive
averts friction
indecisive
crunch situations
painstaking
conscientious
polishes
to worry unduly
reluctant
single-minded
self-starting
on a narrow front
dwells on
technicalities
trait
resolving conflict
soothing hurt feelings

10.3.3 Team skills

From the table, it is clear that one of the most important attributes of a good teamworker is flexibility, since the demands made on each individual will change as the team develops and as the project moves on, creating new challenges and requiring team members to take on new roles.

Another crucial trait is interpersonal awareness, the ability to observe and analyze such roles and relationships within the team and the reactions of clients and other stakeholders in the project. Interpersonal skills mean that such an observer can also react appropriately, quickly identifying tensions and resolving conflict, soothing hurt feelings and restoring motivation. Clearly, an important component of interpersonal skills is self-awareness – understanding your own motives and the effects that your behaviour has on others. Members of successful teams value and support each other and believe that they can learn from each other.

[4] Belbin. (2011). *Team Role Summary Descriptions*. Retrieved from http://www.belbin.com/content/page/49/BELBIN(uk)-2011-TeamRoleSummaryDescriptions.pdf

Key words & phrases

paradoxically
as a matter of course
day-to-day
conveyed

Paradoxically, working on a team project requires a great deal of autonomy. Because the team is autonomous, all the team members have to be self-directing, self-monitoring and self-evaluating. Any team leader that emerges is not there to tell everyone what to do, but to coordinate effort and maintain motivation. Information and tasks must be shared, but each team member has to take initiatives and monitor his or her own progress. It is also important to be able to learn fast from experience, so that mistakes can be quickly corrected and avoided in future.

Communication skills also have a high priority. Not only does the team have to communicate their work in written reports and oral presentations to university tutors, but also to stakeholders outside the university, such as clients or the general public. The skill of negotiation will be in great demand and diplomacy is a vital component of this. Communication within the team must also be excellent since failure to communicate sensitively and diplomatically leads to misunderstandings and conflict. Decisions have to be agreed and properly documented as a matter of course, but also day-to-day practical details might prove critical if not conveyed to the whole team.

Source: Argent, S. (2013). *From high school to university: A handbook for EAP students.* Summerford: Gateway University Press.

Task 8 Thinking critically to apply learning

Using what you have just read about group development, group roles and group skills, you should now be in a position to review your personal evaluation of your group's performance in the Marshmallow Challenge.

Look back at Task 2 and add more evaluative comments. Think about the way your group developed as a team, the different roles that team members played and the skills and abilities you demonstrated.

Compare your evaluation with the other students in your Marshmallow Challenge group.

Task 9 Writing: keeping a record of what you have learnt

Write advice to yourself about working in teams to remind you of what you need to know when you do your first group project.

Self study

* Find group project briefs for university courses in your discipline — if possible, for courses you are intending to follow. Prepare questions about the projects, analyze the requirements and think about how you would perform as a team member. Prepare to report to the class.
* Record key vocabulary for talking about group projects in your field.

Section 3 Reflection for assessment

What the university expects:
- autonomy – set goals and direct your own learning; self-assess rigorously and conscientiously; critical reflection – critically evaluate the quality and impact of your own and others' work

Contexts:
- projects for study and work which require peer and self-assessment

Aims:
- to understand the importance of reflection in academic and professional life
- to develop frameworks for presenting personal reflection for assessments
- to use key vocabulary for reflecting on group projects

Task 1 Thinking critically: personal reflection using a theoretical framework

1.1 Which role in the table on page 274 best describes your preferred role in class? What evidence can you provide that this is your usual role?

1.2 Work in pairs with a student who you know well. Which role in the table do you think best describes your partner's usual role in class? Make a note of your choice, giving supporting evidence.

1.3 Compare your self-evaluation with your partner's peer evaluation.

1.4 Discuss these questions as a class:

   a How does it feel to try to categorize yourself?

   b How does it feel to have a classmate categorize you?

   c Is such a framework helpful? What are the problems with using a theoretical framework to describe people?

   d When is it important to be able to describe yourself?

Study smart: recording your reflections

Preparing for and starting at university is a time of great change and challenge. It is useful to write your reflections regularly in a notebook, diary or journal so that you record how you understand and meet these challenges. In addition to developing your writing and vocabulary, this record of your self-reflection will provide valuable material whenever you need to describe yourself, for example in an assessed group project or for a job application. Keep this record with your CV or resumé and develop it throughout your university career to give your personal statements real depth and quality.

Task 2 Writing: starting a reflective diary

If you are applying for a job or applying to study a university course, you usually have to support your application with a personal statement. You can collect ideas for this by keeping a reflective diary.

Using ideas from Task 1, draft a text in which you describe yourself. Explain your strengths, describe how you manage your weaknesses and how you feel you perform in a team. Keep this as the first entry in a reflective diary. You will have an opportunity to review and expand your writing at the end of the section.

Task 3 Reading to identify assessment requirements

3.1 Read the first section of the extract below quickly to answer the question *What aspects of a group project are you asked to reflect on for assessment?*

3.2 Read the first section again carefully to identify what tutors are looking for in a reflective commentary on a group project. Make notes of any criteria used by tutors and compare your notes with another student.

3.3 Find any useful strategies that you could use to help in developing a reflective commentary.

Chapter 10 Group work (Continued)

10.4 The criteria for critical reflection

A UK university gives the following outline of one of its key developmental aims for its students.

Critical self-awareness and personal literacy

Understanding how one learns, the ability to assess the work of oneself and others, and to identify one's strengths and weaknesses. The ability to organize oneself and perform as an autonomous, effective and independent learner. The ability to relate to other people and function collaboratively in diverse groups, including the development of appropriate interpersonal skills, emotional intelligence and adaptive expertise[5].

The reflective commentary in assessed group work is an important indicator of a student's capacity to learn from experience and is graded on its quality and depth. Effective personal reflection on a group project is valued within and beyond the university context because it demonstrates professional competence in two respects. Firstly, there is the ability to analyze rigorously all aspects of the project you have been engaged in. Well thought-out comments about these aspects and how group members functioned in the task show observational and analytical skill, much more so if they include suggestions about how problems could be avoided next time. Secondly, an honest and conscientious exploration of your own performance, particularly how you have overcome problems and what you have learnt, demonstrate your personal awareness of what you can achieve and where you have to improve, indicating your potential as a recruit to a professional position.

10.4.1 Reflecting on the process

The whole process through which the project develops, from the initial brief to the deliverables at the deadline, needs to be described, analyzed and critically evaluated. Information is best recorded on a regular basis in a diary or journal as the project evolves, regardless of whether this is a requirement for assessment, because this document will be a rich source of commentary for any reflective report. Reflection

---

Key words & phrases

emotional intelligence

adaptive expertise

---

[5] Oxford Brookes University. (2011). *Brookes graduate attributes*. Retrieved July 2, 2012, from http://www.brookes.ac.uk/services/ocsld/sese/graduate_attributes.pdf

on how the group as a whole completed each stage of the discipline-specific work on the project is absolutely critical to the particular field of study and allows you to demonstrate a deep and developing understanding of your subject and its application. In addition, the management of the process has to be reviewed in detail, from planning to completion, from decision making to tea making and from time keeping to conflict resolution. Marking criteria reflect the depth and detail of analysis and the quality of evaluation, so few marks are gained by simply describing what happened. Every group will meet problems in the course of their project and it is the way that the team worked through these that is important.

10.4.2 Reflecting on peer contributions

The reflective component of a group project usually includes an evaluation of the contribution of each member of the team. The group may have to decide together on the grade that each of them is to receive for their personal contribution, and so it is important to apply valid criteria fairly. The team may be given criteria to apply in their peer assessment. They may or may not be able to read each other's commentaries.

Generally speaking, for a high grade, a really good team member interacts well with other team members in a tactful way, gets unpopular things done, manages time well and produces good-quality work to meet deadlines. Such a person is engaged with the project and willing to do extra work in his/her own time to make sure that tasks are achieved. He/she also motivates and supports other team members and is keen to learn.

At the very least, a team member should make and maintain workable relationships with others, contribute to tasks and work dependably on regular tasks. All team members should observe deadlines and attend team meetings.

The sort of behaviour which results in a low grade from peers is generally the kind of behaviour which means that others have to step in to take over tasks, e.g., laziness, lack of interest, failure to communicate. A really weak team member does not interact well with others and usually remains silent in meetings. He or she misses deadlines, especially when pressure builds, wastes time and is not interested in developing new skills to support the project.

10.4.3 Reflecting on your own contribution

An important benefit of working in teams is the potential for self-discovery, and this forms an important component of the reflective assessment grade. Through careful reflection on their own performance, each team member can identify valuable lessons learnt about their own strengths and weaknesses, abilities they never suspected they had and attributes such as flexibility and capacity for hard work.

It is useful to start by outlining what you hope to gain from the project, setting yourself some objectives and personal goals so that these can form a framework for assessing your own learning. However, be flexible, as there will inevitably be some unexpected challenges and therefore some surprises in what you discover about yourself. Again, it is crucial not just to describe or summarize what happened, but to make connections with your own previous experience and with theories you have read about, reflect on any difficulties you had, clarify what you have learnt and examine how you learnt it.

Follow any guidelines you are given, for example, headings to use. Also use criteria for peer contributions in assessing your own contribution. Evidence any claims you make using your documentation of the project, particularly your personal diary or journal. This is one type of academic writing where your personal response to situations is important and so do not be afraid to use the pronoun *I*. However, you may still be expected to use and reference ideas from published sources too, because they show a depth of research into aspects such as team roles and motivation.

Key words & phrases

tactful
workable relationships
dependably
to step in
pressure builds
self-discovery
to make connections

Source: Argent, S. (2013). *From high school to university: A handbook for EAP students.* Summerford: Gateway University Press.

Task 4 Applying criteria for reflecting on the process

Here are some reflective comments from students evaluating their group's success on the Marshmallow Challenge.

4.1 **Rank them in order from the most to the least reflective.**

4.2 **Work in pairs to compare the order in which you have ranked the comments, and justify your choices using the criteria you identified in the first part of the extract on page 277.**

4.3 **What should each student do to make their commentary richer and therefore worth more marks?**

Student 1: It was a disaster. The teacher didn't explain clearly enough what we had to do, or give us enough time. Nobody finishes when it's a group, but I could do it well on my own.

Student 2: We spent too long talking about it. We need to be faster at seeing the solution. Perhaps each group member could make a design first, because there are probably lots of different ways to do it.

Student 3: We broke some of the spaghetti pieces by accident and so they were too small to use. The marshmallow was too heavy when we put it on our structure and it just wouldn't stand up.

Student 4: John saw the solution straight away, no problem. We just did what he said. And it was OK until we put the marshmallow on top, then it crashed and time had run out.

Task 5 Understanding criteria for reflecting on peers

The table on page 280 shows a set of marking criteria for students to use for peer assessment on a group project, together with the instructions for grading performance.

5.1 Each attribute (A–D) has two sentences missing from the criteria.

Complete the table using the following criteria. Compare your answers.
- Pursues development activities in own time.
- Does not prioritize.
- Is receptive to other team members' ideas.
- Always waits to the last minute.
- Can lose concentration when pressure increases.
- Is frequently late or absent for reasons others consider trivial.
- Stays calm during periods of pressure.
- Uses tact and diplomacy.

5.2 **Think of your class as a team and reflect on how your peers perform in the class team.**

Your teacher will give you peer review forms for a number of your classmates. Using the table on page 280 to guide you, give each classmate a mark from 1–5 for each attribute. Write comments as appropriate.

5.3 **What did you find most difficult about assessing your classmates and awarding grades for team performance?**

Instructions for team peer assessment: *For each other member of your team, allocate a mark for each attribute according to their performance. Marks such as 3.5 are allowed. The maximum number of marks is 20. Your own aggregate score will be determined as an average of the marks given to you by your peers.*

Team peer assessment criteria:

attribute	mark				
	1.0	2.0	3.0	4.0	5.0
A. Working with others Effectiveness in relating and co-operativeness with others	Impatient listener. Does not consider other people's opinions. Loses their interest and support.	Sometimes fails to share ideas to gain support or does not support others well.	Makes and maintains workable relationships with others.	_____. Always makes helpful suggestions and co-operates.	Initiates and cultivates key contacts. _____. Gets unpopular things done.
B. Planning and organizing Establishes realistic goals and uses resources	Reluctant to plan ahead. _____. Frequently misses deadlines.	_____. Spends too much time on nonessential items.	Organizes work to keep productively occupied, but sometimes deadlines cause rushed work.	Carefully plans so that support is available when needed and deadlines are met comfortably.	Always on top of things and in control. Handles difficulties smoothly.
C. Effectiveness under stress Ability to work under pressure of changing load and deadlines	Easily gets confused and anxious when given more than one assignment to do.	Keeps work flowing smoothly in normal situations. _____.	_____. Maintains steady output.	When a crisis occurs, can rapidly adjust priorities to produce high-quality work.	Smoothly produces high-quality work to meet each new and existing deadline.
D. Commitment to job Diligence, involvement and interest in work	_____. Does not contribute ideas in meetings.	Produces what is asked for, but does not devote time to develop new job skills.	Works dependably on regular assignments, but does not take on extra work.	Very attentive to responsibilities. Discourages casual conversation when there's work to be done.	Eagerly seeks new assignments and challenges. _____.

Task 6 Applying peer assessment criteria to a case study

Julia is a member of a team which has just completed a group project for Environmental Science. She has written a reflective commentary on each of her team members.

6.1 Study Julia's reflective commentary on the members of her team and use the criteria from the table on page 280 to give marks to Erica, John, Maysoun, Jian Min and Gordon.

6.2 Most students are reluctant to criticize their team mates, but assessment can be expressed diplomatically. Find Julia's diplomatic strategies in commenting on her classmates.

6.3 How could Julia improve her commentary?

6.4 Look again at your peer reviews of your classmates. Make your comments diplomatic, but honest. Return them to the teacher and then study your peers' reviews of you.

Erica

Erica is a hard-working, extremely supportive and helpful team member. She is patient and fair at all times and has great diplomatic skills. Erica's presentation skills are excellent, but during the presentation she struggled with some of the questions which took her away from her specific area (however, the questions aimed at Erica were far from clear). This may have been due to the fact that she lacks confidence. However, her contribution of ideas, work and diplomacy skills were highly respected by the group and she was a valuable team member.

John

John is sometimes a hard-working member of the group with a great enthusiasm for countryside management. However, when he does not understand something, he does not always ask for clarification and this often led to the wrong work being done. John's attitude to academic work was in conflict with others and he had different expectations and priorities. He would miss meetings or not finish his share of the work unless reminded by other members of the group. John contributed and communicated better with the group in the second semester after common goals and deadlines had been set out.

Maysoun

Maysoun is a hard-working, supportive and enthusiastic team member. She can be undiplomatic and impatient towards group members, but never without good reason. Though this could be seen as a negative trait in some situations, it was necessary as the rest of the group could be too passive and non-confrontational when problems arose. Maysoun has excellent presentation skills and copes professionally under pressure (for example, when handling difficult questions). Maysoun is a good coordinator who is able to maintain focus and delegate effectively.

Jian Min (Johnny)

Johnny is a quiet, studious and supportive member of the group. He is an organized and calm person who has good diplomatic and motivational skills. His contribution to meetings is limited and this can appear as lack of interest, but we discovered that this was just shyness. If there are issues to be dealt with or work to plan, Johnny will quietly make sure they are tackled. Johnny's technical skills were a valuable asset to the group when working on improving the PowerPoint presentation slides. He is a very supportive team member who is sensitive to people's moods and is good at using humour to relax tensions.

Gordon

Gordon is an enthusiastic team member. He is hard-working when a task is delegated to him and is keen that workloads are shared fairly. He can lose concentration and be disorganized, which led to meetings being interrupted, delayed or missed. He lacks confidence in his own knowledge and can be hesitant to voice an opinion. However, during the preparations for the presentation, Gordon was adept at passing his presentation skills and experience on to other members of the group. He is an excellent diplomat under pressure.

Task 7 Understanding criteria for assessing self-reflection

For another project, Julia's team had to create, deliver and review a morning's input for a primary school class on the environmental impacts of food.

7.1   Their tutor has given them four criteria for assessing self-reflection: *setting goals, analyzing, evaluating* and *narrating*.

   Complete in the table below by reading the explanations and inserting the criteria in the appropriate place.

criteria	explanation
	the clarity with which you describe the experience in question and the extent to which the description motivates and leads to the subsequent analysis, evaluation and goal-setting stages
	the extent to which you can identify connections with your previous knowledge and experience, and with the learning outcomes of the programme
	your ability to explain the quality of your experience, give insights into how learning has taken place and state reasons for any judgements made
	the extent to which you can identify practical steps for improvements in areas discussed in evaluation; you will be able to specify short and long-term goals which are clearly stated

7.2   **What additional points were made in the last section of the extract on page 278 for writing a good self-reflective commentary?**

Task 8 Applying criteria for assessing self-reflection in a case study

Read Julia's self-reflective commentary and evaluate it using the criteria and strategies identified in Task 7. What is good about her commentary and what would improve it?

Group project: Create, deliver and review a morning's input for a primary school class on the environmental impacts of food.

Self-reflective commentary

My learning objectives

1   Develop confidence in my creativity.

2   Challenge my negative perceptions about reviewing activities; experience them from the facilitator's point of view and make them work.

I feel I achieved objective 1 as I'm pleased with the amount I contributed to the group creatively, and this was a real surprise for me. I was pleased that the group was so positive about my ideas and actually used many of them for the main activity and the reviewing. I discuss this in more depth in the 'Conclusion' section of my Learning Log.

I don't feel that I achieved my second objective regarding reviewing, but I tried hard and I have now experienced reviewing sessions from a facilitator's point of view and learnt something about how they can be improved.

My role within the group

At the first meeting, the group settled quickly into the sort of roles defined by Belbin (1981) (from Weightman, 1999, p. 115); the chair (myself), the shaper, the ideas person, the resource investigator, the team worker and other roles associated. I felt that I had taken on a leadership role. I was worried about this; however, as the meetings progressed I felt more comfortable.

Personal strengths

*   My organizational skills throughout this task I feel were very beneficial and helped to keep the group moving towards the same goal.

*   My previous experience working with children in an educational setting was useful and was complemented by the experience of some of the other group members.

*   I was concerned for the welfare of the team. An example of this was shortly before the first session at the school. Most of the team had been up all night on another assignment. I wanted to make sure no-one went to teach on an empty stomach so I organized breakfast.

Personal weaknesses

*   In the peer reviews, someone said that I listened more to one person's opinions more than the others.

*   I found it very difficult to relax and allow others to work at their own pace. I found it difficult to hide my frustration.

Personal analysis of how I learn

I thrive when I am thrown in at the deep end and have a range of problems to tackle. I also learn best by experience and find group work is a fantastic opportunity to learn skills from your peers.

What I have learnt

*   It is possible to be a leader and still be liked within the group and that I am not the dictator I am always concerned I am.

*   I worry far too much about things beyond my control. I need to accept that I do not have responsibility or control over what other people have agreed to do.

*   At times I was concerned I focused too much on things like research, paper work and meetings with the group. However, the feedback from the class teacher was that these aspects were much appreciated and we ourselves realised when the event ran smoothly that all the meetings to iron out problems had been very beneficial.

Building from the experience

For future group work, I aim to do the following things differently:

*   Approach members personally and respectfully to discuss any problems.

*   Attempt to relax about the pace that others work and trust that things will be done when they need to be done.

*   Ensure that I listen to advice from everyone and avoid relying too obviously on one member.

Key words & phrases

negative perceptions

the facilitator

learning log

complemented

the welfare

been up all night

on an empty stomach

frustration

thrown in at the deep end

dictator

beyond my control

iron out problems

Task 9 Thinking critically about your response to group work

Read the students' comments about their experience of group work, and choose a comment that you either can identify with or find particularly surprising. Work in pairs to discuss why you think this.

It was hard – we argued a lot and it felt very uncomfortable. Sometimes we really did not want to meet and discuss things, but I knew I had to get on with it.

It was a good feeling when we looked after each other.

I felt challenged to give my best.

We got motivated by this project – we wanted to take it further.

The best thing was actually working in a team and doing a professional report. We felt good about ourselves.

It was really good to work with people we hadn't worked with before. No one had a group of friends to relate to, so we all started on an equal footing and no one felt excluded.

You have to be really independent to work in a team.

Don't worry about what you say, just talk: if you don't start talking early, you'll get left behind.

We learnt to trust each other.

Task 10 Redrafting your self-reflective commentary

Use what you have learnt in this section, particularly the criteria for self reflection, to redraft and expand your diary entry from Task 2.

> **Study smart:** graduate attributes
>
>
> At the beginning of this book, you were introduced to the concept of graduate attributes: … *the skills, knowledge and abilities of university graduates, beyond disciplinary content knowledge, which are applicable to a range of contexts and are acquired as a result of completing any undergraduate degree.*
>
> Throughout the book, you have explored seven graduate attributes by investigating what the university expects of students and by working towards meeting these expectations. You have only just begun your journey, but you have taken the first steps.

[7] Barrie, S. (2004). A research-based approach to generic graduate attributes policy. *Higher Education Research and Development*, 23(3), 217.

Graduate Attributes

1. Critical reflection
- understand complex relationships between observations, evidence and theories
- analyze and evaluate problems, solutions, claims and evidence
- critically evaluate the quality and impact of your own and others' work

2. Awareness of how knowledge is advanced
- develop criteria for evaluating knowledge
- tolerate temporary and conditional viewpoints
- consider opposing positions

3. A spirit of enquiry
- pursue knowledge for its own sake
- seek sources of information
- persist in efforts to secure answers and knowledge
- respond flexibly and positively to unfamiliar situations

4. A global and ethical understanding
- identify your global responsibilities
- take responsibility for your actions
- respond sensitively in cross-cultural contexts
- demonstrate a high level of ethical commitment

5. Effective communication
- present complex ideas in response to the needs and expectations of an audience
- listen and respond to the ideas of others
- take a stance and defend it
- negotiate effectively with others

6. Autonomy
- set goals and direct your own learning
- use feedback to improve performance
- self-assess rigorously and conscientiously

7. Teamworking
- encourage and advise others
- contribute positively to teamwork
- take on a variety of roles in a team

Task 11 Reflecting on your EAP journey

Reflect on what you have learnt on your EAP course.

What are the most important ways in which you think you have changed?

Are you ready to enter university?

What further goals do you have?

Our very best wishes for the future!

Transcripts

⊕T01 Unit 1, Section 1, Task 3

GUY: Hi, Chen. Did you get anything by e-mail yet about the flat? I just got a call from this guy Khalid Othmani. He sounds really interested.

CHEN: Yes, two. I printed them off. Haven't replied yet. What did Khalid say?

GUY: He's a postgrad, from Libya. He's only here for one semester. He's doing Robotics, I think he said.

CHEN: Wow, cool! Robotics is so interesting! Why only one semester?

GUY: It's a European Master's, done in three universities. He's so lucky! Last semester he was in France somewhere and next summer he goes to Spain. He could stay on campus if he wanted, but he said it's too noisy in the halls of residence[1]. He's leaving to find a quieter place to study. Do we want someone for only one semester, though? It will mean we have to start looking again in May and our contract is until next January.

CHEN: Yeah, I guess so. But most undergrads will want to go home for the summer, too, so we'll probably have to re-advertise then anyway.

GUY: Right. What about your e-mails?

CHEN: I've got them here. This is Cao Yong Qiang, Matt, and he's doing Building and Estate Management. He's in the first year of his BSc. He seems very nice and friendly. He was on campus last semester, but he's like me – he wants to share a flat to save money for his parents. Actually, I would really like to help him, but I think we would speak Chinese too much!

GUY: No! That would be good for me! I've got my first exam this semester!

CHEN: Oh yeah! I forgot about your Chinese module.

GUY: And the other one?

CHEN: This is Dimitri. He's a third-year student[2], doing a BA in Business Studies. He did his first two years by open learning at home in Athens. He's living at his uncle's house in Summerford. It's too crowded and he hasn't got enough room to study properly. He says he's a 'mature student' – what does he mean?

GUY: He's older than us. That could be why he studied by open learning. He probably has a job and a family at home.

CHEN: Oh! Yeah, he does seem old from his e-mail.

GUY: No problem – he'll be nice and quiet. So … no girls to cook and clean the flat, then?

CHEN: No chance. Just think of Xiaohua – her room's a mess and she can't even cook rice! And she is definitely not quiet!

GUY: Ha ha! I'll tell her you said that! So, we've got three so far. We can't afford to wait any longer. Let's interview them this evening and take them around the flat.

CHEN: OK. We have to ask them some questions so that we can choose two.

GUY: Yes, but they might be … er, wrong, you know … All three of them might be unsuitable.

CHEN: Or they might not like the flat! Let's write some questions now. How should we contact them? By phone? They've all got mobile[3] numbers.

Key words & phrases

a postgrad
a semester
robotics
European
a contract
undergrads
to re-advertise
Building and Estate Management
module
open learning
a mature student
a mess
can't even
can't afford to
interview
unsuitable
to contact
mobile

---

[1] *dormitories* in US English
[2] In English and Welsh universities, degrees are usually three years because students spend an extra year in the sixth form at high school.
[3] *cell phone* in US English

T02 Unit 1, Section 5, Task 1

MAYSOUN: Hello, I'm Maysoun. Can I tell you about this important lecture on Tuesday evening? That's the 25th of January. It's by Professor Dedi Mogea. He's a visiting professor from Indonesia who is going to teach postgraduates in my department. There are notices on all the noticeboards with the details. We are really lucky because he's a world expert on tropical rainforests. His first lecture is open to everyone. It's a basic introduction and it's called 'A visit to the tropical rainforest'.

Key words & phrases

a world expert

a basic introduction

T03 Unit 1, Section 5, Task 2

MAYSOUN: He's going to talk about its climate and geography, and explain how plants and animals have adapted to life there, resulting in the richest biodiversity on Earth. He's also going to talk about some of the threats from human activity and how we are all involved as consumers ... yes, consumers of the rainforest.

Key words & phrases

geography

have adapted

consumers

T04 Unit 1, Section 5, Task 5

MAYSOUN: Good afternoon, everyone. Welcome to Gateway University and to the second Rachel Carson public lecture on the world's most important ecosystems. Last semester you heard from Dr Collingwood about the polar ecosystems, but today you are invited to visit a very different place by Professor Dedi Mogea. We are very fortunate to have Professor Mogea as a visiting professor to our Department because of his outstanding research. I will now let Professor Mogea start our visit.

PROF MOGEA: Yes. Thank you, Maysoun. So, er ... I am Dedi Mogea and we are going to visit a very different place. It's hot and humid, dynamic and teeming with noise and life ... Here it is in Slide 2: the Equatorial, or tropical, rainforest.

Now, this is just a start, an introductory lecture, so I will try to keep it non-technical – a simple overview. Look at Slide 1 here. First, I'll define 'tropical rainforest' and briefly describe the key locations and the major types of forest. OK? Next, I'll outline its structure, how the ecosystem appears to be organized in layers. This is important because you need to understand the structure so that I can explain the next part – some of the adaptations of plants and animals. I want to show how their dynamic struggle to maintain a place in the ecosystem has resulted in the richest biodiversity of any system on Earth. And finally, I will outline some of the threats to this biodiversity and explain how we are all responsible.

Key words & phrases

polar

hot and humid

dynamic

teeming with

equatorial

structure

struggle

maintain

T05 Unit 1, Section 5, Task 6

PROF MOGEA: Now, strictly speaking, the tropical rainforest that you see here on slide 2 is a biome – that's B-I-O-M-E. What we mean by a biome is an ecosystem defined by its geography and climate. In terms of geography, tropical rainforest is found on the continents and islands that lie in a broad band near the equator in a region often referred to as 'the tropics'. Look at the map on the next slide ... Here the solar radiation that falls on the Earth is at its most intense. It doesn't vary much throughout the year and so neither does the climate – as you see here in slide 4. The constant, intense solar radiation provides enough heat energy to drive a daily cycle of evaporation, thunder clouds and precipitation, or rain. So, this cycle ensures frequent, heavy rainfall throughout the year. The climate is described as 'ever wet' and shows little seasonal variation, which makes it quite different from any other regions of the world. OK. Now, the high humidity and high intensity of solar radiation in this region are ideal for plant growth, and this means that the natural climax vegetation – that is, without any disturbance – is forest. In fact, huge trees, among the tallest in the world.

So, tropical rainforest is forest that develops in the equatorial regions of the Earth where there is abundant, year-round rainfall and intense solar radiation. Where are they and how do they vary?

There are three main locations in the world that have these regions and hence have important tropical rainforests: South America, Africa and South East Asia. Look again at the map ... OK? So, within these regions we have all kinds of places: coasts, mountains, swamps. So we can classify rainforest further according to geographical factors such as altitude, topography and proximity to the ocean. Look at

Key words & phrases

biome

continents

solar radiation

intense

vary

evaporation

precipitation

regions

climax vegetation

huge

abundant

mountains

swamps

geographical factors

altitude

topography

proximity

this diagram on slide 5 now. In terms of altitude, for example, lowland and montane tropical rainforest are distinguished. There are also swamp forests, which are permanently or periodically flooded, and mangrove forests that occur along the coast in all equatorial regions. What distinguishes these forests from each other are their characteristic species: the tropical rainforests of my country, Indonesia, support a very different range of flora and fauna – plants and animals – than those of the Congo in Africa or the Amazon in South America. Also, the lowland forest has different species from montane forest, and so on. Yet the tropical rainforests of all these regions share many common features.

So, what do they all have in common? Well, as I've already said, the dominant life form is trees. In lowland forest in particular, there are very tall, in fact massive, trees that take hundreds of years to grow. But before I can say much more about rainforest characteristics, I need to explain the layered structure of the forest.

Look at slide 6 now. It helps to think of the forest in layers, although you don't really see these layers as you walk through the forest. The tallest trees in the forest form the uppermost layer, or canopy – the top of the structure. Some trees stand many meters higher than the others, and these are known as the 'emergents' because they emerge from the forest and stand out. You can see them quite clearly from the air. Emergents are not just one species, but can be several different species. Below these emergents are understorey layers of shorter trees. Now, some of these trees are shorter by nature – they have grown to their normal mature height. But the rainforest ecosystem is very dynamic – always on the move, always changing. So some of them are immature emergent species and these will keep growing until they eventually grow above the rest. OK? Now the ground …

At ground level, it's cool, dark and wet. Here, the ground is open, with not much obvious plant life. Small plants such as grasses are relatively rare. The reason is that it's so dark, we don't get enough light down here. Conditions are not good for photosynthesis, unlike the top of the canopy where the emergents enjoy full tropical sunshine and can photosynthesize all day, all year round. Are you OK with photosynthesis? From school? Plants need light to combine CO_2 and water to make carbohydrates, for example, sugar, for their growth.

So, the rainforest ecosystem has horizontal layers in which growing conditions are different. It is cool, wet and dark near the floor, becoming warmer, drier and lighter towards the top.

⊕T06 Unit 2, Section 1, Task 2

DR MALIK: Hello, Guy, come in and sit down. How are things?

GUY: Hello, Doctor Malik. Fine, thanks.

DR MALIK: Let's see … the last time we met to review your studies was at the beginning of Semester 1, and we talked about the exams you had to resit in the summer.

GUY: Yes, I was pretty worried about them. I didn't think … I didn't think I would get through, but I did. It was such a relief.

DR MALIK: Mmm … I remember. And we also discussed your attitude to your studies in your first year, didn't we?

GUY: Yes, I know I didn't have a good attitude in my first year – I thought it would just be a repeat of things I learnt at school so I didn't try very hard. But failing my exams and having to do resits made me change my ideas. I think now … I think I've got a much better idea of what's involved in studying at university. I think I understand how hard I have to work to get the grades I want.

DR MALIK: Well, it's good to hear that you can learn from your mistakes and that you now understand what you have to do to be successful. You have a better idea what you are capable of.

GUY: Yes, I think I do … definitely.

DR MALIK: Now, I've got a note here of your action plan for the first semester. You said you would try to organize your time better and study smarter this year. What happened about that?

GUY: I think I did study smarter last semester. My friend Chen gave me some help – about making a study plan – so I could organize my time better. That was really useful. I put all my lectures and seminars in the plan so I didn't miss any of them, and I put specific times in the plan to read and prepare for the seminars. That made me feel more confident because I was in control, so I'm going to do that again – make another study plan for this semester.

DR MALIK: Good idea. I noticed that you made some useful contributions in seminars last semester – and without any prompting from me. I was pleased to see that. Now, I also remember we talked about using the library. You said, I think, that you were a little bit afraid to go to the library, so … what happened about that?

GUY: Well, I went with Chen and our other friend Maysoun to a lecture. It was a lecture given by one of the librarians about how to use the library. So, after that I wasn't afraid to go there anymore. I spent a lot of time in the library … I probably spent more time there last semester than in my whole first year at university! It's nice and quiet there and easy to study, and this semester, I'm sharing a flat with Chen and two other students, so I'll probably go to the library whenever I need quiet study time.

DR MALIK: Good – it sounds like your friends are having a good influence on you and, looking at your grades, it seems to have worked. You got an A grade for that essay you wrote for me on the co-operative movement and 75 per cent in the International Marketing exam, so that's an A grade, too. Well done!

GUY: Thanks. I was pretty surprised because I didn't see myself as an A-grade student. But actually, I think it was because I really enjoyed writing that essay. Because, you know, I work in the Summerford Co-op sometimes and the manager is really friendly. He's doing an MBA and we chat – we compare what we're learning in our Business Studies classes. He talks to me about how the theories and ideas we study in class relate to a real company like the Co-op. I think that really motivated me because the ideas weren't only from books, but I could see them in practice.

DR MALIK: Excellent! That's exactly what we want you to understand by the end of your degree – how the theories we teach you can be applied to practice in the real world. OK, so I can see that you've got some good study strategies in place now and you also have a much better idea about the scope of a degree – by that I mean what kind of thinking and learning is involved and what you personally have to do to be successful. But I can see that you also have a much better attitude towards your studies, probably because you know which parts of the course interest you.

GUY: Yes, I really want to focus on the practical things that interest me. So, actually, could I ask you about that? I was thinking about changing my elective module. I registered for the Legal Studies elective at the beginning of the year, but I don't think I want to do that one now, really. I wondered if there was another elective I could do – something a bit more practical?

DR MALIK: Well, in fact, we have started a new elective module this semester on Change Management. That one's very practical. The lecturer is Dr Simpson - she's new in our department and she has some very innovative ideas. She's actually going to get members of staff from one of the big insurance companies to come into class and talk to students about how they managed all the changes to the company in the recent merger.

GUY: That sounds great. I think I'd really enjoy it. How do I change my elective?

DR MALIK: Well, first you need to look at the module outline and the assessment to be sure about your choice. You can find it on the department intranet. Then you need to complete this change of module form and take it to the undergraduate office on the ground floor. So, I think that's all we need to talk about today. Here is the record I've made of our meeting and your plans for the semester. Have a look at it and make sure that it's correct.

GUY: Yes, I think that's what we agreed.

DR MALIK: OK, fine. Later in the term we'll have another meeting to look ahead to next year and your honours dissertation – get you thinking about that so you can do some reading over the summer. But remember, in the meantime, any problems, just send me an e-mail to make an appointment so we can discuss them.

GUY: Thanks a lot. I'll do that.

Key words & phrases

made useful contributions

any prompting

having a good influence on

an A-grade student

that motivated me

in practice

be applied to practice

good study strategies

the scope of a degree

my elective module

registered for an elective

innovative ideas

recent merger

change of module form

undergraduate office

honours dissertation

⊙T07 Unit 2, Section 2, Task 2

DR MICHAELSON: Hello, good to see you, Chen. Come in and have a seat. Sit over here next to my desk so I can hear you – I'm a bit deaf you know, so you might have to speak loudly.

CHEN: Thanks, I'll try, but you know speaking loudly is a problem … I'm not confident to speak loudly.

DR MICHAELSON: Really? Tell me some more about that.

CHEN: Well, you know … my English is not so good … but, you know … because I'm Chinese and in our culture we don't like to speak out … stand out from a group, so I don't like to give my opinion in class.

DR MICHAELSON: Hmm … that's interesting. Are you happy with that – I mean being silent in class? Is that OK for you?

CHEN: I don't know … not really, I think. When other students speak I think, 'I know that! I could say that!' But I don't manage to answer quickly and I'm not confident to speak loudly, so the tutor doesn't notice me.

DR MICHAELSON: OK, so you say that you want to speak in class – in seminars – because often you know the answer, but you don't speak because you don't feel confident to speak loudly enough to make the tutor pay attention to you. Is that right?

CHEN: Erm … yes.

DR MICHAELSON: Is this – speaking in class – important to you? Something that you would like to change? Would you like to discuss it now?

CHEN: Erm … yes. I don't know if I can change, but I would like to try.

DR MICHAELSON: OK. Well, we can think about it in terms of coaching … you know, like a football coach helps the players in his team to play better. I am like the coach and you are like a player. I can't play football for you, or speak in seminars for you, because you have to do that for yourself. But I can help you to think about your goal and how you can reach it. So tell me, what would you like to be different about speaking in seminars?

CHEN: I would like to feel easy to speak out in seminars. Like in my software development seminar, there is a student from Greece and he is usually the first one to speak. You know he doesn't always know the answer, but he just speaks anyway! I would like to feel confident to give my point like that.

DR MICHAELSON: OK, so your goal is to feel confident contributing in seminars – like the Greek student.

CHEN: Yes. I would like to be as confident as him.

DR MICHAELSON: Good. So tell me, what stops you speaking? What happens now when you know the answer and you want to say something?

CHEN: Well … I try to make a sentence … and, you know … to check my grammar is OK, but I … there isn't enough time and another student answers before I can answer.

DR MICHAELSON: OK, so you think that you need to check the grammar of your answer before you speak, but that slows you down and you miss the chance to speak. What would happen if you said an answer with grammar mistakes?

CHEN: I think … maybe people would laugh at me.

DR MICHAELSON: Really? What about the Greek student? Does he always speak with correct grammar?

CHEN: No … at least I think … he sometimes makes grammar mistakes.

DR MICHAELSON: OK, so he sometimes makes mistakes … and do people laugh at his mistakes?

CHEN: No … well … no, they don't. I think they sometimes want him to stop talking! But that's because he doesn't give the right answer.

DR MICHAELSON: So if it's OK for the Greek student to make mistakes and to give the wrong answer, is it OK for you to do that, too?

CHEN: I guess … maybe … I'm not sure.

DR MICHAELSON: Perhaps we can think about the football players again. Is it OK for them to miss a goal or to lose the ball to another player?

CHEN: Yes … that's just part of the game.

DR MICHAELSON: So is making grammar mistakes or giving the wrong answer in seminars part of the game, too?

Key words & phrases

have a seat

a bit deaf

being silent

manage to answer

in terms of coaching

do that for yourself

software development

seminar

anyway

as confident as him

what happens

slows you down

miss the chance

miss a goal

lose the ball

part of the game

ACCESS EAP: Frameworks • Transcripts

CHEN: I guess ... yes, I see what you mean.

DR MICHAELSON: Good, but the football players who miss the goal or lose the ball ... what do they do about that?

CHEN: I suppose they go and practise kicking goals more accurately and running with the ball to improve their skills.

DR MICHAELSON: Yes, good, so what should you do about your contributions in seminars?

CHEN: Well ... I should try to do more speaking ... actually, I have some friends – I speak with them a lot. It's not a problem because I'm comfortable to speak with them. I know they don't laugh at my mistakes. They want me to be successful.

DR MICHAELSON: OK, so your friends don't laugh at you. Do you think you could imagine that the people in your seminars are like your friends? They also want you to be successful. The lecturer certainly wants you to succeed in your studies.

CHEN: I can try.

DR MICHAELSON: Good, but I think you need some specific practice activities ... you know, just like the football players, to make you feel more confident. Speaking with your friends is good, but you say it's easy for you. What could you do that requires more effort?

CHEN: Well ... actually, my friend Guy persuaded me to go to the international students meeting last semester. I could join the meeting again and try to contribute ... try to say more at the meeting.

DR MICHAELSON: I have another suggestion that you could think about. There's no need to decide right now. You might know that in our department we have a student–staff liaison committee. It consists of staff members and students who represent all our different degrees. Its purpose is to make sure that students have a say in how our degrees are run. The committee discusses any problems students have with the courses and tries to come up with solutions. We need a new student representative this semester. Do you think you could do that?

CHEN: Oh ... I'm not sure ... Do I have enough knowledge about the courses and the department?

DR MICHAELSON: Don't worry about that – you learn as you go along.

CHEN: Can I think about it? Maybe discuss it with my friends and let you know?

DR MICHAELSON: Of course. In the meantime, I want you to think about our discussion and then send me an e-mail so I have a record of our conversation. I would like you to tell me what your goal is and what the current reality is – by that, I mean what things are like now. Then I want you to say what options there are for you to make changes and what you will do to make those changes happen.

CHEN: OK ... thanks. I'll do that this afternoon.

⊛T08 Unit 3, Section 2, Task 1

XIAOHUA: Hi, Matt! How's things? What are you doing?

MATT: I'm good, thanks. Just got something I did for Jenifer – you know, the writing teacher? Want a coffee?

XIAOHUA: No need, I'm meeting Chen here – I'll get coffee when he comes. He's always late! Probably messing with his computer again.

MATT: I don't understand! What's wrong with this word? *Malicious*. Chen talks about malicious code in viruses – means *bad*, right? But Jenifer, see, put 'WW', 'wrong word' here.

XIAOHUA: Oh yeah, it means *bad*. But she put 'NNS', too. That's a clue. NNS means she can understand what you mean, but a native speaker – English, I mean – doesn't say it like that. NNS is 'not native speaker'. Like it's the wrong collocation. One of her favourite things!

MATT: Collocation? I never heard that!

XIAOHUA: Word partners. Like *malicious* and *code*. What word did you put with *malicious*?

MATT: *Effects* ... *malicious effects*. Sounds OK to me. I thought it was kind of advanced!

Key words & phrases

I see what you mean

practise kicking

to improve skills

what should you do

should try

do you think you could

imagine that

practice activities

requires more effort

persuaded

have another suggestion

there's no need to

a student–staff liaison

committee

consists of

represent

to make sure that

have a say

to come up with

a student representative

learn as you go along

in the meantime

reality

options

⏍T09 Unit 3, Section 2, Task 2

MATT: *Effects … malicious effects*. Sounds OK to me. I thought it was kind of advanced!

XIAOHUA: Yeah, but maybe you should check first.

MATT: I did. I checked in my dictionary and it said *bad*, but *bad*'s a common word. I think I must use rare words.

XIAOHUA: Oh no, it's not like that with academic words. They're not always rare. You have to use the words that the lecturers and professors use a lot – learn to use their vocabulary. It's not like high school, where the teachers like you to find new, rare words. Lecturers don't want surprising words. They want frequent, academic words.

MATT: That's so different from my English essays at school.

XIAOHUA: Yeah, and you have to use the right collocations – word partners that go together frequently.

MATT: Oh no! How do I find all this stuff?

XIAOHUA: Does your dictionary give collocations for *malicious* or *effects* – some words that they go with?

MATT: I didn't see that … Yes, *malicious rumour*. I don't understand that. And *malicious girl* … OK … and for *effects* we got *bad, harmful, negative, detrimental, adverse*. Wow! That's a lot! I like *detrimental*.

XIAOHUA: Yeah, maybe. There's a neat way to check this. What's your assignment topic? I mean, what makes the bad effects?

MATT: It's about health checks for workers in construction. They sometimes work with hazardous materials – you know, dangerous. And these might have bad effects on their health, so the manager has to make sure they get checked for these bad effects.

XIAOHUA: Right. I'll show you this website we learnt about in EAP class. You can use it to see what words go with *effects*. You can even see real academic examples. Here's the handout to explain the website.

⏍T10 Unit 3, Section 2, Task 4

XIAOHUA: Type in this URL from my handout. I'll get you a copy later. Click on *Enter*. You can do some searches straight away, but after that you have to set up a username and password. But it's free.

Here on the left side you can choose what you want to do, then the answer comes up on the right side of the screen. First we can see if these two words – *malicious effects* – go together frequently. Click *List* in the top left and type in the search string box *malicious effects,* and click on *Search*.

What answer? Oh! Don't have it. Not there. So you better use another word.

MATT: What? I want to write *something effects*.

XIAOHUA: We can check those words from your dictionary same way. What are they again?

MATT: *Bad, harmful, negative, detrimental, adverse*. But how I can choose the most academic word?

XIAOHUA: Ah, see where it says *Sections*? Choose *academic*! Then search.

MATT: OK. Now an academic search. I put in *bad effects* and search … Wow, only 4! Not academic! I was right! Ha ha! *Harmful*, 12 – better! *Negative*, 13; *detrimental*, only 12 again; *adverse* … wow, 75! That's the one!

XIAOHUA: Good! But we need to check some examples for *adverse effects*, to make sure the meaning is correct for your sentence. Click on the blue words *adverse effects* in the result window. There, you can look at KWIC. That's K-W-I-C: key word in context. All 75 examples in the academic texts! You might find medical ones if you scroll down and look at the left-hand side – it tells you what academic subject the example comes from. And if you want to see more of the text, like the whole sentence, click on the number of the example.

MATT: Great. Thanks, Xiaohua. This is really useful!

T11 Unit 3, Section 4, Task 2

JACK CURTIS: Good evening, everyone. I'm Jack Curtis, from the Department of Mathematics here at Gateway. Welcome to this series of ten lectures to introduce the basics of mathematical modelling to students across the university. Copies of the programme are at the back of the hall, for those who haven't got one. And there's a handout for each lecture, but everything is on the Mathematics website, so you can always get them there.

You'll be glad to hear I'm going to assume that you know only basic mathematics. That is, high school maths[1]. But I will have to teach a little more advanced stuff as we go. However, I'm sure you'll manage to keep up with me, especially when you see how relevant it is to your own subject and your own research. This first lecture is a basic introduction to the idea of modelling; the key mathematical concepts. Later, we will look at how computers have revolutionized research in all disciplines through modelling. By the end of the lecture series, you'll know about some of the important software tools that you can apply in your own research and you'll be able to start using them.

Let's start with a simple definition. A mathematical model is a description of a system using a set of variables, together with the equations, or functions, that relate the variables. The variables can include a range of values, for example, measurements such as height, numbers, time values. So a mathematical model is really a whole series of equations that show how the different variables in the system are related. Economists might be interested in using a model like this to represent a system such as trade in a particular commodity. Environmentalists model ecosystems and meteorologists model climate change. Mathematical models are also used to put engineering systems through large numbers of virtual tests

Right, mathematical models use mathematics to describe and investigate systems. These models are used in fields as diverse as biology, computing, economics and geography. A model often starts as a kind of metaphor, or analogy, to represent a system in the real world. For example, when biologists talk about *the tree of life*, they don't mean a real tree, but a system in which there are branches from a main trunk. Computer science has many analogies, for example, *array*, *binary tree*, *list* and *dictionary*, to explain systems such as data structures. I'm sure all you business students are familiar with metaphors like stock *market crashes*, *credit crunch* and *price squeeze*. Even names like the *knapsack problem* and the *travelling salesman problem* are analogies for mathematical problems. Metaphors and analogies link new ideas to familiar ones that we all know.

When these analogies are elaborated, I mean, worked out in mathematical detail, they become models. There are three main purposes for working with such models: explanation, prediction and evaluation. Firstly, models are used to explain how a system works by representing the system as something familiar, with well-understood components and processes. Secondly, if a model is accurate, it can predict future events or what will happen if something is changed, using different scenarios – climate change models have this important function. Thirdly, models are used to evaluate new inventions or methods. It is particularly useful to test new materials and devices using computer models because computers allow thousands of virtual test runs without any expensive loss or damage. So, researchers use models to explain, predict and evaluate.

Incidentally, there's another good example of the second purpose, predicting. Stephen Hawking's research into black holes depended on him finding a mathematical way of cancelling various infinites that cropped up in his equations. He predicted that black holes would emit radiation, which sounded bizarre at the time. Nevertheless, Hawking Radiation was subsequently discovered and named after its predictor.

OK, I see that some of you are feeling uncomfortable! Back to basics, then. A simple mathematical model that you probably already know is this growth curve on Slide 3. It's a typical one. Here's some measure of time, say hours or days, on the horizontal or *x* axis, and some variable we are investigating on the vertical or *y* axis. The *y* variable might be number of bacteria, number of people, prices, etc. This typical shape of the curve is due to the mathematical relationship between the *x* and *y* variables. In other words, how something changes over time. I'll give you an easy example.

Now, think first of a microbe – a bacterium. In 24 hours, it divides into two, and each of these bacteria splits into two in the next 24 hours. The pattern you get over a week is: 1, 2, 4, 8, 16, 32, 64, 128.

Key words & phrases

to assume
keep up with
software tools
a set of variables
equations
functions
commodity
meteorologists
virtual
diverse
trunk
binary
stock market
credit
knapsack
are elaborated
scenarios
new inventions
devices
test runs
black holes
infinites
cropped up
emit radiation
sounded bizarre
Back to basics, then
x axis
y axis
curve
microbe
bacterium

---

[1] *math* in US English

Plotted on a graph, like this, it looks a bit like the letter J. There is a steep increase, here. This model is called exponential or geometric growth. This pattern happens when the rate of growth is proportional to the amount or number. Then you have the mathematical relationship: r proportional to n, where r is the rate of growth and n is the number or amount. Do you know this special symbol? To show proportionality? Of course, if you plot rate of growth against number, you get a straight line and that's the basis of linear regression, for example, for estimating trends. It's very important in statistical analysis, but I'll say more about that in the next lecture. Put simply, with exponential growth, the larger a quantity gets, the faster it grows.

This type of growth describes many systems apart from the growth of bacteria. It describes potential human population growth and the potential spread of infectious disease, as one person infects, say, three people and each of them infects three others, and so on. In physics, there is the nuclear chain reaction, the concept which is the basis for nuclear weapons. In economics, we have the concept of compound interest, and you may also know of pyramid selling schemes – or scams, as they should really be known. Both involve exponential or geometric growth. In computing, the spread of the Internet can be plotted on this kind of curve. Then, also in computing, there's the exponential decrease in size of computerized devices – a reverse 'J' curve, if you like. This is a consequence of Moore's law, which states that the number of transistors that can be included in an integrated circuit doubles every two years. Turing, in 1950, predicted exponential growth in the size of computer memory. These are just a few examples from different fields. I'm sure that most of you will know about an application of this model in your particular field.

By the way, there's an interesting traditional story that illustrates this model, about grains of rice on a chess board. It's famous in most cultures, so you may already know it. A clever guy did something to earn a reward from the emperor. When the emperor asked him what he wanted, he asked for a chess board on which grains of rice were arranged as follows: one on the first square, double that amount on the second (2 grains), double again on the third (4 grains), 8 on the fifth, and so on. This amounted to more rice than existed in the whole world!

Of course, our growth curve for bacteria is only a model: bacteria don't increase to take over the entire surface of the Earth, infectious diseases don't kill everyone, and pyramid selling schemes collapse. Why is this? Sometimes the variable gets used up completely and so the growth stops, as in the pyramid scheme when there are no more people to recruit. There is also the example of a chemical reaction that has used up one of the chemical reagents completely. In these situations, growth doesn't suddenly stop. As the pool of potential pyramid sellers diminishes, it takes longer to find new recruits. As the chemical reagents are consumed by the reaction, it takes longer for reacting molecules to find each other. The rate of growth now slows in proportion. This situation is represented by an 'S' curve, as we can see here on Slide 6, known as a logistic curve.

In nature, though, exponential growth stops mainly because of limiting factors: the bacteria don't have enough food to keep multiplying; people are immunized against infectious diseases, and this has the effect of slowing down rates of infection. The model has to take account of these factors if we want to understand particular systems in order to make predictions.

So, you see how a mathematical model has to include key components of the system that is being investigated. You don't have to include all the known components. For example, you don't necessarily have to model the granularity of the stones in the tarmac of a road to accurately model a truck's behaviour. We may know a lot about how tarmac interacts with rubber tyres, but a friction coefficient will be sufficient. Also, mathematical models of a planetary system are generally two-dimensional, even though we obviously exist in a three-dimensional universe. However, if the model doesn't fit the observable system very well, if it doesn't describe the required elements of a system closely enough, then it has to be adjusted. It has to be changed in some way until it does, and that tells the researcher a lot about the system. So this is where mathematical modelling gets really interesting!

Often, an overly complicated model is a big hint that you are heading in the wrong direction. I'll give you an ancient example of this: the ancient Greeks' epicycles for planetary motion. Circles were the perfect shape to them. When it was discovered that some heavenly bodies did not move in circles, that is, the planets, they added circles within circles – epicycles – to model the behaviour. More accurate

ACCESS EAP: Frameworks • Transcripts

models meant adding more epicycles and greatly complicating the mathematics of the model. It took a long time, but eventually Copernicus put the Sun (rather than the Earth) at the centre of the planetary system, and Kepler used the mathematics of an ellipse to describe planetary motion to a very high degree of accuracy. Both these fundamental changes to the mathematical model made it simpler but more accurate and also, so it turns out in the age of space travel, closer to the truth.

On the other hand, useful models sometimes have to be refined rather than discarded. Newtonian physics was improved by Einstein, but we still use it. Most of the time it's fine, for example, for predicting movement of fairground rides, cars, planes, etc., but not in strange situations such as a long way from the Earth's surface, or next to a huge object or when travelling very fast. GPS systems have to use the theory of relativity – rather than Newtonian physics – as they rely on satellites which are up in orbit and so, according to the theory of relativity, experience a very slightly faster rate of time than someone on Earth.

Now, with computers to do the calculations, the process for you is relatively easy. Once you know what the key components of the system are, you can enter sets of data – the key variables – and run scenarios to model their interactions. You can see if the model fits with real observations, you can make predictions, test run inventions and also see how materials will behave under different conditions …

⊕T12 Unit 4, Section 1, Task 1

CARMEN RODRIGUEZ: Welcome, everyone! We are just a small group for this first seminar, but we'll be running more of these informal sessions around the campus over the next few weeks and we hope you'll encourage your friends and classmates to come to them – of course, if you find this one useful that is. Let me introduce my colleagues. On the left is Victor O'Leary.

VICTOR O'LEARY: Hello.

CARMEN RODRIGUEZ: He is the subject librarian for Environmental Sciences, and next to Victor is Paula Kahn.

PAULA KAHN: Hi.

CARMEN RODRIGUEZ: She deals with Computer Science. And I'm Carmen Rodriguez – I am the specialist librarian for Business Studies. Before we start, can I just ask – how many of you have already been to consult your subject librarian? Hmm … no-one yet – well, I hope that after today you'll understand how we can help you get started on your research and you'll feel confident to come and talk to us. Since there are only five of you, could I ask you to go round and say your name and why you decided to come to this session?

MAYSOUN: Well, I'm Maysoun and I'm doing the Master's in Environmental Studies and I would like to do some research about my country – I come from Syria – because my father, you know, he works for the Ministry of Irrigation. So he can get me lots of statistics, you know, that they collect to monitor the water and pollution and things like that.

GUY: I'm Guy. To be honest, I haven't really thought about research because I'm an undergraduate. I'm on the International Business degree, but this is only my second year so it's too early to think about research. I only came really because Maysoun wanted some company.

KHALID: Hi, I'm Khalid and I came with my friends Guy and Maysoun and Dimitri. I'm doing a European Master's in Robotics but I don't do any research until I get to Spain for my third stage next summer. It seems a long way off.

DIMITRI: Hello, my name is Dimitri. Actually, I have tried to think about research and it's a big problem for me. I studied the first part of my degree as an external student of Gateway University. I was also working as an accountant in Athens. When you are an external student, you get everything you need in a manual and so you don't need to go to a library. Now I'm in the final year and they expect me to do a research project and find the resources by myself. I really don't know how to start.

PETER: Hi, I'm Peter. I'm an undergraduate, too – in my second year like Guy – but on the Marine Science degree. I haven't really thought about research, but I was intrigued by the idea of going on a research journey, so I've come along to find out more about that.

CARMEN RODRIGUEZ: Thanks everyone for those introductions. I'm sure we can offer something for all of you here – even the ones like Khalid, Guy and Peter who think they don't need us yet. But we also have Maysoun, who's started thinking about data collection, and Dimitri, who's not sure yet how to get started. I thought we could begin by defining what we mean by research – what research involves. Then we can go on to look at one of the comparisons – or metaphors – that are used to try to simplify and explain this complex concept. That way we can show you where the subject librarians fit into the research process and how we can help. This is an informal session so we can take questions as we go along.

So, let me ask you first, what is research? What do you think is involved in doing research and how is research different from, say, journalism?

MAYSOUN: Research is finding out something new and – well, you need to collect data for research and journalists don't collect data. They are just looking for stories.

GUY: Yes, I'd agree that research goes deeper than journalism somehow. Journalists talk about research, but really the kind of research they do is like I do when I write an essay. I go to the library or search on the Internet to find facts.

DIMITRI: I think you need some kind of aim or maybe problem. Like when I'm doing an audit of company accounts, I'm looking for problems with the accounts. Of course, I guess journalists start with problems as well.

CARMEN RODRIGUEZ: Good! You've come up with interesting ideas and I'd like to pick up on some of them. Research does involve problems, as Dimitri said. You try to explore problems and puzzles – things you don't understand – in order to explain them. Maysoun's right – usually, you collect and analyze data which will support your explanation of the problem or puzzle. A key difference with journalism is that the process is systematic. That means you have a goal and a plan which you try to follow. Journalists just respond to events – the news; they don't control what happens. Another difference is the kind of questions that you can ask about your problem or puzzle. Journalists mainly ask 'what', 'when', 'where', 'who' kinds of questions, but in research you are more interested in 'how' and 'why'. Of course, these questions are harder to answer because you don't just describe, you have to explain. However, the one difference that we haven't mentioned so far is that research has to relate to theory – it adds to knowledge in your field by testing established theories or models against events in the real world. Journalism, on the other hand, is a series of unconnected events in the real world and there is no body of knowledge that journalists add to each time they research a story. Now, there are several metaphors that people use to talk about research …

ⓣT13 Unit 4, Section 1, Task 5

CARMEN RODRIGUEZ: Now, there are several metaphors that people use to talk about research and we're going to look at just one of them today. We can think of research as a journey. Paula will explain this in more detail and then Victor will explain how your subject librarian can help you to begin your research journey. After that we can take some of your questions. So, over to Paula.

PAULA KAHN: Thanks, Carmen. OK, so, research as a journey. First, I'm going to ask you to think about journeys. What makes you go on a journey? Why not just stay at home?

GUY: Usually you want to get somewhere – you have a destination.

PETER: That's true, but you might just like travelling – the freedom to explore new places.

KHALID: Or you might not want to travel, but you have to – to get away from a difficult situation or problem.

PAULA KAHN: Yes, good, all those ideas are useful for thinking about research. As Carmen said, research often does start with a problem or something you can't explain and the journey is your search for an explanation – and obviously if you find a satisfactory explanation, then you've reached your destination. Peter mentioned the enjoyment of travelling and the freedom to explore. The same is true for research. You can find yourself in uncharted territory that no-one has explored before. This is what people mean when they talk about the excitement of research. But think about what you do before you set off on a journey – how do you prepare?

MAYSOUN: We need to plan which way we will go. My husband usually buys maps and plans for the trip. I can get my son ready and think about what to take with us.

DIMITRI: In my profession – accounting – time is money. You have to know exactly where to go so you don't take the wrong road and waste time. Maps are essential.

PAULA KAHN: Precisely – we normally plan journeys so we get to our destination as quickly as possible. Research is like that, too, in some ways. It's certainly important to have an accurate map of your starting position. That lets you see which paths are well known and which still need to be explored. But it's also important to be ready to deviate from the path if something interesting or unexpected happens. You certainly need to have a destination in mind, but you won't always know exactly how you are going to get there. You have to keep an open mind. A journey has stages and so does research. Now, Maysoun mentioned collecting data from her father's ministry. Data collection is one of the stages, but it is not the best place to start. Starting with data would be like parachuting into an unknown country and trying to find your way out – and without a map, too!

DIMITRI: So where should we start?

PAULA KAHN: Well, you have to find out what researchers are currently working on in your field. You start by reading – most important – and preparing a map of what is already known so you can find out the kinds of journeys that other researchers have made to get to that point. They sometimes give you suggestions for new avenues of research, too. By finding out what has been done, you can also find out what has not been done that you could do. This is the gap – the missing part of the map, if you like – that you want to identify. When you've found this gap, then you can plan your own research to add another section to that particular research avenue. The process is also iterative, so each stage is refined by the results of the previous stage – by that, I mean that as you read, your ideas about what you want to research become clearer and this helps you to read in a more focused way.

MAYSOUN: But I thought I had to do something new that no-one has done before?

PAULA KAHN: Not completely new. You have to build on what other researchers have done before you. Perhaps you might develop an existing method and use it to collect more reliable data. Or you might collect data in a different context – in your case Syria – and compare it with data from other countries or regions which have been published in the literature. That shows to what extent findings can be generalized to different contexts.

KHALID: The comparison, the metaphor, doesn't work completely though, does it? I mean if you start your journey with a problem, you run away from it, but in research it seems you run towards the problem.

PAULA KAHN: You're right, of course, and that's where the metaphor breaks down and the comparison stops being useful. Seeing research as a journey shows that it has a starting point and a destination with a plan about how to get from one point to the other, but there is never an exact correspondence between the two concepts that are being compared in a metaphor. We could probably think of lots of other ways that journeys are not like research and that's also helpful to understand the concept, too. But you have to get started on your research journey to really understand what is involved, so I'll hand over to Victor now. He's going to talk about how the subject librarians can help you to begin to prepare the map of your starting point.

VICTOR O'LEARY: Thanks, Paula. OK, so Paula talked about research as a journey and the need for an accurate map of your starting position so you know which paths are well known and which still need to be explored – what has not been done that you could do. Reading is the first stage of your research journey and that's where the subject librarians fit in because we can help you to find the literature that you will use to map your starting position. The final result of any research project is always a report of some kind – a paper presented at a conference or published in a journal, or an unpublished dissertation stored in the university library. There is absolutely no point in doing research unless you publish your findings for the research community to read. Now, the subject librarians know the kinds of places – the databases of journals or conference proceedings or dissertations – where these reports are listed and catalogued. We can show you these databases and help you to search them to find relevant sources to read around your topic. We can show you how to use online search tools that can make your search for sources more effective. As it happens, I'm doing a lunchtime workshop tomorrow about searching online databases, so if you're free at 12:30, come along.

Key words & phrases

time is money
take the wrong road
precisely
as … as possible
in some ways
lets you see
to deviate from the path
to get there
to keep an open mind
parachuting into
new avenues
the gap
iterative
reliable data
can be generalized
breaks down
an exact correspondence
a paper
a conference
a journal
unpublished dissertation
databases
conference proceedings
catalogued
to read around your topic
online search tools

CARMEN RODRIGUEZ: Thanks, Victor. So I hope we've been able to clarify what research involves and how you get started, but I'm sure you'll have some questions. Yes, Maysoun?

MAYSOUN: What happens if I do my research and then I discover that someone has done the same thing before me? How can I be sure that my research has never been done before?

CARMEN RODRIGUEZ: Well, this is where reading the research literature plays such an important role. As Victor said, the final outcome of a research project has to be a report. Researchers can only contribute to the body of knowledge in their field if other researchers read about their work and accept their findings and conclusions. Research published in journals and books shows the current state of the art in a field – if you like, how far they have got with mapping the territory. So that's why you need to find and read this published work – to make sure you know what has already been done. However, your task is made a little bit easier because researchers publishing in a particular research area will mostly review the same key studies. You get a good idea about this if you compare the lists of references at the end of a series of papers. There will be several papers which appear in all the lists because these studies have helped to move the field forward and so everyone refers to them. Now, the online databases allow you to do a special kind of search starting with these key studies and looking for all the more recent sources that refer to or cite them. It's a quick way to find recent studies that are relevant to your topic. Victor will talk more about this type of search tomorrow when he shows you how to search the databases. Guy, you have a question?

GUY: Well, this is interesting for Maysoun and Khalid and maybe Dimitri, but I don't see how it's relevant for an undergraduate in the second year, like me or Peter. I mean, I've only just got used to finding my way around the library and looking for books to get ideas for my essays and reports. I don't do research and I find the whole thing really quite scary and off-putting. You talk about journeys and maps and destinations, but what's that got to do with my essays and assignments?

PETER: Yeah, I agree with Guy – research is definitely a postgraduate thing. I can't do research yet because I don't know enough about my subject. I don't have all the skills and knowledge I need.

CARMEN RODRIGUEZ: I understand how you feel and that's why we want you to come and use our services in the library – so you feel more comfortable with the research tools when you start to do your own research. However, you do in fact do research already – you just don't recognize it. Most of the ideas you study have been developed through research activities. For example, in Guy's case, you learn about management theories which were derived from research that observed the behaviour of workers in factories. And in Peter's case, you learn about the findings of research expeditions to chart the seabed and identify marine species living there. But, also, your lecturers set problems for you to solve or questions which require explanations and you use sources such as books to find how other people solved these problems or found explanations. When you synthesize ideas from books to answer a question for an assignment, then you are in effect reviewing the literature relating to that question and your essay is similar to a literature review. It's only a small step from answering a question set by the lecturer to choosing your own research question to answer.

Well, I guess that's all we have time for today, but – whether you're a postgraduate or undergraduate – please come to Victor's talk tomorrow or visit your subject librarian, and we'll show you how you can start your research journey.

⊕T14 Unit 4, Section 2, Task 1

VICTOR O'LEARY: Hello and welcome everyone, and particularly the students who attended our lunchtime seminar yesterday. I'm pleased to see you've come to the library to consult your subject librarian about your research. Today we're looking at online resources and how to search them to find sources of information.

So, yesterday we compared doing research to going on a journey, and I'm just going to tell you a little story about that.

There was a tourist travelling in Ireland – in the south, you know – and he was lost, so he stopped a local farmer to ask the way: 'Can you tell me how to get to Drogheda?' 'Ah well,' says the farmer, 'If I wanted to get to Drogheda, I wouldn't start from here!' So, a funny story, but with a serious point because, just like the tourist on his journey to Drogheda, for your research journey you have to start from where you are, but that isn't always the best place to start. The task for your subject librarian is to show you a better place to start and that's my main point in this talk. First, I'll talk a little about the places where you can find information online, then I'll demonstrate how to search for it. After that you can try it for yourself.

Now, as I'm sure you know, there's an awful lot of information on the Internet these days and it's growing all the time. So the first thing to consider is how to search effectively for what you want. You've got two places to start. You can start with Google or other search engines such as Yahoo! or Bing, or you can start with the online databases that I mentioned yesterday – effectively, these are like huge catalogues of electronic sources. But let's start with where you probably are: Google. Did you know that this search engine was actually developed by two postgraduate students as part of their research? Google is similar to other search engines because it looks for all the pages on the Internet which contain your search term. However, it uses a PageRank algorithm to rank or sort the pages it finds in a special way. The more links to a page, the higher its ranking. A page with many links from other pages has been effectively rated useful by other users. Google has other useful applications, too – I wonder if you know about Google Books and Google Scholar – I'll talk about those a bit later.

So, Google is definitely a good place to start, but it's not the only place. Google is good for practising your search skills so you can use these to search the large number of databases that you can find online. Databases are different from Google because someone – a librarian or an information scientist – has already evaluated and selected the information before adding it to the database. Anyone can put anything online, whereas not everything gets onto the databases. They only include content which meets certain criteria, for example, journals which might influence the way a field develops and up to-date papers that have been peer reviewed. They also try to include papers from around the world – of course, these papers have to be written in English so that excludes a lot of research published in other languages. But all this means that you start closer to where you want to end up – closer to Drogheda, if you like – and your search is already more focused.

I'm going to show you how to use one of the largest databases: the Web of Science. Once you know how to use that, your subject librarian can show you the more specialist databases for your subject. But first, let's start where many of you are – with Google. I'll just bring up the familiar standard search screen on the monitor here … and I'm going to click this link on the right for *Advanced search*.

So, now you can see you have some options to refine your search and these are presented to you in everyday language that's easy to understand. At the top, we can see 'Find web pages that have' and then 'all these words' so you can type several words in this box and Google will find pages that have all of them anywhere on the page. Underneath the first box you have an option to search for an exact phrase or string of words. This is useful for finding pages with particular expressions or phrases that are used regularly in your field, like 'climate change' or 'advanced driver assistance systems'. You should be able to see that both these options produce a smaller number of results – in other words, you use them to narrow your search. Now, on the next line you can see the word OR separating the three boxes. That's a different kind of search because it finds pages with any one of the search terms you enter rather than only pages with all of them. You use this option to broaden your search and get more results. Finally, above the next box you can see the instructions 'don't show pages that have' and then 'any of these unwanted words', so you can use this search to exclude word meanings that you don't want. For example, you might want to find information about Java, a programming language, but not about Java, a type of coffee.

Now, you could do all these operations in the standard search box by using what are known as Boolean operators to connect your search terms. There are three main operators, AND, OR and NOT, and for search strings you use inverted commas just like direct quotes. You don't need to know about these operators in Google advanced search because it uses everyday words, but you will see them when you search the online databases. So let's look at the Web of Science now. I'll just bring that up on the screen … there it is – and you can see it has a similar look to Google advanced search, but instead of the everyday words to show the type of search, we have the Boolean operators next to the search boxes. The drop-down menus give you a choice of which operator to use and the menus on the right give you more options for narrowing your search. So now you're not just looking for a word on a page, but perhaps for a word in a title in combination with an author or a particular publication, and there are several more options in each menu. You can also narrow your search by looking only in a certain

Key words & phrases

demonstrate

catalogues

electronic sources

postgraduate students

search term

PageRank algorithm

to rank

has been rated

search skills

an information scientist

content

up to date

peer reviewed

excludes

the Web of Science

advanced search

options

to refine your search

everyday language

a string of words

to narrow

to broaden

a programming language

the standard search box

Boolean operators

bring that up

instead of

the drop-down menus

in combination with

time period, say after 2000, or by choosing only one of the databases. There are helpful examples under each box to show you how to type your search terms and these also show you another useful search tool: truncation. Notice how the example has an asterisk after *spill* in 'oil spill* Mediterranean'. This search will bring up all the members of this word family, for example, *spill* or *spills* or *spilled* or *spillage*. So this is another way of broadening your search by truncating – that's cutting – the end of a word and adding an asterisk.

So, I said I would come back to some of Google's other applications and you can see these in the drop-down menu labelled 'more' at the top of the Google page. Let's get it back up on the screen …

There we can find two particularly useful tools for researchers: Google Books and Google Scholar. Google Books is an online collection of books, and Google Scholar contains a more restricted set of webpages which Google has identified as academic. Let's look at the advanced search in Google Scholar. The search boxes are the same as for standard Google, but with extra boxes to do similar searches to the ones that we saw in the Web of Science. So, we can now search just in the title of a page and we can look for an author or a particular publication over a specific period of time. When we click the *Search Scholar* button, we get the familiar Google results page, but with some differences. The same PageRank algorithm is used to rank pages, but different criteria are used to decide which pages are listed first in the results. The ranking is determined not only by the number of links from other pages, but also by the journal which published the articles or by the author. Another important criterion is how often articles are referred to in other literature. Google Scholar shows this underneath each result using a link – 'cited by' – and a number. The number refers to the number of articles Google Scholar found which all have citations to the article that you selected. If you follow the link labelled 'cited by', you get a second list of search results – a much shorter list – showing articles which have the one you selected in their list of references.

I hope you can see that this is a powerful way to really focus your search and find the most relevant papers to map the start of your research journey. You can do the same kind of citation search in the Web of Science by selecting the link 'cited reference search' at the top of the page beneath the tabs. But before I talk about that, I think you should try searching with Google Scholar and see what you come up with.

⊙T15 Unit 5, Section 1, Task 1

NICK: Hi, everyone. Guy and Chen, here are some friends of mine. This is Pam, Heather, Neal and Kate.

PAM, HEATHER, NEAL & KATE: Hi!/G'day!

GUY & CHEN: Hi!

NICK: Guy's hoping to go overseas for a gap year.

NEAL: Great!

NICK: I know how much you lot love to start a conversation with 'When I was in Timbuktu …'. Anyway, I told him you'd have some interesting stories about your experiences.

NEAL: Where are you going, Guy? What are you hoping to do?

GUY: Well, I'd really like to work with producer co-operatives, maybe some kind of development project. I'm thinking of going somewhere in Africa.

KATE: Oh! Nice!

PAM: Well my first teaching job was in Africa, too. In a tropical part, in fact. It was a lot different from what they told us to expect in the orientation sessions. For a start, the university was still being built.

NICK, HEATHER, NEAL & KATE: Oh yes!/Been there!/Tell me about it!

PAM: I remember I had to teach speaking skills one afternoon each week, and my class was timetabled in a temporary classroom with a tin roof – you know, metal. Well, every afternoon we had a tropical rainstorm – not just a shower, big heavy drops, a real downpour. On a tin roof, the noise is deafening! No way could we hear each other. It was impossible. You couldn't predict the exact time, but once it started it lasted at least an hour. I didn't know what to do – I was a new teacher and I thought I was supposed to cope. I was too embarrassed to complain.

NICK: Yeah, it never turns out the way they tell you, Guy. For my first job, I went to Japan straight after my teacher training. I had an evening class of four students who were all really, really nice and I was doing exactly what I'd been taught on my teacher training course. I set them up with a speaking task, listened as they talked and then gave them feedback at the end. I felt really good about how things were going.

PAM: Pride comes before a fall, eh?

NICK: Yes, absolutely! Then – just by chance, I have to say – I asked them if they thought the classes were okay and one woman said she wasn't happy. This was a big thing in Japan, and to do this to the teacher in front of the other students a big, big thing – and this isn't recently, this is at least 20 years ago – so I asked why and was a bit taken aback by her answer. She said that she wanted me to speak and not just to listen and then correct. And she said that they paid all this money for a native speaker, but I hardly said anything! I felt angry and confused. I thought, what's gone wrong? Wow, I've done this wonderful course, with all this great methodology from the experts – was it completely useless?

HEATHER: Yeah, it's hard because you get such a short training course and then you're expected to be an expert. I mean, it can really knock your confidence, and that's a big issue when you're away from home. I should've learnt some of the language before I went to teach English in China – I didn't realize how much my confidence would suffer because I hadn't. I was in a place where very few people spoke English. I could buy things in a little local supermarket, because you don't need to speak – things like spoons, plates, eggs. It was okay as long as everything went smoothly, but I couldn't always tell what I was buying. Once I thought I had bought some shampoo, but it turned out to be something for cleaning the toilet! And there was a big argument one day when I tried to pay with a forged banknote.

NICK: What a talented woman! Where did you learn to forge banknotes?

CHEN: Sad to say, they are found in my country, but easy to see, you know.

HEATHER: No, Nick! I didn't know the note was forged, of course. Yes, easy to see, but they do catch us foreigners out. Anyway, everyone crowded round and seemed to be shouting. The assistant was so angry and that really upset me. I had to go into that supermarket every day. I didn't have a cooker in my room and I was too shy to try and order food in restaurants. I lost a lot of weight because I wasn't eating enough. I got really depressed – it was a big part of my culture shock.

NEAL: Yeah, knowing the local culture is very important, even when you think you've got it cracked things can go wrong. I don't know if this is relevant to your situation, Guy, but one problem a lot of teachers have is cheating. In one place I taught, I felt I got on very well with my students – in fact, most were very good at English. Some other UK and US teachers told me that students in this country had a bad reputation for cheating. I was sure my students were different.

KATE: There's a *but* coming …

NEAL: You're right – *but* they were extremely worried about their exam and the class representative kept telling me that everyone in the class had to pass my English exam at the end of the year. If they didn't, they would have to repeat the whole year. I tried to reassure them and told them I would only test them on what we had covered in class – they were sure to pass. During the exam, I caught them texting on their mobile phones. These were the best students in the class, with no reason to cheat. I ran round very angrily, confiscating the phones. I was so disappointed in them …

KATE: I had a funny cheating incident when I was teaching girls in a high school in Turkey, although it wasn't funny at the time! In my first week, I gave them a vocabulary test. Some of them hadn't learnt the words and wrote absolutely nothing on their answer papers, so when I marked these I gave them a 'zero'. That's what you do, isn't it – no answers, no marks? I wrote a big fat 'nothing' by each name on their blank sheets. When I gave the papers back, there was uproar – some of these girls screamed and ran out of the room and the remaining students sat in stunned silence. I went to see the principal, who explained that the 'zero' grade was reserved for students caught cheating, she said. In Turkey, cheating is just as serious as it is here. I had accused them of cheating! I was so annoyed – no one had bothered to tell me this fact. A bit more information would have helped.

GUY: Oh no! It all sounds so difficult!

Key words & phrases

a bit taken aback
methodology
knock your confidence
went smoothly
a forged banknote
talented
catch … out
depressed
culture shock
got it cracked
cheating
had a bad reputation for
to reassure
confiscating
a big fat nothing
uproar
in stunned silence
no one had bothered

GUY: Oh no! It all sounds so difficult!

NEAL: Don't look so worried, Guy. It's not that bad. We could've given up and gone home to the UK, but we didn't. There's always a solution and it's all good experience – part of 'life's rich pattern', as they say – and very useful for job interviews. The more experience you have, the more you have to say.

KATE: So tell us what you did, Neal. Did you fail all your exam cheats?

NEAL: I was just going to say when you interrupted with your story! No, I didn't. It turned out that I had it all wrong! At the end of the exam, the class representative came to retrieve the phones. She explained that they didn't think I understood the situation and so they couldn't rely on my promise to pass everyone. They were texting the weakest students to help them with the answers. I felt ashamed of my hasty judgement – they weren't cheating for themselves, but they were helping their classmates. I changed my marking system by including a percentage for attendance and that meant I could pass them all, even the weakest ones.

CHEN: Cool!

GUY: Nice one!

NEAL: What was your solution, Kate?

KATE: Well, I had to apologize and re-mark the blank papers, giving them all one mark, but I wasn't happy that no one had told me. It often comes down to poor communication – they just don't know what you don't know and what they should tell you. The more you know about the systems they're using, the less likely you are to have problems.

PAM: Of course!

HEATHER: I'm interested in Nick's problem. We all know how the experts tell us we should teach, but sometimes it doesn't seem to fit the situation. Who did you listen to, Nick – your students or the experts?

NICK: The students, of course! It was all fine in the end, as I changed what I did and they were really pleased. I changed my approach with other classes, too, and the students got much more benefit from these classes. I suppose I could've ignored the student who complained, but she must've been very determined to speak out like that. I was actually really lucky that she'd said this right at the beginning, because the sooner you find out about a problem, the less damage you do. But what about Pam? Did you ever teach a successful speaking class, then?

PAM: Yes. The other teachers knew about the problem with the rain, of course, and I got a lot of help from them. They must've noticed my voice had got croaky because I'd been shouting to be heard above the noise of the rain. After the first week, they kindly offered to swap classrooms with me when they could. Fortunately, we got a lovely new classroom complete with language lab and aircon the following term. And the experience taught me to speak up on behalf of my students as well as myself and not be afraid to discuss with other teachers any problems I'm having.

CHEN: Heather, were you very depressed all the time in China?

HEATHER: No, but it took some time. I think the International Officer might've said something to my classes, as some of my students helped me to go shopping. They were really kind, but I couldn't rely on them all the time. I just had to learn enough language to be independent. So I started to learn some basic vocabulary, and gradually my confidence improved. Eventually I really enjoyed bargaining in the market and commenting on things like the weather and the traffic, asking other shoppers how to use products, or whether clothes would fit me. I learnt how to spot forged banknotes, too! I never did get used to the huge crowds of people everywhere, though!

Key words & phrases

life's rich pattern
it turned out that
to retrieve
hasty judgement
it is down to
to fit the situation
croaky
to swap
aircon
on behalf of
to spot

⊕T17 Unit 5, Section 2, Task 1

NICK: Guy's hoping to go overseas for a gap year [...] I know how much you lot love to start a conversation with 'When I was in Timbuktu ... '. Anyway, I told him you'd have some interesting stories about your experiences.

⊕T18 Unit 5, Section 2, Task 3

PAM: My first teaching job was in Africa, too.

NEAL: Where are you going, Guy? What are you hoping to do?

PAM: ... not just a shower, big heavy drops ...

⊕T19 Unit 5, Section 2, Task 3

PAM: ... the university was still being built.

NICK: I told him you'd have some interesting stories about your experiences.

HEATHER: ... your students or the experts?

NEAL: ... they weren't cheating for themselves, but they were helping their classmates.

HEATHER: I thought I had bought some shampoo, but it turned out to be something for cleaning the toilet!

NICK: Where did you learn to forge bank notes?

⊕T20 Unit 5, Section 2, Task 5

CARMEN RODRIGUEZ: Good! You've come up with interesting ideas and I'd like to pick up on some of them. Research does involve problems, as Dimitri said.

PAULA KAHN: Yes, good, all those ideas are useful for thinking about research. As Carmen said, research often does start with a problem or something you can't explain and the journey is your search for an explanation ...

CARMEN RODRIGUEZ: However, you do in fact do research already – you just don't recognize it.

⊕T21 Unit 5, Section 2, Task 5

HEATHER: ... they do catch us foreigners out.
I never did get used to the huge crowds of people everywhere, though!

⊕T22 Unit 5, Section 2, Task 7

NICK: Oh yes!/Been there!

HEATHER: Tell me about it!

PAM: Of course!

NEAL: Great!

KATE: Oh! Nice!

NICK: Wow ...

CHEN: Cool!

GUY: Nice one!

⊕T23 Unit 5, Section 4 Task 1

HEATHER: I could buy things in a little local supermarket, because you don't need to speak – things like spoons, plates, eggs. It was okay as long as everything went smoothly, but I couldn't always tell what I was buying. Once I thought I had bought some shampoo, but it turned out to be something for cleaning the toilet!

T24 Unit 5, Section 4, Task 2

so [level tone]

so [fall tone]

so [rise tone]

so [rise-fall tone]

so [fall-rise tone]

T25 Unit 5, Section 4, Task 3

NICK: This is Pam, Heather, Neal and Kate.

HEATHER: … things like spoons, plates, eggs.

NICK: I told him you'd have some interesting stories about your experiences.

PAM: My first teaching job was in Africa, too.

PAM: … not just a shower, big heavy drops …

T26 Unit 5, Section 4, Task 4

NICK: This is Pam, Heather, Neal and Kate.

Walls are built for privacy, security and warmth. They are made of wood, concrete or steel. You can get your exam results online, from your tutor, or at the office.

T27 Unit 5, Section 4, Task 5

HEATHER: … things like spoons, plates, eggs.

… for example, books, pens, paper.

… such as essays, reports, presentations.

T28 Unit 5, Section 4, Task 6

NICK: I told him you'd have some interesting stories about your experiences.

T29 Unit 5, Section 4, Task 7

NICK: I had this evening class of four students who were all really, really nice and I was doing exactly what I'd been taught on my teacher training course.

NICK: … one woman said she wasn't happy. This was a big thing in Japan, and to do this to the teacher in front of the other students a big, big thing – and this isn't recently, this is at least 20 years ago – so I asked why and was a bit taken aback by her answer. She said that she wanted me to speak and not just to listen and then correct. And she said that they paid all this money for a native speaker, but I hardly said anything!

NICK: Wow, I've done this wonderful course, with all this great methodology from the experts – was it completely useless?

NEAL: … they were extremely worried about their exam […] everyone in the class had to pass my English exam at the end of the year. If they didn't, they would have to repeat the whole year. I tried to reassure them and told them I would only test them on what we had covered in class – they were sure to pass […] I was so disappointed in them …

KATE: Some of them hadn't learnt the words and wrote absolutely nothing on their answer papers …

ⓐT30 Unit 5, Section 5, Task 1

NICK: It was all fine in the end, as I changed what I did and they were really pleased. I changed my approach with other classes, too, and the students got much more benefit from these classes. I suppose I could've ignored the student who complained, but she must've been very determined to speak out like that. I was actually really lucky that she'd said this right at the beginning …

ⓐT31 Unit 5, Section 5, Task 2

NICK: This is Pam, Heather, Neal and Kate.

HEATHER: … things like spoons, plates, eggs.

NICK: I told him you'd have some interesting stories about your experiences.

PAM: My first teaching job was in Africa, too …

PAM: … not just a shower, big heavy drops …

ⓐT32 Unit 5, Section 5, Task 3

PAM: My first teaching job was in Africa, too.

ⓐT33 Unit 5, Section 5, Task 3

STUDENT A: We're going to the lecture.

STUDENT B: We're going to the lecture, too.

STUDENT A: I'm worried about the exam.

STUDENT B: I'm worried about the exam, too.

STUDENT A: I'm studying engineering.

STUDENT B: My brother's studying engineering, too.

ⓐT34 Unit 5, Section 5, Task 4

HEATHER: … your students or the experts?

NICK: … this isn't recently – this is at least 20 years ago …

NEAL: … they weren't cheating for themselves, but they were helping their classmates.

HEATHER: I thought I had bought some shampoo, but it turned out to be something for cleaning the toilet!

ⓐT35 Unit 5, Section 5, Task 6

KATE: No answers, no marks.
        No pain, no gain.
        No win, no fee.

ⓐT36 Unit 5, Section 5, Task 7

NEAL: The more experience you have, the more you have to say.

KATE: The more you know about the systems they're using, the less likely you are to have problems.

NICK: … the sooner you find out about a problem, the less damage you do.

🎧T37 Unit 5, Section 5, Task 7

SPEAKER A: The sooner it's fixed, the less it costs.

SPEAKER B: Where there's a will, there's a way.

SPEAKER A: The higher you climb, the further   you fall.

SPEAKER B: The bigger the better.

SPEAKER A: The more the merrier.

SPEAKER B: The more you pay, the more you get.

🎧T38 Unit 6, Section 1, Task 4

ADMIN OFFICER: Right, now, can you tell me what course you are studying here?

STUDENT: Accounting.

ADMIN OFFICER: Sorry, can you say that again?

STUDENT: Accounting.

ADMIN OFFICER: Can you tell me what is your major?

STUDENT: Accounting.

ADMIN OFFICER: You mean you don't know yet?

🎧T39 Unit 6, Section 2, Task 2

GUY: Sorry, Dr Malik, can I ask you something? Have you got time?

DR MALIK: Hello, Guy. I'm a bit pushed at the moment – will it take long? I've got to chair a Finance Committee meeting in five minutes.

GUY: Yes, yes, I'll be quick. You know the *Managing change* module you recommended? I'm really enjoying that. I like working through the case studies – it's so practical.

DR MALIK: Good, good, I'm glad, but I'm …

GUY: And I'd like to look at change on a bigger scale, you know, economic development. I've been reading how the co-operative movement is involved – it often chimes with local tradition, you know – and I found out the Department of Agriculture has a module called *Co-operative societies as an instrument of change in the developing world*.

DR MALIK: Ah yes, I know the one, but can we talk about this another time, Guy? I …

GUY: But it starts in two weeks. Could I just do it as another elective?

DR MALIK: Have you checked with the Department of Agriculture? I mean, it's OK as far as we're concerned, as long as there are spare places and it doesn't clash with anything else on your timetable.

GUY: Oh, I thought you might have to … er … I thought I might need a letter or something.

DR MALIK: Why don't you check it out yourself first, Guy, and e-mail me if you need anything like that. Sorry, I must get a move on!

GUY: Right. Thanks. I'll let you know, shall I?

Key words & phrases
a bit pushed
on a bigger scale
chimes with
an instrument of change
clash
get a move on

🎧T40 Unit 6, Section 2, Task 2

MARGARET ELLIS: Hello, Department of Agriculture. Margaret Ellis speaking.

GUY: Hi. I'd like to ask about your new module *Co-operative societies as an instrument of change in the developing world*. Is this module available across the university? I'm a student in the Business School, but I'm really interested in doing my honours dissertation in this field. My tutor, Dr Malik, said I could do it. I mean, if there are spare places.

MARGARET ELLIS: I see. I'm not sure. This is a full module with continuous assessment and an exam.

GUY: Oh no! It's full?

Key words & phrases
a full module
continuous assessment

MARGARET ELLIS: No, no, I didn't say it was full. It's a full module – not a half module: 100 effort hours with assessment and exam, so there's a fee. Will you be paying for it yourself or will the Business School pay?

GUY: Oh, I see. How much would it be?

MARGARET ELLIS: £550. You'd better check how you are going to pay.

GUY: Right. And when is it timetabled?

MARGARET ELLIS: Lecture then seminar every Tuesday at 3 p.m. There's more on the VLE, but the lecturer can tell you about that.

GUY: Oh dear, that's a timetable clash for me.

MARGARET ELLIS: Sorry, not my problem.

GUY: No, no, of course not! Could you tell me where I can find him – the lecturer?

MARGARET ELLIS: Let me see … Actually, he's not based at Gateway. He's a visiting lecturer from the ICRF, so he's not based here. You'll have to contact him directly.

GUY: Could you repeat that, please? I need to write it down.

MARGARET ELLIS: I-C-R-F. It's a research foundation.

GUY: What does it stand for?

MARGARET ELLIS: Well, I think it's … yes, International Co-operative Research Foundation.

GUY: And the lecturer's name?

MARGARET ELLIS: Here it is. Dr Carbrook, Dr Alice Carbrook.

GUY: Thanks very much for your help.

MARGARET ELLIS: Bye bye.

⊕T41 Unit 6, Section 2, Task 2

GUY: Hello, Dr Bailey? Are you busy? I'm Guy. Did you get my e-mail?

JEREMY BAILEY: Er … yes, I did. Hello, Guy. Let me see if I've got this right. You want us to pay £550 for you to study this new module and you want to move your core module lectures, International Economics 2, to another day?

GUY: Yes, I thought I could go to any lectures I want within the university, but the Department of Agriculture charge a fee for their modules.

JEREMY BAILEY: Well, in principle, I think you can go to the lectures for free, but in practice, timetables don't always accommodate these ideals! Anyway, it's the assessments that cost the department money.

GUY: Oh, okay, so I could just go for the input – the lectures and seminars?

JEREMY BAILEY: Maybe – it's up to them. But you still have to make sure you get enough module credits to complete your year. And this timetable clash … well, it's just not possible! It's a substantial group – over 200 – we can't move the lectures to another day just for you! Besides, that big lecture room is heavily used – not many empty slots.

GUY: Oh dear! What do you suggest?

JEREMY BAILEY: Sorry, I can't help I'm afraid. Maybe you could see if you can get a reading list for the module. Why not contact the lecturer? At least you could show him how keen you are!

GUY: Thanks, that's a good idea.

⊕T42 Unit 6, Section 3, Task 1

GUY: Sorry, Dr Malik – can I ask you something?

DR MALIK: Sorry, I must get a move on!

MARGARET ELLIS: Sorry, not my problem.

JEREMY BAILEY: Sorry, I can't help I'm afraid.

⊚T43 Unit 6, Section 3, Task 2

Part 1

GUY: … can I ask you something?

GUY: Have you got time?

DR MALIK: … will it take long?

GUY: Is this module available across the university?

Part 2

DR MALIK: I'm a bit pushed at the moment …

MARGARET ELLIS: I'm not sure.

JEREMY BAILEY: … it's just not possible!

JEREMY BAILEY: Sorry, I can't help I'm afraid.

⊚T44 Unit 6, Section 3, Task 3

[Repeat of T43]

⊚T45 Unit 6, Section 3, Task 4

Part 1

SPEAKER: You gave me the wrong change.

Part 2

MARGARET ELLIS: I'm not sure.

JEREMY BAILEY: … it's just not possible!

JEREMY BAILEY: Sorry, I can't help I'm afraid.

⊚T46 Unit 6, Section 4, Task 2

CHAIR (Nabil): The next item on the agenda, 5.1, is 'Feedback on exams'. There's been a pretty vigorous postcard campaign by the Student Union on this, and I believe they collected hundreds of signatures on their petition, too. Chen here is our student representative for Maths and Computer Science undergraduate courses. Chen, you put this item on the agenda – would you like to speak about it?

CHEN: Thanks, Nabil – I mean, Chair. Yes, MACS student–staff committee asked me to check what happens in other universities – especially what's good practice – and I put some points together for you. Then we want this committee to ask the university Learning and Teaching Strategy Committee for a response.

CHAIR (Nabil): OK. Good idea. What did you find out, Chen?

CHEN: First, it's very different what students get for exam feedback, not just different universities, but different departments in one university. A very mixed picture. Especially here at Gateway, it doesn't have a clear policy for the whole university – I mean, not like what we got for plagiarism or equality policy. Everybody, we all have to read them and sign up! So, when students have worries about exam results and talk to friends, they are shocked to find some departments give so much and others nothing. I mean, Geography and Molecular Biology and Biotechnology are really good. First-year Geography students can even get their papers back to keep. But Philosophy department won't let students ever see papers after marking or even discuss with each student. And this …

DR MICHAELSON: Sorry, but I'm just curious. I thought that exam scripts were covered by data protection.

Key words & phrases

a vigorous campaign

signatures

their petition

speak about

good practice

ask for a response

a mixed picture

a clear policy

equality policy

covered by

data protection

STUDENT A: You mean they are confidential? No one is allowed to see them?

DR MICHAELSON: Not really – the opposite. I thought that you have a right to see your script because it's your personal data. The Data Protection Act basically says you have a right to see what information the university has about you.

CHEN: It's not sure, people are a bit confused on that point, I think, Dr Michaelson. I looked on many university websites and some say that exams are not under Data Protection Act. But one university didn't want to show any papers to students in any department and is having a big argument with the Law Department on this. Yes, I was surprised. Very famous university. This university Law Department says that law students can see their exam papers. So I checked with our Law professors here at Gateway. They agree. All students have a right to see their papers, but must be a correct system – I mean, procedure – to do it. Although it's not data protection, strictly. I think they just want to be fair. Anyway, but sorry, that's not the point. The point is this: do we want Gateway to have best practice or worst practice?

CHAIR (Nabil): Good point, Chen. What was the best practice you found, then? Who's doing it right?

CHEN: Seems to me that policies in some Australian universities are very good, and explain clearly to students. Example: In one university there, you can see your exam paper for any subject and every department must make sure everyone knows the procedure how to do it. But examiners' comments, what they write about your answer, might not be on the paper and that makes me ask, 'How useful is that?'. Some places maybe have to pay a small charge to see or get a copy, a few dollars. Also Canada, it's similar. So Gateway …

CHAIR (Nabil): Could I just ask, what do international students expect? I wonder what happens in other universities, for example, Chinese universities, Chen?

CHEN: Yes, I checked this, too. I don't have experience in Chinese university, but my contacts say generally students are not allowed to see their marked exam scripts unless they are strongly suspicious about their grades. They need to apply for the permission, but I think they do it a lot. School is different though, as I know in my experience. In senior high school in China, the students' marked exam scripts are given back to them, and problems arising from the exams are discussed and explained in class. The teachers want everyone to get best scores!

DR MICHAELSON: So that's quite a difference between high school and university.

CHEN: Yes, true. But to go back to your question about international students, what do they expect? We can see on their webpage the International Student Association made a recommendation – students should be able to see correct answers to exam questions. So we know they expect that, but only some departments do it. Honestly, I think this is important for the university, to be more up to date in policy on this. I want to put points for improving in three groups: general feedback, for whole class or year group, personal feedback for each student, but also important teaching how to use feedback. OK? So, number one, correct answers to exam questions, this is general feedback. It can be solutions to the exam questions, like maths, or model answers like essays. General comments from the examiners, too, very useful. But, even before we take exams, we need to know how it will be marked – what they are looking for. That's part of general feedback, too.

DR MICHAELSON: Yes, you mean marking criteria, what you have to do to get a good mark. Examiners usually have some kind of guidelines for this. I suppose it would be helpful for students to see that sort of thing, too.

CHEN: Exactly. With all this we are clear where we have to aim. But we also need to know if we miss the target! That's the second group, personal feedback.

STUDENT B: Yes, I'm interested in what you said, Chen, about markers' comments. My friend at Nottingham University, right, she gets a copy of the marker's comments for her own paper, automatically – she doesn't have to ask for it. She says it's great. What do you think?

CHEN: She's doing History?

STUDENT B: Yeah! How did you know?

CHEN: They are trying out this new system in that department at Nottingham and the students really like it. I think one thing the guy said … Let me see … Nick Thomas, yes, is really important. I want to read it:

Key words & phrases

confidential
have a right to
personal data
best practice
worst practice
my contacts
strongly suspicious
made a recommendation
up to date
marking criteria
miss the target
automatically

'Obviously exam technique and essay technique are very different things, and we've particularly had student feedback saying that it's changed the way they have approached exams, it's changed the way they revise, it's changed the way they write in exams and it's meant that they have got a clear idea of what we're looking for.'

See, they got a lot of feedback for coursework, but exams are different. We need that exam feedback.

DR MICHAELSON: Yes, but there are a lot of practical problems with giving exam feedback to hundreds of students all at once.

STUDENT A: I guess lecturers just want to mark exams then forget about them. We're asking them to do more work.

CHEN: People find solutions when they try. I think what you say is, 'Where there's a will there's a way'. And some changes, when you try them, they're not really problems. I found some good examples. You can ask me!

CHAIR (Nabil): Right, Chen's challenged us to anticipate reasons not to change the present system. First, there's the numbers problem, Chen. How can examiners write comments on each student's paper? And how can tutors discuss papers with every student, especially right at the end of a semester or year?

CHEN: OK. Question one, writing comments on every student's paper …

⊕T47 Unit 6, Section 4, Task 2

CHEN: OK. Question one, writing comments on every student's paper. External examiners ask departments to do this to help them see reasons for grades. So they supposed to do it anyway. Not always exactly on the paper. It might be on a special marking sheet – one for each student, but gives reasons for grade. Lots of universities do that. Nick Thomas has this system for marking, but no need to photocopy. The marking sheet has got carbon copies behind it. Old-fashioned, but perfect solution. Second question, too many students to discuss with each one in a tutorial …

⊕T48 Unit 6, Section 4, Task 2

CHEN: Second question, too many students to discuss with each one in a tutorial.

Some universities do this and say only maybe ten per cent of students ask for this tutorial. Also they put on a time limit to make students work out exactly what to ask a tutor and not to waste time. Anyway, tutors want to speak to students, too, especially if students got problems. It's true, some departments had to re-organize the way to file and store exam papers. Because it's usually not names, only numbers on papers. Got to be easy to retrieve them, and it took time. But after they did this, the process could speed up. And if they plan carefully and everyone knows about it, time is not wasted. Any more questions?

DR MICHAELSON: You said that in China, students are sometimes suspicious about their marks. They want to challenge the grade. I think many departments see this as a potential problem.

⊕T49 Unit 6, Section 4, Task 2

DR MICHAELSON: You said that in China, students are sometimes suspicious about their marks. They want to challenge the grade. I think many departments see this as a potential problem.

CHEN: Yes, I see. One of them here talks about that. It says they do it and only a 'very tiny minority' want to argue about marks.

CHAIR (Nabil): Do you think lecturers will write model answers for their essay questions? I mean in subjects like English and History? It will take too much time.

CHEN: In most universities, it's policy to provide an answer when you set a question, for external examiner. But could be an outline, you know, main points for a good answer. But I'm not sure. Does this happen everywhere at Gateway, Dr Michaelson?

DR MICHAELSON: Yes, it's a university policy. In fact, all exam questions have to conform to guidelines from the Teaching and Learning Committee.

STUDENT B: Could you tell us about your third group of points?

CHEN: Right. So, if everyone has arranged everything to give exam feedback to students, students need to know what to do about the feedback. Also, how to think about questions to ask tutor, even how not to show feelings too much – be objective. I found Australian universities very good on this, particularly the ANU website. They go into this very deeply for students. Gateway can do some training like this for students, too. I think that's everything I got to say. I can give you this summary with my sources.

CHAIR (Nabil): Thanks very much for that very thorough research and analysis, Chen. If everyone here agrees, I'll send your summary for circulation before the next LTSC and I'll speak about it at that meeting.

ALL: OK./Yes, all right.

⊕T50 Unit 6, Section 4, Task 5

CHEN: Obviously, exam technique and essay technique are very different things, and we've particularly had student feedback saying that it's changed the way they have approached exams, it's changed the way they revise, it's changed the way they write in exams and it's meant that they have got a clear idea of what we're looking for.

⊕T51 Unit 6, Section 4, Task 6

DR MICHAELSON: I thought that exam scripts were covered by data protection.

NABIL (Chair): Chen, you put this item on the agenda – would you like to speak about it?

DR MICHAELSON: Not really …

STUDENT A: You mean they are confidential? No one is allowed to see them?

CHEN: … but sorry, that's not the point. The point is this …

CHEN: … do we want Gateway to have best practice or worst practice?

STUDENT B: Yeah! How did you know?

⊕T52 Unit 6, Section 4, Task 7

CHEN: … but sorry, that's not the point. The point is this: do we want Gateway to have best practice or worst practice?

⊕T53 Unit 7, Section 2, Task 1

IRINA PAVLENKO: Hello, and welcome to this first lecture on ethics in research. My name is Irina Pavlenko and I am a lecturer in the Computer Science Department here at Gateway University. I am a member of the Ethics Committee that considers the proposals for all the research that is done in my department – that's research by undergraduates, postgraduates and doctoral students, as well as the research that my colleagues – your lecturers – do. Making sure that we do research according to ethical principles is very important for all the departments across the university. Now, I think we have got people from a range of different disciplines here today – is that right? OK, so I'm not going to go into a great deal of detail about specific disciplines, but I'll give out some case studies at the end of the session, which I want you to think about for the second session. Now, I hope you've all got a copy of my presentation slides. So, in the first slide you can see the overview of my talk today. My main aim is to explain that ethics involves choices between right and wrong behaviour; it's about the different options we have in our lives, and how we can decide a course of action by assessing the consequences or results of choosing one option rather than another – both direct and indirect results – but also how we can use standards to evaluate those choices. Most of the lecture will be about illustrating the points on these slides with specific examples to help you to see how these abstract concepts relate to choices and consequences in your everyday social, academic and professional lives. At the end, I'll say a little bit about ethics in research, but we'll go into that in more detail in later sessions. And I'll give you some case studies to think about.

⊕T54 Unit 7, Section 2, Task 2

IRINA PAVLENKO: OK, let's start with some definitions in Slide 2: the top one – Blackburn, 1996 – is from the *Oxford Dictionary of Philosophy,* and the other – Newall, 2005 – is from a website of essays; the references are at the end of the slides, if you want to read more. People sometimes make a difference between *morals* and *ethics*, but these two terms are really interchangeable because, in fact, they come from Latin and Greek words which both mean *habit*, so we are not going to distinguish any difference in meaning today. It's enough to say that when we make ethical or moral choices, we are concerned with decisions about right or wrong ways to act towards other people in our societies. Now, it's important to remember that ethics are not the same as laws. Ethics are more universal norms of behaviour, but it is true to say that at different historical periods, cultures have had different views about how people in their societies should behave. So ethical concepts have been used to criticize or interpret laws. For example, in the 19th and early 20th centuries, women in Western societies campaigned for the right to vote and protested against the law that said only men who owned property could vote. As a result of this and other political campaigns, Western societies now view peaceful protests as an ethical way to express political viewpoints. Other societies do not share this view, however.

So, I've summarized the key points here in Slide 3: ethics is about competing moral choices – which often arise in periods of change – and the consequences or results of making those choices. We can see this if we continue with the example about votes for women. When women did not have the right to vote, society considered them to be inferior to men. Men generally thought that if women were given the vote, this would change the relationship between men and women and cause chaos in society. Men became really worried about the potential for civic disorder, but the more they resisted the change, the more violently women protested until one woman was killed during a protest. However, in the First World War, women contributed considerably to the war effort and society came to see their contribution as being equal to that of men. After the war, many women were not prepared to go back to their former subservient roles and campaigned more fiercely for equality with men and the right to vote. In the UK, the government recognized their contribution to the war and passed a law in 1918 which gave all women over 30 years of age the right to vote. These days, the right to vote for all citizens is one of the laws in the United Nations' Universal Declaration of Human Rights.

OK, moving on to the next slide. I've referred to the Declaration of Human Rights because it's one example of a moral code – that's like a set of standards – against which we can evaluate options and make ethical choices. Societies have tried throughout history to establish these kinds of standards by specifying rules such as *Do not lie, Do not cheat, Do not kill*. However, it's not as easy as this because very often ethical choices involve accepting a small amount of bad for a greater good. For example, in Nazi Germany, many citizens strongly disagreed with Adolf Hitler's policies towards Jewish members of their society and they helped their Jewish neighbours to hide and escape from the Nazis. If these people had been discovered, the Nazis would have killed both the Jews and their protectors. So in this situation, lying to the authorities was essential in order to save people's lives. But this illustrates a basic general principle underlying all ethical choices: behave towards others as you want them to behave towards you. If you'd been Jewish in Nazi Germany, I think you would have wanted your neighbours to conceal you from the Nazis.

So, I'm going to simplify things quite a lot and say that for our purposes, we have two approaches to ethical problems. We can assess the consequences of different choices and choose the least worst option, or we can attempt to establish a set of standards which can help us to choose between competing options. In practice, we usually do both these things together, but I'll consider them separately. Let's take an example from my own field, robotics. This is a field that has developed rapidly in recent times so we now have robots that can move about and work beside people in their homes, in offices and in hospitals. We can imagine a future – one that so far we have only read about in science

ACCESS EAP: Frameworks • Transcripts

fiction – where robots are as common as PCs are today, but also where they are increasingly able to act like humans. What are the ethical consequences of this? The first important consequence concerns privacy. If robots become common in our homes, then they can be used to collect information about us which we might want to keep private. Home robots would have sensors to help them to navigate around their environment, including cameras, sound recording equipment and global positioning systems. Data from these sensors would be transmitted wirelessly to a PC or the Internet to control the robot. However, if the robot control system was not secure, hackers could gain access to it to control the robot or eavesdrop on our conversations. If this private information was stored, governments might be able to force individuals to make it available, for example, in court. Another consequence we need to consider is robots as social actors, employed to care for vulnerable people such as the elderly or disabled or children. On the face of it, this seems like a good idea. Robots do not get tired and they have endless patience. They can even be programmed to express human emotions. Indeed, people are more likely to accept care from robots if these machines look and behave like humans, at least to some extent. But again, this has ethical implications. If robots appear too much like humans, vulnerable people might become emotionally dependent on them.

So, in 2010, Research Councils in the UK drafted a set of five ethical rules for robotocists – that's the people who design robots. If you're interested in this research area, you can look up the online reference and read about the rules in more detail. These rules are quite controversial, but the team who prepared them wanted to stimulate the ethical debate in this field. The key aspect was to view robots not as accountable or ethical entities, but simply as complex tools – the rules assume that robots cannot be ethical, but their human designers can. Robotocists should be required to design robots which conform to human rights and freedoms, which are safe to use and which do not exploit humans. It should always be obvious that a robot is not a human and it should be clear who is legally responsible for a robot.

Finally, a word about research: ethics is about integrity – being honest, trustworthy and accurate – and this definitely applies to research. The Research Council *Framework for Research Ethics* states that research should be undertaken in a way that ensures its integrity and quality. In other words, your research should not be trivial, but it should have the potential to add new knowledge in your discipline, and the research design and data collection should be valid and reliable in order to produce accurate results. Doing poor quality research, or research which is not honest or trustworthy, has the potential to cause harm. It could give misleading findings, which might be applied with adverse results. You risk wasting time – not least, for your participants. If the research is funded, you are also wasting money.

Now, just to summarize the main ideas I want you to take away from my talk today: when you investigate an ethical issue, you need to identify the problem or issue and the opposing positions as clearly as possible, and make sure you have all the relevant information about each position. You need to outline the different options and choices that are available and try to decide what the consequences would be of making those choices. You can also use ethical codes or rules to help you decide the best option. So, I'm now going to hand out some case studies relating to a variety of disciplines and I'd like you to prepare one of these for discussion next week …

⊕T55 Unit 7, Section 4, Task 2, 3 and 4

CLIVE SANDERS: OK, we're all here, so we can start. This is a meeting of the Academic Misconduct Board held on the 18th of June to consider category B, or minor, offences. Noah, this is Susan Bailey, our new clerk for this committee, and Susan, this is Dr Noah Ojukwu, who sits with me to discuss the cases. This board hears the minor offences and if there are any major cases we cannot resolve here, these go to the University Discipline Committee. So I think we've got six cases to hear today, is that right?

SUSAN BAILEY: Yes, one from Construction Management, two from Urban Design and three from Building and Estate Management.

Key words & phrases

privacy
to keep private
sensors
to navigate around
to transmit data
wirelessly
hackers
to gain access to
to eavesdrop on conversations
in court
social actors
vulnerable people
the elderly
the disabled
on the face of it
have patience
to express emotions
at least to some extent
ethical implications
emotionally dependent
drafted a set of rules
controversial
to stimulate debate
accountable
entities
to conform to
exploit
legally responsible
integrity
trustworthy
to undertake research
trivial
have the potential to
poor quality
misleading findings

NOAH OJUKWU: All undergraduate degrees?

SUSAN BAILEY: Yes, I've scheduled the postgrad cases together next week.

CLIVE SANDERS: OK, so what are we dealing with today?

SUSAN BAILEY: Most of them are fairly straightforward. We've got Turnitin reports as clear evidence of plagiarism for four of them. There's one case of a student taking notes into an exam. The invigilator saw the student consulting the notes and confiscated them, so we have those as evidence. But there's also a case of a student that we think has bought an essay from the Internet, and this might be rather more tricky because he's not owning up to it. We don't have direct evidence, just circumstantial evidence from the student's grades. In semester 1 he got a C, two Ds and an E, but he's submitted a grade A essay.

CLIVE SANDERS: OK, so for that case, if he continues to deny wrongdoing and we can't get him to admit to using unfair means, we may have to refer him higher up to the University Discipline Committee. The others should be straightforward, though. Let's look at the documents for the first student. Oh, I see this one was submitted by you, Noah, for a Construction Management assignment. We have a Turnitin report which shows evidence of large-scale copying, but the assignment instructions clearly explain what plagiarism is with a reference to the handbook, so the student can't claim he didn't know.

NOAH OJUKWU: Yes, this one is from my module in Construction Management. This student actually copied one of my own papers. In fact, this has happened to me before. I give out this paper in the lecture as follow-up reading and I must admit I got a bit fed up with students copying it, so I uploaded it to Turnitin myself. The thing is, I warn the students that I've put it into Turnitin and we discuss what that means and what will happen if they do not use this source correctly in their assignment. So obviously, this student didn't understand or perhaps he didn't attend that lecture.

CLIVE SANDERS: Yes, it may well be the case that he didn't attend the lecture. We've got his written statement here saying he was ill and returned to his own country for treatment at the beginning of semester 2. He says he wrote his assignment in hospital.

NOAH OJUKWU: Has he submitted a medical certificate for this period of illness?

SUSAN BAILEY: No, I checked with his tutor.

CLIVE SANDERS: OK, I think we're ready to see him now.

Welcome to this meeting. I'm Dr Sanders and these are my colleagues, Dr Ojukwu – I think you know – and Ms Bailey, who records the decisions of this meeting. Now, we've called you here today to discuss an allegation of plagiarism. Your tutor has provided us with evidence that you copied quite a lot of your essay from a handout he gave you in class and from an Internet source. Can you tell us something about the construction of this piece of work – how did you put it together? Were you aware of copying?

STUDENT: First I want to say sorry, I'm sorry. Yes, I admit I copied, but I had a lot of problems this semester and I didn't know it was wrong. My father died and I went home to be with my family, and then I got ill and I went to hospital and I was there for three weeks. And now I have problems about money and I started doing a job so I miss time for assignments. But also I'm not familiar with the system here and it is different in my country, you know.

CLIVE SANDERS: OK, so you're suggesting that you had family problems and you were under some financial stress, and also you were ill in hospital for three weeks. Did you submit a medical certificate to the course administrator for that period?

STUDENT: No, I didn't know about that or what I should do.

CLIVE SANDERS: Well, if you have a legitimate reason for being away from your studies, like being in hospital, you must tell your tutor so the exam board can take this into account when they look at your grades. Can you get a medical certificate now for the period you were in hospital?

STUDENT: Yes, I mean no … I don't know. Maybe no. But really I don't understand the education system here.

NOAH OJUKWU: What in particular about the system here is difficult for you?

STUDENT: Turnitin is all new. We don't have Turnitin. In my country, you can copy. The lecturer tells you 'learn the book and write what it says'.

NOAH OJUKWU: So you're suggesting that in your previous education system, it would be OK to copy. What kind of work did they ask you to do in high school?

STUDENT: Exams, all exams no coursework.

CLIVE SANDERS: Despite that, while you were copying, did you think it was OK to do that?

STUDENT: I know it was not OK, but I don't know what else to do. I was ill, my father died, I have to work hard to get money for my studies.

CLIVE SANDERS: Well, thanks for being honest with us. I don't think there's anything else we need to ask you. Noah?

NOAH OJUKWU: No, nothing.

CLIVE SANDERS: Do you have any questions for us?

STUDENT: Please, sir, what will happen to me? When I got this e-mail, I was really frightened. Is there a problem with my degree?

CLIVE SANDERS: No, it's not that level of misconduct. This is a minor offence. You've admitted that what you did was wrong and this is your first time to come before this board.

STUDENT: Please, sir, what do I have to do?

CLIVE SANDERS: You'll need to wait for a few days. We have to discuss your case and make a decision, and then that decision, has to be approved by the Dean. Then Ms Bailey will write to you and tell you what the decision is, and you will probably be required to do another assignment.

SUSAN BAILEY: I'll send you the letter by e-mail, so please check your e-mail regularly and if you don't understand the letter or the instructions, please contact me for clarification.

CLIVE SANDERS: So that's all we need from you. You can go now. OK. So, Susan, an explanation for your benefit. We've got three levels of penalty at this board: misunderstanding, where he really did not know that he was doing something wrong; misuse, where he has admitted that he did know, but there are extenuating circumstances – in this case, he was under a lot of pressure; and the third more serious one is intentional cheating, where the intention is to deliberately deceive to gain unfair advantage.

NOAH OJUKWU: I think he knew that what he was doing was wrong. I wasn't convinced by what he said about the system in his country.

CLIVE SANDERS: Well, he said that he didn't have to do assignments, just exams, so perhaps he never learnt to reference at high school. But I think you're right, this is a case of misuse. He didn't set out deliberately to cheat, but he was aware that what he was doing was wrong. However, he clearly has a lot of issues, with family and financial problems. I suggest we ask him to resubmit another assignment. We'll need to offer him the opportunity to do this within the next two weeks to allow him the possibility to progress within the normal timeframe. If he can't manage that, then we can consider a further arrangement.

OK, so who have we got next?

⊕T56 Unit 8, Section 1, Task 1

MAURICIO: Thanks for telling me about these lectures – they are going to be a big help with my thesis.

GUY: Have you got a title yet?

MAURICIO: Well, I work in Public Health Policy, on nutrition, and I'm interested in traditional foods in South America, particularly Peru, my home country. You know, kids get sick when they don't have a balanced diet, but our traditional diet was balanced. Now parents are forgetting it. So it will be about combating child malnutrition in poor areas. Probably through case studies or something like that.

GUY: Will you get data from any other countries?

> **Key words & phrases**
>
> public health
>
> traditional foods
>
> a balanced diet
>
> combating
>
> malnutrition

MAURICIO: Brazil and Argentina. My supervisor is involved in a World Food Programme project in Peru. But he's hoping to start another project in Africa, so I might go there, too.

GUY: Really? Which country?

MAURICIO: Angola. It's on the west coast, south of the equator.

GUY: Great. I'm hoping to do my final-year project in Malawi this summer. That's a bit further east, between Zambia and Mozambique.

MAURICIO: What are Chen and Khalid doing in the summer?

GUY: Chen's going home to China, to Qingdao. That's up in the north I think, on the east coast. They did the sailing there for the Beijing Olympics. Khalid's going home, too, to Libya. He's invited me to stop over with him in Tripoli if I can.

MAURICIO: That's right on the Mediterranean coast – lovely and hot!

⊕T57 Unit 8, Section 5, Task 1

GUY: You know your assignment about the carbon footprint of a mobile phone? Do you think your lecturer's trying to make you give up your mobile phone to reduce your carbon footprint?

CHEN: Maybe, he's kind of green, but no way I'm doing that! Anyway, my footprint's smaller than yours! I cycle everywhere. You use your dad's old car. That's why I'm fitter – race you to that bus stop over there!

GUY: OK, I guess you've got a point. But your country's carbon footprint is bigger. China's got a bigger carbon footprint than the UK.

CHEN: Well, maybe, but China's footprint isn't as big as the USA.

GUY: Are you sure about that?

CHEN: No, but anyway, you can't compare countries like that – it's not so simple.

GUY: Well, let's look for some data when we get back and see who's right.

⊕T58 Unit 8, Section 5, Task 4

CHEN: Let's search for 'carbon footprint by nation'. There's a *Guardian* article. Oh dear, it says *China speeds ahead of the rest.*

GUY: Let's scroll down to the data. Look! There, I was right! China produced over 7,700 million tonnes of CO_2. Compare that to the USA, where it's under 5,500 million.

CHEN: But per capita, you have to see what each person is responsible for. USA has 17.67 tonnes for each person. That's over three times more polluting than China. And China is much lower than the UK – look, 5.83 tonnes per capita compared with 8.35.

GUY: It's total emissions that count for climate change.

CHEN: I know, but if you want to reduce carbon overall, you have to show individual people what they can do. So per capita data makes much more sense. My carbon footprint is much smaller than yours! It's much easier for people in Australia and the US to reduce by a few tonnes each, than for people in poor countries with very low carbon emissions already.

GUY: Yes, I suppose so, especially a hugely wealthy country like the USA. But China's population is enormous. There have to be national targets.

CHEN: We can't ignore development. Western countries like UK and USA had industrial development a long time ago – you've done massive polluting, but now you don't need to. We need to catch you up.

GUY: Yes, you're right. We should look at development – the UN has lots of data on that. OK, here's the 2011 Human Development Report. They give the tables in a separate file.

CHEN: What's this, H-D-I?

GUY: It's Human Development Index. I've just been reading about that in Economics. That's what Amartya Sen is famous for. With a guy from Pakistan, another economist called Ul Haq, they worked out a way to measure human development that wasn't just about wealth and industrialization. It takes into account the standard of living for poor people in a country. It includes health and education.

CHEN: That's what we need. These countries are ranked for HDI.

GUY: If development is important, maybe we should look at the BRIC countries – the ones with the most rapidly developing economies: Brazil, Russia, India and China.

CHEN: And some really poor countries for comparison. What about these three?

GUY: Papua New Guinea, Yemen, Zimbabwe. Yes, a good geographical spread. We need to see the bigger picture. It's not just about who's got the biggest footprint, but who needs to change most and how.

CHEN: And how do they calculate it? I mean, I make you a cell phone and generate CO_2, then I sell it to you. Does that go on my footprint or yours?

GUY: Good point, man – find out for your essay!

Key words & phrases

ranked for
a geographical spread
the bigger picture
good point

⊙T59 Unit 9, Section 2, Task 2

ROBERT DOUGLAS: Hello, everyone. I'm Robert Douglas, and I'm from the Department of Psychology here at Gateway. I'd just like to welcome everyone to this series of ten seminars in which we are going to pair up researchers from different disciplines to discuss their work. We hope this will help us to find common ground with our colleagues in other departments so that we can forge links and perhaps develop some joint research projects. I'm particularly interested in promoting cross-disciplinary research because I've actually done quite a lot of boundary crossing myself. I started out as a physical chemist, but then I switched to linguistics and became interested in how our brains learn language. Now I'm working in the field of cognitive science. I'm pleased to see so many research students here today. Research in the future is highly likely to involve collaboration with colleagues from other disciplines, so you may find yourselves following a similar career path to mine.

OK, I'm going to kick off with an exploration of the 'big picture' because this is where I think the different disciplines have most in common, and it will also give us a point of reference for exploring specific differences in the next few seminars. I've called this lecture 'What counts as evidence?' and I'm going to be talking about the kind of research evidence that is collected in different fields in order to build knowledge. What I'm going to argue is that the process of research and knowledge building is similar across disciplines, even though the objects of study or types of problems that are the focus of research and the specific evidence, in other words the data, that are collected are very different. In the seminars which follow this one, you'll hear about different research approaches, so you'll be able to evaluate this thesis and decide to what extent you agree with me.

Key words & phrases

to pair up
to find common ground
to forge links
joint research projects
boundary crossing
a physical chemist
switched to
linguistics
cognitive science
a career path
to kick off
a point of reference
thesis

⊙T60 Unit 9, Section 2, Task 4

ROBERT DOUGLAS: I'll start from my own perspective, which is a psychology perspective. We can view humans as pattern-seeking animals. What do I mean by that? Well, we use our senses to observe the world around us and to identify patterns which enable us to predict what might happen in the future. Obviously, in early human societies, being able to predict the behaviour of predators or the abundance of food supplies was useful as a survival mechanism. This has left us with an innate curiosity and a desire to explain why things are the way they are. However, if you think about it, our primary senses are rather unreliable: birds can see much further and in more detail than us and they can use the earth's magnetic field to navigate. Insects and some birds can see a wider range of the ultraviolet spectrum than us, and dogs can smell and hear better than we can. What we are good at is creating tools to extend the range of our senses and our capabilities, and because we have language, we're also good at speculating, generalizing, communicating and sharing ideas, and this is how we create knowledge.

So what kinds of patterns do I mean? Well, early humans observed the natural world, for example, the stars, and speculated about the reasons for the patterns they found there. They formulated models, such as the astrological system of star signs, and then they linked these to personality types and used them to predict likely events. I'm sure you're familiar with this model in popular magazines today. Some time later, scholars developed new research tools, such as the telescope, and this greatly extended the range of possible observations. Over centuries, they built up a wealth of data which they used to formulate theories that would allow them to explain the observations. Eventually, Johannes Kepler was able to look at the data in a different way and formulate mathematical laws that explained

Key words & phrases

pattern-seeking
predators
the abundance of
a survival mechanism
an innate curiosity
primary senses
the earth's magnetic field
the ultraviolet spectrum
the astrological system of star signs
the telescope
a wealth of data
to formulate laws

planetary motion. Isaac Newton extended this work to propose a general law of gravitation – Newton showed that the motions of objects on earth and of planets are governed by the same set of universal laws. In the three centuries since then, scientists have extended and applied this knowledge to put men on the moon, change the shape of our environment, and design computers that vastly extend the range of our natural senses and abilities.

I've presented this story of the search for new knowledge in the field of astronomy as one of continual progress in research, which is often the way the history of science is told at school, but we know that it doesn't happen in this linear fashion at all. Instead, it proceeds through leaps of imagination and creativity on the part of researchers who are often competing to discover new phenomena and formulate different theories to explain them. Scientists take it for granted that the physical world has an objective reality which is independent of our ability to think about it. However, our knowledge of that physical world is personal knowledge. By that, I mean that it is based on individual judgements influenced by the perspective of the current accepted theory, which may turn out to be inaccurate. For this reason, scientists publish their work within a research community and argue about the findings of other studies which may contradict their own results. It is the clash of competing claims about the meaning of research findings which refines and improves understanding and builds knowledge and theory in an iterative cycle. For example, Kepler's laws were not universally accepted until they were tested against observations of the planets Venus and Mercury and found to make accurate predictions. Much later, Einstein developed the theory of relativity as a refinement of Newton's universal laws to account for extremely large or small or fast-moving objects.

Now, the laws and theories developed by Kepler, Newton and Einstein have a wealth of empirical data which validates them, so that gives them a great deal of explanatory and predictive power. This has contributed to a widely held view that the right way to do research is the way physicists do it. I'm sure you'll be aware of the so-called 'hierarchy of sciences', with physical sciences at the top, social sciences at the bottom and biological sciences somewhere in between. This hierarchy was proposed at least 200 years ago by a French philosopher called Auguste Comte, who suggested that sciences differed in their complexity and level of development and the precision with which they could be studied. Comte's proposal is still controversial. More recent writers tend to refer to 'hard' and 'soft' sciences, depending on the kind of approach that researchers are able to take. So, for example, the physical sciences can more easily take a deductive approach, using established theory to formulate hypotheses for testing. The social sciences, on the other hand, often adopt an inductive approach, collecting data and looking for patterns and regularities in order to formulate tentative hypotheses which can later be tested.

However – if you think about it – the inductive approach is just what the early astronomers were using when they observed the stars. So it is probably better to think of inductive and deductive approaches to research as two sides of a circle – or even a spiral if you like, a progressive circle – and these two sides feed in to each other as the research field develops. Research initially proceeds from data collection in specific contexts to tentative hypotheses and general theories which might apply to many contexts. Then these theories can be used to formulate hypotheses to be tested by collecting more data. The older and more developed a research field is, the more agreement there is about the core theories and methodologies. That makes it more likely that researchers will be able to adopt a deductive approach. Now, of course, it is true that there is a much higher level of agreement about the core theories and methodologies in the physical sciences compared to the social sciences, but at the frontiers of research in these disciplines there are probably similar levels of uncertainty and disagreement.

Without wanting to offend my colleagues from physics and chemistry or to downplay the spectacular achievements in these fields, I think you'd have to agree that the physical sciences deal with the simplest objects in the entire universe: atoms and their constituents. They have relatively stable properties and can be described using mathematical laws and models. In contrast, social scientists study extremely complex systems within multiple networks affected by large numbers of variables, which are hard to identify. Perhaps instead of hard and soft we should relabel the physical sciences easy and the social sciences difficult. This isn't my insight, by the way. I first came across the idea in an article written by Jared Diamond for Discover magazine way back in August 1987. He was talking about the tendency for hard scientists to ridicule research approaches in the soft sciences. This

Key words & phrases

planetary motion
a general law of gravitation
the motions of objects
are governed by
universal laws
vastly extend
astronomy
continual progress
independent of
in this linear fashion
leaps of imagination
on the part of
take it for granted
an objective reality
a research community
the clash of competing claims
an iterative cycle
were tested against
the theory of relativity
empirical data
validates
predictive power
a widely held view
hierarchy of sciences
to formulate hypotheses
feed in to
the core theories
methodologies
the frontiers of research
to offend
to downplay
you'd have to agree
the entire universe
stable properties

came about because the concepts under investigation tended to be familiar ones on which everyone claimed to have expertise. He gave 'social frustration' as an example – we all think we know what that is, but how would you measure it? You can find the article online and it's well worth reading. I'm going to quote him in full here because his ideas are clearly relevant today. He was talking about the relationship between theory and research-based evidence and how you turn theoretical concepts into variables that you can measure. He said:

To compare evidence with theory requires that you measure the ingredients of your theory. For ingredients like weight or speed it's clear what to measure, but what would you measure if you wanted to understand political instability? Somehow, you would have to design a series of actual operations that yield a suitable measurement – i.e., you must operationalize the ingredients of theory[4].

Now, he used a nice expression: 'ingredients of theory'. By that, he meant the components of theory or theoretical concepts. He gave a simple example of two cavewomen unable to decide which tree had more fruit and was therefore the one they should climb to get food. Without a number system to operationalize their concept of 'more', the two cavewomen could never prove to each other which tree offered better pickings.

I'll use another example to get you thinking about how different disciplines operationalize 'the ingredients of their theories', as Jared Diamond puts it, and just how difficult this is to do with precision. Let's consider the measurement of distance. Physical scientists can measure distance directly using some kind of ruler with an agreed unit of measurement, for example, a metre. Of course, it's important to have a standard of measurement so that everyone agrees about the distance between two points. The current standard for the metre makes use of the theory of relativity, which states that the speed of light in a vacuum is constant. The metre has thus been defined as the length of the path travelled by light in a vacuum during a time interval of – let me write this up – one 299,792,458 millionths of a second.

Now, a measurement of distance is also used by ecologists, but they use it to make an indirect measurement of the turbidity – that's cloudiness or murkiness – of the water in a pond or lake. This relates to the amount of suspended solids or tiny creatures in the water and I think you can well imagine, this would be very difficult to measure directly. So they also make use of light and distance with a simple device called a Secchi disk, invented by an Italian astronomer, Angelo Secchi. The disk has alternate black and white quarters and is suspended on a pole or line, which is lowered slowly down into the water. The depth at which the pattern on the disk is no longer visible to a human observer is taken as a measure of the turbidity of the water. So this is an example of the use of a direct measurement of distance to operationalize the concept of turbidity. Obviously, this is only a correlation, not an exact measure, and it can also be affected by the amount of sunlight reflecting off the water or the eyesight of the person taking the readings. To get round these variations, the process for taking the measurement is standardized as much as possible; usually the same person takes all the measurements at the same time of day.

Finally, I'll take an example from the social sciences. In the 1960s, the anthropologist Edward Hall was interested in the experience of social and personal space – as it is shaped by culture – because he suggested that this determines the interactions and relationships between people. He used measures of distance to define the edges of four distinct areas radiating out from each person – what he called expanding and contracting fields. These could be associated with different social interactions: intimate space, personal space, social space and public space. Hall did not suggest that these measurements translated precisely to human behavior, but rather that they constituted a system for gauging the effect of distance on communication and how the effect varies among individuals and cultures. Having defined these areas, he could list the different sensory experiences available in each one – smell, touch, sight, loudness of voice, for example. He could then use this delineation of personal space to explore differences between personality types – introverts and extroverts – and between cultures. So this was a simple and elegant way to operationalize complex concepts such as personal and social space.

Well, from these examples, I hope you can see that differences between disciplines relate to the

[4] Diamond, J. (1987). Soft sciences are often harder than hard sciences. *Discover*. Retrieved from http://bama.ua.edu/~sprentic/607%20Diamond%201987.htm

---

Key words & phrases

under investigation
social frustration
to quote him in full
the ingredients of your theory
operationalize
the speed of light
in a vacuum
a time interval
ecologists
the turbidity
murkiness
suspended solids
to measure directly
the anthropologist
radiating out
constituted
for gauging
sensory experiences
a simple and elegant way
lending themselves more

objects they study and the precision of measurement they can achieve. The objects of study in the physical sciences are relatively simple and constant, thus lending themselves more easily to direct measurements and a deductive approach to knowledge creation. Research in the social sciences, however, requires more sophisticated, but often less clear-cut approaches that yield probabilistic answers through statistical analysis. In all disciplines, researchers publish their findings and argue about what these mean in relation to the theories and methodologies that their discipline has established and the findings of other researchers. A large part of this argument centres around methodology and the quality of evidence or data which supports the findings: whether the ingredients of theory have been operationalized appropriately and whether there are any limitations in the data-collection methods.

So now that I've laid the groundwork for our discussions, next week we'll be welcoming two colleagues from Computer Science and Political Science to discuss a joint research project …

⊙T61 Unit 9, Section 4, Task 3

BARBARA JOHNSON: Thanks very much for taking the time to talk to me today. As I mentioned in my e-mail, the purpose of this discussion is to find out more about the approach to research in different disciplines, and what I hope is that we will find similarities across the different fields. I'm planning to use the results to improve what we teach to students coming on to our summer pre-sessional courses. So, I wonder if I could start by asking you to briefly introduce yourselves and say what your discipline is. That way, the person transcribing the discussion will be able to distinguish our different voices. Perhaps I can start. I'm Barbara and I run the summer pre-sessional courses for international students here at Gateway University.

DR RUTHERFORD: I'm Chris and I'm the course director for the Logistics and Supply Chain Management degree in the Faculty of Business Management.

PROF FOWLER: Hi, my name is Ruth, and I'm programme director for the Food Science programme in Life Sciences. We have degrees in Food Science and Nutrition, and Food Science Safety and Health.

DR O'DONOVAN: Hello, I'm Tadhg from Engineering. I teach Fluid Mechanics and Heat Transfer, and that's also my research area, with applications in anything from bio heat to electronics cooling or even solar thermals, so that's renewable energies.

DR BROWN: Hi, I'm Caroline from Urban Studies. I teach Town Planning, Real Estate and Property Surveying to third-year undergraduates.

BARBARA JOHNSON: Thanks for that. So perhaps I can start by asking how a student goes about doing research in your discipline.

DR O'DONOVAN: Well, I guess it depends on the kind of research you're talking about. I think it's fair to say when you do engineering research projects, there are different categories out there – one which can be very heavy literature review based, and one which would be perhaps experimental, whether that's numerical or actual physical experiments, or simulations. And I perhaps tend to throw in another one – design-and-build projects. So you're making a prototype design and testing it to see if it works in reality.

PROF FOWLER: Yes, I'd agree – that classification is a bit like what we do in Life Sciences. Normally with Food Sciences, the students do what we call 'dry' projects – that's like a literature review. We refer to them as dry because they're in the library and not in a lab. Wet projects are based in the lab. Probably the best way to describe wet projects is they're like being in a kitchen – like cooking, really. You have to have a menu that you know works, you have to be organized, and you have to have specific ingredients. And then the way you mix them, the order you mix them, the temperature and how long you incubate things for, are important. And using sterile techniques – making sure that things are not contaminated – is crucial. We also do field observations for subjects like plant biology.

DR BROWN: We tend to use observation a lot in Urban Studies. Increasingly, in our field, people are moving towards the methodologies of observing the environments in neighbourhoods. It's called 'systematic social observation'. We often get students to take photographs that they can compare with historical photos. It's about observation accuracy – noting all the things that they've seen on the ground that might have an influence, and connecting that to government policy and planning documents relating to those sites. That connection between the actual location and the policy is really important. We also want them to think about urban spaces in relation to the wider theoretical body of literature. So look at what's happening in Summerford High Street and link that to some of the big issues like the changing face of global retail and the government's attitude to planning for retail. There are big debates in planning theory and real estate around this issue.

DR RUTHERFORD: In Logistics, we might use observation, too, maybe go out and count the trucks arriving at a distribution centre. A lot of people forget about observation, but it is a good triangulation method. Our research is probably more applied and less theoretical, I'd say. Often what we're doing is trying to solve a problem for a company. Say a company might have a problem with on-shelf availability of their products and they are suffering from poor sales as a result. The students will come in and do an investigation – root-cause analysis is a typical technique – to find out what's causing the problem. And then, through interviews or historical data and documentation, they try and figure out what the opportunities are for improvement and come up with some recommendations. Hopefully, in a really good project, we'd see an evaluation of the impact of those recommendations in cost terms – performance terms – and that often involves some sort of cost modelling. Some of our students are capable of doing this kind of case study really well, but quite a lot of students are far less capable in research terms. So those weaker students would tend to do a structured literature review project, which they can complete within three months. We tend to steer the weaker students towards that methodology.

DR O'DONOVAN: Yeah, we would encourage the weaker students to do a literature project as well. Normally, I'm not very keen on literature review projects. Really, the students get kind of overwhelmed by the amount of reading they have to do and they end up putting the report together in a rush without any real critical analysis of what they've read. But a design project or a simulation takes so long to set up and test, and a lot of students run out of time, so they end up doing the literature project.

BARBARA JOHNSON: And how would a student find a topic? Do you have a list of topics that they choose from or do they find their own topic?

DR O'DONOVAN: With us, we normally give them a list of topics because we need them to work on something we can supervise. So the supervisors all write project proposals and the students can choose one of these.

PROF FOWLER: We give them the option. We like them to choose something they're interested in, but we give suggestions if they can't come up with anything.

DR RUTHERFORD: At the moment students choose their own topics, but we also provide a list of topics that reflect lecturers' different interests. When it comes to a case study within a company, sometimes students go out and find their own companies, but companies also approach us with a specific project they want investigated.

DR BROWN: We tend to get students looking at sites and identifying problems within the environment. They have to decide what specific aspects of the problem to focus on and find the policy documents and theoretical papers which will provide the higher-level view and the overall evaluation of the case. The link between the physical location, government policy and the theoretical literature is crucial.

BARBARA JOHNSON: So case study methodology is something that students in Town Planning and Logistics could do?

PROF FOWLER: And Food Science. They could also do case studies in Food Science. For example, in the management of food safety, we have a process approach called Hazard Analysis and Critical Control Points, or HACCP. Students might look at a particular food production line and identify critical control points, or they might have to produce a scheme of work for a particular production line.

DR O'DONOVAN: We can do case studies in Engineering as well, in fact. I've sometimes asked students to choose an engineering disaster – you know, the Tay Bridge railway disaster or the Fukushima nuclear power plant, and analyze the causes and consequences from an engineering perspective. What aspect of the design was faulty or what safety issues were overlooked?

BARBARA JOHNSON: So once students have chosen their topic or have got an idea of what they are interested in, what comes next?

PROF FOWLER: Once they have a topic, they need to pose a question. Usually I say to them, 'OK,

Key words & phrases

go out and count
a triangulation method
root-cause analysis
come up with
overwhelmed
in a rush
end up doing

you've identified a topic, now you need to ask a question because it'll make it much easier for you to structure what you're going to write if you have a question that you need to answer – even if you don't come to a definitive conclusion, you need to be able to discuss it'. The question helps to frame that discussion. Often students come up with a very general topic and I say, 'Well, you need to focus it, so try to ask a specific question. It's much easier to select the different sources for your literature review if you have a question'.

DR BROWN: Yes, absolutely. A question – or questions, really – are essential. Your research questions inform your literature review and that informs your data collection and how you analyze your results according to your research objectives and aims. It's quite simple, but a lot of students just don't get that.

DR O'DONOVAN: I'd definitely agree with that, but I'd bring it right down to having a question for each source you read. For an experimental type project, or a design project, you need an awful lot of literature, but it tends to be very focused and it has to be critically analyzed for you to be able to design and test an experiment. I think you really have to focus: Why are you reading this paper? What are you trying to find out of this paper? It needs to do something for you – it needs to help you make a decision about an experimental method or a product design.

DR RUTHERFORD: Yes, something that I find Logistics students battle with – especially when they've decided what their methodology is going to be … you know, data collection by interview – maybe a semi-structured interview – is how they devise those interview questions. There is quite often a gap between the literature they've read, the frameworks or models they've drawn from the literature and then the design of their interview questions. You think, where do they get these questions from?

DR BROWN/PROF FOWLER: Yeah – there's no connection.

DR RUTHERFORD: They're just kind of plucked out of the air.

BARBARA JOHNSON: So they've done all this work and read the literature, but there's no link to the interview questions?

DR RUTHERFORD: That's right, there's no logical argument to justify the choice of questions. They've just kind of appeared out of nowhere. And when you see the research questions on one page – so they've come up with their research questions – and you see their questionnaire questions on the next page, you can't see the relationship. You can't see which of those interview questions will answer the research questions, and my biggest bugbear with thesis projects is they just don't get it.

BARBARA JOHNSON: Is it because they have so much information it just gets too confused in their heads?

DR O'DONOVAN: I think they just don't know what a literature review is for and what we're expecting. I mean, the major no-nos are taking a paper and simply summarizing it. Then taking the next paper and summarizing that, too, and going on for 200 pages. I even had one student who wrote something like 'The first paper I read was … the second paper I read …'. He had no idea why he was reading and summarizing the literature. And quantity seems to be another criterion. They say to you, 'I've written a really thick report', as if we weighed them and we gave them marks accordingly!

PROF FOWLER: I certainly think that it would be useful for students to analyze what the structure of a literature review is, so that they realize that they have to have a topic; ask a question; define some aims and objectives – in order to limit the scope of their research; give the background; give the evidence – from other studies – and cite the references for that evidence; discuss and make a conclusion, and then maybe suggest areas for further research. That sort of structure is actually quite hard to get across to students. That's not just me being picky; that's what you actually have to do.

DR O'DONOVAN: It's the scientific method: you read the literature and find a gap; you have a hypothesis; your understanding of the literature helps you to work out how you can collect data in order to confirm or redefine the hypothesis, so it's always closing that circle.

BARBARA JOHNSON: So as I understand it, the problem is that what you often see is a complete lack of connection between the research question and the literature review, and this is quite often where students fall down.

DR RUTHERFORD: Yes, it's quite often a weakness in the thesis stage of the programme. Maybe quite a nice assignment would be to give students a research question and tell them to go away and read the literature, and put a literature review together and then design a survey.

DR BROWN: What questions would you need to ask to get the data you need to answer the research question?

DR RUTHERFORD: For example, they could think about what goes through the mind of a consumer when they stand at a shelf deciding which product to take. How would you go about finding out how a person decides that? And that's probably the easiest one – I'm not saying it's the easiest thing to do, but because everybody's a consumer, it's likely that all students would get something out of that.

BARBARA JOHNSON: That would be an accessible project. They could do a literature review and survey questions, and that would be the right scope for a pre-sessional project. How would that work for Urban Studies students?

DR BROWN: Mmm, that would be OK, yes, but we were talking earlier of actually getting them out looking at a site and making a link to the planning policy. So you might take the same location, say Summerford High Street, but different students would look at different sectors, like transport, or retailing or open space, or the historical environment. So the research questions might be, how well is planning or transport or retailing policy working in this location? Or what impact have changes in policy had? This is the kind of research a lot of our students will go on to do as part of their work. Central government and local governments often commission research into the impact of their policies and it's usually done by consultants.

BARBARA JOHNSON: Well, I see our time is up, so we need to call a halt there, but I'd like to thank you all very much. You've given me some really concrete ideas to get our pre-sessional students thinking in more research-minded ways.

Key words & phrases

goes through the mind of
go about finding out
get something out of
an accessible project
go on to do
to call a halt
research-minded

The authors and publisher would like to thank the following for permission to reproduce copyright material:

Page 23: *Issues in robot design*, reproduced with kind permission of Fitsum Akilulu Reda, student at Heriot Watt University, 2007.

Pages 23 & 54: Definition of *robotics*, taken from Siciliano, B., & Khatib, O. (Eds.). (2008). *Springer Handbook of Robotics*. Berlin: Springer (pp. 2–3).

Page 28: Photo of rain in the rainforest, reproduced with kind permission of Dr. Peter Wilkie, Royal Botanic Garden Edinburgh.

Pages 39–49, 51–52 & 203: Texts and tables, Lindgren, A., Chen, F., Jordan, P. W., & Zhang, H. (2008). Requirements for the design of Advanced Driver Assistance Systems: The differences between Swedish and Chinese drivers. *International Journal of Design, 2*(2), 47. Reproduced with kind permission of Anders Lindgren Walter.

Pages 63 & 66: Screenshots and concordance lines taken from the British National Corpus, reproduced with kind permission of Brigham Young University.

Page 65: Dictionary definitions reproduced with kind permission of *Macmillan Dictionary*, www.macmillandictionary.com.

Pages 77–80, 186, 188–189, 205 & 241: Reproduced by permission of SAGE Publications, London, Los Angeles, New Delhi and Singapore, *Critical reading and writing for postgraduates*, Copyright (© Mike Wallace and Alison Wray, 2006).

Page 87: Screenshot of a Google Advanced Search. Google and the Google logo are registered trademarks of Google Inc., used with permission.

Page 88: Screenshot of the ISI Web of Knowledge, reproduced with kind permission of Thomson Reuters.

Page 90: Screenshot of a Google Scholar search. Google and the Google logo are registered trademarks of Google Inc., used with permission.

Pages 102 & 238: Abstract 1, taken from Abdulla, F. A., & Al-Omari, A. S. (2008). The impact of climate change on the monthly runoff of a semi-arid catchment: Case study Zarqa river basin (Jordan). *Journal of Applied Biological Sciences, 2*(1), 43–50. Reproduced with kind permission of Fayez Abdulla, Ph.D.

Page 102: Abstract 2, taken from Bou-Zeid, E. R., & El-Fadel, M. (2002). Climate change and water resources in Lebanon and the Middle East. *Journal of Water Resources Planning and Management, 128*(5), 343–355. Reproduced with permission from ASCE, http://ascelibrary.org/doi/abs/10.1061/%28ASCE%290733-9496%282002%29128%3A5%28343%29.

Page 102: Abstract 3, taken from Evans, J. P. (2009). 21st century climate change in the Middle East. *Climatic Change, 92*(3–4), 417–432. Reproduced with kind permission of Dr Jason Evans.

Page 103: Abstract 4, taken from Hreiche, A., Bocquillon, C., Najem, W., & Dandach, D. (2005). The potential impact of future climate change on Lebanese river basin hydrology using scenarios. In T. Wagener et al. (Eds.), *Regional Hydrological Impacts of Climatic Change*, 103–110. Conference proceedings from International Association of Hydrological Science. Reproduced with kind permission of Taylor and Francis, http://dx.doi.org/10.1623/hysj.52.6.1119.

Page 103: Abstract 5, from article entitled 'Climate Change and Water Resources Management in Arid and Semi-arid Regions: Prospective and Challenges for the 21st Century' by Ragab Ragab and Christel Prudhomme ©NERC (CEH).

Page 103: Abstract 6, reprinted by permission from Macmillan Publishers Ltd: Nature Journals (358:119–122), copyright (1992).

Page 108: Photo of a supermarket in China, © ValeStock/Shutterstock.com

Page 121: Case study, from INTERCULTURAL COMMUNICATION: A PRACTICAL GUIDE by Tracy Novinger, Copyright © 2001. By permission of the University of Texas Press.

Pages 132 & 133: Text, from INTERCULTURAL COMMUNICATION: A PRACTICAL GUIDE by Tracy Novinger, Copyright © 2001. By permission of the University of Texas Press.

Page 133: Text B, reproduced with kind permission from The University of Queensland.

Page 134: Text, reproduced with kind permission from Communicaid Group Ltd., 2011.

Page 136: The Ethical Volunteering Guide, reproduced with kind permission from Ethical Volunteering.

Page 146: Task 2 audio, taken from Thomas, N. (2007) *Feedback on exams: written sheets in History*, Promoting Enhanced Student Learning video resource. [video online]. Available at: http://www.nottingham.ac.uk/pesl/resources/assessment/feedback610. Reproduced with kind permission of Dr Nick Thomas, University of Nottingham.

Pages 148 & 192: Task 5 text and audio, taken from Thomas, N. (2007) *Feedback on exams: written sheets in History*, Promoting Enhanced Student Learning video resource. [video online]. Available at: http://www.nottingham.ac.uk/pesl/resources/assessment/feedback610. Reproduced with kind permission of Dr Nick Thomas, University of Nottingham.

Page 168: Turnitin text and logo, reproduced with kind permission of Turnitin.

Page 183: Source A, Keenan, F. G. (1992). *Large vocabulary syntactic analysis for text recognition*. (Unpublished PhD thesis). Nottingham Trent University, Nottingham.

Page 183: Source B, adapted from the European Association for Machine Translation. (n.d.). *What is machine translation?* Retrieved on February 29, 2012, from www.eamt.org/mt.php. Reproduced with kind permission from the European Association for Machine Translation (EAMT).

Page 197: Text, reproduced with kind permission of The University of Wollongong.

Page 199: Source A, Pfaff, B., & David, K. (1998). *Society and open source. Why open source software is better for society than proprietary closed source software.* Retrieved October 10, 2012, from http://benpfaff.org/writings/anp/oss-is-better.html. Reproduced with kind permission of Ben Pfaff and Kenneth David, PhD (University of Chicago) Professor, Anthropology & Transcultural Project Studies, Michigan State University.

Page 200: Source D, taken from Kassab, Y. (2009). *Why is open source better than commercial software?* Retrieved March 19, 2012, from http://ezinearticles.com/?Why-is-Open-Source-Better-Than-Commercial-Software?&id=2895035.

Page 211: Text by Niyi Awofeso, reproduced with kind permission of Professor Niyi Awofeso, University of Western Australia.

Page 211: Text by Jennie Naidoo and Jane Wills. This article was published in *Health promotion: Foundations for practice*, Jennie Naidoo and Jane Wills, Chapter 1: Concepts of health, Copyright Baillière Tindall/Elsevier 2009.

Page 211: Text by WHO, the World Health Organization (WHO) definition of health, http://www.who.int/about/definition/en/print.html. Reproduced with kind permission of WHO.

Page 211: Text by Derek Yach, extract taken from text by Derek Yach, The Vitality Institute.

Page 216: Extract 1, taken fom Wiedmann, T., & Minx, J. (2008). A definition of 'carbon footprint'. In C. C. Pertsova (Ed.), *Ecological economics research trends* (pp. 1–11). Hauppauge NY, USA: Nova Science Publishers. Retrieved October 3, 2012, from http://www.censa.org.uk/docs/ISA-UK_Report_07-01_carbon_footprint.pdf. Reproduced with kind permission of Dr Tommy Wiedmann.

Page 217: Extract 2, taken from Wright, L. A., Kemp S., & Williams, I. (2011). 'Carbon footprinting': Towards a universally accepted definition. *Carbon Management, 2*(1), 61–72. Retrieved April 21, 2012, from http://www.future-science.com/doi/abs/10.4155/cmt.10.39. Reproduced with kind permission of the publisher, Future Science Ltd.

Page 218: Extract 3, taken from Williams, I., Kemp, S. Coello, J. Turner, D.A., & Wright, L.A. (2012). A beginner's guide to carbon footprinting. *Carbon Management*, Special report, *3*(1), 55–67. Reproduced with kind permission of the publisher, Future Science Ltd.

Page 220: CO_2 emissions table, taken from United Nations. (2011). *Human Development Statistical Annex.* Retrieved from http://hdr.undp.org/en/media/HDR_2011_EN_Tables.pdf (Full UN Human Development Reports (1990–2011) available at http://hdr.undp.org/en/). Reproduced with kind permission from The Human Development Report Office. Additional source: U.S. Energy Information Administration.

Pages 221 & 222: Chapter 2 and scatter graphs, taken from United Nations. (2012). *Human Development Report 2011.* Retrieved April 26, 2012, from http://www.undp.prg/content/ham/undp/library/corporate/HDR/2011%20Global%20HDR/English/HDR_2011_EN_Chapter2.pdf. Reproduced with kind permission from The Human Development Report Office.

Pages 227 & 228: *Mail Online* articles and logos. Bates, C. (2012, March 10). The heart drug with an unusual side effect ... it could make you less RACIST. *Mail Online.* Retrieved from http://www.dailymail.co.uk/health/article-2111600/Blood-pressure-drug-combats-racism-unusual-effect and Thornhill, T. (2012, February 10). Surprise status update: More adults like Facebook and Twitter than teenagers. *Mail Online.* Retrieved from http://www.dailymail.co.uk/sciencetech/article-2099442/Surprise-status-update-More-adults-like-Facebook-Twitter-teenagers.html. Both articles and accompanying logos reproduced with kind permission of *The Mail Online*.

Pages 227 & 228: *The Telegraph* article and logo, Fleming, N. (2007, August 30). Mobile phone use and cancer linked. The Telegraph. Retrieved from http://www.telegraph.co.uk/news/uknews/1561675/Mobile-phone-use-and-cancer-linked.html. Article and logo reproduced with kind permission of *The Telegraph*, © Telegraph Media Group Limited 2007.

Page 229: Bar graph, *The Pew Research Center's Internet & American Life Teen-Parent survey*, reproduced with kind permission of The Pew Research Center.

Page 231: Goldacre, B. (2011, June 4). Are mobiles a health risk? There's no answer yet. *The Guardian.* Retrieved from http://www.guardian.co.uk/commentisfree/2011/jun/04/bad-science-ben-goldacre-mobile-phone-health. Reproduced with kind permission of *The Guardian* newspaper. Copyright © Guardian News & Media Ltd 2007.

Page 234: Text, taken from Fanelli, D. (2010). 'Positive' results increase down the hierarchy of sciences.' *PLoS ONE*, 5(4): e10068. DOI:10.1371/journal.pone.0010068. Reproduced with kind permission of Daniele Fanelli, PhD.

Page 236: Hall's diagram of personal space, based on Wikipedia image, http://commons.wikimedia.org/wiki/File:Personal_Spaces_in_Proxemics.svg. Modified and used under the CC-BA-SA 3.0 license, http://creativecommons.org/licenses/by-sa/3.0/legalcode.

Page 238: Abstract 2, *Teens, kindness and cruelty on social network sites*, reproduced with kind permission of The Pew Research Center.

Page 239: Abstract 4, taken from Terbeck, S., Kahane, G., McTavish, S., Savulescu, J., Cowen, P. J., & Hewstone, M. (2012). Propranolol reduces implicit negative racial bias. *Psychopharmacology*, 22(3), 419–424. Published online February 28, 2012. DOI: 10.1007/s00213-012-2657-5.

Page 239: Abstract 3, Lindgren, A., Chen, F., Jordan, P. W., & Zhang, H. (2008). Requirements for the design of Advanced Driver Assistance Systems: The differences between Swedish and Chinese drivers. *International Journal of Design, 2*(2), 47. Reproduced with kind permission of Anders Lindgren Walter.

Pages 240 & 242: Abstract 1, taken from Kelly, P., & Moogan, Y. (2012). Culture shock and higher education performance: Implications for teaching. *Higher Education Quarterly, 66*(1), 24–46. Reproduced with kind permission of John Wiley & Sons, Inc.

Pages 240 & 242: Abstract 2, taken from Lebcir, R. M., Wells, H., & Bond, A. (2008). Factors affecting academic performance of international students in project management courses: A case study from a British post-92 university. *International Journal of Project Management, 26*(3), 268–274. Reproduced with kind permission of Dr Mohamed Lebcir, University of Hertfordshire.

Pages 243–249: Text, taken from Kelly, P., & Moogan, Y. (2012). Culture shock and higher education performance: Implications for teaching. *Higher Education Quarterly, 66*(1), 24–46. Reproduced with kind permission of John Wiley & Sons, Inc.

Pages 244 & 245: Text, taken from Lebcir, R. M., Wells, H., & Bond, A. (2008). Factors affecting academic performance of international students in project management courses: A case study from a British post-92 university. *International Journal of Project Management, 26*(3), 268–274. Reproduced with kind permission of Dr Mohamed Lebcir, University of Hertfordshire.

Page 251: Definition g, sourced from Wikipedia, http://en.wikipedia.org/wiki/Hazard_analysis_and_critical_control_points. Text has been modified and used under the CC-BA-SA 3.0 license, http://creativecommons.org/licenses/by-sa/3.0/legalcode.

Page 251: Definition h, taken from Ingram, H., Teare, R., Scheuing, E., & Armistead, C. (1997). A systems model of effective teamwork. *The TQM Magazine, 9*(2), 118–127. Published by and reproduced with kind permission of Emerald Group Publishing Limited.

Page 253: Extract 1, taken from Abdulla, F. A., & Al-Omari, A. S. (2008). The impact of climate change on the monthly runoff of a semi-arid catchment: Case study Zarqa river basin (Jordan). *Journal of Applied Biological Sciences, 2*(1), 43–50. Reproduced with kind permission of Fayez Abdulla, Ph.D.

Page 254: Extract 2, taken from Lebcir, R. M., Wells, H., & Bond, A. (2008). Factors affecting academic performance of international students in project management courses: A case study from a British post-92 university. *International Journal of Project Management, 26*(3), 268–274. Reproduced with kind permission of Dr Mohamed Lebcir, University of Hertfordshire.

Page 254: Extract 3, taken from Terbeck, S., Kahane, G., McTavish, S., Savulescu, J., Cowen, P. J., & Hewstone, M. (2012). Propranolol reduces implicit negative racial bias. *Psychopharmacology, 22*(3), 419–424. Published online February 28, 2012. DOI: 10.1007/s00213-012-2657-5.

Pages 255 & 256: *A mechanical model of electricity for teaching students*, taken from the dissertation of and reproduced with kind permission of Christopher Steele, University of Sheffield, 2005.

Page 257: *The mechanisms and application of microbial enhanced oil recovery*, reproduced with kind permission of Wu Le, Heriot-Watt University.

Pages 260 & 261: *The Common European Framework of Reference for Languages (CEFR)* and Reading and Writing 'Can do' statements, reproduced with kind permission of The Council of Europe, © *Council of Europe*.

Pages 262 & 264: Information in table on IELTS, TOEFL – iBT and PTE Academic, reproduced with kind permission from the Educational Testing Service. Copyright © 2013 Educational Testing Service. www.ets.org. Information also reproduced with kind permission of Pearson, © 2013 Pearson plc.

Page 266: The Marshmallow Challenge, based on information from http://marshmallowchallenge.com/Welcome.html.

Pages 268 & 271: *Group Projects for Assessment and Computer Science: Software Design and Engineering*, taken from the University of Cambridge. (2011). *Group Design Project 2011–2012: Project Briefing*. Retrieved June 26, 2012, from http://www.cl.cam.ac.uk/teaching/group-projects/StudentBriefing_1112.pdf. Reproduced with kind permission of the University of Cambridge.

Page 274: *Belbin Team Roles* and *Team Skills*, Belbin. (2011). *Team Role Summary Descriptions*. Retrieved from http://www.belbin.com/content/page/49/BELBIN(uk)-2011-TeamRoleSummaryDescriptions.pdf. Reproduced with kind permission from www.belbin.com.

Page 277: *Critical self-awareness and personal literacy*, taken from Oxford Brookes University. (2011). *Brookes graduate attributes*. Retrieved July 2, 2012, from http://www.brookes.ac.uk/services/ocsld/sese/graduate_attributes.pdf. Reproduced with kind permission of Oxford Brookes University.

Pages 281–283: Student descriptions and commentary, reproduced with kind permission of Jennifer Argent, 2013.